Assessment Guide

Grade 1

Harcourt
Orlando Austin Chicago New York Toronto London San Diego

Visit *The Learning Site!*
www.harcourtschool.com

Printed in the United States of America

ISBN 0-15-336537-4

9 10 022 10 09 08 07

CONTENTS

TESTS

INTRODUCTION

Assessment in Harcourt Math

Harcourt Math provides a wide range of assessment tools to measure student achievement before, during, and after instruction. These tools include:

- Entry Level Assessment
- Progress Monitoring
- Summative Evaluation
- Test Preparation

Entry Level Assessment

Inventory Tests—These tests, provided on pages AG1–AG8 in this *Assessment Guide*, may be administered at the beginning of the school year.

Assessing Prior Knowledge ("Check What You Know")—This feature appears at the beginning of every chapter in the *Harcourt Math* Pupil Edition. It may be used before chapter instruction begins to determine whether students possess crucial prerequisite skills. Tools for intervention are provided.

Pretests—The Chapter Tests, Form A (multiple choice) or Form B (free response), may be used as pretests to measure what students may already have mastered before instruction begins. These tests are provided in this *Assessment Guide*.

Progress Monitoring

Daily Assessment—These point-of-use strategies allow you to continually adjust instruction so that all students are constantly progressing toward mastery of the grade-level objectives. These strategies appear in every lesson of the *Harcourt Math* Teacher's Edition, and include the Quick Review, Lesson Test Prep, and the Assess section of the lesson plan.

Intervention—While monitoring students' progress, you may determine that intervention is needed. The Intervention and Extension Resources page for each lesson in the Teacher's Edition suggests several options for meeting individual needs.

Student Self-Assessment—Students evaluate their own work through checklists, portfolios, and journals. Suggestions are provided in this *Assessment Guide*.

Summative Evaluation

Formal Assessment—Several options are provided to help the teacher determine whether students have achieved the goals defined by a given standard or set of standards. These options are provided at the end of each chapter and unit and at the end of the year. They include

Chapter Review/Test in the *Pupil Edition*
Chapter Tests in this *Assessment Guide*
Unit Tests in this *Assessment Guide*
Chapter Test Prep, in the *Pupil Edition*

Performance Assessment—Two performance tasks for each unit are provided in the *Performance Assessment* book. Scoring rubrics and model papers are also provided in the *Performance Assessment* book. The tasks also appear in the *Pupil Edition* at the end of each unit.

Harcourt Assessment System—This technology component provides the teacher with the opportunity to make and grade chapter and unit tests electronically. The tests may be customized to meet individual needs or to create standards-based tests from a bank of test items. A management system for generating reports is also included.

Test Preparation

Test Prep—To help students prepare for tests, the Lesson Test Prep, at the end of most lessons, provides items in standardized-test format. In addition, the Chapter Test Prep pages at the end of each chapter in the *Pupil Edition* provide practice in solving problems in a standardized test format.

ASSESSMENT OPTIONS AT A GLANCE

ASSESSING PRIOR KNOWLEDGE

Check What You Know, *PE*
Inventory Test, Form A, *AG*
Inventory Test, Form B, *AG*

TEST PREPARATION

Chapter Test Prep, *PE*
Lesson Test Prep, *PE*
Study Guide and Review, *PE*

FORMAL ASSESSMENT

Chapter Review/Test, *PE*
Inventory Tests, *AG*
Pretest and Posttest Options
Chapter Test Form A, *AG*
Chapter Test Form B, *AG*
End-of-Year Tests, *AG*

Unit Test Form A, *AG*
Unit Test Form B, *AG*

Harcourt Assessment System—
CD-ROM

DAILY ASSESSMENT

Quick Review, *PE*
Lesson Test Prep, *PE*
Number of the Day, *TE*
Problem of the Day, *TE*
Lesson Quiz, *TE*

PERFORMANCE ASSESSMENT

Performance Task A, *PA*
Performance Task B, *PA*

STUDENT SELF-ASSESSMENT

How Did Our Group Do?, *AG*
How Well Did I Work in My Group?, *AG*
How Did I Do?, *AG*
A Guide to My Math Portfolio, *AG*
Math Journal, *TE*

Key: AG=*Assessment Guide*, TE=*Teacher's Edition*, PE=*Pupil Edition*, PA=*Performance Assessment*

PREPARING STUDENTS FOR SUCCESS

Assessing Prior Knowledge

Assessment of prior knowledge is essential to planning mathematics instruction and to ensure students' progress from what they already know to higher levels of learning. In *Harcourt Math*, each chapter begins with Check What You Know. This tool to assess prior knowledge can be used to determine whether students have the prerequisite skills to move on to the new skills and concepts of the subsequent chapter.

If students are found lacking in some skills or concepts, appropriate intervention strategies are suggested. The *Intervention • Skills* and *Intervention • Problem Solving* ancillaries provide additional options for intervention. The *Teacher's Edition* of the textbook provides references for reteaching, practice, and challenge activities as well as suggestions for reaching students with a wide variety of learning abilities.

Test Preparation

With increasing emphasis today on standardized tests, many students feel intimidated and nervous as testing time approaches. Whether they are facing teacher-made tests, program tests, or state-wide standardized tests, students will feel more confident with the test format and content if they know what to expect in advance.

Harcourt Math provides multiple opportunities for test preparation. At the end of most lessons there is a Lesson Test Prep, which provides items in a standardized-test format. Chapter Test Prep pages at the end of each chapter provide practice in problem solving presented in a standardized-test format. Test-taking tips also appear in this *Assessment Guide* on pages AG xlvii and AG xlviii.

FORMAL ASSESSMENT

Formal assessment in *Harcourt Math* consists of a series of reviews and tests that assess how well students understand concepts, perform skills, and solve problems related to program content. Information from these measures (along with information from other kinds of assessment) is needed to evaluate student achievement and to determine grades. Moreover, analysis of results can help determine whether additional practice or reteaching is needed.

Formal assessment in *Harcourt Math* includes the following measures:

- Inventory Tests, in this *Assessment Guide*
- Chapter Review/Tests, in the *Pupil Edition*
- Chapter Tests, in this *Assessment Guide*
- Unit Tests, in this *Assessment Guide*
- End-of-Year Tests, in this *Assessment Guide*

The **Inventory Tests** assess how well students have mastered the objectives from the previous grade level. There are two forms of Inventory Tests—multiple choice (Form A) and free response (Form B). Test results provide information about the kinds of review students may need to be successful in mathematics at the new grade level. The teacher may use the Inventory Test at the beginning of the school year or when a new student arrives in your class.

The **Chapter Review/Test** appears at the end of each chapter in the *Pupil Edition*. It can be used to determine whether there is a need for more instruction or practice. Discussion of responses can help correct misconceptions before students take the chapter test.

The **Chapter Tests** are available in two formats—multiple choice (Form A) and free response (Form B). Both forms assess the same content. The two different forms permit use of the measure as a pretest and a posttest or as two forms of the posttest.

The **Unit Tests**, in both Form A and Form B, follow the chapter tests in each unit. Unit tests assess skills and concepts from the preceding unit.

The **End-of-Year Tests** assess how well students have mastered the objectives in the grade level. There are two forms of End-of-Year Tests—multiple choice and free response. Test results may provide a teacher help in recommending a summer review program.

The **Answer Key** in this *Assessment Guide* provides reduced replications of the tests with answers. Two record forms are available for formal assessment—an Individual Record Form (starting on page AG xxviii) and a Class Record Form (starting on page AG xliv).

Students may record their answers directly on the test sheets. However, for the multiple-choice tests, they may use the **Answer Sheet**, similar to the "bubble form" used for standardized tests. That sheet is located on page AG xlix in this *Assessment Guide*.

DAILY ASSESSMENT

Daily Assessment is embedded in daily instruction. Students are assessed as they learn and learn as they are assessed. First you observe and evaluate your students' work on an informal basis, and then you seek confirmation of those observations through other program assessments.

Harcourt Math offers the following resources to support informal assessment on a daily basis:

- Quick Review in the *Pupil Edition* on the first page of each lesson
- Lesson Test Prep in the *Pupil Edition* at the end of each skill lesson
- Number of the Day in the *Teacher's Edition* at the beginning of each lesson
- Problem of the Day in the *Teacher's Edition* at the beginning of each lesson
- Assess in the *Teacher's Edition* at the end of each lesson

Quick Review allows you to adjust instruction so that all students are progressing toward mastery of skills and concepts.

Lesson Test Prep provides review and practice for skills and concepts previously taught. Some of the items are written in a multiple-choice format.

Number of the Day and **Problem of the Day** kick off the lesson with problems that are relevant both to lesson content and the students' world. Their purpose is to get students thinking about the lesson topic and to provide you with insights about their ability to solve problems related to it. Class discussion may yield clues about students' readiness to learn a concept or skill emphasized in the lesson.

Assess in the Teacher's Edition at the end of each lesson includes three brief assessments: Discuss and Write—to probe students' grasp of the main lesson concept, and Lesson Quiz—a quick check of students' mastery of lesson skills.

Depending on what you learn from students' responses to lesson assessments, you may wish to use **Problem Solving, Reteach, Practice**, or **Challenge** copying masters before starting the next lesson.

PERFORMANCE ASSESSMENT

Performance assessment can help reveal the thinking strategies students use to work through a problem. Students usually enjoy doing the performance tasks.

Harcourt Math offers the following assessment measures, scoring instruments, and teacher observation checklists for evaluating student performance.

- Unit Performance Assessments and Scoring Rubrics, in the *Performance Assessment* book
- Project Scoring Rubric in this *Assessment Guide*
- Portfolio Evaluation in this *Assessment Guide*
- Problem Solving Think Along Response Sheets and Scoring Guides in this *Assessment Guide*

The **Performance Assessment** book includes two tasks per unit. These tasks can help you assess students' ability to use what they have learned to solve everyday problems. For more information see the *Performance Assessment* book.

The **Project Scoring Rubric** can be used to evaluate an individual or group project. This rubric can be especially useful in evaluating the Problem Solving Activity that appears in the *Teacher's Edition* at the beginning of every chapter. The project is an open-ended, problem-solving task that may involve activities such as gathering data, constructing a data table or graph, writing a report, building a model, or creating a simulation.

The **Problem Solving Think Along** is a performance assessment that is designed around the problem-solving method used in *Harcourt Math*. You may use either the Oral Response or Written Response form to evaluate the students. For more information see pages AG xxii–AG xxvi.

Portfolios can also be used to assess students' mathematics performance. For more information, see pages AG xviii–AG xx.

STUDENT SELF-ASSESSMENT

Research shows that self-assessment can have significant positive effects on students' learning. To achieve these effects, students must be challenged to reflect on their work and to monitor, analyze, and control their learning. Their ability to evaluate their behaviors and to monitor them grows with their experience in self-assessment.

Harcourt Math offers the following self-assessment tools:

- Math Journal, ideas for journal writing found in the *Teacher's Edition*
- Group Project Evaluation Sheet
- Individual Group Member Evaluation Sheet
- End-of-Chapter Individual Survey Sheet

The **Math Journal** is a collection of student writings that may communicate feelings, ideas, and explanations as well as responses to open-ended problems. It is an important evaluation tool in math even though it is not graded. Use the journal to gain insights about student growth that you cannot obtain from other assessments. Look for journal icons in your *Teacher's Edition* for suggested journal-writing activities.

The **Group Project Evaluation Sheet** ("How Did Our Group Do?") is designed to assess and build up group self-assessment skills. The Individual Group Member Evaluation ("How Well Did I Work in My Group?") helps the student evaluate his or her own behavior in and contributions to the group.

The **End-of-Chapter Survey** ("How Did I Do?") leads students to reflect on what they have learned and how they learned it. Use it to help students learn more about their own capabilities and develop confidence.

Discuss directions for completing each checklist or survey with the students. Tell them there are no "right" responses to the items. Talk over reasons for various responses.

Project Scoring Rubric

Check the indicators that describe a student's or group's performance on a project. Use the check marks to help determine the individual's or group's overall score.

Score 3 Indicators: The student/group

_______ makes outstanding use of resources.
_______ shows thorough understanding of content.
_______ demonstrates outstanding grasp of mathematics skills.
_______ displays strong decision-making/problem-solving skills.
_______ exhibits exceptional insight/creativity.
_______ communicates ideas clearly and effectively.

Score 2 Indicators: The student/group

_______ makes good use of resources.
_______ shows adequate understanding of content.
_______ demonstrates good grasp of mathematics skills.
_______ displays adequate decision-making/problem-solving skills.
_______ exhibits reasonable insight/creativity.
_______ communicates most ideas clearly and effectively.

Score 1 Indicators: The student/group

_______ makes limited use of resources.
_______ shows partial understanding of content.
_______ demonstrates limited grasp of mathematics skills.
_______ displays weak decision-making/problem-solving skills.
_______ exhibits limited insight/creativity.
_______ communicates some ideas clearly and effectively.

Score 0 Indicators: The student/group

_______ makes little or no use of resources.
_______ fails to show understanding of content.
_______ demonstrates little or no grasp of mathematics skills.
_______ does not display decision-making/problem-solving skills.
_______ does not exhibit insight/creativity.
_______ has difficulty communicating ideas clearly and effectively.

Overall score for the project. _______

Comments: ____

____

Project ______________________ Date ________
Group members ________________________

How Did Our Group Do?

Discuss the question. Then circle the score your group thinks it earned.

How well did our group	Great Job	Good Job	Could Do Better
		SCORE	
1. share ideas?	3	2	1
2. plan what to do?	3	2	1
3. carry out plans?	3	2	1
4. share the work?	3	2	1
5. solve group problems without seeking help?	3	2	1
6. make use of resources?	3	2	1
7. record information and check for accuracy?	3	2	1
8. show understanding of math ideas?	3	2	1
9. demonstrate creativity and critical thinking?	3	2	1
10. solve the project problem?	3	2	1

Write your group's answer to each question.

11. What did our group do best? ______________________________

____

____

12. How can we help our group do better? ______________________

____

____

Name ______________________ Date _____

Project ______________________________

How Well Did I Work in My Group?

Circle **yes** if you agree. Circle **no** if you disagree.

1.	I shared my ideas with my group.	yes	no
2.	I listened to the ideas of others in my group.	yes	no
3.	I was able to ask questions of my group.	yes	no
4.	I encouraged others in my group to share their ideas.	yes	no
5.	I was able to discuss opposite ideas with my group.	yes	no
6.	I helped my group plan and make decisions.	yes	no
7.	I did my fair share of the group's work.	yes	no
8.	I understood the problem my group worked on.	yes	no
9.	I understood the solution to the problem my group worked on.	yes	no
10.	I can explain to others the problem my group worked on and its solution.	yes	no

Name ______________________ Date ______

Chapter ______________________________

INDIVIDUAL END-OF-CHAPTER SURVEY

How Did I Do?

Write your response.

1. I thought the lessons in this chapter were

____

2. The lesson I enjoyed the most was

____

3. Something that I still need to work on is

____

4. One thing that I think I did a great job on was

____

5. I would like to learn more about

____

6. Something I understand now that I did not understand before these lessons is

____

7. I think I might use the math I learned in these lessons to

____

8. The amount of effort I put into these lessons was

____

(very little some a lot)

PORTFOLIO ASSESSMENT

A portfolio is a collection of each student's work gathered over an extended period of time. A portfolio illustrates the growth, talents, achievements, and reflections of the learner and provides a means for the teacher to assess the student's performance and progress.

Building a Portfolio

There are many opportunities to collect students' work throughout the year as you use *Harcourt Math*. Suggested portfolio items are found throughout the *Teacher's Edition*. Give students the opportunity to select some work samples to be included in the portfolio.

- Provide a folder for each student with the student's name clearly marked.
- Explain to students that throughout the year they will save some of their work in the folder. Sometimes it will be their individual work; sometimes it will be group reports and projects or completed checklists.
- Have students complete "A Guide to My Math Portfolio" several times during the year.

Evaluating a Portfolio

The following points made with regular portfolio evaluation will encourage growth in self-evaluation:

- Discuss the contents of the portfolio as you examine it with each student.
- Encourage and reward students by emphasizing growth, original thinking, and completion of tasks.
- Reinforce and adjust instruction of the broad goals you want to accomplish as you evaluate the portfolios.
- Examine each portfolio on the basis of individual growth rather than in comparison with other portfolios.
- Use the Portfolio Evaluation sheet for your comments.
- Share the portfolios with families during conferences or send the portfolio, including the Family Response form, home with the students.

Name ______________________________

Date ______________________________

PORTFOLIO GUIDE

A Guide to My Math Portfolio

What is in My Portfolio	What I Learned
1.	
2.	
3.	
4.	
5.	

I organized my portfolio this way because ______________________________

____

____

Name ______________________________

Date ______________________________

PORTFOLIO EVALUATION

Evaluating Performance	Evidence and Comments
1. What mathematical understandings are demonstrated?	
2. What skills are demonstrated?	
3. What approaches to problem solving and critical thinking are evident?	
4. What work habits and attitudes are demonstrated?	

Summary of Portfolio Assessment

For This Review			Since Last Review		
Excellent	Good	Fair	Improving	About the Same	Not as Good

Date ________________________

Dear Family,

This is your child's math portfolio. It contains work samples that your child and I have selected to show how his or her abilities in math have grown. Your child can explain what each sample shows.

Please look over the portfolio with your child and write a few comments in the blank space at the bottom of this sheet about what you have seen. Your child has been asked to bring the portfolio with your comments included back to school.

Thank you for helping your child evaluate his or her portfolio and for taking pride in the work he or she has done. Your interest and support is important to your child's success in school.

Sincerely,

____
(Teacher)

- -

Response to Portfolio:

____
(Family member)

ASSESSING PROBLEM SOLVING

Assessing a student's ability to solve problems involves more than checking the student's answer. It involves looking at how students process information and how they work at solving problems. The problem-solving method used in *Harcourt Math*—Understand, Plan, Solve, and Check—guides the student's thinking process and provides a structure within which the student can work toward a solution. The following instruments can help you assess students' problem-solving abilities:

- Think Along Oral Response Form (copy master) p. AG xxiii
- Oral Response Scoring Guide p. AG xxiv
- Think Along Written Response Form (copy master) p. AG xxv
- Written Response Scoring Guide p. AG xxvi

The **Oral Response Form** (page AG xxiii) can be used by a student or a group as a self-questioning instrument or as a guide for working through a problem. It can also be an interview instrument the teacher can use to assess students' problem-solving skills.

The analytic **Scoring Guide for Oral Responses** (page AG xxiv) has a criterion score for each section. It may be used to evaluate the oral presentation of an individual or group.

The **Written Response Form** (page AG xxv) provides a recording sheet for a student or group to record their responses as they work through each section of the problem-solving process.

The analytic **Scoring Guide for Written Responses** (page AG xxvi), which gives a criterion score for each section, will help you pinpoint the parts of the problem-solving process in which your students need more instruction.

Name ______________________________

Date ______________________________

Problem-Solving Think Along: Oral Response Form

Solving problems is a thinking process. Asking yourself questions as you work through the steps in solving a problem can help guide your thinking. These questions will help you understand the problem, plan how to solve it, solve it, and then look back and check your solution. These questions will also help you think about other ways to solve the problem.

Understand

1. What is the problem about?
2. What is the question?
3. What information is given in the problem?

Plan

4. What problem-solving strategies might I try to help me solve the problem?
5. What is my estimated answer?

Solve

6. How can I solve the problem?
7. How can I state my answer in a complete sentence?

Check

8. How do I know whether my answer is reasonable?
9. How else might I have solved this problem?

Name ____

Date ____

Problem-Solving Think Along:

Scoring Guide • Oral Responses

Understand *Criterion Score 4/6* *Pupil Score* ______

______ **1.** *Restate the problem in his or her own words.*

2 points Complete problem restatement given.
1 point Incomplete problem restatement.
0 points No restatement given.

______ **2.** *Identify the question.*

2 points Complete problem restatement of the question given.
1 point Incomplete problem restatement of the question given.
0 points No restatement of the question given.

______ **3.** *State list of information needed to solve the problem.*

2 points Complete list given.
1 point Incomplete list given.
0 points No list given.

Plan *Criterion Score 3/4* *Pupil Score* ______

______ **1.** *State one or more strategies that might help solve the problem.*

2 points One or more useful strategies given.
1 point One or more strategies given but are poor choices.
0 points No strategies given.

______ **2.** *State reasonable estimated answer.*

2 points Reasonable estimate given.
1 point Unreasonable estimate given.
0 points No estimated answer given.

Solve *Criterion Score 3/4* *Pupil Score* ______

______ **1.** *Describe a solution method that correctly represents the information in the problem.*

2 points Correct solution method given.
1 point Incorrect solution method given.
0 points No solution method given.

______ **2.** *State correct answer in complete sentence.*

2 points Complete sentence given; answer to question is correct.
1 point Sentence given does not answer the question correctly.
0 points No sentence given.

Check *Criterion Score 3/4* *Pupil Score* ______

______ **1.** *State sentence explaining why the answer is reasonable.*

2 points Complete and correct explanation given.
1 point Sentence given with incomplete or incorrect reason.
0 points No explanation given.

______ **2.** *Describe another strategy that could have been used to solve the problem.*

2 points Another useful strategy described.
1 point Another strategy described, but strategy is a poor choice.
0 points No other strategy described.

TOTAL 13/18 *Pupil Score* ______

Name ______________________________

Date ______________________________

WRITTEN RESPONSE FORM

Problem Solving

Understand

1. Retell the problem in your own words. ______________________________

2. Restate the question as a fill-in-the-blank sentence. ______________________________

3. List the information needed to solve the problem. ______________________________

Plan

4. List one or more problem-solving strategies that you can use. ______________________________

5. Predict what your answer will be. ______________________________

Solve

6. Show how you solved the problem. ______________________________

7. Write your answer in a complete sentence. ______________________________

Check

8. Tell how you know your answer is reasonable. ______________________________

9. Describe another way you could have solved the problem. ______________________________

Problem-Solving Think Along:
Scoring Guide • Written Responses

Understand — *Criterion Score* 4/6

Indicator 1: Student restates the problem in his or her own words.

Scoring:
- 2 points Complete problem restatement written.
- 1 point Incomplete problem restatement written.
- 0 points No restatement written.

Indicator 2: Student restates the question as a fill-in-the-blank statement.

- 2 points Correct restatement of the question.
- 1 point Incorrect or incomplete restatement.
- 0 points No restatement written.

Indicator 3: Student writes a complete list of the information needed to solve the problem.

- 2 points Complete list made.
- 1 point Incomplete list made.
- 0 points No list made.

Plan — *Criterion Score* 3/4

Indicator 1: Student lists one or more problem-solving strategies that might be helpful in solving the problem.

Scoring:
- 2 points One or more useful strategies listed.
- 1 point One or more strategies listed, but strategies are poor choices.
- 0 points No strategies listed.

Indicator 2: Student gives a reasonable estimated answer.

- 2 points Reasonable estimate given.
- 1 point Unreasonable estimate given.
- 0 points No estimated answer given.

Solve — *Criterion Score* 3/4

Indicator 1: Student shows a solution method that correctly represents the information in the problem.

Scoring:
- 2 points Correct solution method written.
- 1 point Incorrect solution method written.
- 0 points No solution method written.

Indicator 2: Student writes a complete sentence giving the correct answer.

- 2 points Sentence has correct answer and completely answers the question.
- 1 point Sentence has an incorrect numerical answer or does not answer the question.
- 0 points No sentence written.

Check — *Criterion Score* 3/4

Indicator 1: Student writes a sentence explaining why the answer is reasonable.

Scoring:
- 2 points Gives a complete and correct explanation.
- 1 point Gives an incomplete or incorrect reason.
- 0 points No sentence written.

Indicator 2: Student describes another strategy that could have been used to solve the problem.

- 2 points Another useful strategy described.
- 1 point Another strategy described, but it is a poor choice.
- 0 points No other strategy described.

TOTAL 13/18

MANAGEMENT FORMS

This *Assessment Guide* contains two types of forms to help you manage your record keeping and evaluate students in various types of assessment. On the following pages (AG xxviii–AG xliii) you will find Individual Record Forms that contain all of the Learning Goals for the grade level, divided by unit. After each Learning Goal are correlations to the items in Form A and Form B of the Chapter Tests. Criterion scores for each Learning Goal are given. The form provides a place to enter a single student's scores on formal tests and to indicate the objectives he or she has met. A list of review options is also included. The options include lessons in the *Pupil Edition* and *Teacher's Edition*, and activities in the Workbooks that you can assign to the student who is in need of additional practice.

The Class Record Form (pages AG xliv–AG xlvi) makes it possible to record the test scores of an entire class on a single form.

Individual Record Form

Grade 1 • Inventory Test

Student Name ____________________

Test	INV
Form A	
Form B	

(The Grade 1 Inventory Test assesses Kindergarten content. Lesson numbers and Learning Goals are provided for your reference.)

Item Number	Lesson Number	Goal #	Learning Goal
1	1.6	1B	To identify, sort, and classify objects by color, shape, size, and kind
2	2.3	2A	To identify, copy, extend, and create simple patterns
3	1.4	1A	To identify positions such as top, middle, bottom; in and out, above below, over and under and right and left
4	3.1	3A	To use one-to-one correspondence to identify when one group is equal to, more than, or fewer than another group
5	3.2	3A	To use one-to-one correspondence to identify when one group is equal to, more than, or fewer than another group
6	3.3	3A	To use one-to-one correspondence to identify when one group is equal to, more than, or fewer than another group
7	3.5	3B	To count objects and write numbers from 0–5
8	3.6	3B	To count objects and write numbers from 0–5
9	4.2	4A	To count objects and write numbers from 0–10
10	4.2	4A	To count objects and write numbers from 0–10
11	5.4	5A	To identify, sort, and classify solid figures and plane shapes
12	5.4	5A	To identify, sort, and classify solid figures and plane shapes

Student Name ____________________

Inventory Test (continued)

Item Number	Lesson Number	Goal #	Learning Goal
13	5.1	5A	To identify, sort, and classify solid figures and plane shapes
14	4.3	4A	To count objects and write numbers from 0–10
15	6.3	6A	To count, recognize, and write numbers 11–30
16	8.2	8A	To identify penny, nickel, dime and their value
17	8.3	8A	To identify penny, nickel, dime and their value
18	9.1	9A	To compare the length, weight, and capacity of objects by making direct comparisons
19	8.8	8B	To identify concepts of time
20	7.8	7D	To identify ordinal numbers first through tenth
21	11.6	11B	To solve simple addition problems using pictures
22	12.6	12B	To solve simple subtraction problems using pictures
23	11.4	11B	To solve simple addition problems using pictures
24	12.4	12B	To solve simple subtraction problems using pictures
25	12.8	12C	To use problem solving strategies and skills such as *act it out* or *choose the operation* to solve problems

Individual Record Form

Grade 1 • Unit 1

Student Name ______________________

Test	Chapter 1	Chapter 2	Chapter 3	Chapter 4	Unit 1 Test
Form A					
Form B					

	GOALS AND LESSONS ASSESSED			CHAPTER TEST FORM A/B				UNIT 1 TEST FORM A/B				REVIEW
	Goal #	Learning Goal	PE/TE Lessons	Test Items	Criterion Score	Student's Score		Test Items	Criterion Score	Student's Score		Workbooks
						Form A	Form B			Form A	Form B	P, R, C, PS
CHAPTER 1	1A	To write the appropriate numbers and mathematical symbols related to addition stories, pictures, and sentences	1.1 1.2	1–3 4–6	4/6			1, 2 17	2/3			1.1 1.2
	1B	To write sums adding zero	1.3	9, 10	2/2			5	1/1			1.3
	1C	To use the problem solving strategy *write a number sentence* to solve problems	1.4	7, 8	2/2			3, 4	2/2			1.4
CHAPTER 2	2A	To write sums by using the Order Property	2.1	1, 2	2/2			6	1/1			2.1
	2B	To write addition sentences to show ways to make numbers to 10	2.2 2.3	3, 4 5, 6	3/4			7 8	2/2			2.2 2.3
	2C	To write addition sentences vertically	2.4	7, 8	2/2			9	1/1			2.4
	2D	To use the problem solving strategy *make a model* to solve problems	2.5	9, 10	2/2			10	1/1			2.5
CHAPTER 3	3A	To write the appropriate numbers and mathematical symbols related to subtraction stories, pictures, and sentences	3.1 3.2 3.3	1, 2 3, 4 5, 6	4/6			11, 12 16 13	3/4			3.1 3.2 3.3
	3B	To subtract all or zero to solve subtraction sentences	3.5	7, 8	2/2			14	1/1			3.5
	3C	To use the problem solving strategy *make a model* to solve problems	3.4	9, 10	2/2			15	1/1			3.4

CHAPTER 4

Goal #	Learning Goal	PE/TE Lessons	Test Items	Criterion Score	Student's Score		Test Items	Criterion Score	Student's Score		Workbooks
					Form A	Form B			Form A	Form B	P, R, C, PS
4A	To write subtraction sentences to show ways to take apart numbers to 10	4.1 4.2	1, 2 3, 4	3/4							4.1 4.2
4B	To write subtraction sentences to solve how many more	4.4	7, 8	2/2			19	1/1			4.4
4C	To write subtraction sentences vertically	4.3	5, 6	2/2			18	1/1			4.3
4D	To use the problem solving strategy *draw a picture* to solve problems	4.5	9, 10	2/2			20	1/1			4.5

KEY: **P-**Practice, **R-**Reteach, **C-**Challenge, **PS-**Problem Solving

Individual Record Form

Grade 1 • Unit 2

Student Name ______________________

Test	Chapter 5	Chapter 6	Chapter 7	Chapter 8	Unit 2 Test
Form A					
Form B					

	GOALS AND LESSONS ASSESSED			CHAPTER TEST FORM A/B				UNIT 2 TEST FORM A/B				REVIEW
	Goal #	Learning Goal	PE/TE Lessons	Test Items	Criterion Score	Student's Score		Test Items	Criterion Score	Student's Score		Workbooks
						Form A	Form B			Form A	Form B	P, R, C, PS
CHAPTER 5	5A	To write sums to 10 by using addition strategies such as *counting on*, *doubles*, and *doubles plus one*	5.1 5.2 5.3	2–4 7, 8 1, 5, 6	5/8			1, 2, 5 12 7, 8	4/6			5.1 5.2 5.3
CHAPTER 5	5B	To use the problem solving strategy *draw a picture* to solve problems	5.4	9, 10	2/2			20	1/1			5.4
CHAPTER 6	6A	To write sums to 10 and to commit the facts to memory	6.1 6.2 6.3	2, 4 5, 6 1, 3	4/6							6.1 6.2 6.3
CHAPTER 6	6B	To use addition rules to complete function tables through sums of 10	6.4	7, 8	2/2			13	1/1			6.4
CHAPTER 6	6C	To use the problem solving strategy *write a number sentence* to solve problems	6.5	9, 10	2/2			16	1/1			6.5

Student Name ______________________

Chapter	Goal #	Learning Goal	PE/TE Lessons	Test Items	Criterion Score	Student's Score Form A	Student's Score Form B	Test Items	Criterion Score	Student's Score Form A	Student's Score Form B	Workbooks P, R, C, PS
CHAPTER 7	7A	To write differences, subtracting from 10 or less, by using the strategy *counting back*	7.1 7.2	1, 4, 6 3, 5, 7	4/6			10	1/1			7.1 7.2
CHAPTER 7	7B	To write and solve related addition and subtraction sentences	7.3	2, 8	2/2			9, 11, 17	2/3			7.3
CHAPTER 7	7C	To use the problem solving strategy *draw a picture* to solve problems	7.4	9, 10	2/2			18	1/1			7.4
CHAPTER 8	8A	To write differences, subtracting from 10 or less, and to commit the facts to memory	8.1 8.2	1–3 4–7	5/7			3 4, 6	2/3			8.1 8.2
CHAPTER 8	8B	To write and solve fact families, subtracting from 10 or less and adding up to 10	8.4	8	1/1			14	1/1			8.4
CHAPTER 8	8C	To use subtraction rules to complete function tables, subtracting from 10 or less	8.3	9	1/1			15	1/1			8.3
CHAPTER 8	8D	To use the problem solving skill *choose the operation* to solve problems	8.5	10	1/1			19	1/1			8.5

KEY: **P**-Practice, **R**-Reteach, **C**-Challenge, **PS**-Problem Solving

Individual Record Form

Grade 1 • Unit 3

Student Name ______________________

Test	Chapter 9	Chapter 10	Chapter 11	Chapter 12	Chapter 13	Chapter 14	Unit 3 Test
Form A							
Form B							

	GOALS AND LESSONS ASSESSED			CHAPTER TEST FORM A/B				UNIT 3 TEST FORM A/B				REVIEW
	Goal #	Learning Goal	PE/TE Lessons	Test Items	Criterion Score	Student's Score Form A	Student's Score Form B	Test Items	Criterion Score	Student's Score Form A	Student's Score Form B	Workbooks P, R, C, PS
CHAPTER 9	9A	To sort and classify objects by attributes	9.1	3	1/1							9.1
	9B	To organize and display data in tally charts	9.4	1, 2	2/2							9.4
	9C	To organize and display data in graphs	9.2 9.3 9.5	 7, 8 4	2/3							9.2 9.3 9.5
	9D	To use the problem solving skill *use data from a graph* to solve problems	9.6	5, 6	2/2			1, 2	2/2			9.6
	9E	To interpret data in graphs	9.7	9, 10	2/2							9.7
CHAPTER 10	10A	To identify groups from 10 to 100; to write the numbers as tens and ones, as standard numerals, and in a variety of other ways	10.1 10.2 10.3 10.4 10.5	3 1, 2 4 5, 6 7, 8	5/8			3 4	2/2			10.1 10.2 10.3 10.4 10.5
	10B	To use the problem solving skill *make reasonable estimates* to solve problems	10.6	9, 10	2/2			5	1/1			10.6
CHAPTER 11	11A	To identify a number that is greater or less than a given number	11.1 11.2	1 2	2/2							11.1 11.2
	11B	To compare numbers using the symbols for less than (<), greater than (>), and equal to (=)	11.3	3, 4	2/2			6	1/1			11.3
	11C	To identify the missing number that comes before, after, or between a given pair of numbers	11.4	5, 6	2/2			7	1/1			11.4
	11D	To count forward or count backward from a given number	11.5	7, 8	2/2							11.5
	11E	To use the problem solving skill *use a model* to solve problems	11.6	9, 10	2/2			8	1/1			11.6

Student Name ______________________

Chapter	Goal #	Learning Goal	PE/TE Lessons	Test Items	Criterion Score	Student's Score Form A	Student's Score Form B	Test Items	Criterion Score	Student's Score Form A	Student's Score Form B	Workbooks P, R, C, PS
CHAPTER 12	12A	To recognize and extend number patterns by using skip-counting or a hundreds chart	12.1 12.2 12.3	1, 2 3 4	3/4			9	1/1			12.1 12.2 12.3
	12B	To identify numbers as even or odd	12.4	5, 6	2/2			11	1/1			12.4
	12C	To use the problem solving strategy *find a pattern* to solve problems	12.5	7, 8	2/2							12.5
	12D	To identify ordinal position through tenth	12.6	9, 10	2/2			10	1/1			12.6
CHAPTER 13	13A	To write sums to 12 and differences from 12 by using strategies such as *counting on*, *doubles*, and *doubles plus one*	13.1 13.2	1, 2 5, 6	3/4			14	1/1			13.1 13.2
	13B	To use the Associative Property to add three numbers for sums to 12	13.3	7, 8	2/2			12, 13	2/2			13.3
	13C	To use the problem solving strategy *write a number sentence* to solve problems	13.4	10	1/1			15	1/1			13.4
	13D	To write differences from 12 by using the strategy counting back	13.5	3, 4	2/2			16	1/1			13.5
	13E	To write differences related to subtraction stories, models, and pictures	13.6	9	1/1			17	1/1			13.6
CHAPTER 14	14A	To write and solve related addition and subtraction sentences	14.1	1, 2	2/2			18	1/1			14.1
	14B	To write and solve related addition and subtraction sentences using the inverse relationship between addition and subtraction	14.2	3, 4	2/2							14.2
	14C	To write sums to 12 and differences from 12	14.3	7, 8	2/2			19	1/1			14.3
	14D	To write and complete number sentences using addition and subtraction	14.4	5, 6	2/2							14.4
	14E	To use the problem solving skill *choosing a strategy* to solve problems	14.5	9, 10	2/2			20	1/1			14.5

KEY: **P**-Practice, **R**-Reteach, **C**-Challenge, **PS**-Problem Solving

Individual Record Form

Grade 1 • Unit 4

Student Name ______________________

Test	Chapter 15	Chapter 16	Chapter 17	Chapter 18	Chapter 19	Chapter 20	Unit 4 Test
Form A							
Form B							

	GOALS AND LESSONS ASSESSED			CHAPTER TEST FORM A/B				UNIT 4 TEST FORM A/B				REVIEW
	Goal #	Learning Goal	PE/TE Lessons	Test Items	Criterion Score	Student's Score		Test Items	Criterion Score	Student's Score		Workbooks
						Form A	Form B			Form A	Form B	P, R, C, PS
CHAPTER 15	15A	To identify, compare, sort, and classify solid figures	15.1 15.2	1, 2 3, 4	3/4			1 2	2/2			15.1 15.2
	15B	To identify, compare, sort, and classify plane shapes	15.3 15.4	5, 6 7, 8	3/4			3 4	2/2			15.3 15.4
	15C	To use the problem solving strategy *make a model* to solve problems	15.5	9, 10	2/2							15.5
CHAPTER 16	16A	To identify open and closed figures	16.1	1, 2	2/2							16.1
	16B	To use the problem solving skill *use a picture* to solve problems	16.2	3, 4	2/2			5, 6	2/2			16.2
	16C	To identify and use terms of orientation	16.3 16.5	5, 6 9, 10	3/4			7	1/1			16.3 16.5
	16D	To identify symmetrical shapes and their lines of symmetry	16.4	7, 8	2/2			8	1/1			16.4
CHAPTER 17	17A	To identify, extend, and create repeating linear patterns	17.1 17.2 17.3	1, 2 3, 4 5, 6	4/6			9 10	2/2			17.1 17.2 17.3
	17B	To use the problem solving skill *correct a pattern* to solve problems	17.4	7, 8	2/2			11	1/1			17.4
	17C	To use the problem solving skill *transfer patterns* to solve problems	17.5	9, 10	2/2							17.5

Student Name ______________________

Chapter	Goal #	Learning Goal	PE/TE Lessons	Test Items	Criterion Score	Student's Score Form A	Student's Score Form B	Test Items	Criterion Score	Student's Score Form A	Student's Score Form B	Workbooks P, R, C, PS
CHAPTER 18	18A	To write sums to 20 using strategies such as *doubles*, *doubles plus 1*, and *make ten*	18.1 18.2 18.3 18.4	1, 2 3 4 5, 6	4/6			12 13	2/2			18.1 18.2 18.3 18.4
	18B	To use the Associative Property to add three numbers for sums to 20	18.5	7, 8	2/2			14	1/1			18.5
	18C	To use the problem solving skill *use data from a table* to solve problems	18.6	9, 10	2/2							18.6
CHAPTER 19	19A	To write differences from 20 by using the strategy *count back*	19.1	1, 2	2/2			15	1/1			19.1
	19B	To write and solve related addition and subtraction sentences by using the inverse relationship between addition and subtraction	19.2 19.3	3, 4 5, 6	3/4			16 17	2/2			19.2 19.3
	19C	To use the problem solving skill *estimate reasonable answers* to solve problems	19.4	7–10	3/4							19.4
CHAPTER 20	20A	To write sums to 20 and differences from 20	20.1 20.2 20.3	1–4 7, 8 5, 6	5/8			18 19	2/2			20.1 20.2 20.3
	20B	To use the problem solving strategy *make a model* to solve problems	20.4	9, 10	2/2			20	1/1			20.4

KEY: **P**-Practice, **R**-Reteach, **C**-Challenge, **PS**-Problem Solving

Individual Record Form

Grade 1 • Unit 5

Student Name ______________________

Test	Chapter 21	Chapter 22	Chapter 23	Chapter 24	Chapter 25	Unit 5 Test
Form A						
Form B						

Chapter	GOALS AND LESSONS ASSESSED			CHAPTER TEST FORM A/B				UNIT 5 TEST FORM A/B				REVIEW
	Goal #	Learning Goal	PE/TE Lessons	Test Items	Criterion Score	Student's Score Form A	Student's Score Form B	Test Items	Criterion Score	Student's Score Form A	Student's Score Form B	Workbooks P, R, C, PS
CHAPTER 21	21A	To identify halves, fourths, and thirds	21.1 21.2 21.3	1, 2 3, 4 5, 6	4/6			1 2	2/2			21.1 21.2 21.3
CHAPTER 21	21B	To use the problem solving strategy *use logical reasoning* to solve problems	21.4	9, 10	2/2			3	1/1			21.4
CHAPTER 21	21C	To identify parts of groups	21.5	7, 8	2/2			4	1/1			21.5
CHAPTER 22	22A	To identify pennies, nickels, dimes, and their values	22.1 22.2	1, 2 3, 4	3/4							22.1 22.2
CHAPTER 22	22B	To count groups of pennies, nickels, and dimes	22.3 22.4	5, 6 7, 8	3/4			5 6	2/2			22.3 22.4
CHAPTER 22	22C	To use the problem solving strategy *make a list* to solve problems	22.5	9, 10	2/2			7	1/1			22.5
CHAPTER 23	23A	To identify the same amount of money and compare values by using different coins	23.1 23.4 23.5	1, 2 7 8	3/4			8	1/1			23.1 23.4 23.5
CHAPTER 23	23B	To identify a quarter and its value	23.2	3, 4	2/2			9	1/1			23.2
CHAPTER 23	23C	To identify a half dollar and its value, and one dollar and its value	23.3	5, 6	2/2			10	1/1			23.3
CHAPTER 23	23D	To use the problem solving strategy *act it out* to solve problems	23.6	9, 10	2/2							23.6

Student Name ____________________

Unit 5 (continued)

Chapter	Goal #	Learning Goal	PE/TE Lessons	Test Items	Criterion Score	Student's Score Form A	Student's Score Form B	Test Items	Criterion Score	Student's Score Form A	Student's Score Form B	Workbooks P, R, C, PS
CHAPTER 24	24A	To identify the parts of a clock, and to write the time to the hour and half hour	24.1 24.3 24.4 24.5	1, 2 5, 6 7, 8 9, 10	5/8			11 13 14	2/3			24.1 24.3 24.4 24.5
CHAPTER 24	24B	To use the problem solving skill *use estimation* to solve problems	24.2	3, 4	2/2			12	1/1			24.2
CHAPTER 25	25A	To identify and order the months of the year and the days of the week, and to sequence events	25.1 25.2	1, 2 3, 4	3/4			15, 16 17	2/3			25.1 25.2
CHAPTER 25	25B	To use the problem solving strategy *make a graph* to solve problems	25.3	5, 6	2/2							25.3
CHAPTER 25	25C	To read a schedule and compare events by using a chart	25.4	7, 8	2/2			18, 19	2/2			25.4
CHAPTER 25	25D	To use the problem solving skill *make reasonable estimates* to solve problems	25.5	9, 10	2/2			20	1/1			25.5

KEY: **P**-Practice, **R**-Reteach, **C**-Challenge, **PS**-Problem Solving

Individual Record Form

Grade 1 • Unit 6

Student Name ______________________

Test	Chapter 26	Chapter 27	Chapter 28	Chapter 29	Chapter 30	Unit 6 Test
Form A						
Form B						

	GOALS AND LESSONS ASSESSED			CHAPTER TEST FORM A/B				UNIT 6 TEST FORM A/B				REVIEW
	Goal #	Learning Goal	PE/TE Lessons	Test Items	Criterion Score	Student's Score Form A	Student's Score Form B	Test Items	Criterion Score	Student's Score Form A	Student's Score Form B	Workbooks P, R, C, PS
CHAPTER 26	26A	To estimate, measure, and compare the lengths of objects by using nonstandard units, inches, and centimeters	26.1 26.2 26.3 26.4 26.5	1, 2 3 4 5, 6 7, 8	5/8			1 4 3 2 5	3/5			26.1 26.2 26.3 26.4 26.5
	26B	To use the problem solving skill *make reasonable estimates* to solve problems	26.6	9, 10	2/2			6	1/1			26.6
CHAPTER 27	27A	To estimate, measure, and compare weight	27.1 27.2 27.3	1, 2 3–5 6–8	5/8			7 8 9	2/3			27.1 27.2 27.3
	27B	To use the problem solving strategy *predict and test* to solve problems	27.4	9, 10	2/2							27.4
CHAPTER 28	28A	To estimate, measure, and compare capacity	28.1 28.2 28.3	1, 2 3, 4 5, 6	4/6			11 10	2/2			28.1 28.2 28.3
	28B	To measure temperature using a Fahrenheit thermometer	28.4	7, 8	2/2			12	1/1			28.4
	28C	To use the problem solving skill *choose the measuring tool* to solve problems	28.5	9, 10	2/2			13	1/1			28.5

Student Name ______________________

Unit 6 (continued)

Chapter	Goal #	Learning Goal	PE/TE Lessons	Test Items	Criterion Score	Student's Score Form A	Student's Score Form B	Test Items	Criterion Score	Student's Score Form A	Student's Score Form B	Workbooks P, R, C, PS
CHAPTER 29	29A	To find sums to 100 by adding or subtracting tens	29.1 29.4	1 2	2/2			14 15	2/2			29.1 29.4
CHAPTER 29	29B	To add or subtract up to 2-digit numbers without regrouping	29.2 29.3 29.5 29.6	3 5, 6 4 7, 8	4/6			18 17 16 19	3/4			29.2 29.3 29.5 29.6
CHAPTER 29	29C	To use the problem solving skill *make reasonable estimates* to solve problems	29.7	9, 10	2/2			20	1/1			29.7
CHAPTER 30	30A	To write predictions, determine, and record outcomes of an event	30.1 30.2 30.3	1–3 4–6 7, 8	5/8			21 22 23	2/3			30.1 30.2 30.3
CHAPTER 30	30B	To use the problem solving skill *make a prediction* to solve problems	30.4	9, 10	2/2			24	1/1			30.4

KEY: **P**-Practice, **R**-Reteach, **C**-Challenge, **PS**-Problem Solving

Individual Record Form

Grade 1 • End of Year Test

Student Name ____________________

Test	EOY Test
Form A	
Form B	

Goal #	Learning Goal	Test Items	PE/TE Lessons
8D	To use the problem solving skill *choose the operation* to solve problems	3, 4	8.5
9B	To organize and display data in tally charts	5	9.4
9C	To organize and display data in graphs	6	9.5
10A	To identify groups from 10 to 100; to write the numbers as tens and ones, as standard numerals, and in a variety of other ways	7 8	10.4 10.5
12A	To recognize and extend number patterns by using skip-counting or a hundreds chart	9	12.1
13B	To use the Associative Property to add three numbers for sums to 12	10	13.3
13E	To write differences related to subtraction stories, models, and pictures	11	13.6
14D	To write and complete number sentences using addition and subtraction	12	14.4
15A	To identify, compare, sort, and classify solid figures	13	15.1
17A	To identify, extend, and create repeating linear patterns	14	17.1
20A	To write sums to 20 and differences from 20	15	20.2
21A	To identify halves, fourths, and thirds	17	21.3
22B	To count groups of pennies, nickels, and dimes	18	22.4

Student Name ______________________

End of Year (continued)

Goal #	Learning Goal	Test Items	PE/TE Lessons
24A	To identify the parts of a clock, and to write the time to the hour and half hour	19	24.4
26A	To estimate, measure, and compare the lengths of objects by using nonstandard units, inches, and centimeters	20	26.5
29B	To add or subtract up to 2-digit numbers without regrouping	16 1	29.3 29.5
30A	To write predictions, determine, and record outcomes of an event	2	30.2

Formal Assessment

Class Record Form

CHAPTER TESTS

School											
Teacher											
NAMES	Date										

Formal Assessment

Class Record Form

UNIT TESTS

School											
Teacher											
NAMES	Date										

Formal Assessment

Class Record Form

INVENTORY/END OF YEAR TESTS

School											
Teacher											
NAMES	Date										

Test-Taking Tips

Being a good test taker is like being a good problem solver. When you answer test questions, you are solving problems. Remember to **UNDERSTAND, PLAN, SOLVE,** and **CHECK**.

Understand

Read the problem.

- Look for math terms and recall their meanings.
- Reread the problem and think about the question.
- Use the details in the problem and the question.
- Each word is important. Missing a word or reading it incorrectly could cause you to get the wrong answer.
- Pay attention to words that are in **bold** type, all CAPITAL letters, or *italics*.
- Some other words to look for are round, about, only, best, or least to greatest.

Plan

Think about how you can solve the problem.

- Can you solve the problem with the information given?
- Pictures, charts, tables, and graphs may have the information you need.
- Sometimes you may need to remember some information that is not given.
- Sometimes the answer choices have information to help you solve the problem.
- You may need to write a number sentence and solve it to answer the question.
- Some problems have two steps or more.
- In some problems you may need to look at relationships instead of computing an answer.
- If the path to the solution isn't clear, choose a problem-solving strategy.
- Use the strategy you chose to solve the problem.

Follow your plan, working logically and carefully.

- Estimate your answer. Look for unreasonable answer choices.
- Use reasoning to find the most likely choices.
- Make sure you solved all the steps needed to answer the problem.
- If your answer does not match one of the answer choices, check the numbers you used. Then check your computation.

Solve

Solve the problem.

- If your answer still does not match one of the choices, look for another form of the number such as decimals instead of fractions.
- If answer choices are given as pictures, look at each one by itself while you cover the other three.
- If you do not see your answer and the answer choices include NOT HERE, make sure your work is correct and then mark NOT HERE.
- Read answer choices that are statements and relate them to the problem one by one.
- Change your plan if it isn't working. You may need to try a different strategy.

Check

Take time to catch your mistakes.

- Be sure you answered the question asked.
- Check that your answer fits the information in the problem.
- Check for important words you may have missed.
- Be sure you used all the information you needed.
- Check your computation by using a different method.
- Draw a picture when you are unsure of your answer.

Don't forget!

Before the Test

- Listen to the teacher's directions and read the instructions.
- Write down the ending time if the test is timed.
- Know where and how to mark your answers.
- Know whether you should write on the test page or use scratch paper.
- Ask any questions you have before the test begins.

During the Test

- Work quickly but carefully. If you are unsure how to answer a question, leave it blank and return to it later.
- If you cannot finish on time, look over the questions that are left. Answer the easiest ones first. Then go back to the others.
- Fill in each answer space carefully and completely. Erase completely if you change an answer. Erase any stray marks.

Name ______________________ Date __________

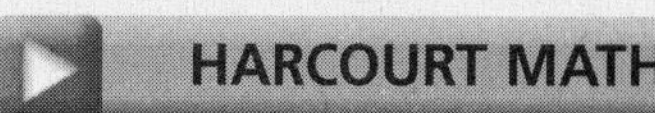

Test Answer Sheet

Test Title ______________________

1. Ⓐ Ⓑ Ⓒ Ⓓ
2. Ⓐ Ⓑ Ⓒ Ⓓ
3. Ⓐ Ⓑ Ⓒ Ⓓ
4. Ⓐ Ⓑ Ⓒ Ⓓ
5. Ⓐ Ⓑ Ⓒ Ⓓ
6. Ⓐ Ⓑ Ⓒ Ⓓ
7. Ⓐ Ⓑ Ⓒ Ⓓ
8. Ⓐ Ⓑ Ⓒ Ⓓ
9. Ⓐ Ⓑ Ⓒ Ⓓ
10. Ⓐ Ⓑ Ⓒ Ⓓ
11. Ⓐ Ⓑ Ⓒ Ⓓ
12. Ⓐ Ⓑ Ⓒ Ⓓ
13. Ⓐ Ⓑ Ⓒ Ⓓ
14. Ⓐ Ⓑ Ⓒ Ⓓ
15. Ⓐ Ⓑ Ⓒ Ⓓ
16. Ⓐ Ⓑ Ⓒ Ⓓ
17. Ⓐ Ⓑ Ⓒ Ⓓ
18. Ⓐ Ⓑ Ⓒ Ⓓ
19. Ⓐ Ⓑ Ⓒ Ⓓ
20. Ⓐ Ⓑ Ⓒ Ⓓ
21. Ⓐ Ⓑ Ⓒ Ⓓ
22. Ⓐ Ⓑ Ⓒ Ⓓ
23. Ⓐ Ⓑ Ⓒ Ⓓ
24. Ⓐ Ⓑ Ⓒ Ⓓ
25. Ⓐ Ⓑ Ⓒ Ⓓ
26. Ⓐ Ⓑ Ⓒ Ⓓ
27. Ⓐ Ⓑ Ⓒ Ⓓ
28. Ⓐ Ⓑ Ⓒ Ⓓ
29. Ⓐ Ⓑ Ⓒ Ⓓ
30. Ⓐ Ⓑ Ⓒ Ⓓ
31. Ⓐ Ⓑ Ⓒ Ⓓ
32. Ⓐ Ⓑ Ⓒ Ⓓ
33. Ⓐ Ⓑ Ⓒ Ⓓ
34. Ⓐ Ⓑ Ⓒ Ⓓ
35. Ⓐ Ⓑ Ⓒ Ⓓ
36. Ⓐ Ⓑ Ⓒ Ⓓ
37. Ⓐ Ⓑ Ⓒ Ⓓ
38. Ⓐ Ⓑ Ⓒ Ⓓ
39. Ⓐ Ⓑ Ⓒ Ⓓ
40. Ⓐ Ⓑ Ⓒ Ⓓ
41. Ⓐ Ⓑ Ⓒ Ⓓ
42. Ⓐ Ⓑ Ⓒ Ⓓ
43. Ⓐ Ⓑ Ⓒ Ⓓ
44. Ⓐ Ⓑ Ⓒ Ⓓ
45. Ⓐ Ⓑ Ⓒ Ⓓ
46. Ⓐ Ⓑ Ⓒ Ⓓ
47. Ⓐ Ⓑ Ⓒ Ⓓ
48. Ⓐ Ⓑ Ⓒ Ⓓ
49. Ⓐ Ⓑ Ⓒ Ⓓ
50. Ⓐ Ⓑ Ⓒ Ⓓ

Name ______________________

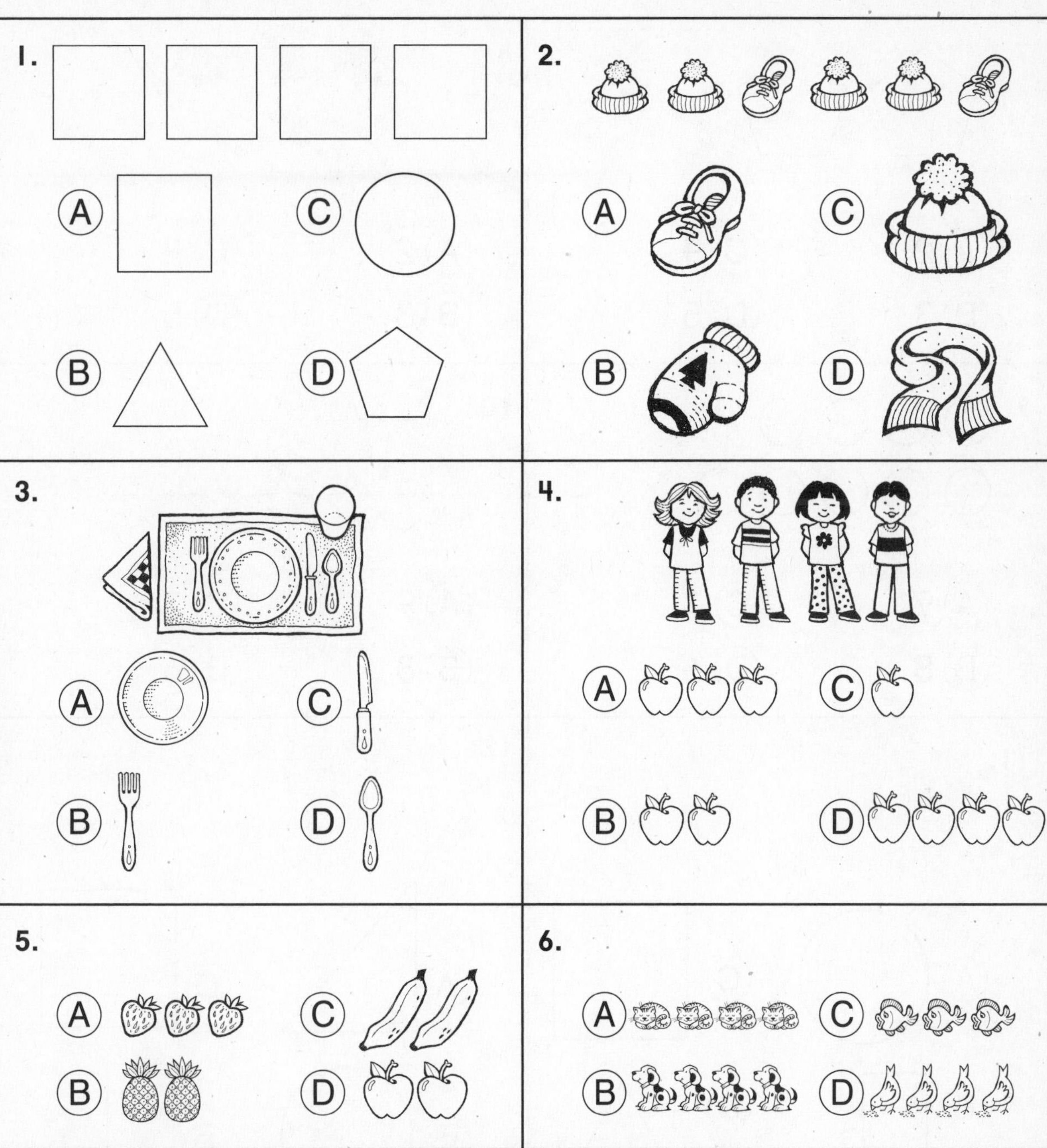

1. Which shape belongs in the group?
2. Find the pattern. Which comes next?
3. Which is on the left side of the plate?
4. Which has the same number of apples as children?
5. Which group has one more than the others?
6. Which group has one less than the others?

Go On

Name ____________________

7.

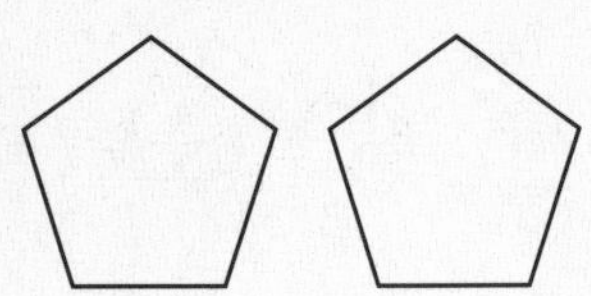

Ⓐ 2 Ⓑ 3 Ⓒ 4 Ⓓ 5

8.

Ⓐ 2 Ⓑ 3 Ⓒ 4 Ⓓ 5

9.

Ⓐ 9 Ⓑ 8 Ⓒ 7 Ⓓ 6

10.

Ⓐ 9 Ⓑ 8 Ⓒ 7 Ⓓ 6

11.

Ⓐ 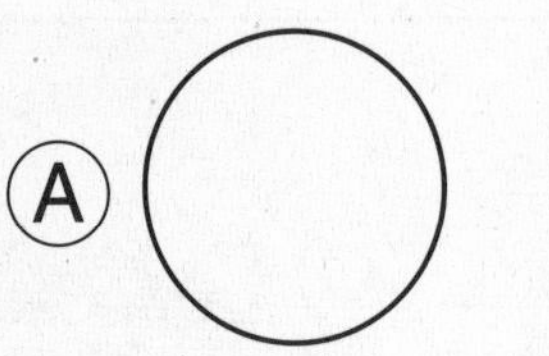

Ⓒ 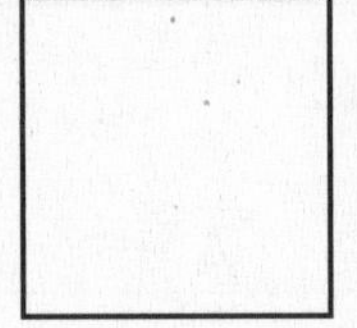

Ⓑ

Ⓓ 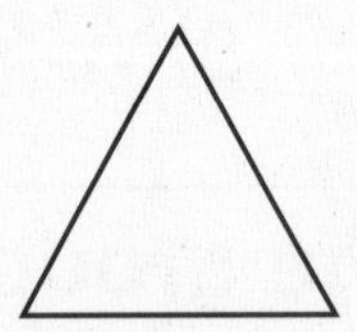

12.

Ⓐ 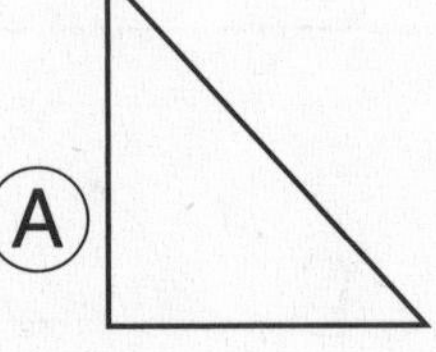

Ⓒ 

Ⓑ

Ⓓ 

7, 8, 9, 10. Which number tells how many there are?
11. Which shape is a square?
12. Which shape is a triangle?

Go On

Name ______________________________

13.

Ⓐ Ⓒ

Ⓑ Ⓓ

14.

Ⓐ Ⓒ

Ⓑ Ⓓ

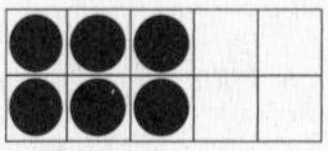

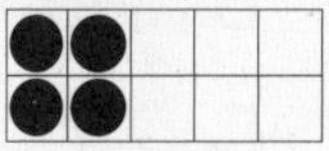

15.

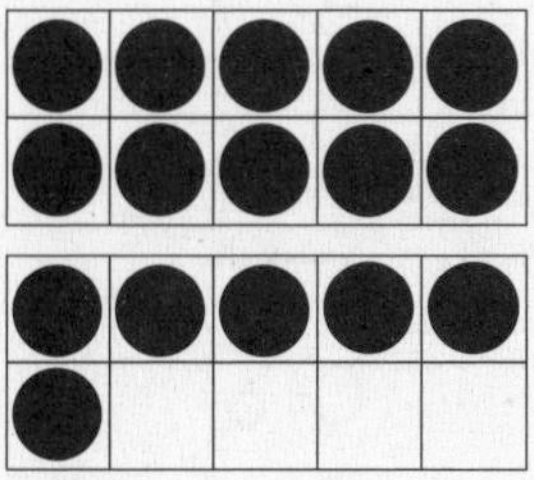

Ⓐ 11 Ⓒ 16

Ⓑ 14 Ⓓ 18

16.

Ⓐ Ⓒ

Ⓑ

17.

Ⓐ 1¢ Ⓒ 10¢

Ⓑ 5¢ Ⓓ 25¢

18.

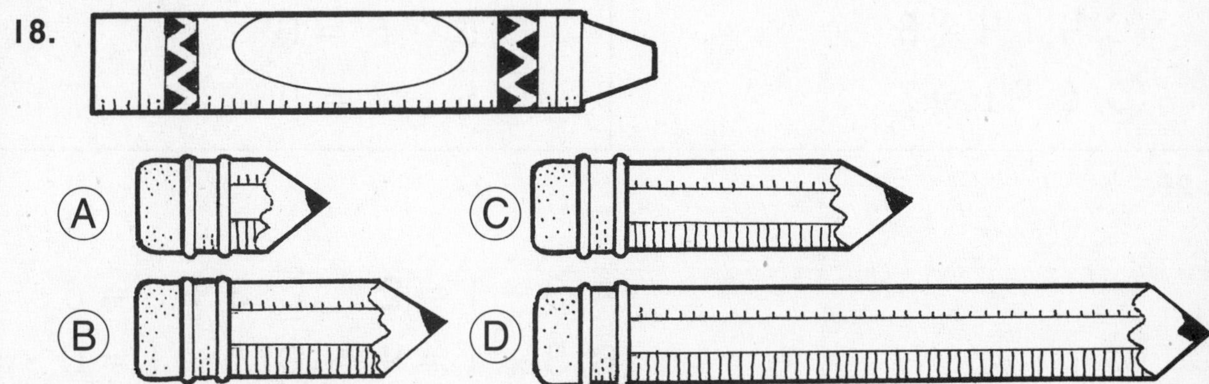

13. Which object is shaped like a cone?
14. Which shows ten?
15. Which number tells how many there are?
16. Which shows a nickel?
17. Which tells how much this coin is worth?
18. Which pencil is longer than the crayon?

Go On

Name ______________________

19.

Ⓐ 12 o'clock
Ⓑ 5 o'clock
Ⓒ 7 o'clock
Ⓓ 6 o'clock

20.

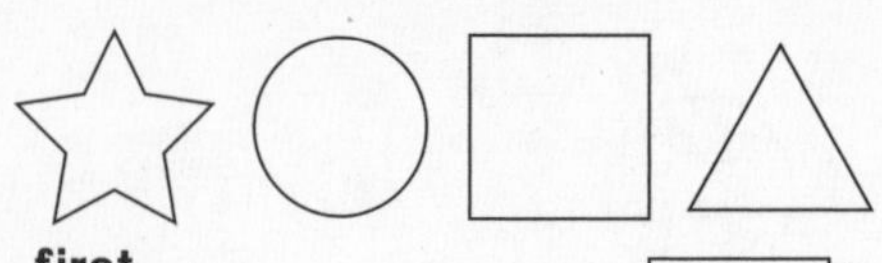

first

Ⓐ Ⓑ Ⓒ Ⓓ

21. $3 + 2 =$ ___

Ⓐ 4 Ⓒ 6
Ⓑ 5 Ⓓ 7

22. $5 - 1 =$ ___

Ⓐ 3 Ⓒ 6
Ⓑ 4 Ⓓ 7

23.

Ⓐ $2 + 4 = 6$
Ⓑ $2 + 2 = 4$
Ⓒ $4 + 4 = 8$
Ⓓ $6 + 1 = 7$

24.

Ⓐ $5 - 2 = 3$
Ⓑ $3 - 2 = 1$
Ⓒ $5 - 5 = 0$
Ⓓ $5 - 1 = 4$

25.

Ⓐ $3 - 1 = 2$ Ⓒ $3 + 3 = 6$
Ⓑ $3 + 1 = 4$ Ⓓ $1 - 1 = 0$

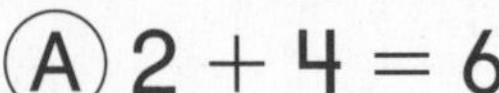

19. What time does the clock show?
20. Which shape is third?
21. Add.
22. Subtract.
23. Which addition sentence matches the picture?
24. Which subtraction sentence matches the picture?
25. Which number sentence matches the picture?

Stop

Name ______________________________

1.

2.

3.

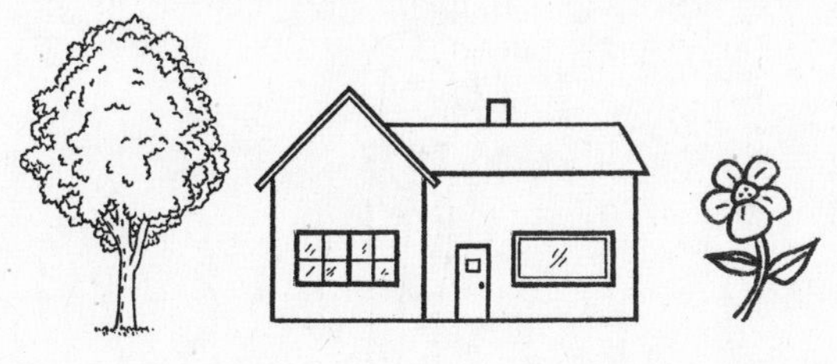

4.

5.

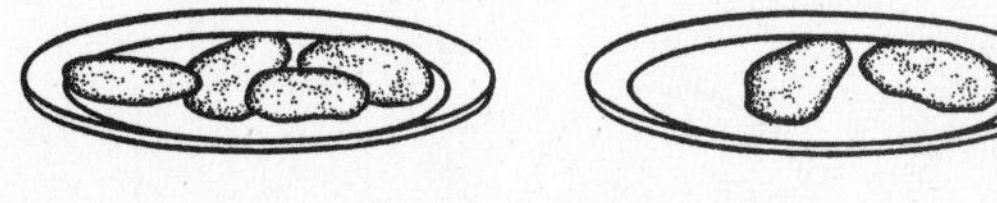

6.

1. Draw another shape that belongs in the group.
2. Draw what comes next in the pattern.
3. Circle the object that is to the right of the house.
4. Draw one bird for each house.
5. Circle the plate that has more cookies.
6. Circle the group that has one less than the other.

Go On

Name ______________________________

7.

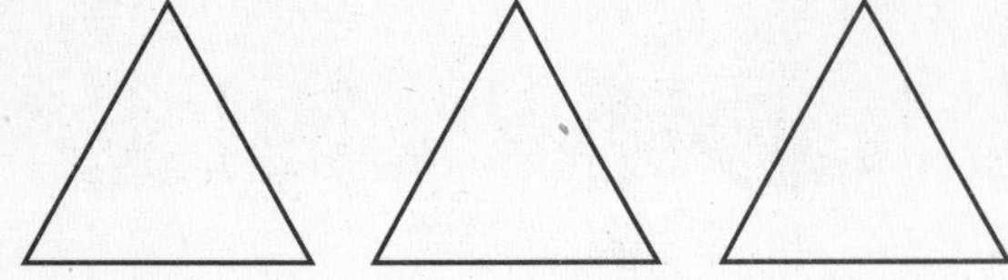

____

8.

____

9.

____

10.

____

11.

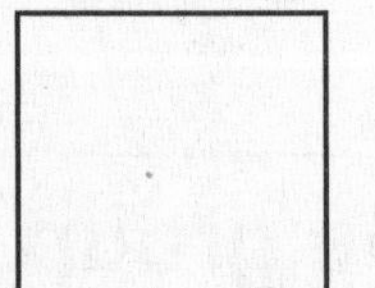

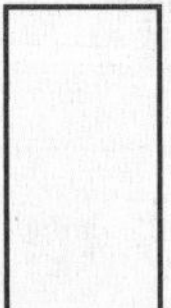

12.

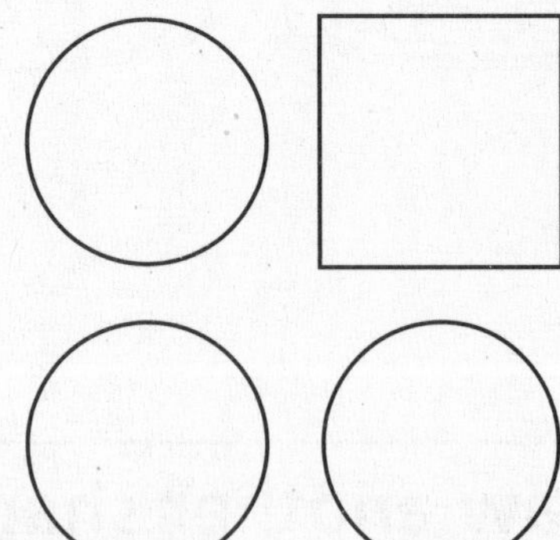

7, 8, 9,10. Write how many there are.
11. Circle the triangle.
12. Mark an X on the shape that is NOT a circle.

Go On

Name ____________________

13.

14.

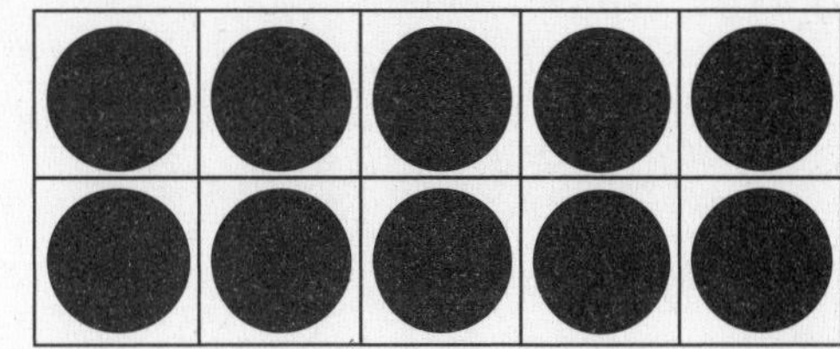

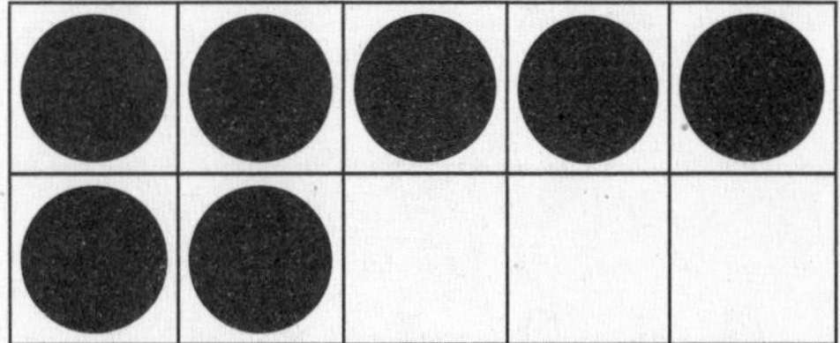

15.

16.

17.

18.

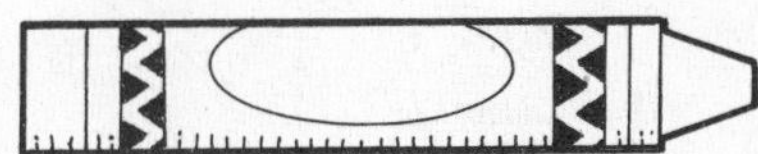

13. Circle the object shaped like a rectangular prism.
14. Mark X on the ten-frame that does NOT show 10.
15. Draw the correct number of counters to show 12.
16. Circle the dime.
17. Circle the coin that is worth 5¢.
18. Draw a line that is longer than the crayon.

Go On

Name ______________________

19.

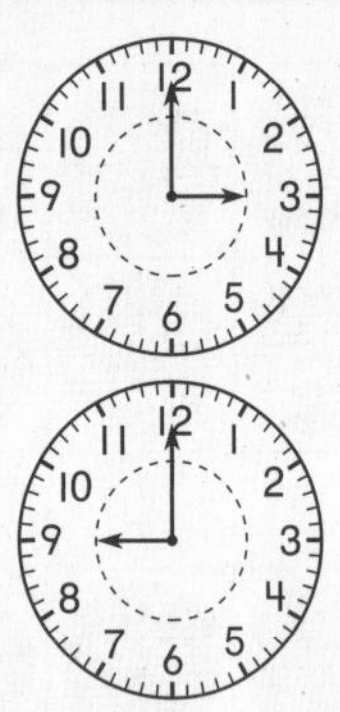

20.

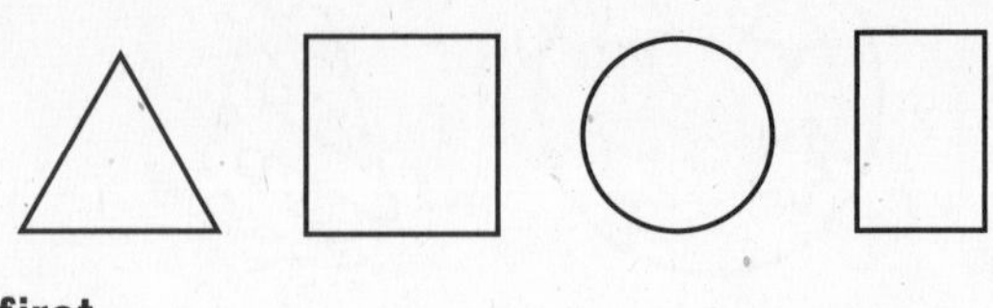

first

21.

4 + 2 = ___

22.

6 − 1 = ___

23.

___ + ___ = ___

24.

5 − ___ = ___

25.

5 + 1 = 6

19. Circle the clock that shows 3:00.
20. Circle the second shape.
21. Add.
22. Subtract.
23. Write the addition sentence that matches the picture.
24. Write the subtraction sentence that matches the picture.
25. Circle the picture that matches the number sentence.

Stop

Name ___________________________

Choose the correct answer.

1. How many are there in all?  2 birds 1 bird ___ in all Ⓐ 9 Ⓒ 4 Ⓑ 6 Ⓓ 3	2. How many are there in all?  2 rabbits 3 rabbits ___ in all Ⓐ 7 Ⓒ 5 Ⓑ 6 Ⓓ 4
3. How many are there in all?  4 fish 2 fish ___ in all Ⓐ 4 Ⓒ 6 Ⓑ 5 Ⓓ 7	4. Add. Find the sum.  $3 + 2 = \_\_\_$ Ⓐ 6 Ⓒ 4 Ⓑ 5 Ⓓ 3
5. Add. Find the sum.  $2 + 4 = \_\_\_$ Ⓐ 3 Ⓒ 5 Ⓑ 4 Ⓓ 6	6. Add. Find the sum.  $2 + 1 = \_\_\_$ Ⓐ 3 Ⓒ 5 Ⓑ 4 Ⓓ 6

Go On

Name ______________________

7. Mark the addition sentence that matches the story.

There are 2 fish.
2 more come.
How many fish are there in all?

___ + ___ = ___

Ⓐ 2 + 2 = 4
Ⓑ 3 + 2 = 5
Ⓒ 4 + 2 = 6
Ⓓ 5 + 1 = 6

8. Mark the addition sentence that matches the story.

There are 2 starfish.
4 more come.
How many starfish are there in all?

___ + ___ = ___

Ⓐ 4 + 4 = 8
Ⓑ 2 + 6 = 8
Ⓒ 6 + 1 = 7
Ⓓ 2 + 4 = 6

9. Find the sum.

3 + 0 = ___

Ⓐ 3
Ⓑ 2
Ⓒ 1
Ⓓ 0

10. Find the sum.

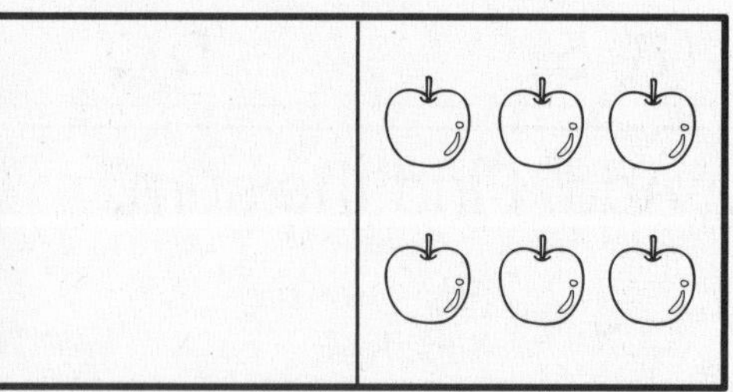

0 + 6 = ___

Ⓐ 0
Ⓑ 2
Ⓒ 6
Ⓓ 8

Stop

Name ______________________

Write the correct answer.

1. How many are there in all?

1 cat　　2 cats　　______ in all

2. How many are there in all?

1 big ball　　3 small balls　　______ in all

3. How many are there in all?

2 birds　　2 birds　　______ in all

4. Add. Write the sum.

3 + 2 = ______

5. Add. Write the sum.

2 + 4 = ______

Go On

6. Add. Write the sum.

4 + 2 = ____

7. Write the addition sentence for the story.

There are 3 clowns. 1 more clown joins them.
How many clowns are there in all?

____ + ____ = ____

8. Write the addition sentence for the story.

There is 1 panda. 4 more pandas come.
How many pandas are there in all?

____ + ____ = ____

9. Find the sum.

4 + 0 = ____

10. Find the sum.

0 + 7 = ____

Stop

Name ______________________________

Choose the correct answer.

1. Add. Mark the sum.

$5 + 1 = 6$

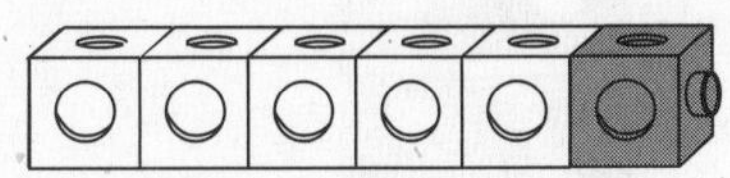

$1 + 5 =$ ___

Ⓐ 7
Ⓑ 6
Ⓒ 5
Ⓓ 2

2. Use cubes. Which two have the same sum?

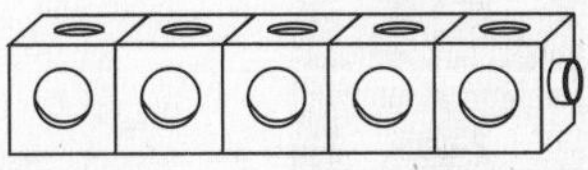

Ⓐ 2 + 3 and 3 + 2
Ⓑ 2 + 3 and 3 + 3
Ⓒ 1 + 5 and 5 + 0
Ⓓ 4 + 2 and 3 + 4

3. Which is a way to make 7?

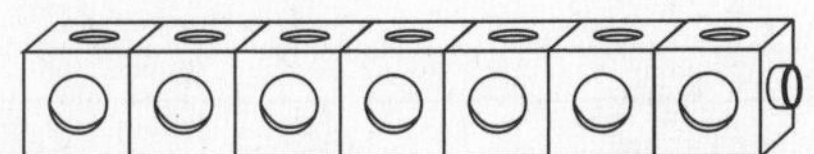

Ⓐ 0 + 8
Ⓑ 7 + 0
Ⓒ 8 + 1
Ⓓ 7 + 2

4. Which is a way to make 8?

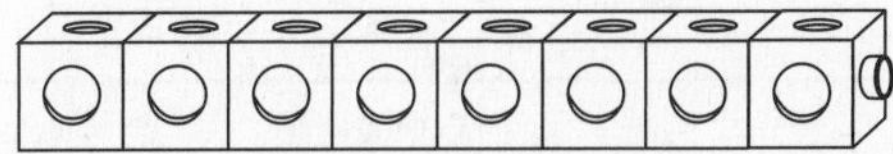

Ⓐ 7 + 0
Ⓑ 8 + 1
Ⓒ 7 + 2
Ⓓ 6 + 2

5. Which is a way to make 9?

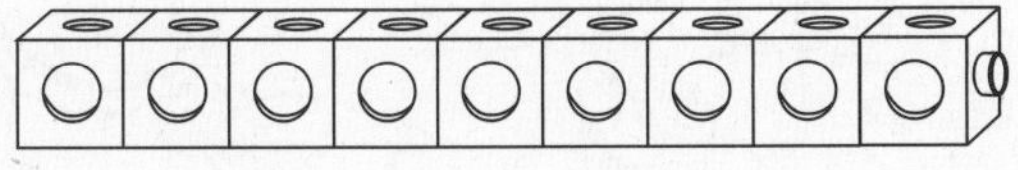

___ + ___ = 9

Ⓐ 4 + 5
Ⓑ 6 + 4
Ⓒ 2 + 9
Ⓓ 9 + 3

6. Which is a way to make 10?

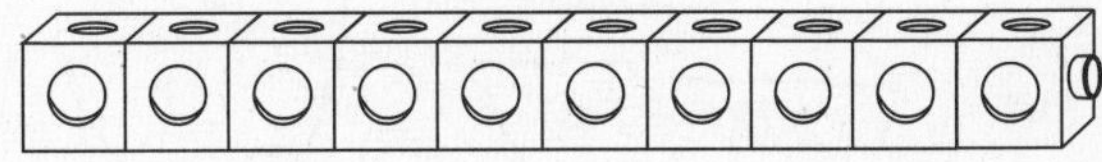

___ + ___ = 10

Ⓐ 3 + 4
Ⓑ 8 + 1
Ⓒ 7 + 3
Ⓓ 10 + 1

Go On

Name ______________________________

7. Which addition problem matches the dots?

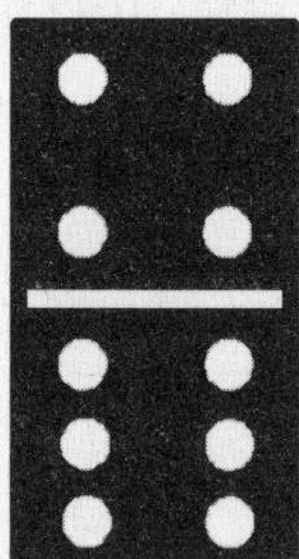

(A) $\begin{array}{r} 4 \\ +\ 2 \\ \hline 6 \end{array}$

(B) $\begin{array}{r} 4 \\ +\ 4 \\ \hline 8 \end{array}$

(C) $\begin{array}{r} 4 \\ +\ 6 \\ \hline 10 \end{array}$

(D) $\begin{array}{r} 2 \\ +\ 2 \\ \hline 4 \end{array}$

8. Which addition problem matches the dots?

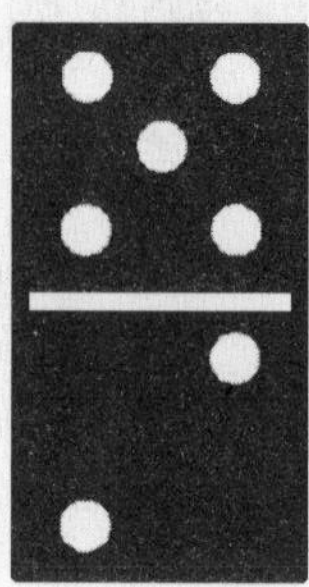

(A) $\begin{array}{r} 2 \\ +\ 2 \\ \hline 4 \end{array}$

(B) $\begin{array}{r} 7 \\ +\ 0 \\ \hline 7 \end{array}$

(C) $\begin{array}{r} 5 \\ +\ 5 \\ \hline 10 \end{array}$

(D) $\begin{array}{r} 5 \\ +\ 2 \\ \hline 7 \end{array}$

9. How much do you spend for both?

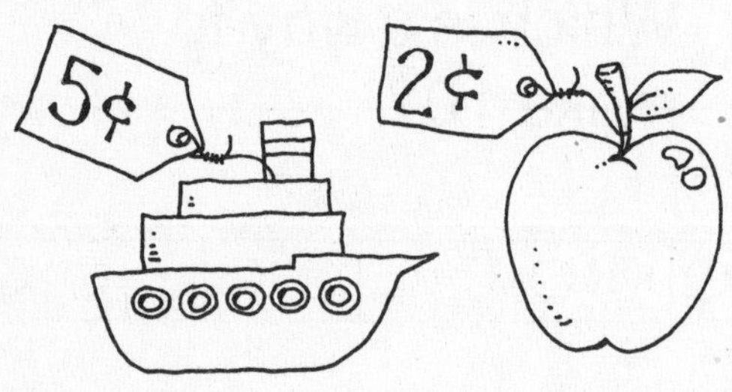

(A) 7¢
(B) 6¢
(C) 5¢
(D) 3¢

10. How much do you spend for both?

(A) 10¢
(B) 9¢
(C) 8¢
(D) 7¢

Stop

Name ____________________

Write the correct answer.

1. Write the sums.

4 + 1 = ___

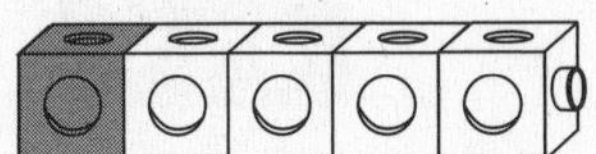

1 + 4 = ___

2. Use cubes to find each sum.

3 + 1 = ___

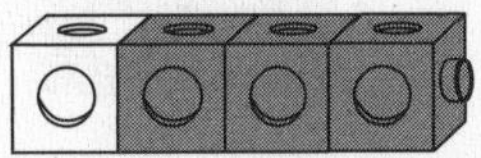

1 + 3 = ___

3. Use two colors.
Color to show a way to make 7.
Complete the addition sentence.

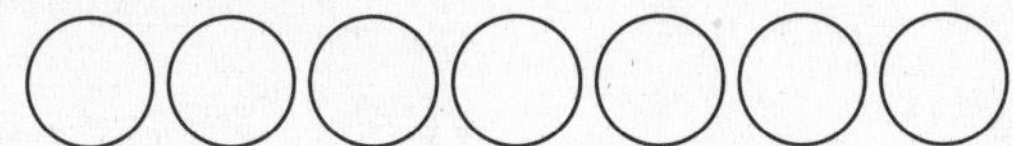

___ + ___ = 7

4. Use two colors.
Color to show a way to make 8.
Complete the addition sentence.

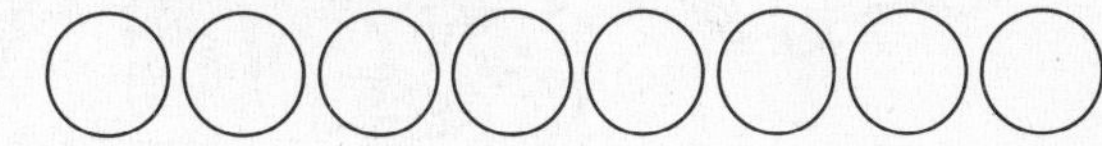

___ + ___ = 8

5. Use two colors.
Color to show a way to make 9.
Complete the addition sentence.

___ + ___ = 9

6. Use two colors.
Color to show a way to make 10.
Complete the addition sentence.

___ + ___ = 10

Go On

Name ______________________________

7. Write the numbers to match the dots.

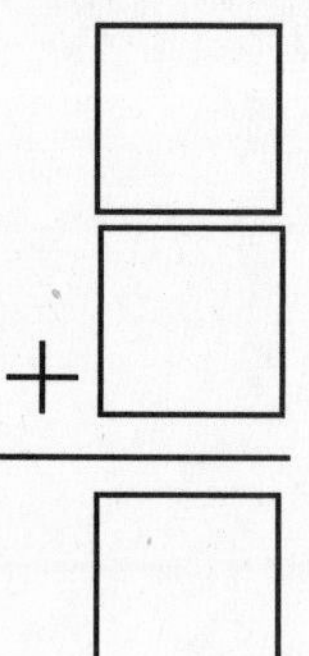

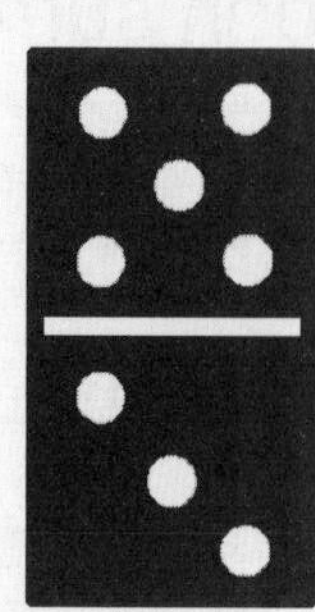

8. Write the numbers to match the dots.

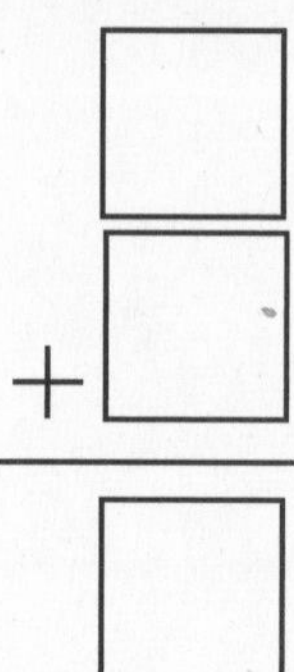

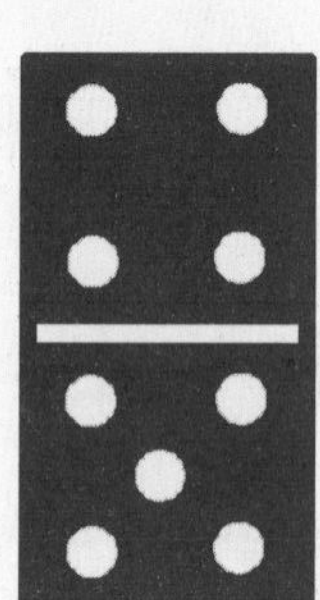

9. Draw the pennies.
Write how much you spend for both.

_____ ¢

10. Draw the pennies.
Write how much you spend for both.

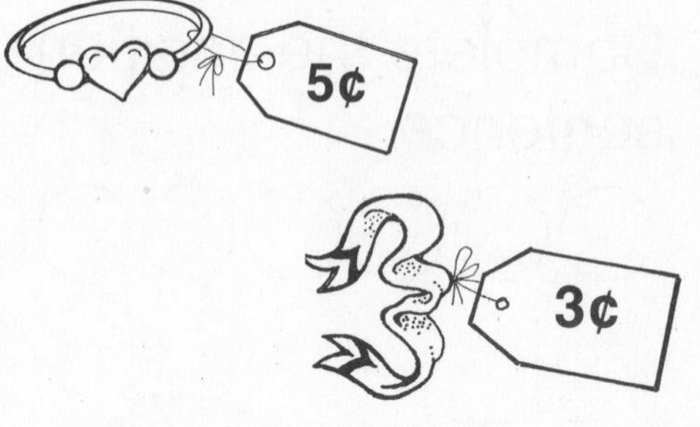

_____ ¢

Stop

Name ______________________

Choose the correct answer.

1. How many are left?

3 dogs 1 walks away

____ are left

Ⓐ 3 Ⓑ 2 Ⓒ 1 Ⓓ 0

2. How many are left?

5 ducks 4 swim away

____ are left

Ⓐ 1 Ⓑ 2 Ⓒ 4 Ⓓ 5

3. Subtract. Write the difference.

$6 - 4 =$ ____

Ⓐ 7 Ⓑ 6 Ⓒ 5 Ⓓ 2

4. Subtract. Write the difference.

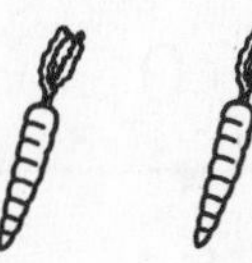

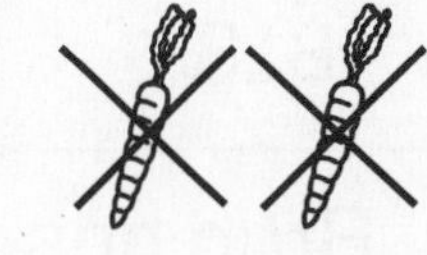

$5 - 2 =$ ____

Ⓐ 5 Ⓑ 3 Ⓒ 2 Ⓓ 0

Go On

Mark the subtraction sentence that matches.

5.  ___ − ___ = ___ Ⓐ 5 − 5 = 0 Ⓑ 6 − 1 = 5 Ⓒ 6 − 5 = 1 Ⓓ 6 − 2 = 4	6.     ___ − ___ = ___ Ⓐ 5 − 3 = 2 Ⓑ 3 − 2 = 1 Ⓒ 4 − 3 = 1 Ⓓ 6 − 2 = 4

Find the difference.

7.     4 − 0 = ___ Ⓐ 4 Ⓑ 3 Ⓒ 2 Ⓓ 0	8.   2 − 2 = ___ Ⓐ 4 Ⓑ 2 Ⓒ 1 Ⓓ 0
9. Brad has 5 apples. He gives 2 away. How many apples are left? Ⓐ 1 Ⓑ 2 Ⓒ 3 Ⓓ 4	10. Kiyo sees 6 cats. 3 run away. How many cats are left? Ⓐ 0 Ⓑ 3 Ⓒ 4 Ⓓ 5

Stop

Name ________________________________

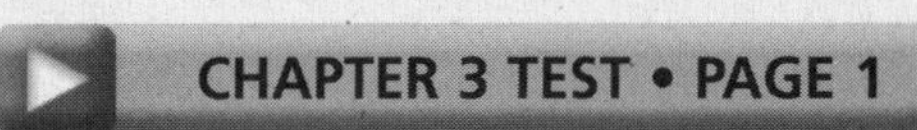

Write the correct answer.

1. Write how many bears are left.

5 bears 3 walk away ___ are left

2. Write how many tigers are left.

4 tigers 1 runs away ___ are left

3. Cross out pictures to subtract.

Write the difference.

5 − 4 = ___

4. Cross out pictures to subtract.

Write the difference.

4 − 2 = ___

Go On

Name ______________________________

5. Write the subtraction sentence.	6. Write the subtraction sentence.
 ____ − ____ = ____	 ____ − ____ = ____
7. Write the difference.	8. Write the difference.
 $6 - 6 =$ ____	 $5 - 0 =$ ____

Use ● to subtract.
Draw the ●. Write the difference.

9. Marta sees 3 birds. 2 fly away. How many birds are left?	10. Lourdes has 4 pencils. She gives 2 away. How many pencils does she have left?
 ____ bird	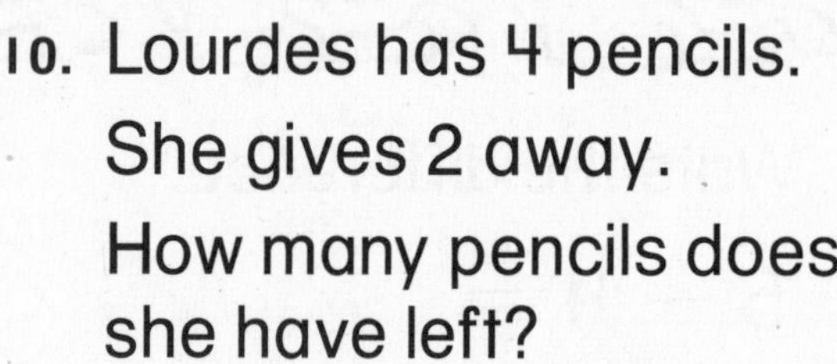 ____ pencils

Stop

Name ____________________

Choose the correct answer.

1. $8 - 6 = \_\_\_$ (A) 6 (C) 2 (B) 3 (D) 1	2. $7 - 3 = \_\_\_$ (A) 1 (C) 3 (B) 2 (D) 4
3. $9 - 9 = \_\_\_$ (A) 0 (C) 9 (B) 1 (D) 10	4. $10 - 7 = \_\_\_$ (A) 1 (C) 3 (B) 2 (D) 4
5. Find the difference. 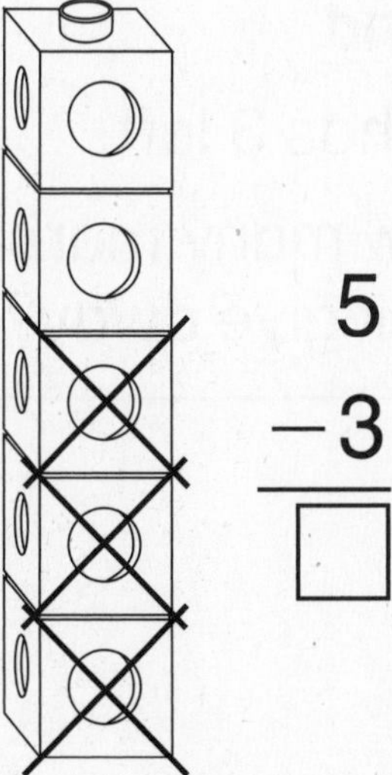 $\begin{array}{r} 5 \\ -3 \\ \hline \square \end{array}$ (A) 5 (C) 2 (B) 3 (D) 0	6. Find the difference. 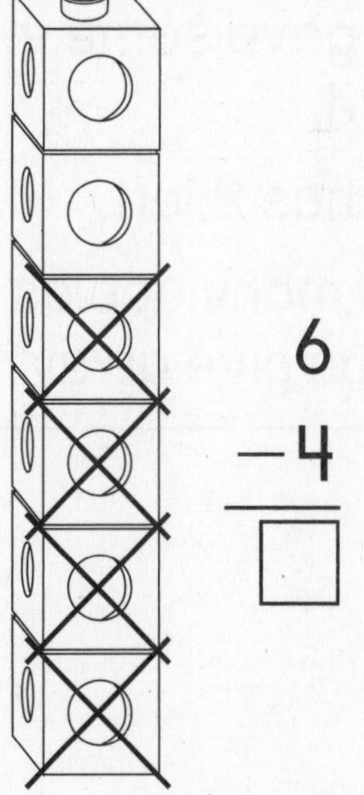 $\begin{array}{r} 6 \\ -4 \\ \hline \square \end{array}$ (A) 2 (C) 6 (B) 4 (D) 10

Go On

Name ___________________________

Choose the correct answer.

7. How many more ■ are there?

$7 - 6 =$ ___

Ⓐ 1 Ⓑ 2 Ⓒ 6 Ⓓ 7

8. How many more bowling pins are there?

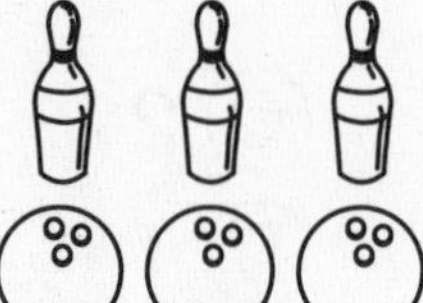

$6 - 3 =$ ___

Ⓐ 1 Ⓑ 2 Ⓒ 3 Ⓓ 6

9. Draw a picture to solve.

Susan had 4 apples.

She gave some to her friend.

She has 2 left.

How many apples did Susan give away?

Ⓐ 4 Ⓑ 2 Ⓒ 1 Ⓓ 0

10. Draw a picture to solve.

Jack had 8 marbles.

He gave some to his friend.

He has 3 left.

How many marbles did Jack give away?

Ⓐ 2 Ⓑ 4 Ⓒ 5 Ⓓ 6

Stop

Name ______________________________

Write the correct answer.

1. $8 - 3 =$ ___	2. $7 - 1 =$ ___
3. $9 - 6 =$ ___	4. $10 - 3 =$ ___
5. Write numbers to match the picture. Write the difference. 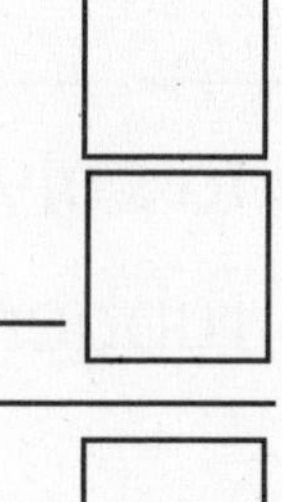 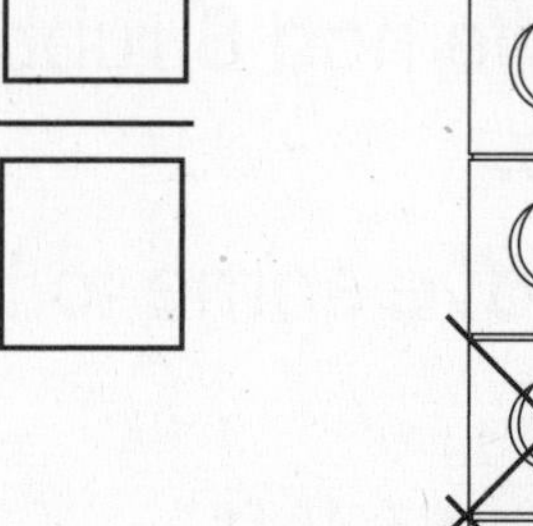 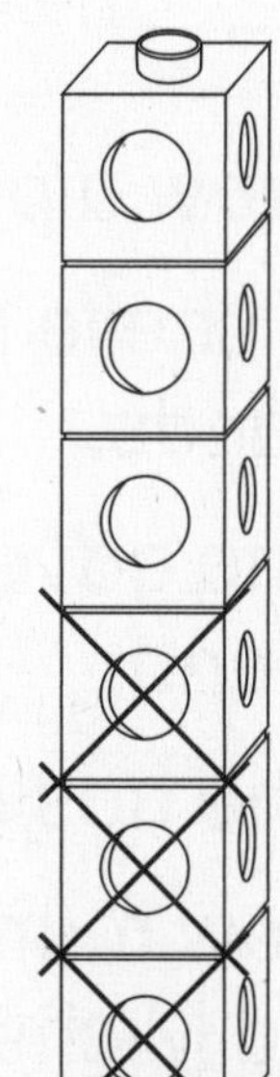	6. Write numbers to match the picture. Write the difference. 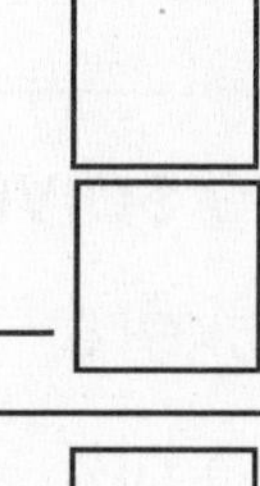 

Go On

Name ______________________

7. Draw lines to match.

Subtract to find how many more.

$4 - 2 = \_\_$

______ more

8. Draw lines to match.

Subtract to find how many more.

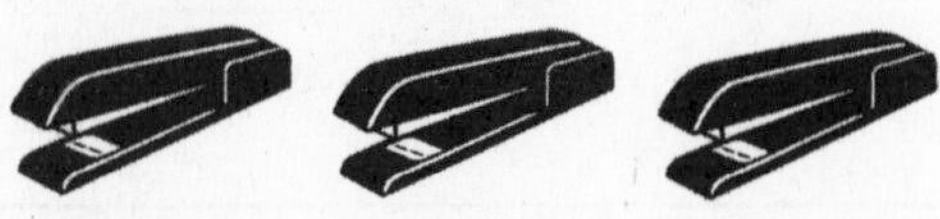

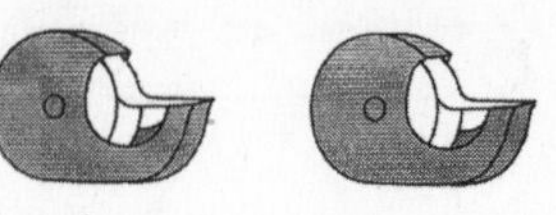

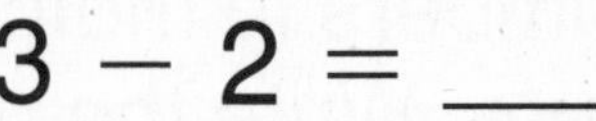

$3 - 2 = \_\_$

______ more

9. Draw a picture to solve.

Josue had 9 stickers.

He gave some to his friend.

He has 4 left.

How many stickers did Josue give away?

______ stickers

10. Draw a picture to solve.

Michelle had 8 rubber bands.

She gave some to her friend.

She has 6 left.

How many rubber bands did Michelle give away?

______ rubber bands

Stop

Name ____________________

Choose the correct answer.

1. How many are there in all?

3 dogs 1 dog ____ in all

Ⓐ 6 Ⓑ 5 Ⓒ 4 Ⓓ 3

2. Find the sum.

4 cats 2 cats

____ in all

Ⓐ 2 Ⓑ 4 Ⓒ 5 Ⓓ 6

3. Mark the addition sentence that matches the story.

Josh has 3 cars. He gets 2 more.
How many cars are there in all?

____ + ____ = ____

Ⓐ $3 + 2 = 5$
Ⓑ $2 + 3 = 5$
Ⓒ $1 + 4 = 5$
Ⓓ $3 + 3 = 6$

4. Mark the addition sentence that matches the story.

There is 1 bus. 4 more come.
How many buses are there in all?

____ + ____ = ____

Ⓐ $4 + 2 = 6$
Ⓑ $4 + 0 = 4$
Ⓒ $4 - 1 = 3$
Ⓓ $1 + 4 = 5$

5. Find the sum.

$5 + 0 =$ ____

Ⓐ 5 Ⓑ 4 Ⓒ 1 Ⓓ 0

Go On

Name ______________________

6. Which addition problems have the same sum?

(A) 2 + 1 = ____ and 2 + 2 = ____
(B) 3 + 1 = ____ and 3 + 2 = ____
(C) 4 + 2 = ____ and 2 + 4 = ____
(D) 4 + 2 = ____ and 4 + 0 = ____

7. Which is a way to make 8?

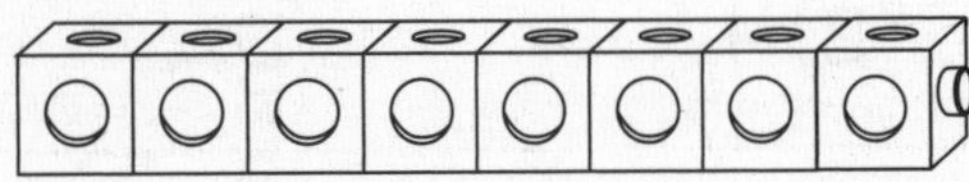

(A) 7 + 0
(B) 8 + 1
(C) 8 + 0
(D) 9 + 0

8. Which addition problem matches the picture?

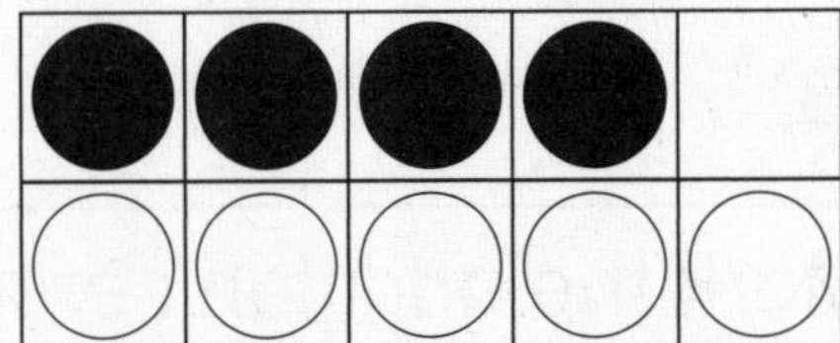

(A) 4 + 5
(B) 5 + 5
(C) 8 + 1
(D) 9 + 0

9. Which addition problem matches the dots?

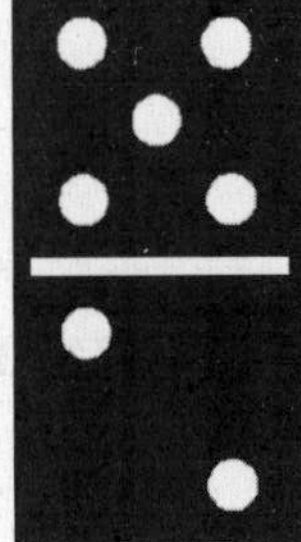

(A) $\begin{array}{r} 5 \\ +\ 7 \\ \hline 12 \end{array}$

(B) $\begin{array}{r} 5 \\ +\ 3 \\ \hline 8 \end{array}$

(C) $\begin{array}{r} 5 \\ +\ 1 \\ \hline 6 \end{array}$

(D) $\begin{array}{r} 5 \\ +\ 2 \\ \hline 7 \end{array}$

10. How much do you spend for both?

(A) 11¢
(B) 10¢
(C) 7¢
(D) 4¢

Go On

Name ____________________

11. How many are left?

6 elephants   3 walk away   ____ are left

Ⓐ 3   Ⓑ 4   Ⓒ 6   Ⓓ 9

12. How many are left?

4 clowns   1 goes away   ____ are left

Ⓐ 0   Ⓑ 2   Ⓒ 3   Ⓓ 4

13. Mark the subtraction sentence that matches.

Ⓐ $5 - 5 = 0$ Ⓒ $6 - 5 = 1$

Ⓑ $5 + 4 = 9$ Ⓓ $5 - 4 = 1$

14. Find the difference.

$5 - 0 =$ ____

Ⓐ 6   Ⓑ 5   Ⓒ 3   Ⓓ 0

15. Sue sees 5 horses.
3 horses run away.
How many horses are left?

Ⓐ 5   Ⓑ 4   Ⓒ 2   Ⓓ 1

Go On

Name ____________________

16. Find the difference.

$8 - 7 =$ ____

Ⓐ 1 Ⓒ 7

Ⓑ 2 Ⓓ 8

17. Find the difference.

$3 - 1 =$ ____

Ⓐ 3 Ⓒ 1

Ⓑ 2 Ⓓ 0

18. Find the difference.

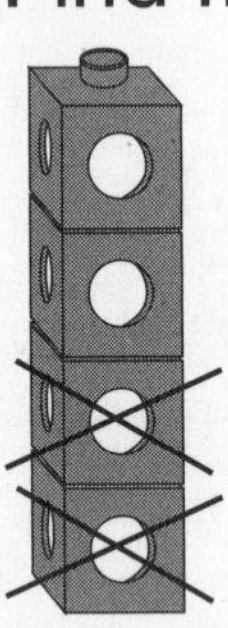

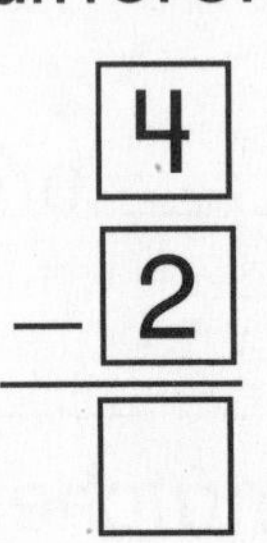

Ⓐ 1

Ⓑ 2

Ⓒ 3

Ⓓ 6

19. How many more are there?

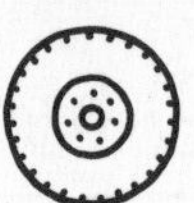
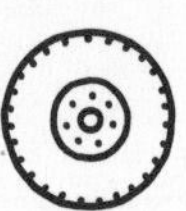
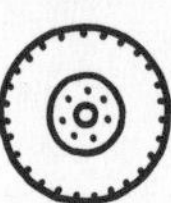
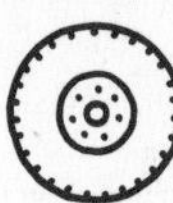

$8 - 6 =$ ____

Ⓐ 8

Ⓑ 6

Ⓒ 3

Ⓓ 2

20. Draw a picture to solve.

Shelly had 7 straws.

She gave some to her friend.

She has 2 left.

How many straws did Shelly give away?

Ⓐ 5

Ⓑ 3

Ⓒ 2

Ⓓ 1

Stop

Name ______________________________

Write the correct answer.

1. How many are there in all?

3 frogs 2 frogs ____ in all

2. Write the sum.

2 mice 1 mouse ____ in all

3. Write the addition sentence that matches the story. Jenna saw 4 bikes. Then she saw 2 more. How many bikes did she see in all?

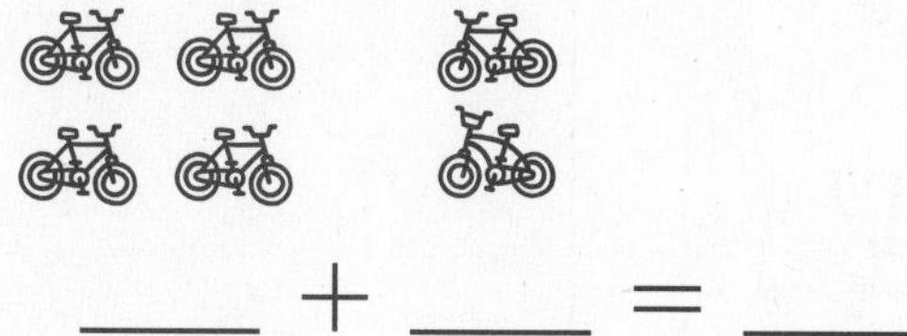

____ + ____ = ____

4. Write the addition sentence that matches the story. Luke saw 2 boats. Then he saw 5 more. How many boats did he see in all?

____ + ____ = ____

5. Write the sum.

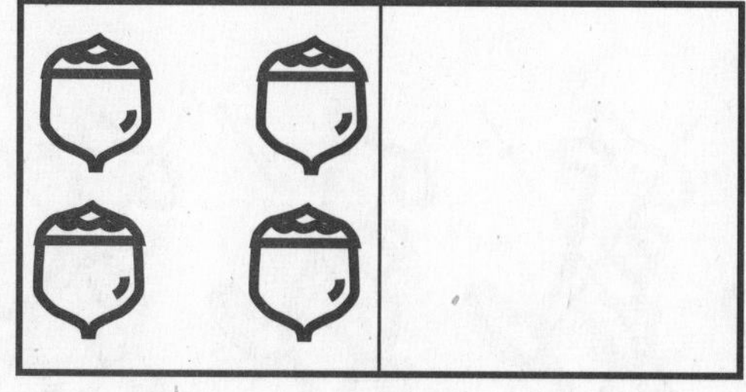

4 + 0 = ____

6. Circle the addition problem that has the same sum as 3 + 4.

3 + 1 = ____

3 + 2 = ____

4 + 3 = ____

Go On

Name ______________________________

7. Draw ◯. Use two colors to show a way to make 8.

Complete the addition sentence.

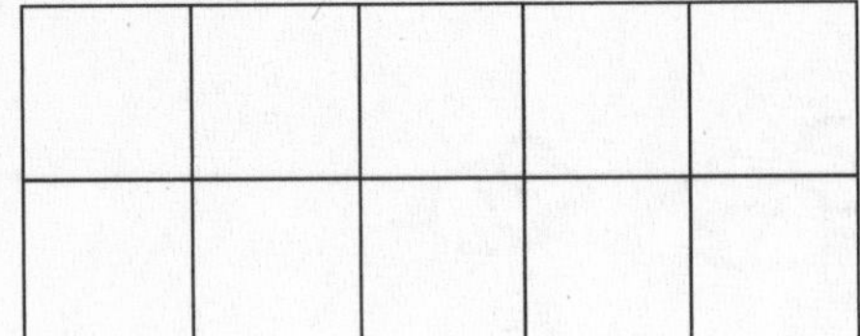

___ + ___ = ___

8. Complete the addition sentence to match the picture.

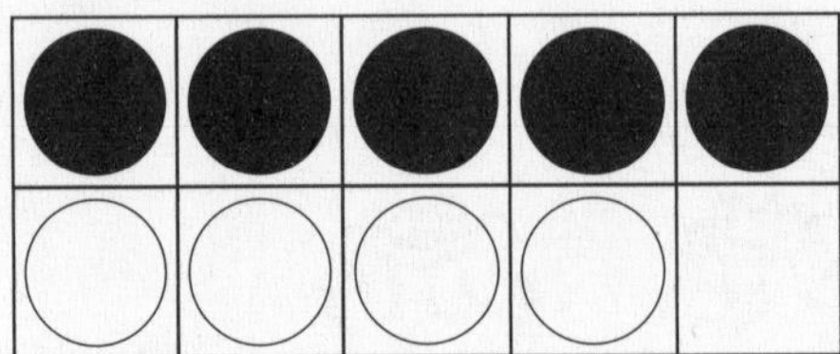

___ + ___ = 9

9. Write the numbers to match the dots.

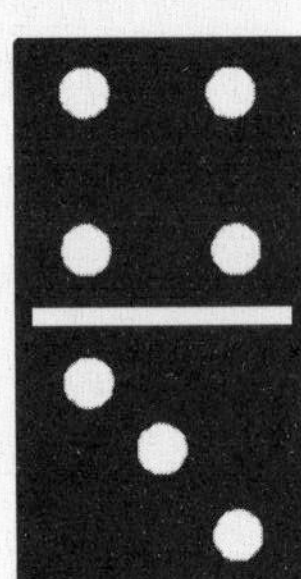

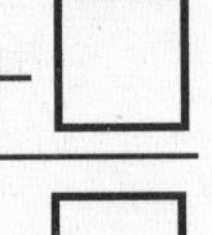

___ + ___ = ___

10. Draw the pennies. Write how much you spend for both.

___ ¢

11. Write how many are left.

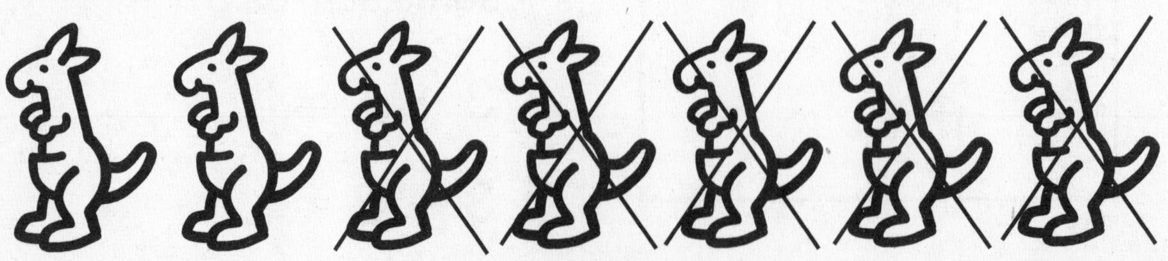

7 kangaroos 5 hop away ___ are left

Go On

Name ______________________

12. Write how many are left.

5 bugs 2 walk away ____ are left

13. Write the subtraction sentence that matches.

____ – ____ = ____

14. Cross out how many fly away. Write the difference.

8 – 8 = ____

15. Brad sees 9 dogs.
6 dogs run away.
How many dogs are left?
____ dogs

16. Write the difference.

5 – 4 = ____

Go On

Name ______________________________

17. Write the difference.

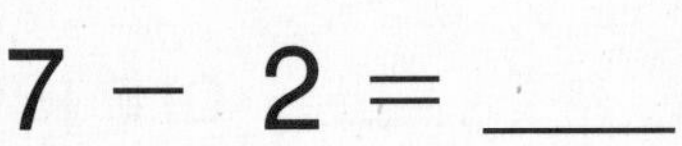

$7 - 2 =$ ____

18. Write the difference.

$$\begin{array}{r} 8 \\ -\ 6 \\ \hline \end{array}$$

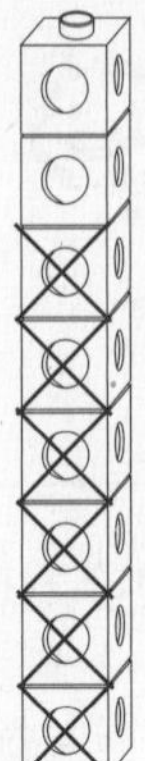

19. Write how many more rabbits there are.

$9 - 3 =$ ____

20. Draw a picture to solve.

Janet had 4 pens.

She gave some to her friend.

She has 1 left.

How many pens did Janet give away?

____ pens

Stop

Name ______________________

Choose the correct answer.

1. Add.

$$\begin{array}{r} 2 \\ +\ 2 \\ \hline \end{array}$$

Ⓐ 2 Ⓑ 3 Ⓒ 4 Ⓓ 5

2. Count on. Find the sum.

$$\begin{array}{r} 3 \\ +\ 1 \\ \hline \end{array}$$

Ⓐ 13 Ⓑ 4 Ⓒ 3 Ⓓ 2

3. Count on. Find the sum.

$$\begin{array}{r} 7 \\ +\ 1 \\ \hline \end{array}$$

Ⓐ 6 Ⓑ 7 Ⓒ 8 Ⓓ 17

4. Count on. Find the sum.

$$\begin{array}{r} 5 \\ +\ 2 \\ \hline \end{array}$$

Ⓐ 6 Ⓑ 7 Ⓒ 8 Ⓓ 9

5. Add.

$$\begin{array}{r} 3 \\ +\ 3 \\ \hline \end{array}$$

Ⓐ 3 Ⓑ 6 Ⓒ 8 Ⓓ 9

6. Add.

$$\begin{array}{r} 5 \\ +\ 5 \\ \hline \end{array}$$

Ⓐ 5 Ⓑ 9 Ⓒ 10 Ⓓ 11

Go On

Name ____________________

7. Use the number line. Count on to find the sum.

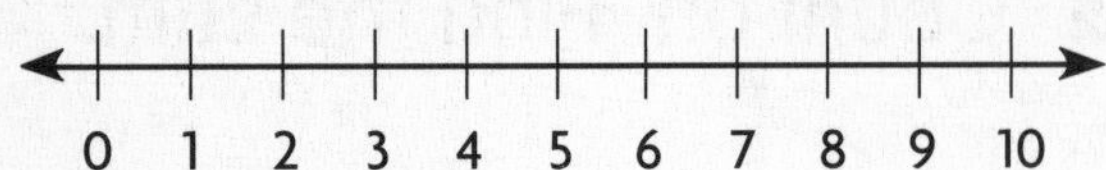

$$\begin{array}{r} 6 \\ +\ 3 \\ \hline \end{array}$$

Ⓐ 10 Ⓑ 9 Ⓒ 8 Ⓓ 7

8. Use the number line. Count on to find the sum.

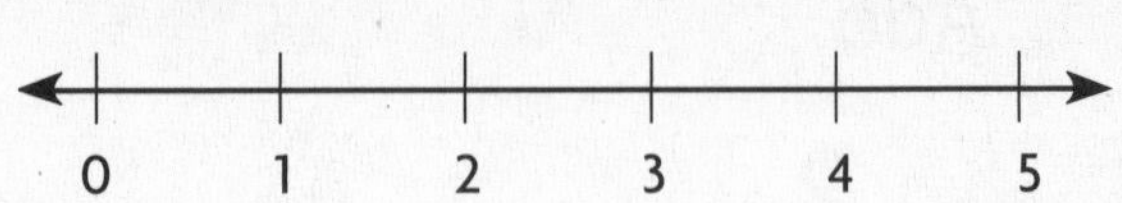

$$\begin{array}{r} 3 \\ +\ 2 \\ \hline \end{array}$$

Ⓐ 5 Ⓑ 4 Ⓒ 3 Ⓓ 2

9. Choose the addition sentence that goes with the picture.

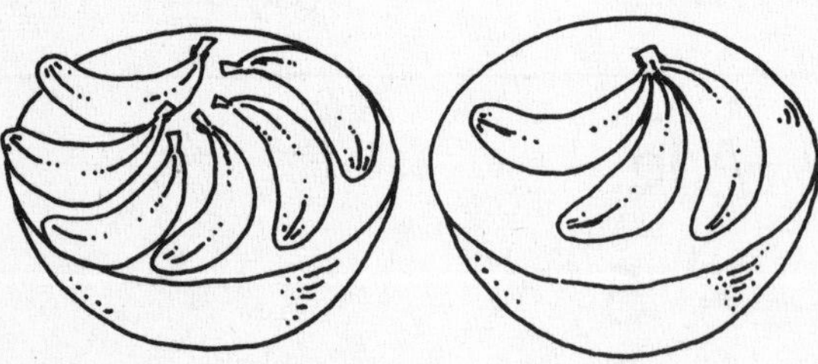

Ⓐ 6 − 3 = 3

Ⓑ 6 + 3 = 9

Ⓒ 6 + 4 = 10

Ⓓ 5 + 3 = 8

10. Choose the addition sentence that goes with the story.

There are 2 plates.

There are 5 🍒 on each plate.

How many 🍒 are there?

Ⓐ 5 + 5 = 10

Ⓑ 5 + 1 = 6

Ⓒ 5 + 0 = 5

Ⓓ 5 − 5 = 0

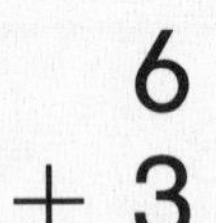

Stop

Name ____________________

Write the correct answer.

1. Add. $\begin{array}{r} 4 \\ +\ 4 \\ \hline \end{array}$	2. Count on. Write the sum. $\begin{array}{r} 3 \\ +\ 2 \\ \hline \end{array}$
3. Count on. Write the sum. $\begin{array}{r} 4 \\ +\ 2 \\ \hline \end{array}$	4. Count on. Write the sum. $\begin{array}{r} 6 \\ +\ 2 \\ \hline \end{array}$
5. Add. $\begin{array}{r} 1 \\ +\ 1 \\ \hline \end{array}$	6. Add. $\begin{array}{r} 3 \\ +\ 3 \\ \hline \end{array}$

Go On

7. Use the number line. Count on to find the sum.

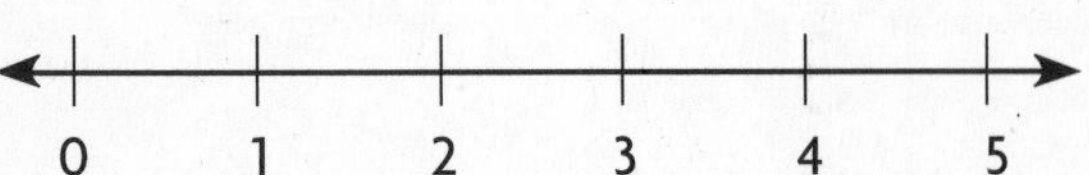

$$\begin{array}{r} 2 \\ +\ 1 \\ \hline \end{array}$$

8. Use the number line. Count on to find the sum.

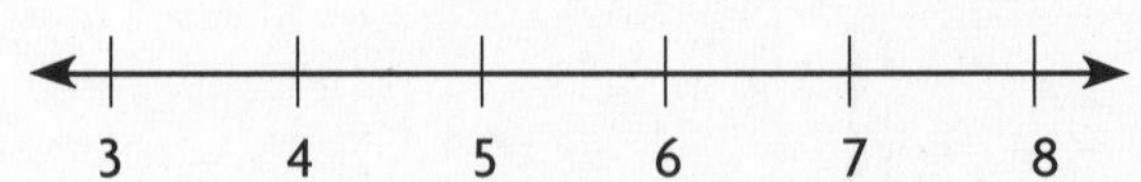

$$\begin{array}{r} 4 \\ +\ 3 \\ \hline \end{array}$$

9. Draw a picture to solve. Then write the addition sentence that matches the story.

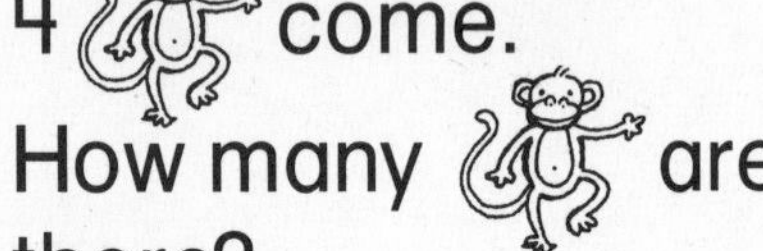

There are 2 monkeys. 4 monkeys come. How many monkeys are there?

____ + ____ = ____

10. Draw a picture to solve. Then write the addition sentence that matches the story.

There are 2 pears on a plate.

There are 2 pears on another plate.

How many pears are there?

____ + ____ = ____

Stop

Name ______________________________

Choose the correct answer.

1. $\begin{array}{r} 8 \\ +\ 2 \\ \hline \end{array}$

Ⓐ 10 Ⓑ 9 Ⓒ 6 Ⓓ 0

2. $\begin{array}{r} 5 \\ +\ 1 \\ \hline \end{array}$

Ⓐ 4 Ⓑ 5 Ⓒ 6 Ⓓ 7

3. Choose the new fact.

$\begin{array}{r} 6 \\ +\ 3 \\ \hline 9 \end{array} \quad \begin{array}{r} 3 \\ +\ 6 \\ \hline \end{array}$

Ⓐ 3 Ⓑ 6 Ⓒ 7 Ⓓ 9

4. $\begin{array}{r} 4 \\ +\ 4 \\ \hline \end{array}$

Ⓐ 4 Ⓑ 6 Ⓒ 8 Ⓓ 10

5. Choose the new fact.

$\begin{array}{r} 4 \\ +\ 3 \\ \hline 7 \end{array} \quad \begin{array}{r} 3 \\ +\ 4 \\ \hline \end{array}$

Ⓐ 1 Ⓑ 5 Ⓒ 7 Ⓓ 9

6. $\begin{array}{r} 4 \\ +\ 1 \\ \hline \end{array}$

Ⓐ 3 Ⓑ 5 Ⓒ 6 Ⓓ 8

Go On

Complete the table.
Follow the rule.

7.

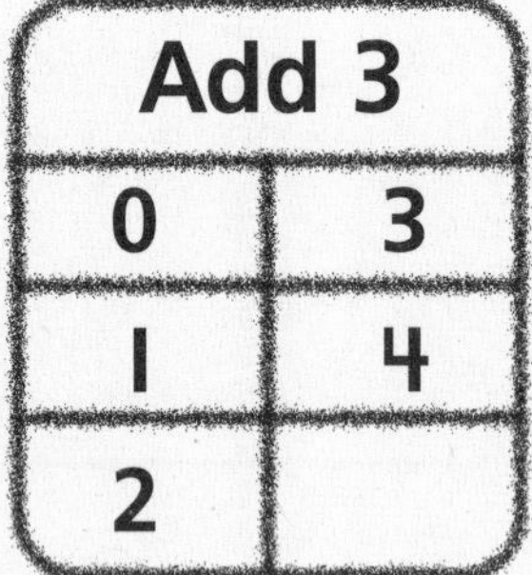

Add 3	
0	3
1	4
2	

Ⓐ 2
Ⓑ 3
Ⓒ 4
Ⓓ 5

8.

Add 1	
2	
4	5
6	7

Ⓐ 2
Ⓑ 3
Ⓒ 4
Ⓓ 5

Choose the correct number sentence to solve the problem.

9. There are 3 red cars.
There are 2 blue cars.
How many cars are there in all?

Ⓐ $3 + 2 = 5$
Ⓑ $3 - 2 = 1$
Ⓒ $5 + 2 = 7$
Ⓓ $5 + 0 = 5$

10. There are 6 dogs.
4 more come.
How many dogs are there in all?

Ⓐ $6 - 4 = 2$
Ⓑ $6 + 0 = 6$
Ⓒ $6 + 3 = 9$
Ⓓ $6 + 4 = 10$

Stop

Name ______________________________

Write the correct answer.

1. $\begin{array}{r} 7 \\ +\ 2 \\ \hline \end{array}$	2. $\begin{array}{r} 6 \\ +\ 1 \\ \hline \end{array}$
3. Write the new fact. $\begin{array}{r} 5 \\ +\ 4 \\ \hline 9 \end{array}$ $\begin{array}{r} 4 \\ +\ 5 \\ \hline \end{array}$	4. $\begin{array}{r} 5 \\ +\ 5 \\ \hline \end{array}$
5. Write the new fact. $\begin{array}{r} 5 \\ +\ 2 \\ \hline 7 \end{array}$ $\begin{array}{r} 2 \\ +\ 5 \\ \hline \end{array}$	6. $\begin{array}{r} 5 \\ +\ 3 \\ \hline \end{array}$

Go On

7. Complete the table. Follow the rule.

Add 0	
1	1
2	2
3	

8. Complete the table. Follow the rule.

Add 2	
4	6
6	8
8	

9. Solve. Write the number sentence that matches the story. Draw a picture to check.

Sue has 4 chicks.

2 more chicks come.

How many chicks are there in all?

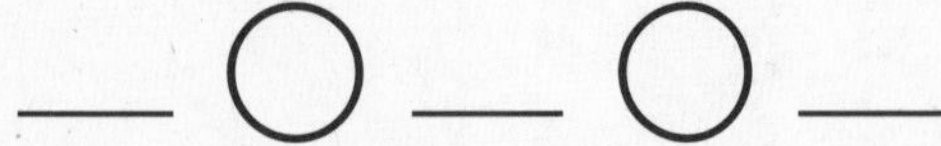

10. Solve. Write the number sentence that matches the story. Draw a picture to check.

There are 5 big birds.

3 little birds come.

How many birds are there in all?

Stop

Name ______________________

Choose the correct answer.

1. Use the number line. Count back to subtract.

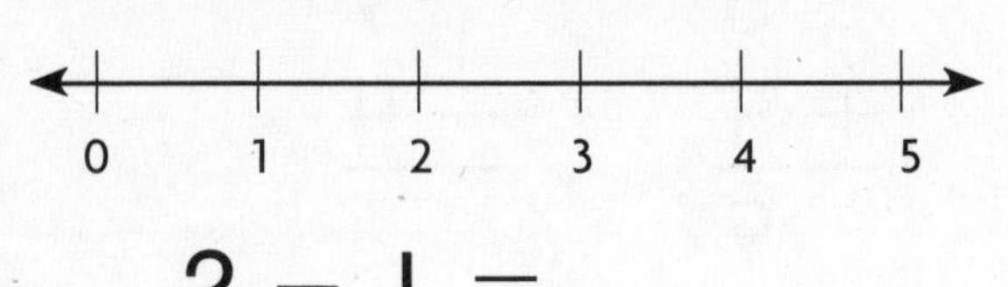

$2 - 1 = \_\_\_$

Ⓐ 0 Ⓑ 1 Ⓒ 2 Ⓓ 3

2. Use the related addition fact to find the difference.

$7 + 2 = 9$

$9 - 2 = \_\_\_$

Ⓐ 9 Ⓑ 7 Ⓒ 2 Ⓓ 1

Count back to subtract.

3. 0 1 2 3 4 5

$$\begin{array}{r} 5 \\ -\ 3 \\ \hline \end{array}$$

Ⓐ 2 Ⓑ 3 Ⓒ 4 Ⓓ 5

4.

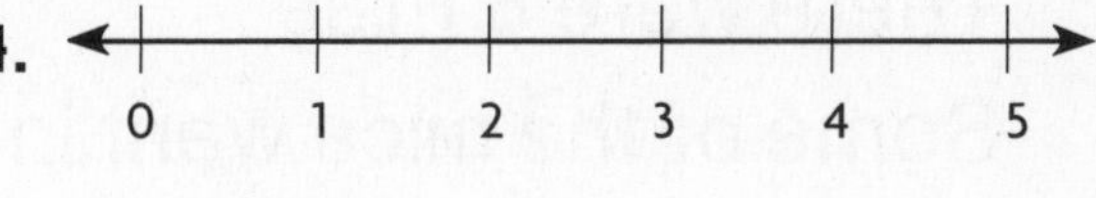

$$\begin{array}{r} 4 \\ -\ 2 \\ \hline \end{array}$$

Ⓐ 1 Ⓑ 2 Ⓒ 3 Ⓓ 6

5.

$$\begin{array}{r} 9 \\ -\ 3 \\ \hline \end{array}$$

Ⓐ 3 Ⓑ 4 Ⓒ 5 Ⓓ 6

6.

$$\begin{array}{r} 6 \\ -\ 1 \\ \hline \end{array}$$

Ⓐ 5 Ⓑ 6 Ⓒ 7 Ⓓ 10

Go On

Name ___________________________

7. Subtract.

$$\begin{array}{r} 3 \\ -\ 2 \\ \hline \end{array}$$

Ⓐ 5 Ⓑ 3 Ⓒ 2 Ⓓ 1

8. Use the related addition fact to find the difference.

$$\begin{array}{r} 5 \\ +\ 4 \\ \hline 9 \end{array} \qquad \begin{array}{r} 9 \\ -\ 4 \\ \hline \end{array}$$

Ⓐ 9 Ⓑ 7 Ⓒ 5 Ⓓ 4

9. Use the picture to solve the problem.

There were 8 mice.

Some of the mice went in a hole.

Now there are 5 mice left.

How many mice went inside the hole?

Ⓐ 8 Ⓑ 5 Ⓒ 4 Ⓓ 3

10. Use the picture to solve the problem.

There were 10 children.

Some of the children got on a bus.

Now there are 4 children left.

How many children got on the bus?

Ⓐ 4 Ⓑ 5 Ⓒ 6 Ⓓ 7

Stop

Name ______________________

Write the correct answer.

1. Use the number line. Count back to subtract. 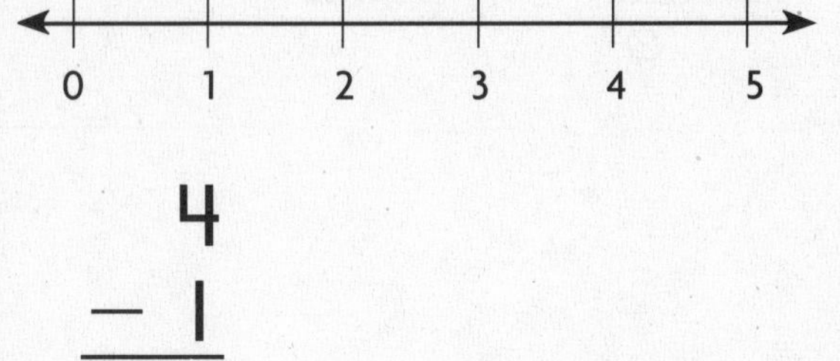 $\begin{array}{r} 4 \\ -\ 1 \\ \hline \end{array}$	2. Use the related addition fact to find the difference. $3 + 5 = 8$ $8 - 3 = \_\_\_$
3. Count back to subtract. $\begin{array}{r} 6 \\ -\ 3 \\ \hline \end{array}$	4. Count back to subtract. $\begin{array}{r} 5 \\ -\ 2 \\ \hline \end{array}$
5. Count back to subtract. $\begin{array}{r} 7 \\ -\ 3 \\ \hline \end{array}$	6. Count back to subtract. $\begin{array}{r} 7 \\ -\ 1 \\ \hline \end{array}$

Go On

Name ________________________________

7. Subtract.

$$\begin{array}{r} 8 \\ -\ 2 \\ \hline \end{array}$$

8. Use the related addition fact to find the difference.

$$\begin{array}{r} 8 \\ +\ 1 \\ \hline 9 \end{array} \qquad \begin{array}{r} 9 \\ -\ 1 \\ \hline \end{array}$$

9. Use the picture to solve the problem.

There were 7 worms inching along.

Some worms went inside an apple.

Now there are 4 left.

How many worms went inside the apple?

____ worms

10. Use the picture to solve the problem.

There were 9 children inside the house.

Some children went outside to play.

Now there are 5 left.

How many children went outside to play?

____ children

Stop

Name ______________________________

Choose the correct answer.

1. $\begin{array}{r} 1 \\ -\ 1 \\ \hline \end{array}$

   (A) 0 (C) 2
   (B) 1 (D) 3

2. $\begin{array}{r} 2 \\ -\ 0 \\ \hline \end{array}$

   (A) 0 (C) 2
   (B) 1 (D) 3

3. $\begin{array}{r} 3 \\ -\ 1 \\ \hline \end{array}$

   (A) 0 (C) 2
   (B) 1 (D) 3

4. $\begin{array}{r} 10 \\ -\ 7 \\ \hline \end{array}$

   (A) 0 (C) 2
   (B) 1 (D) 3

5. $\begin{array}{r} 5 \\ -\ 3 \\ \hline \end{array}$

   (A) 1 (C) 3
   (B) 2 (D) 4

6. Find the missing number.

   $8 - 5 = \bigcirc$

   $8 - \bigcirc = 5$

   (A) 3 (C) 5
   (B) 4 (D) 7

Go On

Name ____________________

7. Subtract.

$$\begin{array}{r} 9 \\ -\ 7 \\ \hline \end{array}$$

Ⓐ 1
Ⓑ 2
Ⓒ 3
Ⓓ 4

8. Which number sentence finishes the fact family?

5 + 4 = 9
4 + 5 = 9
9 − 5 = 4

Ⓐ 9 − 4 = 5
Ⓑ 8 − 3 = 5
Ⓒ 10 − 6 = 4
Ⓓ 8 − 4 = 4

9. What number is missing from the table?

Follow the rule.

Subtract 5	
6	1
7	2
8	

Ⓐ 0
Ⓑ 3
Ⓒ 4
Ⓓ 5

10. Choose the correct number sentence to solve.

There are 6 lions.
3 more lions join them.
How many lions are there now?

Ⓐ 6 − 3 = 3
Ⓑ 6 − 4 = 2
Ⓒ 6 + 1 = 7
Ⓓ 6 + 3 = 9

Stop

Name ________________________________

Write the correct answer.
Subtract to find the difference.

1. $\begin{array}{r} 4 \\ -\ 1 \\ \hline \end{array}$	2. $\begin{array}{r} 5 \\ -\ 0 \\ \hline \end{array}$
3. $\begin{array}{r} 4 \\ -\ 2 \\ \hline \end{array}$	4. $\begin{array}{r} 10 \\ -\ 9 \\ \hline \end{array}$
5. $\begin{array}{r} 9 \\ -\ 5 \\ \hline \end{array}$	6. Write the missing number in the circles. $7 - 4 = \bigcirc$ $7 - \bigcirc = 4$

Go On

7. Subtract.

$$\begin{array}{r} 9 \\ -\ 3 \\ \hline \end{array}$$

8. Write the number sentence that finishes the fact family.

$2 + 5 = 7$

$5 + 2 = 7$

$7 - 5 = 2$

___ − ___ = ___

9. Complete the table. Follow the rule.

Subtract 4	
8	4
9	5
10	

10. Solve. Write the number sentence.

There are 3 bears.
7 more bears join them.
How many bears are there now?

___ ◯ ___ ◯ ___

Stop

Name ____________________

Choose the correct answer. Add or subtract.

1. $2 + 3 =$ ___ (A) 2 (C) 4 (B) 3 (D) 5	2. $5 + 2 =$ ___ (A) 5 (C) 7 (B) 6 (D) 8
3. $4 - 1 =$ ___ (A) 1 (C) 3 (B) 2 (D) 4	4. $9 - 3 =$ ___ (A) 5 (C) 7 (B) 6 (D) 8
5. $7 + 1 =$ ___ (A) 9 (C) 7 (B) 8 (D) 6	6. $8 - 2 =$ ___ (A) 6 (C) 9 (B) 7 (D) 10

Go On

7. $5 + 5 =$ ___

Ⓐ 8 Ⓑ 9 Ⓒ 10 Ⓓ 11

8. $3 + 3 =$ ___

Ⓐ 7 Ⓑ 6 Ⓒ 5 Ⓓ 4

9. Which of these is a related subtraction fact for $2 + 7 = 9$?

Ⓐ $9 - 2 = 7$

Ⓑ $7 - 2 = 5$

Ⓒ $10 - 1 = 9$

Ⓓ $7 - 5 = 2$

10. $7 - 1 =$ ___

Ⓐ 5 Ⓑ 6 Ⓒ 7 Ⓓ 8

11. $8 - 6 = 2$

$8 - 2 =$ ___

Ⓐ 8 Ⓑ 6 Ⓒ 3 Ⓓ 0

12. Find the sums.

$$\begin{array}{r} 7 \\ +\,3 \\ \hline \end{array} \qquad \begin{array}{r} 3 \\ +\,7 \\ \hline \end{array}$$

Ⓐ 10 Ⓑ 9 Ⓒ 8 Ⓓ 7

Go On

Name ____________________

13. Complete the table. Follow the rule.

Add 4	
1	5
2	
3	7

Ⓐ 9
Ⓑ 8
Ⓒ 7
Ⓓ 6

14. Which number sentence finishes this fact family?

5 + 4 = 9
9 − 4 = 5
4 + 5 = 9

Ⓐ 9 − 6 = 3
Ⓑ 5 − 4 = 1
Ⓒ 3 + 6 = 9
Ⓓ 9 − 5 = 4

15. Complete the table. Follow the rule.

Subtract 3	
8	
6	3
5	2

Ⓐ 5
Ⓑ 4
Ⓒ 3
Ⓓ 2

16. Choose the correct number sentence to solve the problem.

Will has 4 mice.
Kate has 2 mice.
How many mice are there in all?

Ⓐ 4 − 2 = 2
Ⓑ 4 + 0 = 4
Ⓒ 4 + 2 = 6
Ⓓ 4 + 4 = 8

Go On

Name ______________________

17. What are the numbers in this fact family?

$3 + 1 = 4$	$4 - 3 = 1$
$1 + 3 = 4$	$4 - 1 = 3$

Ⓐ 1, 2, 3 Ⓒ 1, 3, 5
Ⓑ 3, 4, 7 Ⓓ 1, 3, 4

18. Use the picture to solve.

There were 9 bees.

Some bees went inside a hive.

Now there are 3 left.

How many bees went inside the hive?

Ⓐ 0 Ⓑ 3 Ⓒ 6 Ⓓ 9

19. Choose the number sentence that goes with the story.

Sam has 8 books.

He gives 4 books to Emma.

How many books does Sam have left?

Ⓐ $8 - 4 = 4$
Ⓑ $12 - 8 = 4$
Ⓒ $12 - 4 = 8$
Ⓓ $8 + 4 = 12$

20. Choose the number sentence that goes with the story.

There are 5 [pear] in a bowl.

Sue puts in 4 more [pear].

How many [pear] are in the bowl?

Ⓐ $5 + 3 = 8$
Ⓑ $7 + 2 = 9$
Ⓒ $5 + 4 = 9$
Ⓓ $5 + 1 = 6$

Stop

Name ________________________________

Write the correct answer. Add or subtract.

1. $6 + 2 =$ ___	2. $4 + 5 =$ ___
3. $5 - 1 =$ ___	4. $7 - 6 =$ ___
5. $8 + 1 =$ ___	6. $5 - 3 =$ ___

Go On

Name ______________________

7. $4 + 4 =$ ___

8. $2 + 2 =$ ___

9. Write a related subtraction fact.

$3 + 5 = 8$

___ $-$ ___ $=$ ___

10. $10 - 2 =$ ___

11. $9 - 1 = 8$

$9 - 8 =$ ___

12. Count on to find the sums.

$$\begin{array}{r} 2 \\ +\,5 \\ \hline \end{array} \qquad \begin{array}{r} 5 \\ +\,2 \\ \hline \end{array}$$

Go On

13. Complete the table. Follow the rule.

Add 3	
1	4
2	
3	6

14. Write the number sentence that finishes this fact family.

4 + 6 = 10
10 − 6 = 4
6 + 4 = 10

___ − ___ = ___

15. Complete the table. Follow the rule.

Subtract 2	
9	
7	5
5	3

16. Write the number sentence that solves the problem.

Maria has 6 fish.

Raoul has 1 fish.

How many fish are there in all?

___ + ___ = ___

Go On

Name ______________________________

17. Write the numbers in this fact family.

$5 + 3 = 8$
$8 - 3 = 5$

$3 + 5 = 8$
$8 - 5 = 3$

___, ___, ___

18. Use the picture to solve. There were 8 bears. Some bears went inside a cave. Now 1 bear is left. How many bears went inside the cave?

___ bears

19. Write a number sentence to solve.

Nick has 9 apples.

He gives 2 apples to Molly.

How many apples does Nick have left?

___ ◯ ___ = ___

20. Write the addition sentence that solves the problem.

There are 6 🍌.

Matt brings 3 more 🍌.

How many 🍌 are there now?

___ + ___ = ___

Stop

Name ______________________

Choose the correct answer.
Use the picture to answer questions 1 and 2.

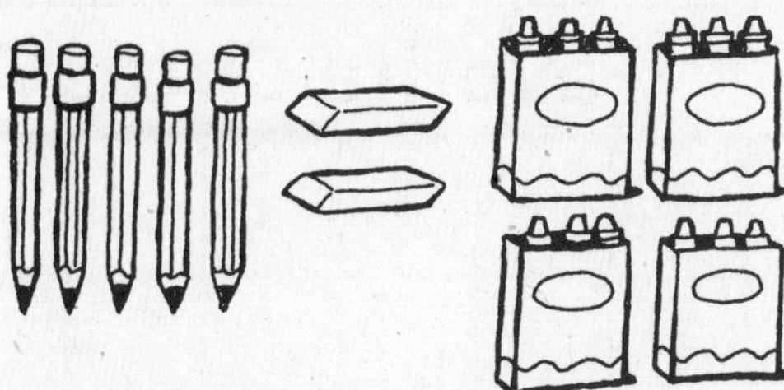

1. Which shows how many pencils there are?	2. Which shows how many boxes of crayons there are?
Ⓐ || Ⓒ ||||	Ⓐ || Ⓒ ||||
Ⓑ ||| Ⓓ ~~||||~~	Ⓑ ||| Ⓓ ~~||||~~

Use the picture to answer question 3.

3. Which shape belongs in the group?

Ⓐ 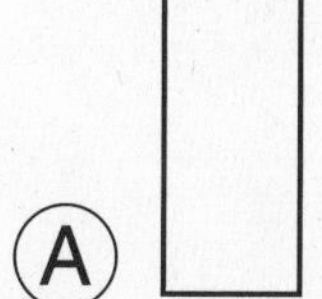 Ⓑ 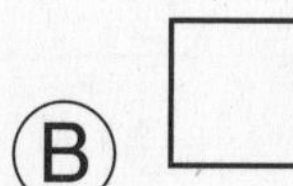 Ⓒ 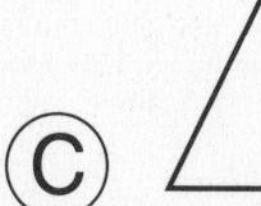 Ⓓ  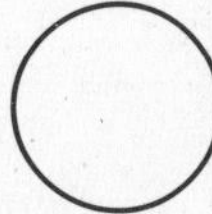

Go On

Use the bar graph to answer questions 4, 5, and 6.

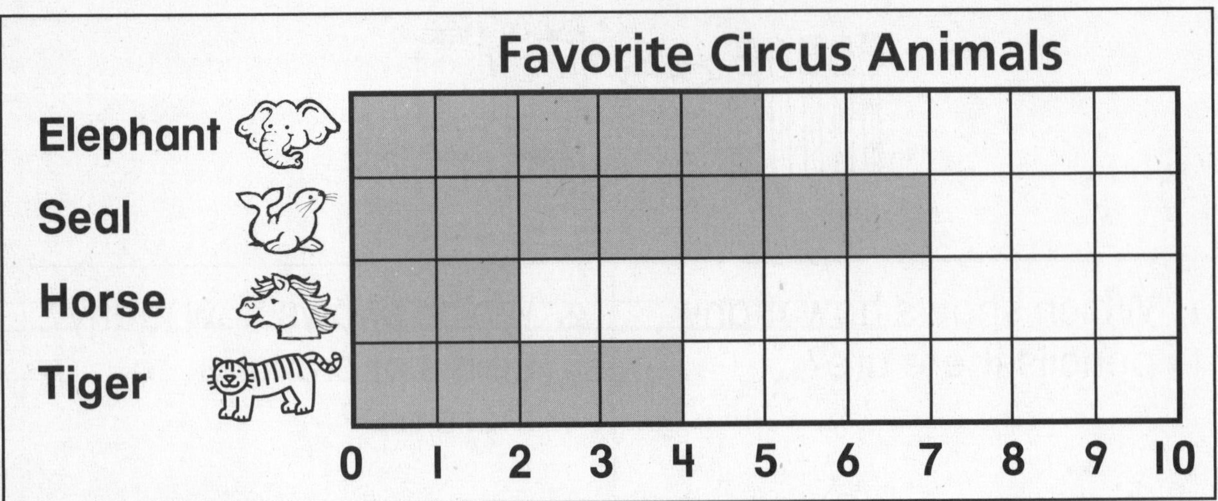

4. Which animal did the **fewest** children choose?

Ⓐ tiger
Ⓑ horse
Ⓒ seal
Ⓓ elephant

5. How many more children chose tigers than horses?

Ⓐ 1
Ⓑ 2
Ⓒ 3
Ⓓ 5

6. How many children chose seals or horses?

Ⓐ 2
Ⓑ 5
Ⓒ 7
Ⓓ 9

Go On

Name ______________________________

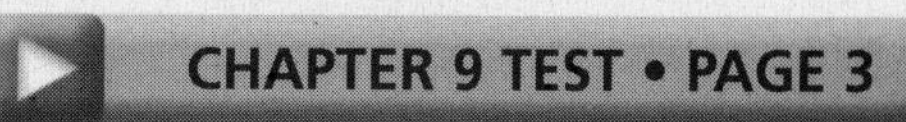

Use the picture graph to answer questions 7 and 8.

Favorite Fruits

Fruit	Count
Apples 🍎	🍎 🍎 🍎 🍎 🍎 🍎
Cherries 🍒	🍒 🍒
Bananas 🍌	🍌 🍌 🍌 🍌 🍌

7. How many children chose apples?

Ⓐ 6
Ⓑ 5
Ⓒ 4
Ⓓ 2

8. How many more children chose bananas than cherries?

Ⓐ 2
Ⓑ 3
Ⓒ 5
Ⓓ 7

Go On

Use the bar graph to answer questions 9 and 10.

Class Pets	
Dog	𝍸 II
Cat	𝍸
Fish	III
Bird	I

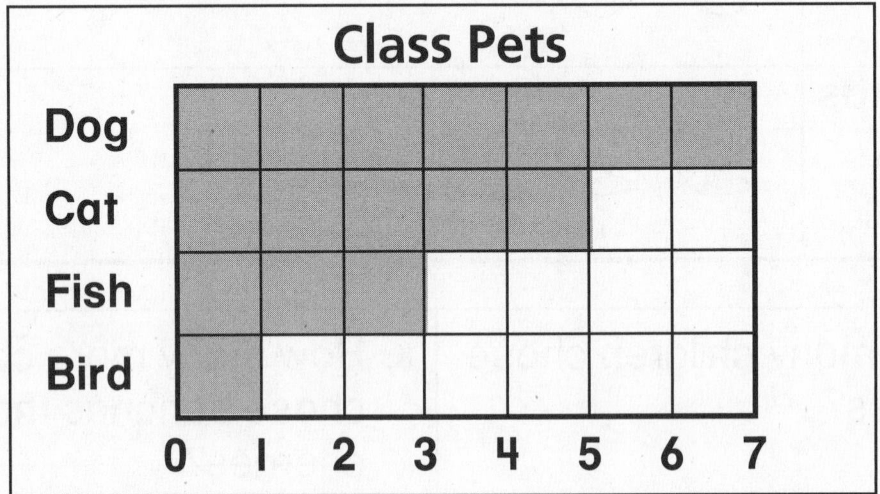

9. Which pet do the **least** number of children have?

Ⓐ dog
Ⓑ bird
Ⓒ cat
Ⓓ fish

10. What is the difference between the **greatest** number of pets and the **least** number of pets?

___ ◯ ___ = ___

Ⓐ 1
Ⓑ 2
Ⓒ 6
Ⓓ 7

Stop

Name ______________________________

Use the picture to answer questions 1 and 2.

1. Make tally marks to show how many 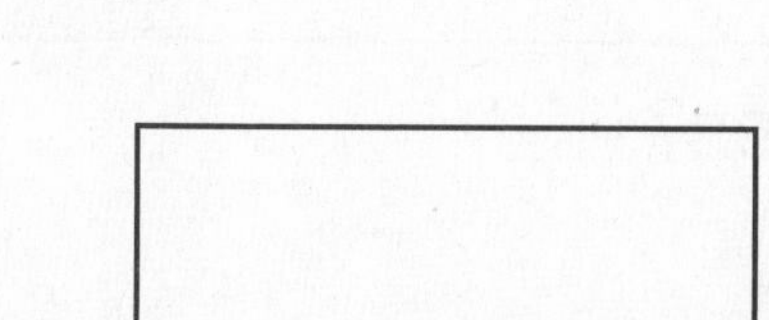 there are.

2. Make tally marks to show how many basketballs there are. 

Use the picture to answer question 3.

3. Draw a line from each shape to the group where it belongs.

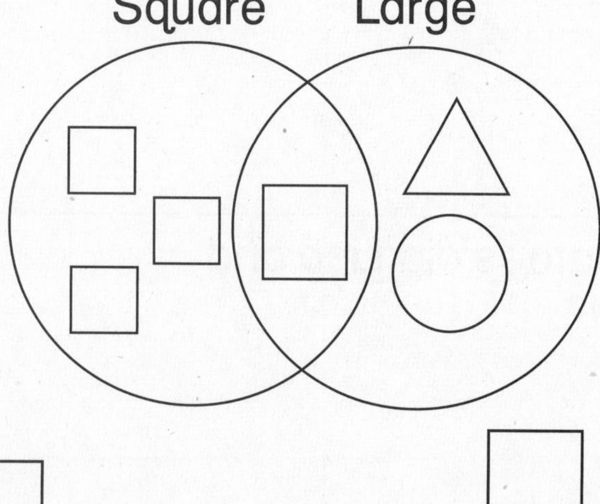

Go On

Name ______________________________

Use the bar graph to answer questions 4, 5, and 6. Mr. Byrd's class grew tomato plants. The graph shows how many tomatoes each child grew.

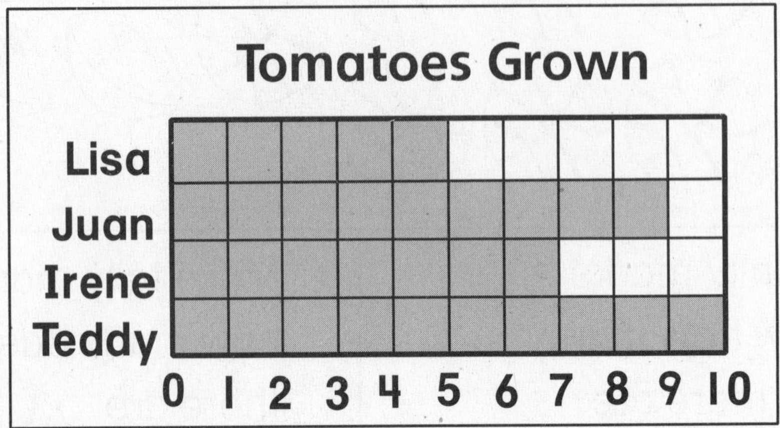

4. Which child grew the fewest tomatoes?

____

5. How many more tomatoes did Teddy grow than Irene?

____

6. How many tomatoes did Lisa and Juan grow in all?

____

Go On

Name ___

Use the picture graph to answer questions 7 and 8.

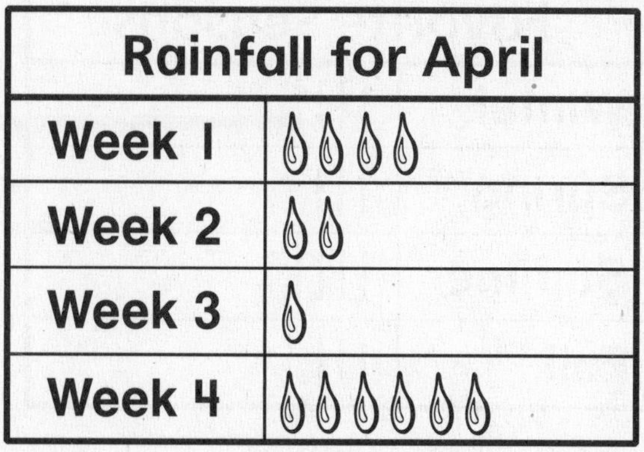

Rainfall for April	
Week 1	💧💧💧💧
Week 2	💧💧
Week 3	💧
Week 4	💧💧💧💧💧💧

Each  💧 stands for 1 inch of rain.

7. Which week had the most rain?

   week ___

8. How many more inches of rain fell in week 1 than in week 2?

   ___ inches

Go On

Name ______________________

Color the bar graph to match the tally table.

Favorite Seasons	
Winter	~~||||~~
Spring	|||
Summer	||||
Fall	|||

Favorite Seasons						
Winter						
Spring						
Summer						
Fall						

0 1 2 3 4 5 6

Use the bar graph to answer questions 9 and 10.

9. How many children voted for winter?

______ children

10. What is the difference between the season with the **greatest** number of votes and the season with the **least** number of votes?

___ ◯ ___ = ___

______ votes

Stop

Name ______________________

For 1–8, mark the one that tells how many there are.

1.

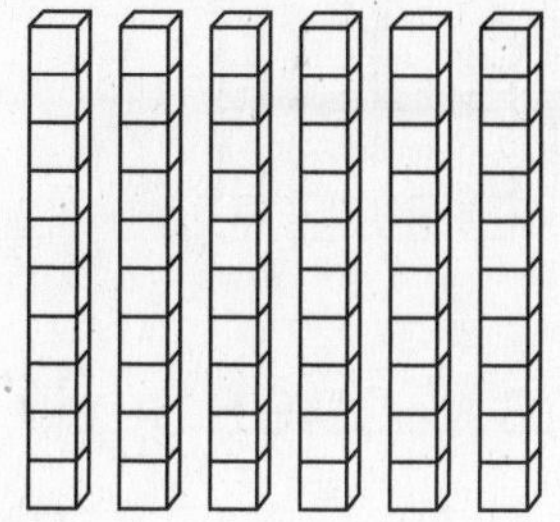

Ⓐ 10 ones = 1
Ⓑ 6 tens = 60
Ⓒ 5 tens = 50
Ⓓ 6 ones = 6

2.

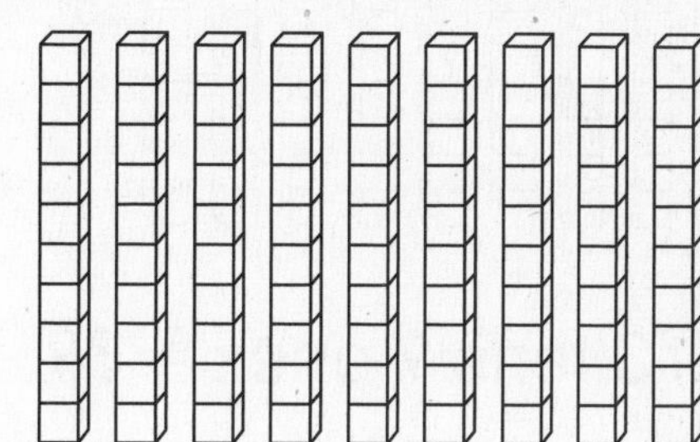

Ⓐ 8 ones = 8
Ⓑ 9 ones = 9
Ⓒ 8 tens = 80
Ⓓ 9 tens = 90

3.

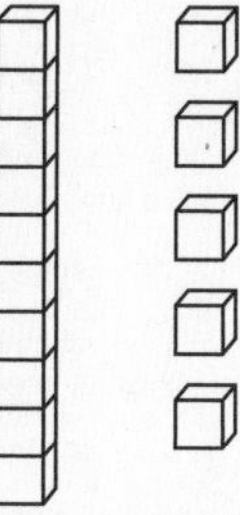

Ⓐ 1 ten 5 ones = 15
Ⓑ 5 tens 5 ones = 55
Ⓒ 5 tens 1 one = 51
Ⓓ 6 ones = 6

4.

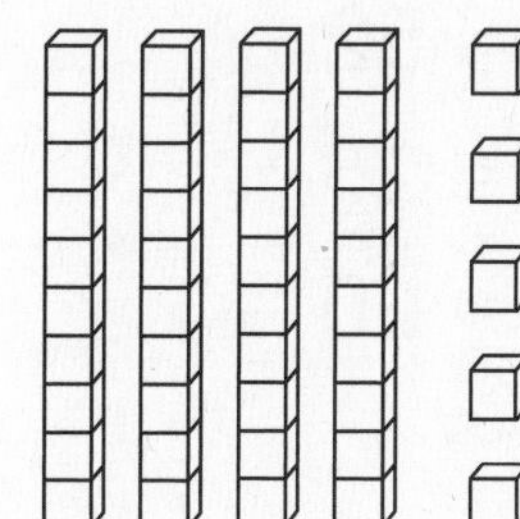

Ⓐ 4 tens 4 ones = 44
Ⓑ 4 tens 5 ones = 45
Ⓒ 5 tens 4 ones = 54
Ⓓ 5 tens 5 ones = 55

Go On

Name ___________________________

5. 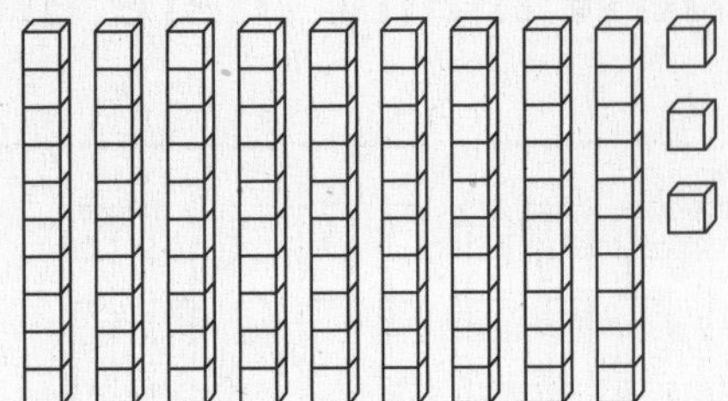

Ⓐ 3 tens 9 ones = 39
Ⓑ 8 tens 3 ones = 83
Ⓒ 9 tens 3 ones = 93
Ⓓ 9 tens 5 ones = 95

6. 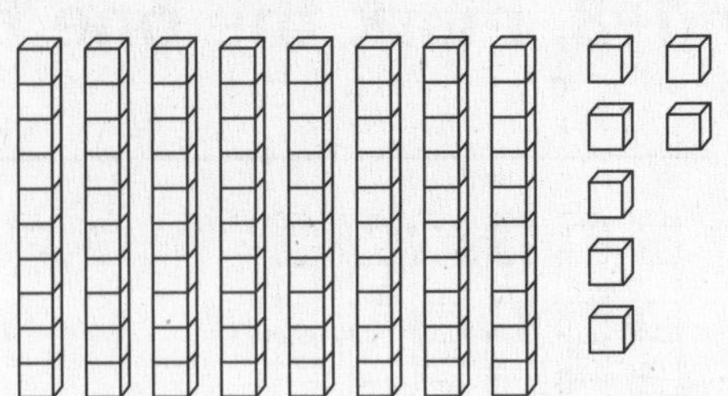

Ⓐ 8 tens 7 ones = 87
Ⓑ 7 tens 8 ones = 78
Ⓒ 7 tens 0 ones = 70
Ⓓ 10 ones = 10

7. 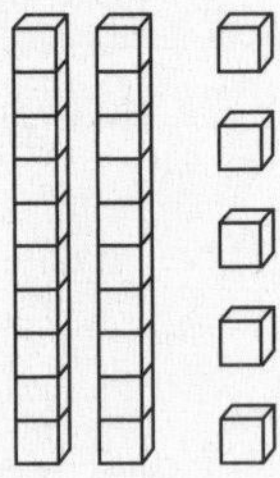

Ⓐ 50 + 2 = 52
Ⓑ 20 + 5 = 25
Ⓒ 20 + 0 = 20
Ⓓ 2 + 5 = 7

8. 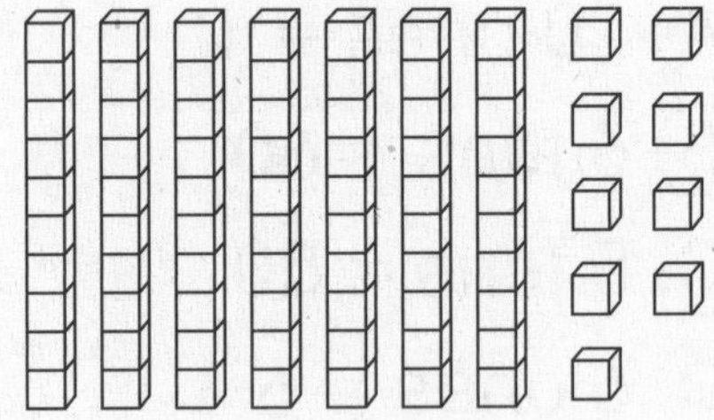

Ⓐ 90 + 7 = 97
Ⓑ 7 + 9 = 16
Ⓒ 70 + 9 = 79
Ⓓ 70 + 0 = 70

For 9–10, choose the closest estimate.

9. About how many (pencil) can you hold in one hand?

Ⓐ about 0 Ⓒ about 50
Ⓑ about 5 Ⓓ about 100

10. About how many  can you fit inside your shoe?

Ⓐ about 0 Ⓒ about 35
Ⓑ about 15 Ⓓ about 50

Stop

Name ______________________________

1. Write how many tens.
Then write the number.

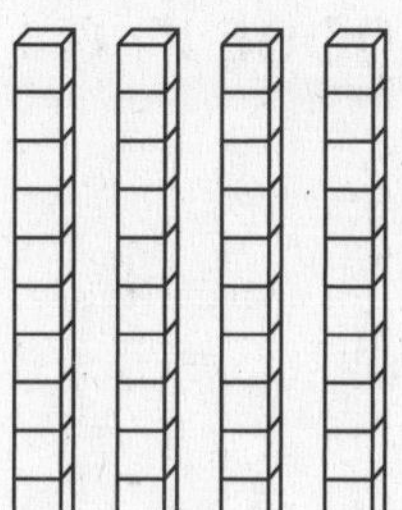

____ tens = ____

2. Write how many tens.
Then write the number.

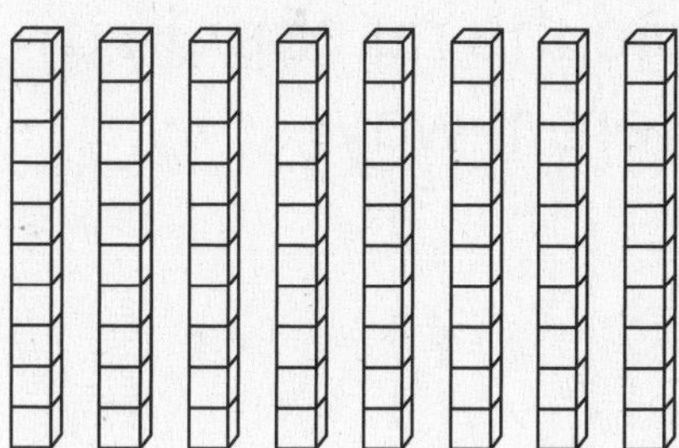

____ tens = ____

Write how many tens and ones there are.
Write the number.

3.

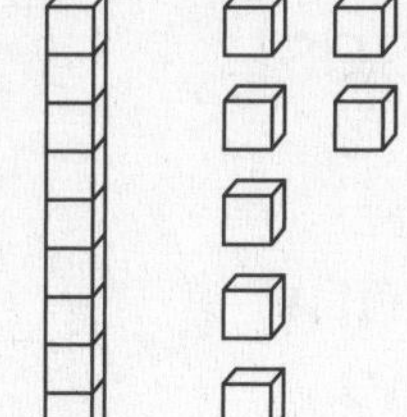

____ tens ____ ones = ____

4.

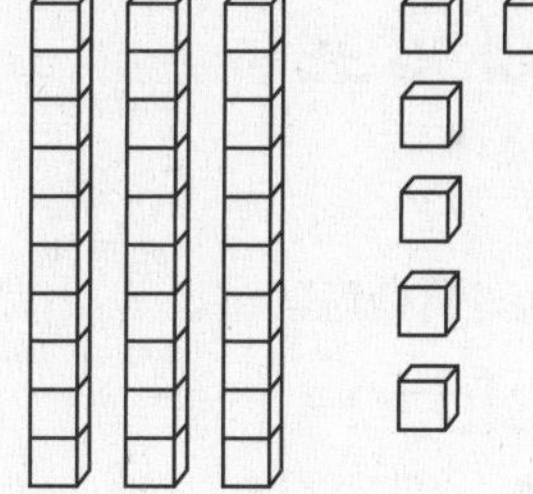

____ tens ____ ones = ____

5.

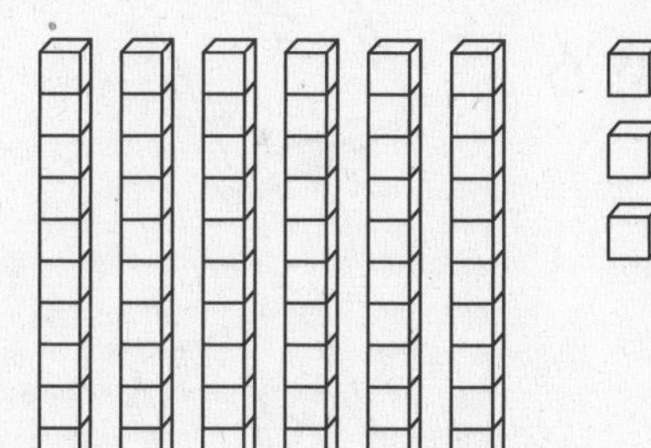

____ tens ____ ones = ____

6.

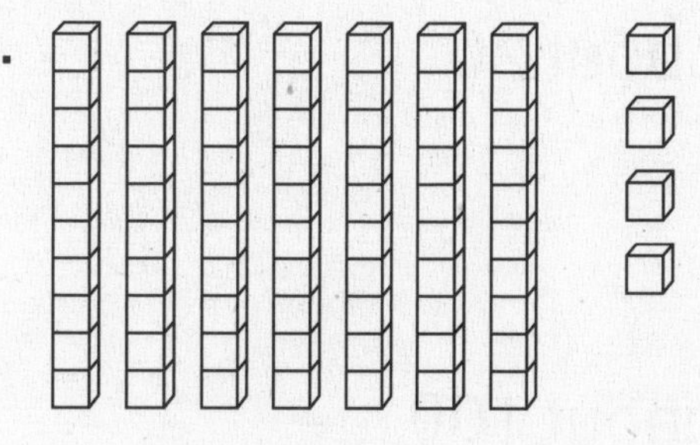

____ tens ____ ones = ____

Go On

7. Write how many tens and ones there are.

Write the number in a different way.

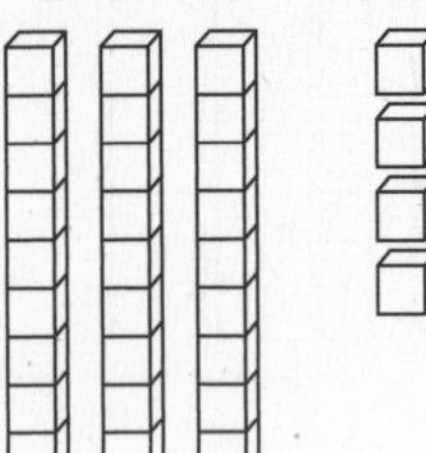

___ tens ___ ones = ___

___ + ___

8. Write how many tens and ones there are.

Write the number in a different way.

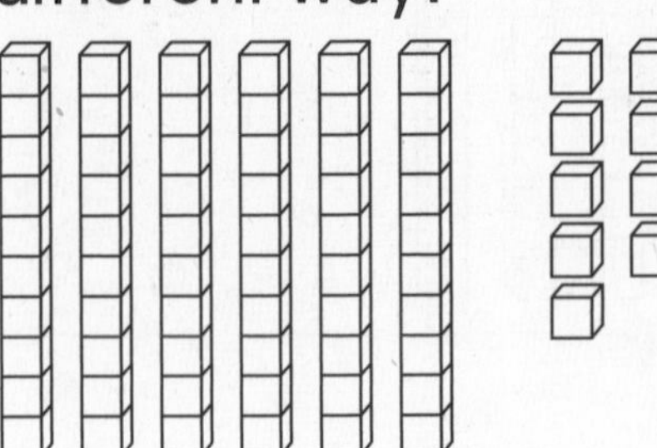

___ tens ___ ones = ___

___ + ___

9. Circle the closest estimate.

About how many  can you hold in one hand?

about 20 

about 100 

10. Circle the closest estimate.

About how many  can you carry?

about 6 

about 60 

Stop

Choose the correct answer.

1. Which number is **greater**?

Ⓐ 38   Ⓑ 13

2. Which number is **less**?

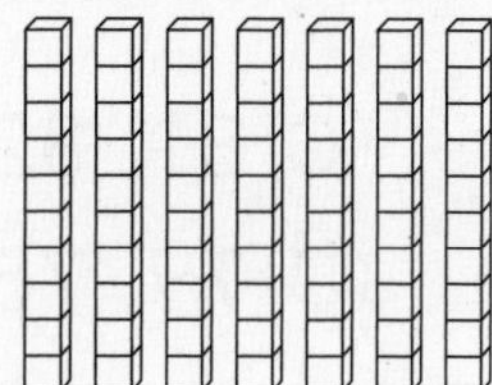

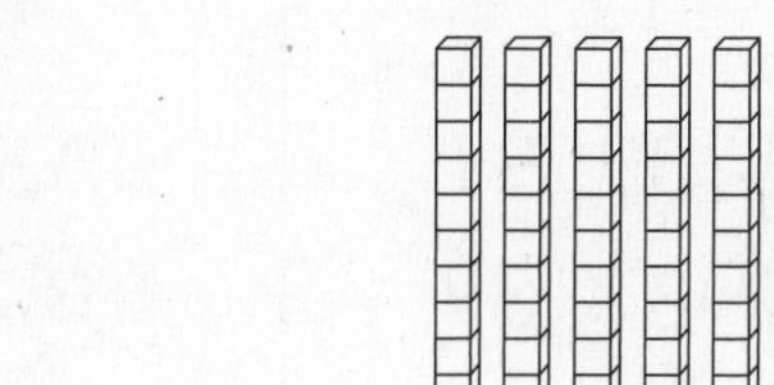

Ⓐ 73   Ⓑ 67

3. Which is correct?

Ⓐ $35 > 26$

Ⓑ $35 < 26$

Ⓒ $35 = 26$

4. Which is correct?

Ⓐ $82 = 80$

Ⓑ $82 < 80$

Ⓒ $82 > 80$

Go On

5. Which number is between?

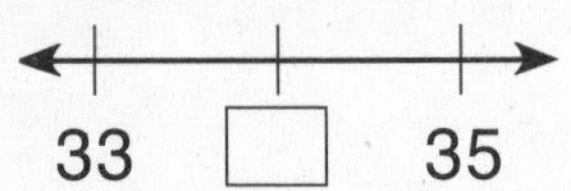

(A) 36 (C) 33
(B) 34 (D) 32

6. Which number is just before?

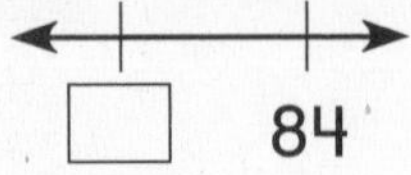

(A) 85 (C) 83
(B) 84 (D) 80

7. Count forward. Which numbers come next?

38, ____, ____

(A) 39, 40 (C) 39, 41
(B) 37, 36 (D) 37, 39

8. Count backward. Which numbers come next?

80, ____, ____

(A) 79, 81 (C) 81, 82
(B) 82, 83 (D) 79, 78

9. Use the model. Find 10 more or 10 less.

Sarah has 29 cards.
Carla has 10 more.
How many cards does Carla have?

(A) 39 (C) 28
(B) 30 (D) 19

10. Use the model. Find 10 more or 10 less.

Sam has 65 can tabs.
Jack has 10 less.
How many can tabs does Jack have?

(A) 75 (C) 55
(B) 64 (D) 50

Stop

Name ______________________________

Write the correct answer.

1. Circle the number that is **greater**.
   Write the numbers.

   44 58

   ____ is greater than ____ .

   ____ > ____

2. Circle the number that is **less**.
   Write the numbers.

   28 33

   ____ is less than ____ .

   ____ < ____

3. Write **less than**, **equal to**, or **greater than**.
   Then write the numbers.

   27 is ______ ______ 26.

   ____ > ____

4. Write **less than**, **equal to**, or **greater than**.
   Then write the numbers.

   66 is ______ ______ 70.

   ____ < ____

Go On

5. Write the missing number that comes between.

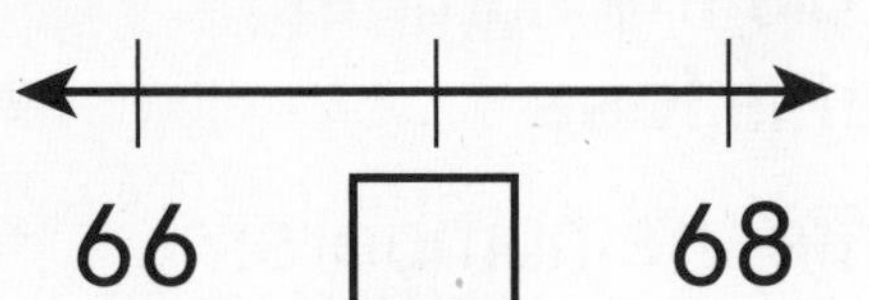

66 ☐ 68

6. Write the missing number that is just after.

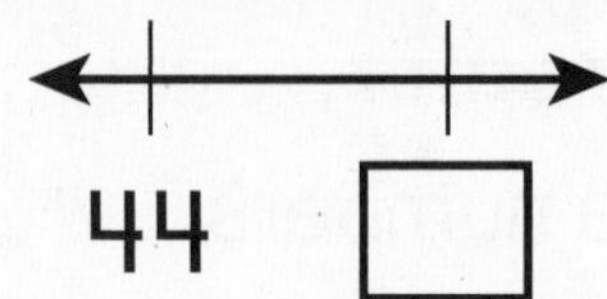

44 ☐

7. Count forward. Write the numbers.

53, ____, ____

8. Count backward. Write the numbers.

12, ____, ____

9. Use the model. Find 10 more or 10 less. Write the number.

Tim has 21 stickers.
Carlos has 10 more.
How many stickers does Carlos have?

____ stickers

10. Use the model. Find 10 more or 10 less. Write the number.

Keiko has 44 gold stars.
Ellen has 10 less.
How many gold stars does Ellen have?

____ gold stars

Stop

Name ___

Choose the correct answer.

1. Count by twos. What number is missing?

2, 4, 6, ___

(A) 2 (B) 4 (C) 6 (D) 8

2. Count by fives. What number is missing?

5, ___, 15, 20

(A) 1 (B) 5 (C) 10 (D) 15

Use the hundred chart to solve 3 and 4.

1	2	3	4	5	6	7	8	9	10
11	12	13	14	15	16	17	18	19	20
21	22	23	24	25	26	27	28	29	30
31	32	33	34	35	36	37	38	39	40
41	42	43	44	45	46	47	48	49	50
51	52	53	54	55	56	57	58	59	60
61	62	63	64	65	66	67	68	69	70
71	72	73	74	75	76	77	78	79	80
81	82	83	84	85	86	87	88	89	90
91	92	93	94	95	96	97	98	99	100

3. Start on 5. Skip count by fives. Find the missing numbers.

5, 10, 15, ___, ___

(A) 25, 30 (B) 20, 30 (C) 20, 25 (D) 5, 15

4. Start on 3. Count forward by tens. What are the next two numbers?

3, 13, 23, ___, ___

(A) 33, 43 (B) 2, 3 (C) 24, 25 (D) 63, 73

Go On

5. Which number is odd?

(A) 4
(B) 5
(C) 6
(D) 8

6. Which number is even?

(A) 13
(B) 9
(C) 7
(D) 4

For 7 and 8, find a pattern to solve.

7. How many shoes are on 5 children?

number of children	1	2	3	4	5
number of shoes	2	4	6	8	?

(A) 5
(B) 7
(C) 8
(D) 10

8. How many petals are on 4 flowers?

number of flowers	1	2	3	4
number of petals	5	10	15	?

(A) 20
(B) 22
(C) 25
(D) 30

9. In which place is the orange?

(A) second
(B) fourth
(C) fifth
(D) eighth

10. In which place is the pineapple?

(A) first
(B) third
(C) ninth
(D) tenth

Stop

Name ______________________

Write the correct answer.

1. Count by twos. Write the missing numbers.

2, ____, 6 , ____, ____

2. Count the toes by fives. Write the missing numbers.

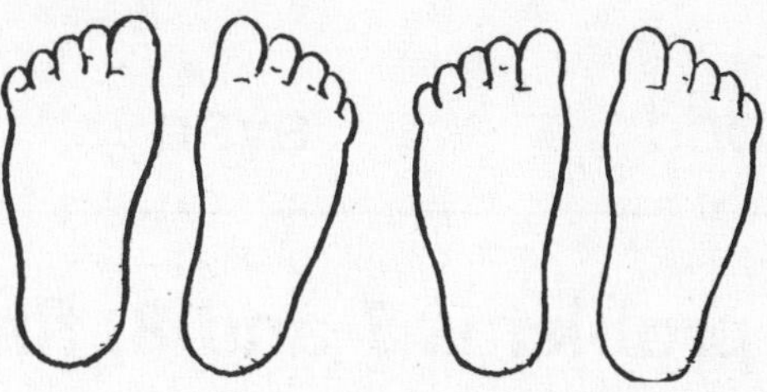

5, ____, ____, ____

Use the hundred chart to solve 3 and 4.

1	2	3	4	5	6	7	8	9	10
11	12	13	14	15	16	17	18	19	20
21	22	23	24	25	26	27	28	29	30
31	32	33	34	35	36	37	38	39	40
41	42	43	44	45	46	47	48	49	50
51	52	53	54	55	56	57	58	59	60
61	62	63	64	65	66	67	68	69	70
71	72	73	74	75	76	77	78	79	80
81	82	83	84	85	86	87	88	89	90
91	92	93	94	95	96	97	98	99	100

3. Start on 6. Count by tens. Write the missing numbers.

6, 16, 26, ____, ____

4. Start on 22. Count by twos. Write the missing numbers.

24, 26, 28, ____, ____

Go On

5. Circle even or odd.

4 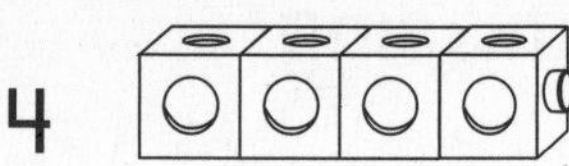

odd even

6. Circle even or odd.

7 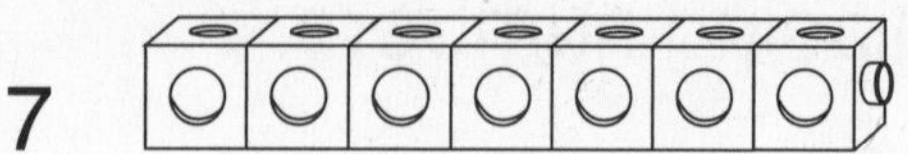

odd even

For problems 7 and 8, find a pattern to solve.

7. How many ears are on 5 cats? Write how many.

number of cats	1	2	3	4	5
number of ears	2	4	6	8	?

_____ ears

8. How many crayons are in 6 boxes? Write how many.

number of boxes	1	2	3	4	5	6
number of crayons	10	20	30	40	50	?

_____ crayons

9. Circle the sixth animal.

first

10. Mark an X on the second animal.

first

Stop

Name ____________________

For 1–4, use the number line. Count on to add. Count back to subtract.

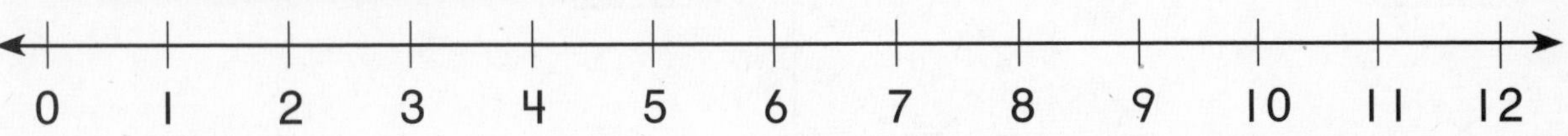

1. $\begin{array}{r} 8 \\ +\ 3 \\ \hline \end{array}$

Ⓐ 8 Ⓑ 9 Ⓒ 10 Ⓓ 11

2. 7 + 1 = ___

Ⓐ 9 Ⓑ 8 Ⓒ 7 Ⓓ 6

3. 8 − 2 = ___

Ⓐ 3 Ⓑ 5 Ⓒ 6 Ⓓ 8

4. $\begin{array}{r} 12 \\ -\ 3 \\ \hline \end{array}$

Ⓐ 9 Ⓑ 10 Ⓒ 11 Ⓓ 12

5. $\begin{array}{r} 4 \\ +\ 4 \\ \hline \end{array}$

Ⓐ 5 Ⓑ 6 Ⓒ 8 Ⓓ 9

6. 4 + 5 = ___

Ⓐ 4 Ⓑ 5 Ⓒ 6 Ⓓ 9

Go On

7.

$$\begin{array}{r} 1 \\ 1 \\ +\ 5 \\ \hline \end{array}$$

Ⓐ 5 Ⓑ 6 Ⓒ 7 Ⓓ 8

8.

$$\begin{array}{r} 2 \\ 3 \\ +\ 5 \\ \hline \end{array}$$

Ⓐ 5 Ⓑ 8 Ⓒ 9 Ⓓ 10

9. Find the difference.

$$\begin{array}{r} 9 \\ -\ 6 \\ \hline \end{array}$$

Ⓐ 15 Ⓑ 9 Ⓒ 5 Ⓓ 3

10. Mark the number sentence that matches the story.

2 girls eat lunch.

5 boys eat lunch, too.

How many children eat lunch?

Ⓐ $2 + 5 = 7$

Ⓑ $7 + 1 = 8$

Ⓒ $5 + 3 = 8$

Ⓓ $5 + 5 = 10$

Stop

Name ______________________

For 1–4, use the number line.
Count on to add.
Count back to subtract.

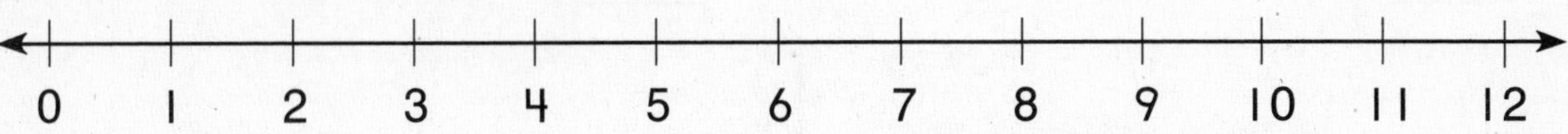

1. $\begin{array}{r} 7 \\ +\ 3 \\ \hline \end{array}$	2. $8 + 2 =$ ___
3. $10 - 3 =$ ___	4. $\begin{array}{r} 11 \\ -\ 2 \\ \hline \end{array}$
5. $\begin{array}{r} 3 \\ +\ 3 \\ \hline \end{array}$	6. $\begin{array}{r} 3 \\ +\ 4 \\ \hline \end{array}$

Go On

Name ______________________

7.	8.
$\begin{array}{r} 1 \\ 3 \\ +\ 4 \\ \hline \end{array}$	$\begin{array}{r} 2 \\ 2 \\ +\ 5 \\ \hline \end{array}$

9. Draw lines to match. Write the difference.

$$\begin{array}{r} 8 \\ -\ 6 \\ \hline \end{array}$$

10. Write a number sentence.

Lee knows 5 songs.

He learns 6 new songs.

How many songs does he know in all?

___ ◯ ___ ◯ ___ songs

Stop

Name ______________________

Choose the correct answer.

1. Which subtraction sentence is related to $8 + 1 = 9$?

   (A) $9 - 1 = 8$
   (B) $9 - 7 = 2$
   (C) $8 - 8 = 0$
   (D) $9 - 9 = 0$

2. Which fact is related to $12 - 4 = 8$?

   (A) $9 + 3 = 12$
   (B) $8 + 4 = 12$
   (C) $12 - 5 = 7$
   (D) $8 - 4 = 4$

3. Which fact belongs in this fact family?

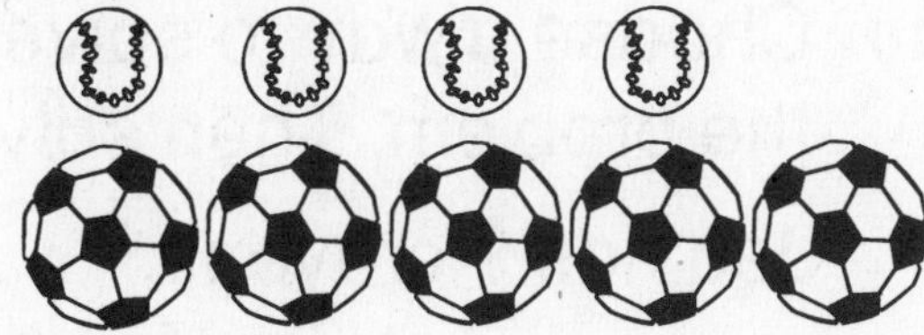

4	5	9

   (A) $5 - 4 = 1$
   (B) $9 - 6 = 3$
   (C) $3 + 6 = 9$
   (D) $4 + 5 = 9$

4. Which fact belongs in this fact family?

6	3	9

   (A) $9 - 6 = 3$
   (B) $6 - 3 = 3$
   (C) $9 - 0 = 9$
   (D) $9 + 3 = 12$

Go On

Name ______________________________

5. What is the missing number? 9 + ___ = 10 10 − 9 = ___ (A) 1 (C) 4 (B) 2 (D) 5	**6.** What is the missing number? ___ + 6 = 12 12 − 6 = ___ (A) 3 (C) 5 (B) 4 (D) 6
7. Find the difference. 11 − 7 = ___ (A) 10 (C) 5 (B) 6 (D) 4	**8.** Find the difference. 12 − 5 = ___ (A) 6 (C) 8 (B) 7 (D) 9
9. Choose a way to solve the problem. Then solve. Betty has 10 books. She gives 4 to Fred. How many are left? (A) 4 (B) 5 (C) 6 (D) 9	**10.** Choose a way to solve the problem. Then solve. Jed has 9 crayons. Mary has 2 crayons. How many are there in all? (A) 12 (B) 11 (C) 10 (D) 7

Stop

Name ______________________

Write the correct answer.

1. Write a related subtraction sentence. 3 + 7 = 10 ___ − ___ = ___	2. Write the sum. Then write a related subtraction fact. 5 + 6 = ___ 
3. Add or subtract. Write the numbers in the fact family. 7 + 2 = ___ 9 − 7 = ___ 9 − 2 = ___ 2 + 7 = ___   	4. Add or subtract. Write the numbers in the fact family. 5 + 3 = ___ 8 − 5 = ___ 3 + 5 = ___ 8 − 3 = ___ 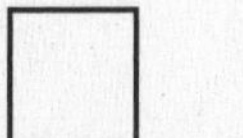 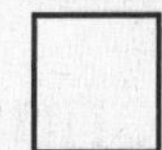

Go On

5. Write the missing number.

$3 + \_\_\_ = 12$

$12 - 3 = \_\_\_$

6. Write the missing number.

$\_\_\_ + 8 = 11$

$11 - 8 = \_\_\_$

7. Write the difference.

$11 - 4 = \_\_\_$

8. Write the difference.

$$\begin{array}{r} 12 \\ -\ 4 \\ \hline \end{array}$$

9. Choose a way to solve the problem. Then solve.

Jill buys 2 bananas.

Jamal buys 7 bananas.

How many bananas do both children buy?

___ bananas

10. Choose a way to solve the problem. Then solve.

There are 11 carrots.

Karen eats 3 of them.

How many are left?

___ carrots

Stop

Name ______________________

Choose the correct answer. Use the bar graph to answer questions 1 and 2.

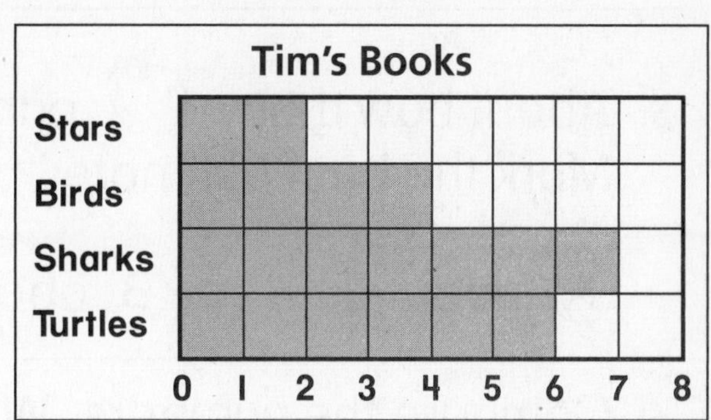

1. About which subject does Tim have 4 books?

   Ⓐ stars
   Ⓑ birds
   Ⓒ sharks
   Ⓓ turtles

2. How many more of Tim's books are about sharks than about stars?

   Ⓐ 1
   Ⓑ 2
   Ⓒ 4
   Ⓓ 5

3. Mark the answer that tells how many.

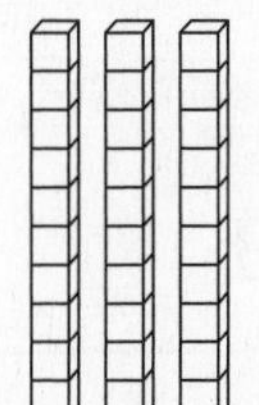

   Ⓐ 5 tens 3 ones
   Ⓑ 2 tens 5 ones
   Ⓒ 3 tens 5 ones
   Ⓓ 3 tens 3 ones

4. Mark the answer that tells the number in a different way.

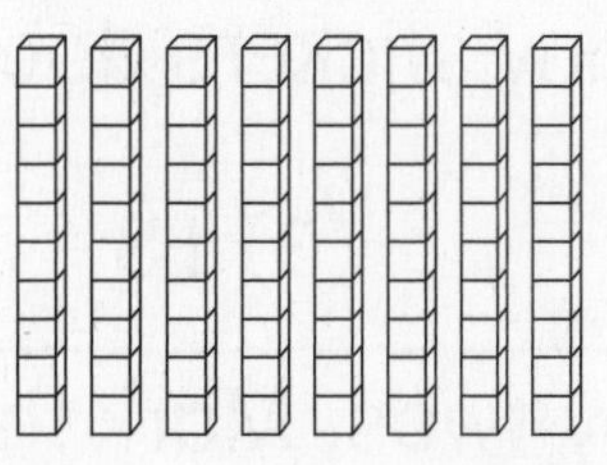

   Ⓐ 8 + 7 = 15
   Ⓑ 70 + 0 = 70
   Ⓒ 70 + 8 = 78
   Ⓓ 80 + 7 = 87

Go On

Name ____________________

5. About how many (apple) can you carry in your hand? Mark the best estimate.

Ⓐ about 2 Ⓑ about 20 Ⓒ about 200

6. Compare the numbers. Which is correct?

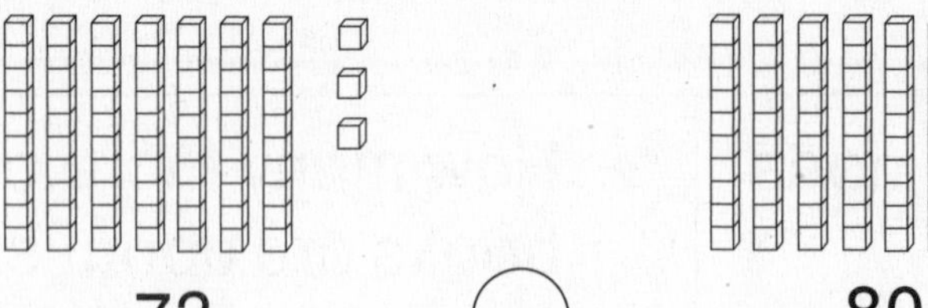

73 ◯ 80

Ⓐ $73 < 80$ Ⓑ $73 > 80$ Ⓒ $73 = 80$

7. Which number is just before?

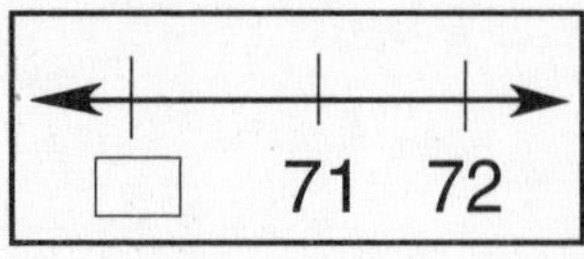

Ⓐ 72 Ⓑ 71 Ⓒ 70 Ⓓ 69

8. Shawna has 23 stickers. Yaritzi has 10 more. How many stickers does Yaritzi have?

Ⓐ 3 Ⓑ 13 Ⓒ 30 Ⓓ 33

9. Count by twos. Mark the missing number.

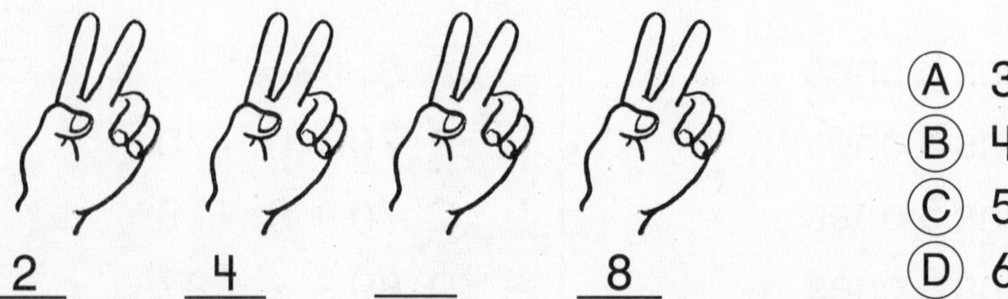

Ⓐ 3
Ⓑ 4
Ⓒ 5
Ⓓ 6

Go On

Name ______________________________

10. In which position is the circled ball?

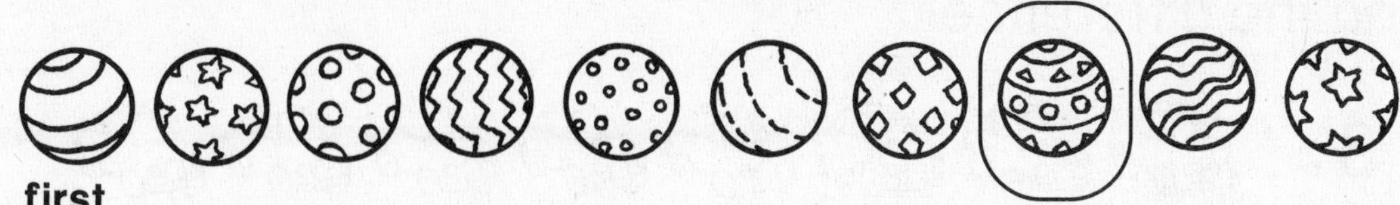

(A) seventh (B) eighth (C) ninth (D) tenth

11. Are the circled numbers **even** or **odd**?

(1) 2 (3) 4 (5)

(A) even (B) odd

12. Find the sum.

$3 + 3 + 6 = \_\_\_$

(A) 9 (B) 10 (C) 11 (D) 12

13. Find the sum.

$6 + 3 + 2 = \_\_\_$

(A) 12 (B) 11 (C) 10 (D) 9

14. Find the sum.

$5 + 6 = \_\_\_$

(A) 1 (B) 10 (C) 11 (D) 12

15. Mark the number sentence that shows the story.

3 ducks go to the pond. 2 more join them.

How many ducks are at the pond?

(A) $2 + 1 = 3$ (B) $3 - 2 = 1$ (C) $3 + 2 = 5$ (D) $6 + 0 = 6$

16. Count back to subtract.

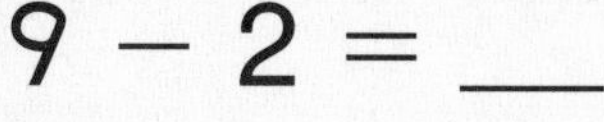

$9 - 2 = \_\_\_$

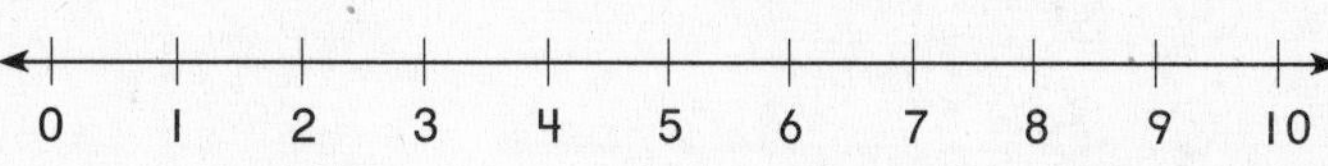

(A) 7 (B) 8 (C) 6 (D) 5

Go On

Name ___________________________

17. How many more cars than boats are there? Find the difference.

$$\begin{array}{r} 8 \\ -\ 4 \\ \hline \end{array}$$

Ⓐ 5　　Ⓑ 4　　Ⓒ 3　　Ⓓ 2

18. Which is a related subtraction fact for 6 + 1 = 7?

Ⓐ 10 − 9 = 1　　Ⓒ 6 − 1 = 5
Ⓑ 7 + 1 = 8　　Ⓓ 7 − 6 = 1

19. Find the difference.

$$\begin{array}{r} 12 \\ -\ 6 \\ \hline \end{array}$$

Ⓐ 2
Ⓑ 5
Ⓒ 6
Ⓓ 11

20. Solve the problem.

There are 6 oranges.

Naomi takes 1 orange.

How many oranges are left?

Ⓐ 6
Ⓑ 5
Ⓒ 2
Ⓓ 1

Stop

Write the correct answer.
Use the bar graph to answer questions 1 and 2.

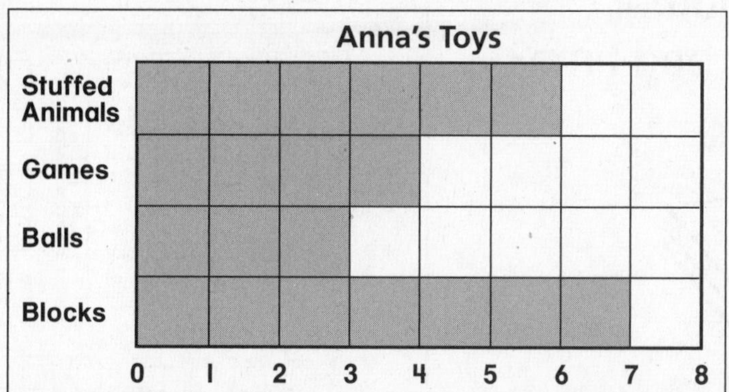

1. How many stuffed animals does Anna have?

____ stuffed animals

2. How many more blocks than games does Anna have?

____ more blocks

3. Write the numbers that tell how many.

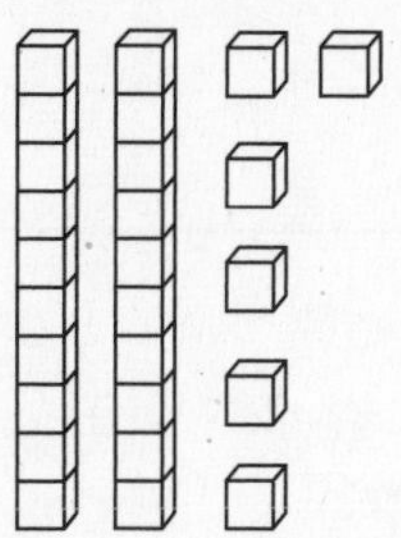

____ tens ____ ones = ____

4. Write the number in a different way.

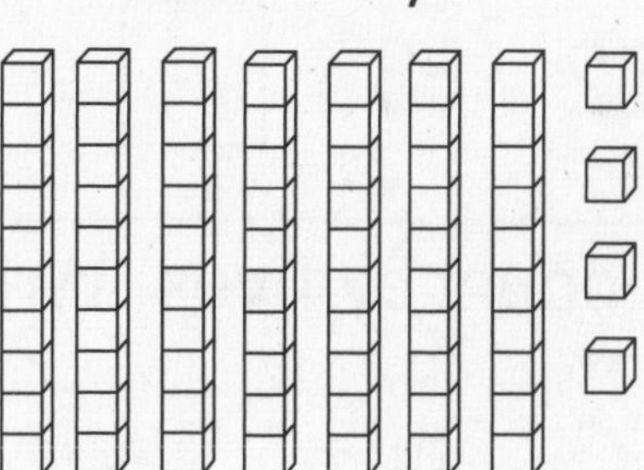

7 tens + 4 ones = 74

____ + ____ = ____

Go On

Name ______________________________

5. Circle the best estimate.

About how many books can Maria's mother read to her at bed time?

about 3
about 30
about 300

6. Compare the numbers. Write >, <, or = in the ○.

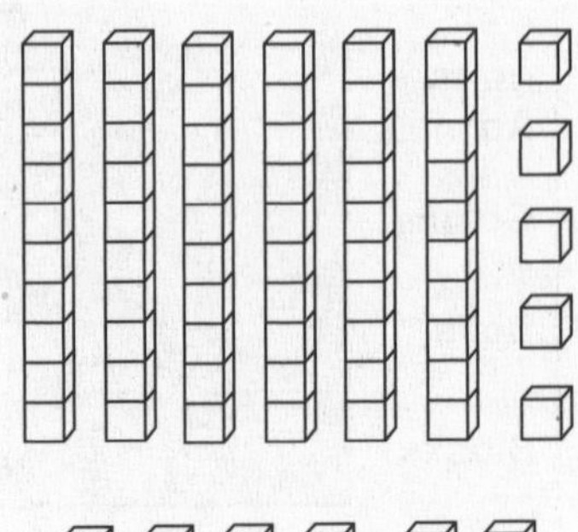

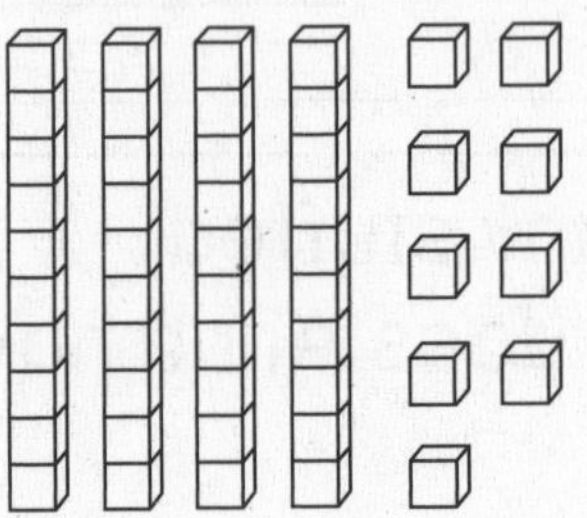

65 ○ 49

7. Which number is just after?

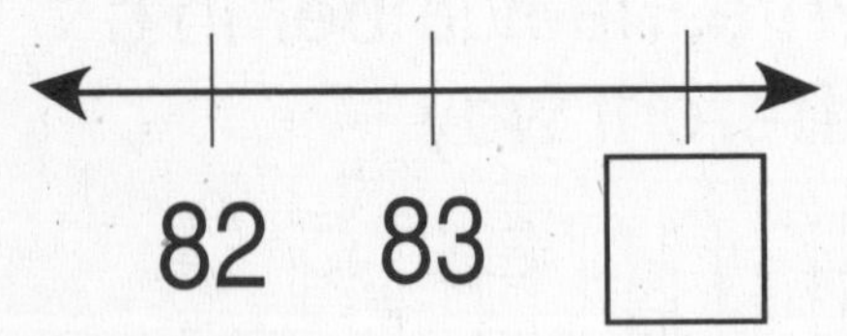

82 83 ☐

8. Josh has 42 cards. Assan has ten less. How many cards does Assan have?

____ cards

9. Skip-count by fives. Write the missing number.

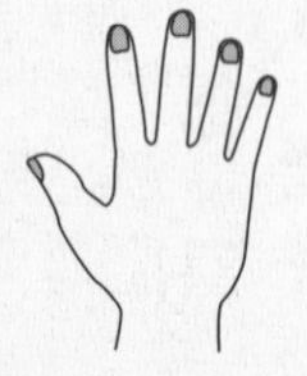
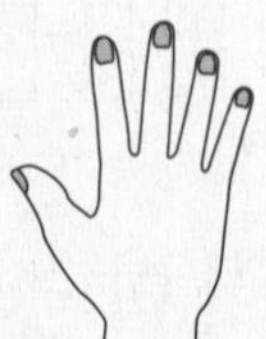
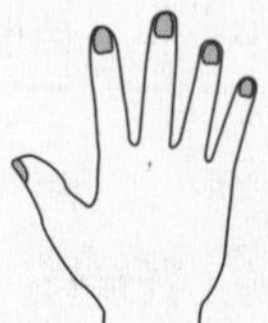
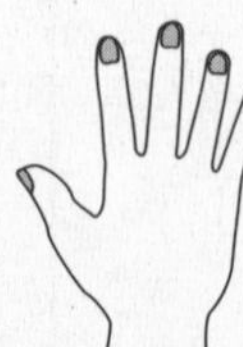

5, 10, 15, ____

Go On

Name ______________________

10. Circle the animal that is ninth.

11. Read the numbers.
Write **even** or **odd**.

2, 4, 8, 10, 12

____

12. Write the sum.

$$\begin{array}{r} 2 \\ 4 \\ +\ 6 \\ \hline \end{array}$$

13. Write the sum.

$5 + 4 + 1 =$ ___

14. Write the sum.

$4 + 3 =$ ___

15. Write the number sentence that shows the story.
4 cats sleep.
2 cats join them.
How many cats are there now?

___ + ___ = ___ cats

16. Count back to subtract.

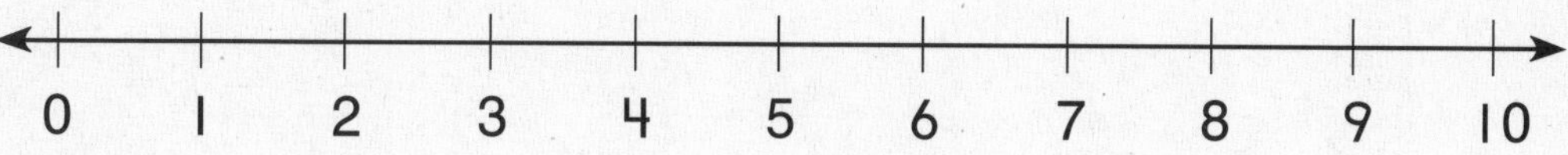

$10 - 3 =$ ___

Go On

17. How many more dogs than cats are there?
Write the difference.

$$\begin{array}{r} 8 \\ -\ 2 \\ \hline \end{array}$$

18. Write the difference.
Then write a related addition fact.

$12 - 3 =$ ____

____ $+$ ____ $=$ ____

19. Write the difference.

$11 - 7 =$ ____

20. Solve. Show your work.
Jim has 10 grapes.
He eats 3.
How many are left?

____ grapes

Stop

Name ____________________

Choose the correct answer.

1. Mark the solid that will stack and roll.

Ⓐ 
Ⓒ 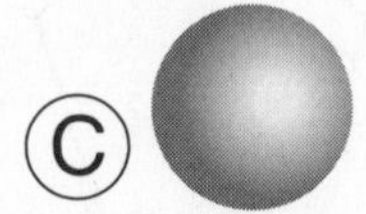
Ⓑ 
Ⓓ 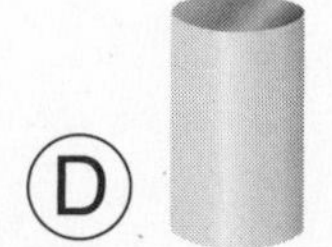

2. Mark the solid that will NOT slide.

Ⓐ 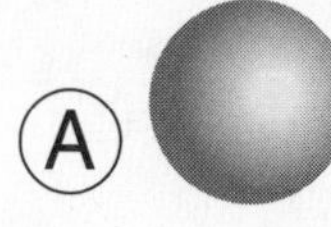
Ⓒ 
Ⓑ 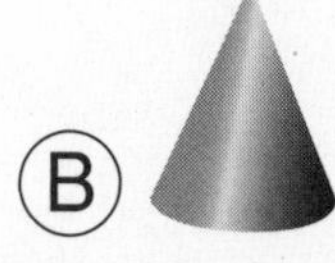
Ⓓ 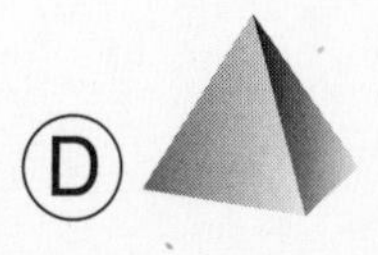

3. How many faces are on a ?

Ⓐ 1 
Ⓒ 5
Ⓑ 4
Ⓓ 6

4. Which solid has only 5 vertices?

Ⓐ 
Ⓒ 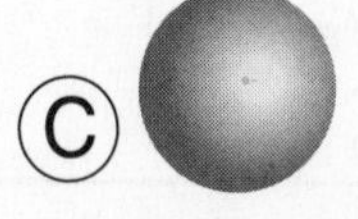
Ⓑ 
Ⓓ 

5. Which shape can you make if you trace around a cylinder?

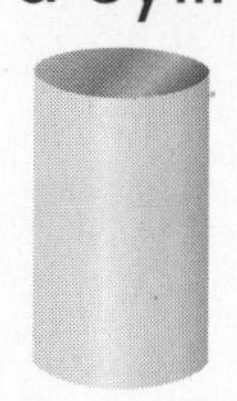
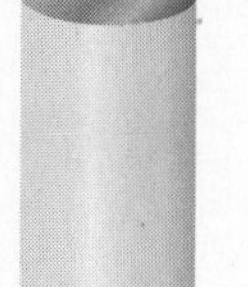

Ⓐ 
Ⓒ 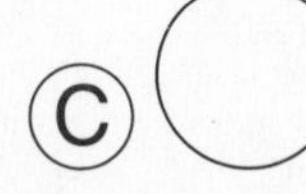
Ⓑ 
Ⓓ 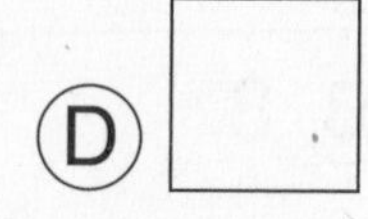

6. Which shape is a triangle?

Ⓐ 
Ⓒ 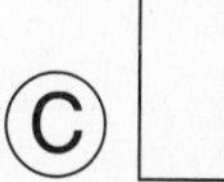
Ⓑ 
Ⓓ 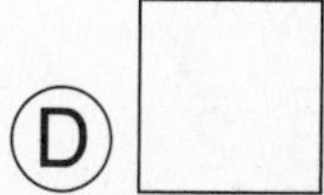

Go On

Name ______________________

7. Mark the shape with 3 vertices and 3 sides.

Ⓐ 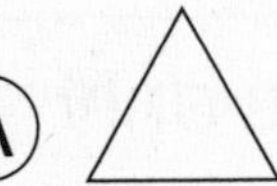

Ⓑ 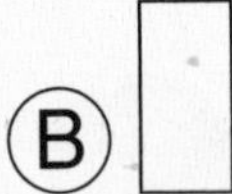

Ⓒ 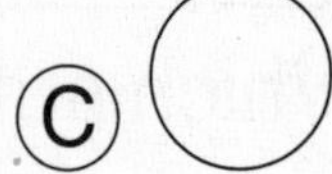

Ⓓ 

8. How many sides and vertices does this shape have?

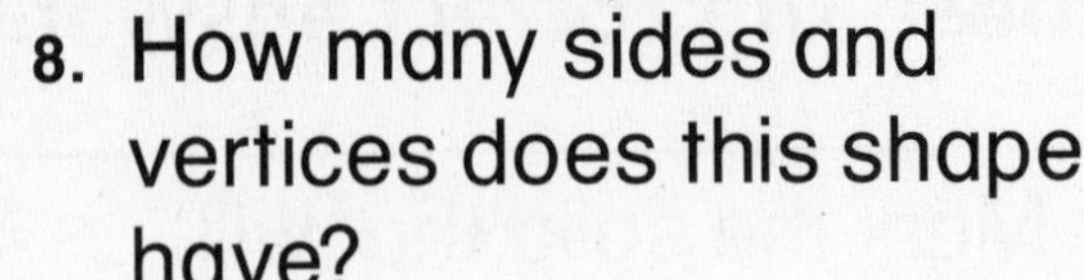

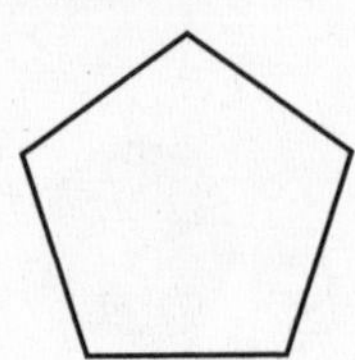

Ⓐ 3

Ⓑ 4

Ⓒ 5

Ⓓ 6

9. How many [right triangles] make a [rectangle]?

Ⓐ 1

Ⓑ 2

Ⓒ 3

Ⓓ 4

10. How many [trapezoids] make a [hexagon]?

Ⓐ 4

Ⓑ 3

Ⓒ 2

Ⓓ 1

Stop

Name ______________________________

Write the correct answer.

1. Circle each solid that will stack.

2. Circle the solid that will NOT roll.

3. How many faces are on a cube?

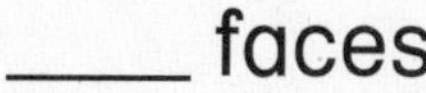

____ faces

4. Circle the solids that have 8 vertices.

5. Which shape can you make if you trace around a cone?

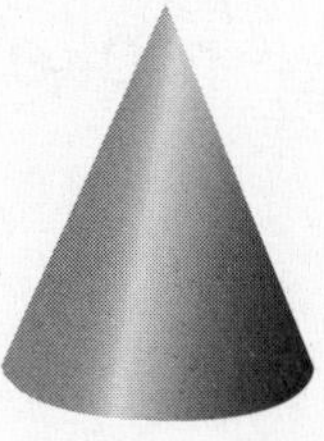

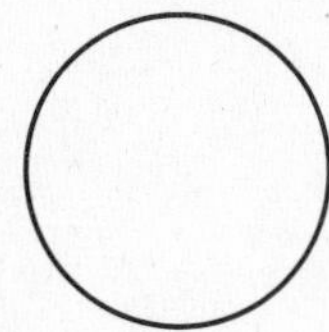 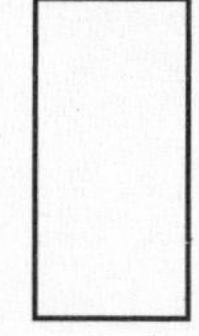

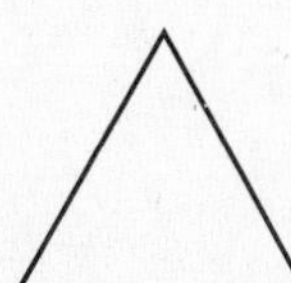 

6. Which shape is a square?

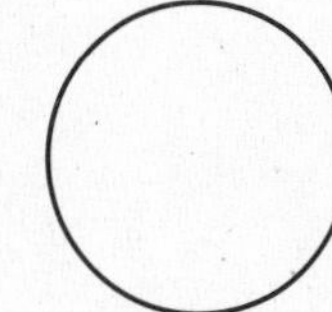 

 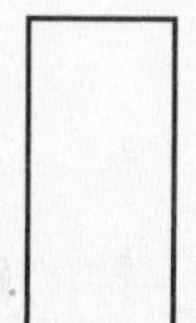

Go On

Name ______________________________

7. Circle the shape with 4 vertices and 4 sides.

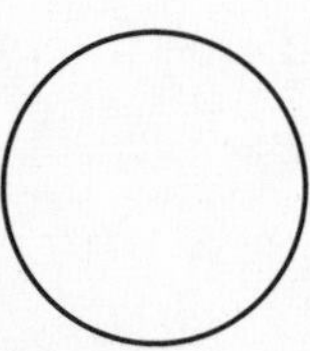
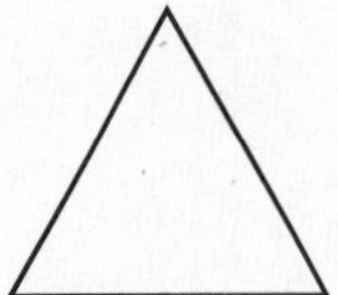
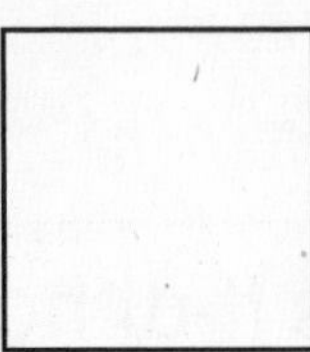
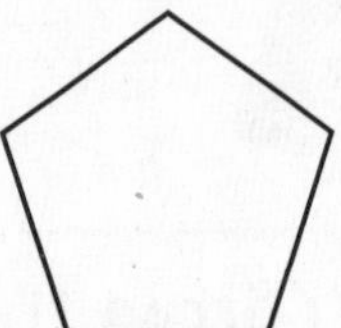

8. How many sides and vertices does this shape have?

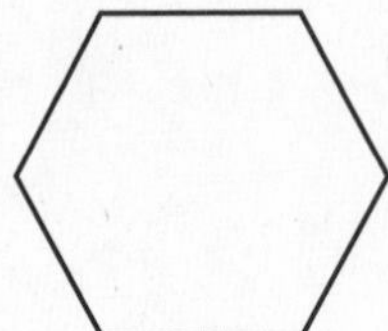

_____ sides

_____ vertices

9. How many △ make a ⏢ ?

_____ triangles

10. How many □ make a ▭ ?

_____ squares

Stop

Name ______________________________

Choose the correct answer.

1. Which shape is a closed figure?

(A) 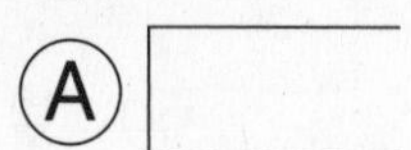
(B)
(C) 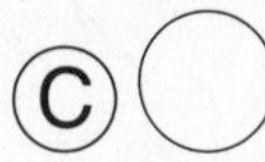
(D)

2. Which shape is an open figure?

(A) 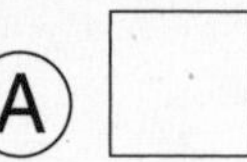
(B)
(C)
(D)

3. Which shows a star to the left of a moon?

(A) 
(B) 
(C) 
(D) 

4. Which shows a bee to the right of a flower?

(A) 
(B) 
(C) 
(D) 

Use the map. Follow the directions. Find the animal.

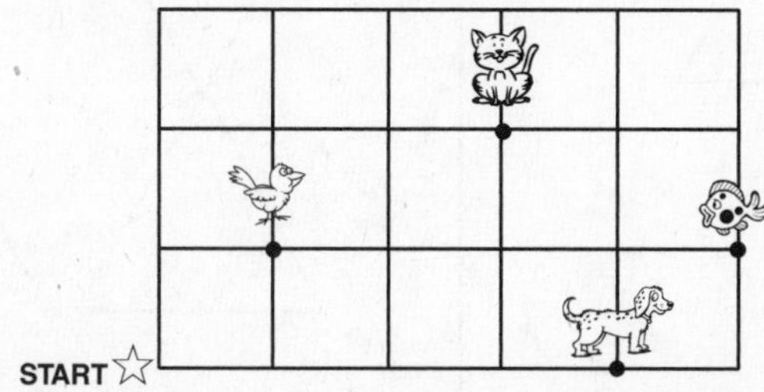

5. Go right 3 and up 2. Where are you?

(A) dog
(B) cat
(C) fish
(D) bird

6. Go right 5 and up 1. Where are you?

(A) dog
(B) cat
(C) fish
(D) bird

Go On

7. Which line makes two parts that match?

8. Which line makes two parts that match?

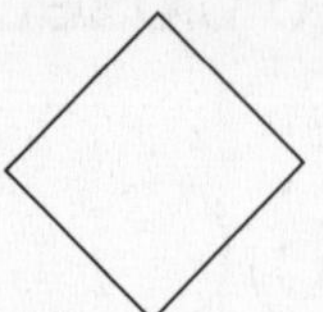

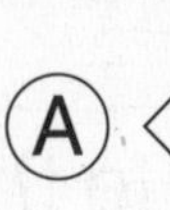
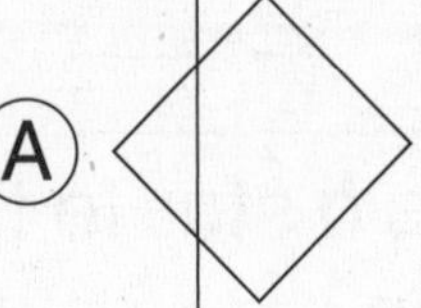

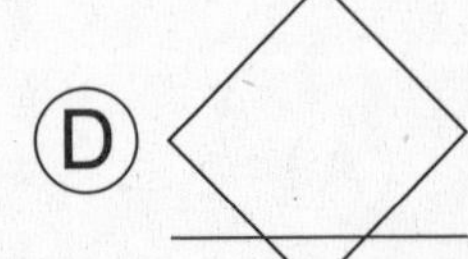

9. Choose the name of the move.

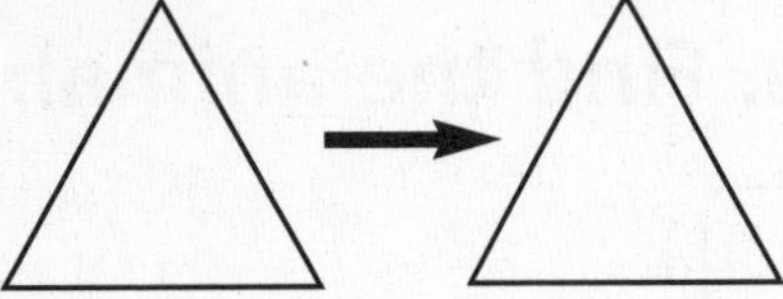

Ⓐ slide
Ⓑ turn

10. Choose the name of the move.

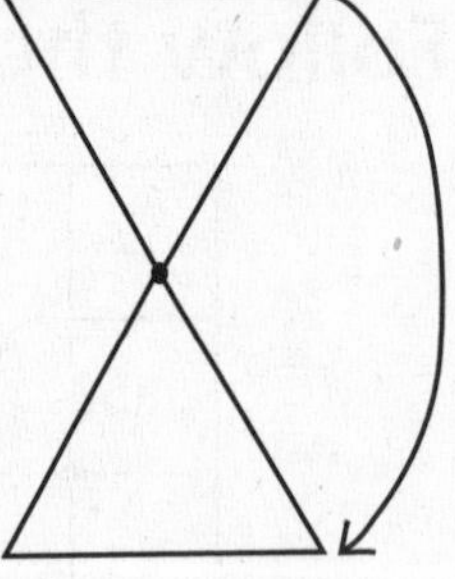

Ⓐ slide
Ⓑ turn

Stop

Name ______________________

Write the correct answer.

1. Circle the closed figures.	2. Circle the open figures.
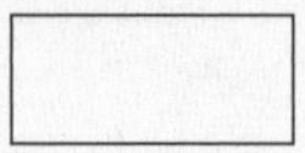 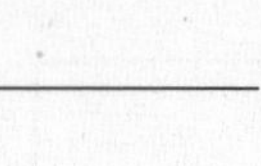	 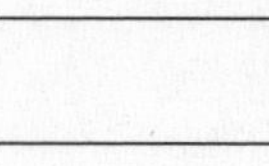 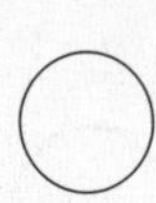  
3. Draw a bone to the right of the dog? 	4. Draw a bird to the left of the tree. 

Use the map. Follow the directions. Draw the shape.

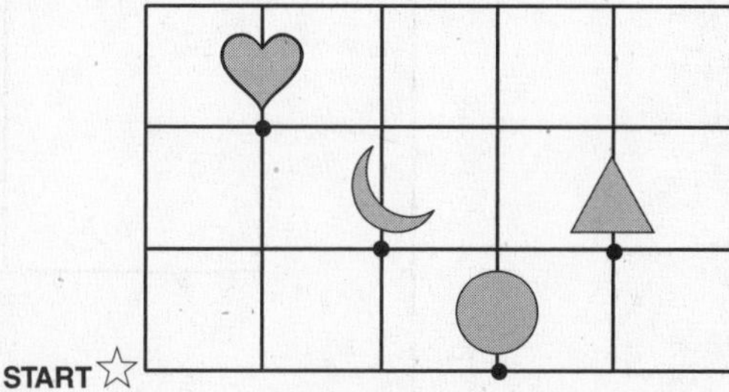

5. Start at the ☆. Go right 1 and up 2. Where are you? ______	6. Start at the ☆. Go right 4 and up 1. Where are you? ______

Go On

7. Draw a line of symmetry to show two matching parts.

8. Draw a line of symmetry to show two matching parts.

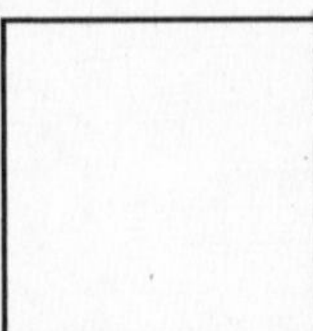

9. Circle **slide** or **turn** to name the move.

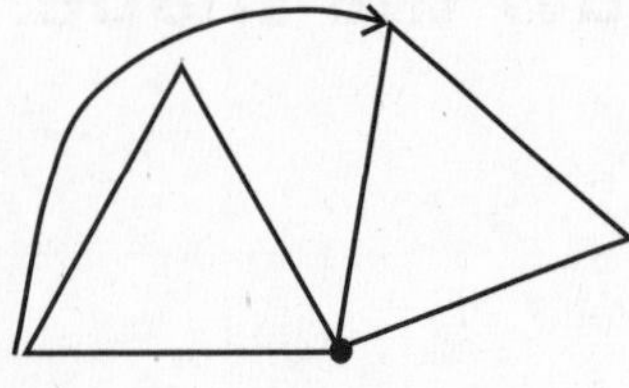

slide
turn

10. Circle **slide** or **turn** to name the move.

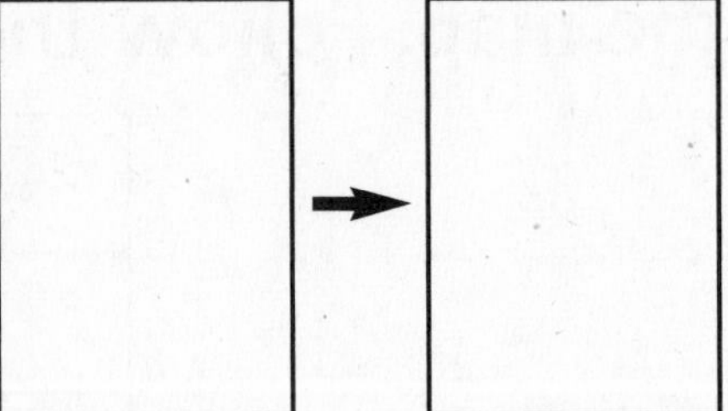

slide
turn

Stop

Name ______________________________

Choose the correct answer.

1. Which shape comes next in the pattern?

Ⓐ Ⓑ Ⓒ Ⓓ

2. Which shape comes next in the pattern?

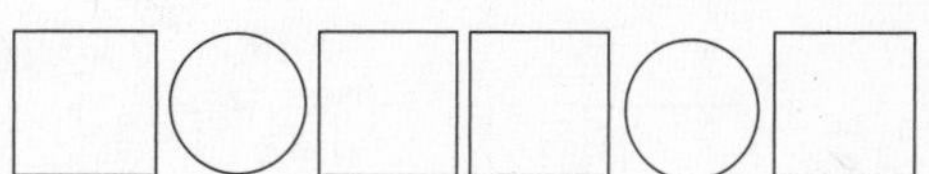

Ⓐ Ⓑ Ⓒ Ⓓ

3. Which is the pattern unit?

Ⓐ Ⓑ Ⓒ Ⓓ

4. Which is the pattern unit?

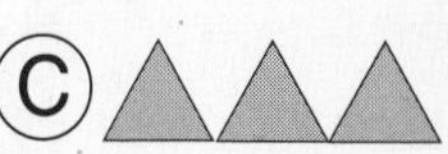

Ⓐ Ⓑ Ⓒ Ⓓ

Go On

Name ______________________

5. Which uses the same shapes as this pattern?

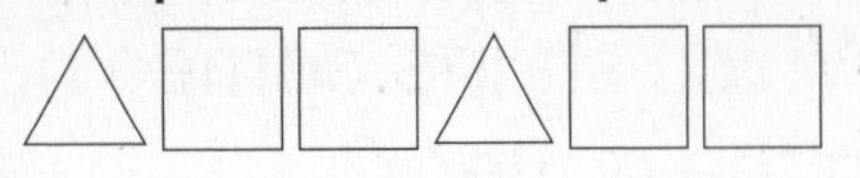

Ⓐ

Ⓑ

Ⓒ

Ⓓ

6. Which uses the same shapes as this pattern?

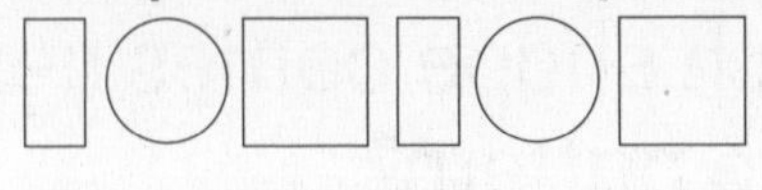

Ⓐ

Ⓑ

Ⓒ

Ⓓ

7. Which shape corrects the mistake in the pattern?

Ⓐ Ⓒ

Ⓑ Ⓓ

8. Which shape corrects the mistake in the pattern?

Ⓐ Ⓒ

Ⓑ Ⓓ

9. Which is another way to show this pattern?

Ⓐ 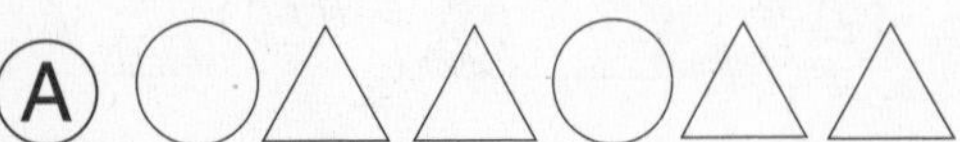

Ⓑ

10. Which is another way to show this pattern?

Ⓐ

Ⓑ

Stop

Name ______________________________

Write the correct answer.

1. Draw the shape that comes next.

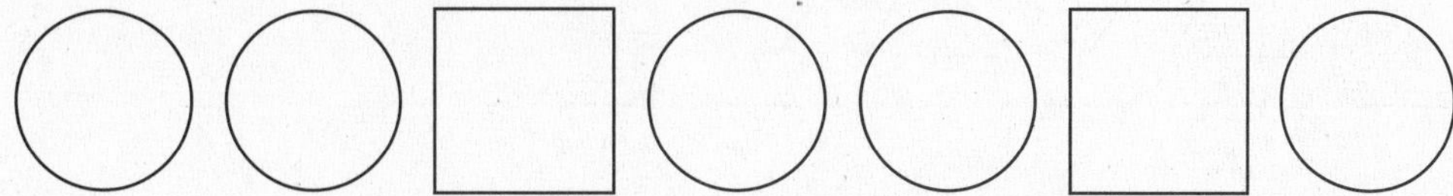

2. Draw the shape that comes next.

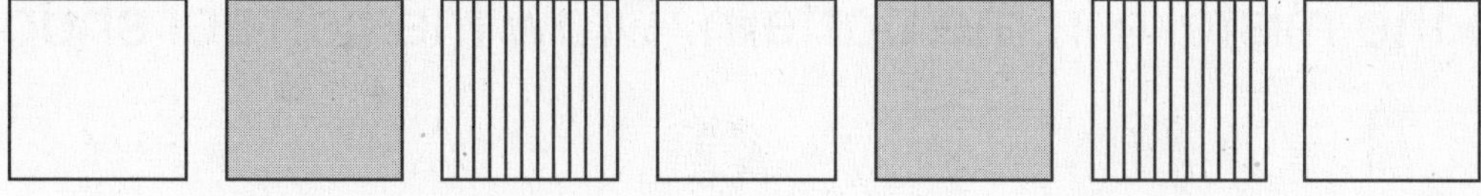

3. Circle the pattern unit.

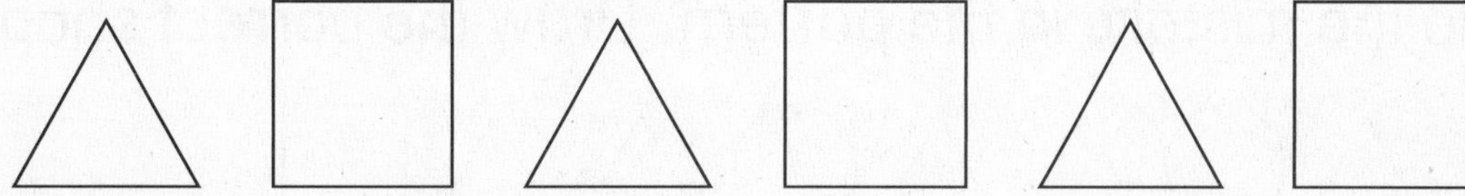

4. Circle the pattern unit.

5. Use the same shapes to make a different pattern. Draw your new pattern.

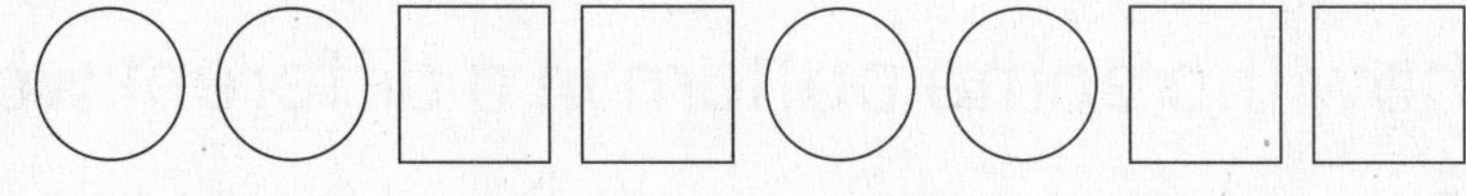

Go On

6. Use the same shapes to make a different pattern.
Draw your new pattern.

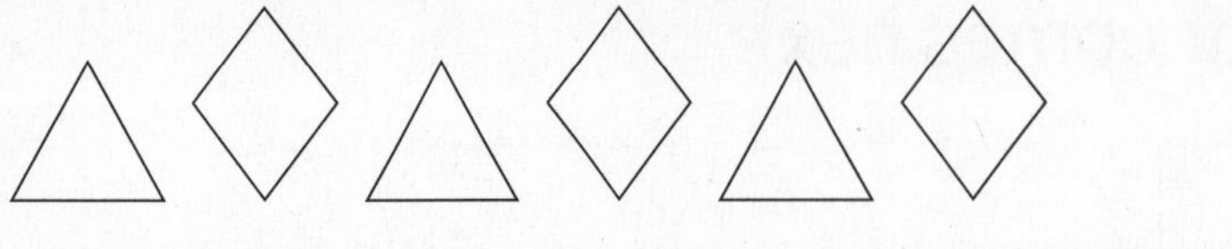

7. Circle the mistake in the pattern. Draw the correct shape.

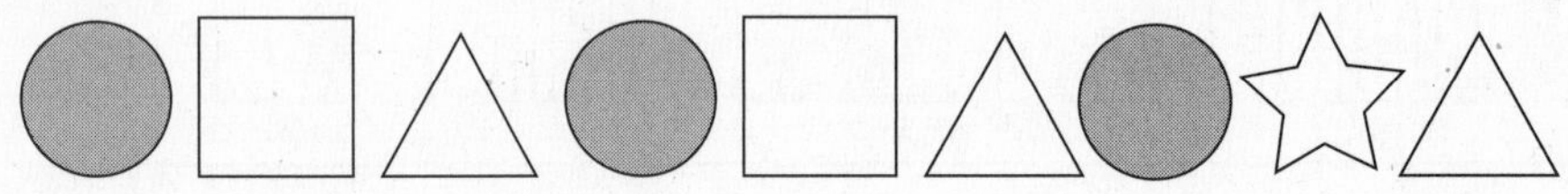

8. Circle the mistake in the pattern. Draw the correct shape.

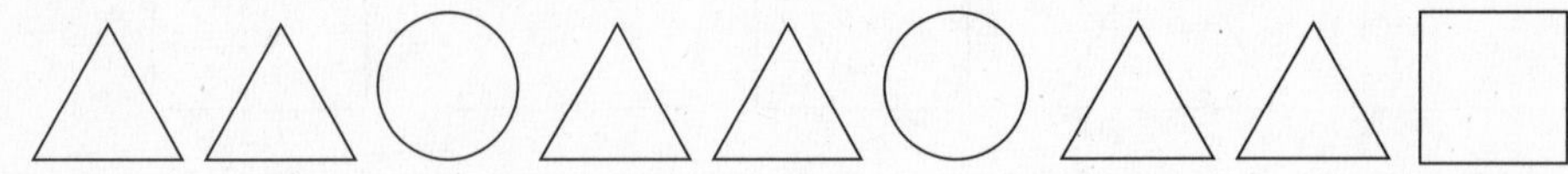

9. Use shapes to show the same pattern in a different way.
Draw the shapes.

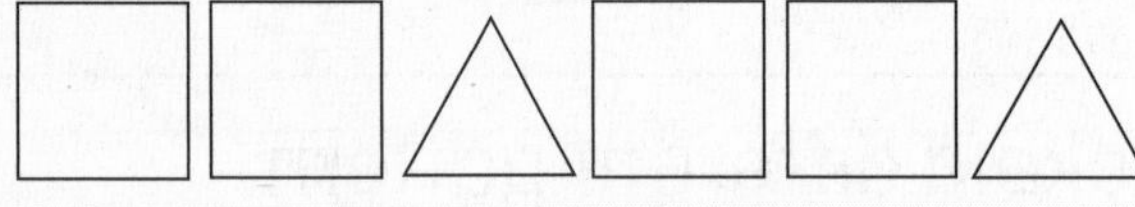

10. Use shapes to show the same pattern in a different way.
Draw the shapes.

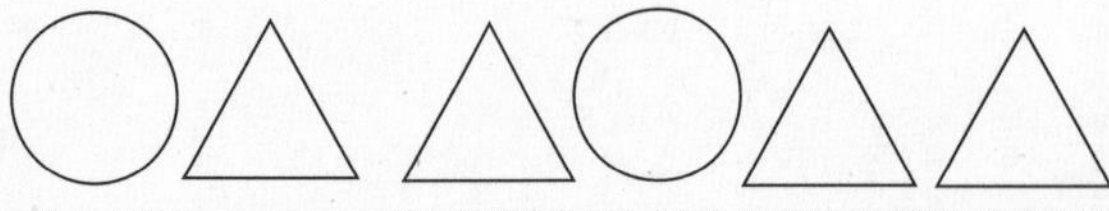

Stop

Name ____________________

Choose the correct answer.

1. $7 + 7 = 14$,
so $7 + 8 =$ ___

Ⓐ 14
Ⓑ 15
Ⓒ 16
Ⓓ 17

2. $6 + 6 = 12$,
so $6 + 7 =$ ___

Ⓐ 15
Ⓑ 14
Ⓒ 13
Ⓓ 12

For 3 to 6, use ● and Workmat 7 to add. Find the sum.

3. 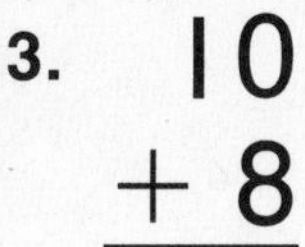

Ⓐ 2
Ⓑ 16
Ⓒ 18
Ⓓ 20

4. 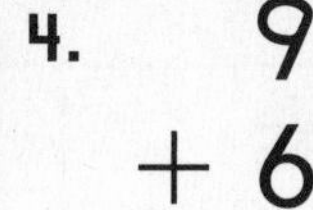

Ⓐ 14
Ⓑ 15
Ⓒ 17
Ⓓ 18

5. $\begin{array}{r} 7 \\ +\ 5 \\ \hline \end{array}$

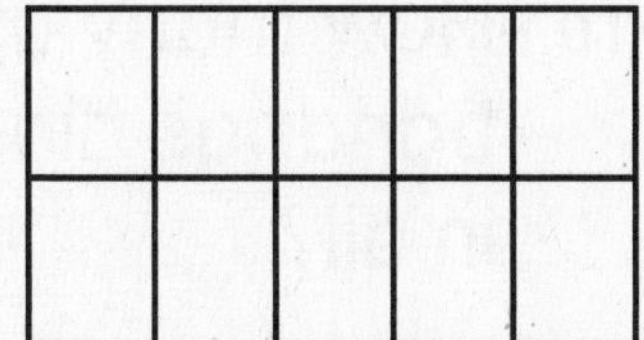

Ⓐ 12
Ⓑ 11
Ⓒ 10
Ⓓ 2

6. $\begin{array}{r} 8 \\ +\ 3 \\ \hline \end{array}$

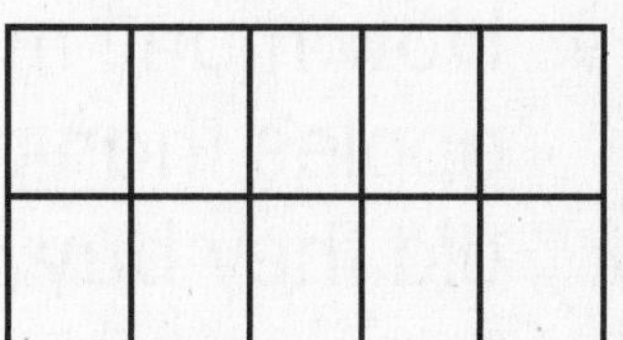

Ⓐ 14
Ⓑ 13
Ⓒ 12
Ⓓ 11

Go On

7.
$$\begin{array}{r} 4 \\ 7 \\ +\ 6 \\ \hline \end{array}$$

Ⓐ 11 Ⓒ 16
Ⓑ 15 Ⓓ 17

8.
$$\begin{array}{r} 3 \\ 8 \\ +\ 2 \\ \hline \end{array}$$

Ⓐ 13 Ⓒ 11
Ⓑ 12 Ⓓ 5

For 9 and 10, use the table.

It tells how many pieces of fruit the children bought.

Fruit	Number
apples	9
peaches	4
bananas	2

9. How many more apples than peaches did they buy?

Ⓐ 8 Ⓒ 5
Ⓑ 6 Ⓓ 4

10. How many apples and bananas did they buy in all?

Ⓐ 12 Ⓒ 8
Ⓑ 11 Ⓓ 6

Stop

Name ______________________________

Write the correct answer.

1. $5 + 5 = 10$, so $5 + 6 =$ ___	2. $8 + 8 = 16$, so $8 + 9 =$ ___

For 3 to 6, use ● and Workmat 7 to add. Write the sum.

3. $\begin{array}{r} 10 \\ +\ 5 \\ \hline \end{array}$

4. $\begin{array}{r} 9 \\ +\ 8 \\ \hline \end{array}$

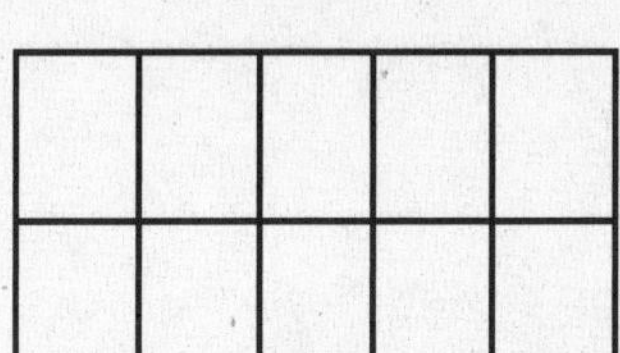

5. $\begin{array}{r} 8 \\ +\ 4 \\ \hline \end{array}$

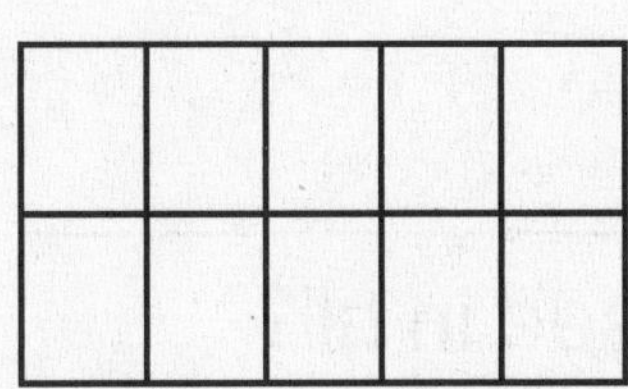

6. $\begin{array}{r} 7 \\ +\ 6 \\ \hline \end{array}$

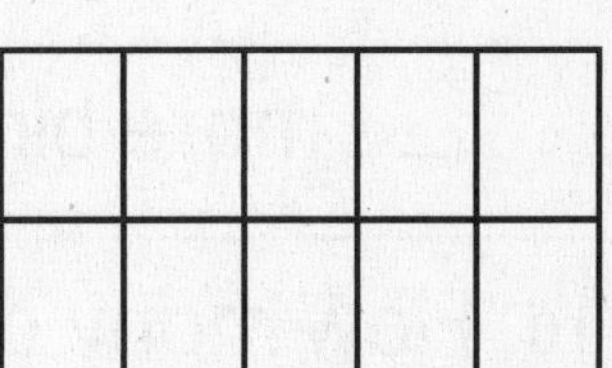

Go On

7. 1 2 + 9	8. 7 3 + 4

For 9 to 10, use the table.

It tells how many animals the children saw in the forest.

Animals	Number
birds	5
squirrels	3
rabbits	2

9. How many more birds than rabbits did they see?

___ ◯ ___ ◯ ___

___ more birds

10. How many animals did they see in all?

___ ◯ ___ ◯ ___ ◯ ___

___ animals

Stop

Name ______________________________

Choose the correct answer.
For 1 and 2, use the number line to subtract.

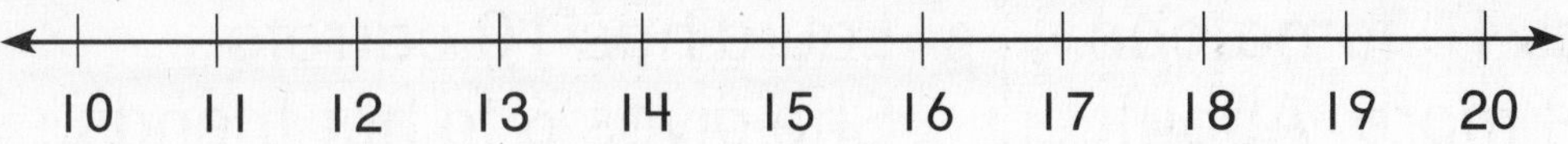

1. 16 − 3 = ___ Ⓐ 13 Ⓒ 19 Ⓑ 14 Ⓓ 20	2. 19 − 3 Ⓐ 14 Ⓒ 16 Ⓑ 15 Ⓓ 17

Use the related fact to help you find sums and differences.

3. 8 + 8 = 16 16 − 8 Ⓐ 6 Ⓒ 12 Ⓑ 8 Ⓓ 16	4. Which is in the same doubles fact family as 9 + 9 = 18? Ⓐ 9 + 6 = 15 Ⓑ 1 + 8 = 9 Ⓒ 19 − 1 = 18 Ⓓ 18 − 9 = 9
5. Which addition fact can help you find the difference for 8 − 4 ? Ⓐ 4 + 0 = 4 Ⓑ 5 + 3 = 8 Ⓒ 4 + 4 = 8 Ⓓ 8 + 4 = 12	6. 12 + 7 = 19 19 − 7 Ⓐ 2 Ⓒ 9 Ⓑ 8 Ⓓ 12

Go On

Name ________________________

Choose the best estimate.

7. Stefan has 10 tomatoes. He finds 4 more. About how many tomatoes does Stefan have now? Ⓐ about 4 Ⓑ about 10 Ⓒ about 15	8. Laura has 10 carrots. She gives 6 to her friends. About how many carrots does Laura have now? Ⓐ about 5 Ⓑ about 10 Ⓒ about 15
9. Rachel picks 6 berries. She needs 15 in all. About how many more berries does Rachel need? Ⓐ about 5 Ⓑ about 10 Ⓒ about 15	10. Rafael picked 13 apples. Celia picked 7 apples. About how many more apples did Rafael pick than Celia? Ⓐ about 5 Ⓑ about 10 Ⓒ about 15

Stop

Name ______________________

Write the correct answer.
For 1 and 2, use the number line to subtract.

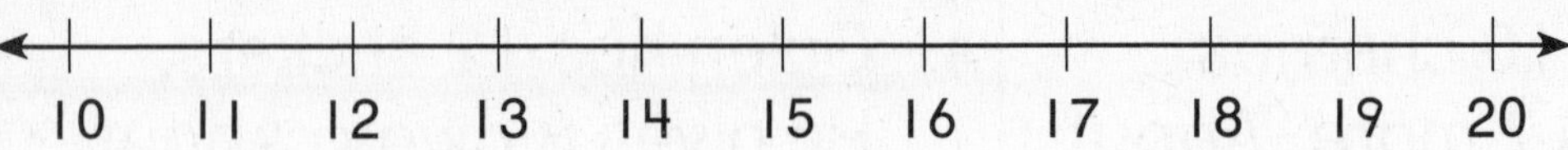

1. 17 − 3 = ___	2. $\begin{array}{r} 18 \\ -\ 2 \\ \hline \end{array}$
3. Write the sum and difference for the pair. $\begin{array}{r} 7 \\ +7 \\ \hline \end{array}$ $\begin{array}{r} 14 \\ -\ 7 \\ \hline \end{array}$	4. Write the fact that is missing from this doubles fact family. 5 + 5 = 10 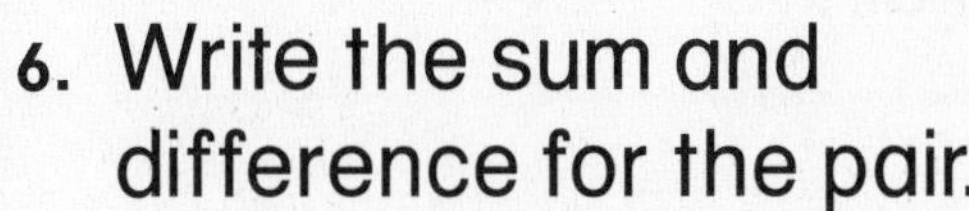
5. Write an addition fact that can help you find the difference for 9 − 5. ___ + ___ = ___	6. Write the sum and difference for the pair. $\begin{array}{r} 3 \\ +8 \\ \hline \end{array}$ $\begin{array}{r} 11 \\ -\ 3 \\ \hline \end{array}$

Go On

Name ______________________

Circle the best estimate.

7. Sara has 10 cherries. She picks 7 more. About how many cherries does Sara have now? about 5 about 15 about 25	8. Galen has 12 stickers. He gives 8 away. About how many stickers does Galen have now? about 5 about 10 about 20
9. Reese sees 5 bugs. Sam sees 6 bugs. About how many bugs do they see in all? about 5 about 10 about 15	10. Mina has 15 paper clips. Kim has 4. About how many more paper clips does Mina have than Kim? about 5 about 10 about 20

Stop

Name ______________________

Choose the correct answer.

1. $8 + 9$

Ⓐ 19 Ⓑ 18 Ⓒ 17 Ⓓ 16

2. $14 - 7$

Ⓐ 6 Ⓑ 7 Ⓒ 8 Ⓓ 9

3. $6 + 5$

Ⓐ 12 Ⓑ 11 Ⓒ 10 Ⓓ 1

4. $12 - 8$

Ⓐ 20 Ⓑ 9 Ⓒ 5 Ⓓ 4

5. Which of these is a way to make 20?

Ⓐ 4 + 10
Ⓑ 3 + 3 + 1
Ⓒ 14 + 6
Ⓓ 10 − 9

6. Which of these is a way to make 14?

Ⓐ 16 − 2
Ⓑ 10 + 3
Ⓒ 12 + 1
Ⓓ 20 − 3

Go On

Name ______________________________

7. Which fact is in the same fact family as
4 + 7 = 11?

(A) 11 − 11 = 0
(B) 11 − 4 = 7
(C) 15 − 4 = 11
(D) 4 + 11 = 15

8. Mark the pair that shows 2 facts that are in the same family.

(A) 9 − 6 = 3
3 + 6 = 9

(B) 6 − 3 = 3
3 + 6 = 9

(C) 9 + 9 = 18
10 + 8 = 18

(D) 8 + 7 = 15
8 − 7 = 1

For 9 and 10, use 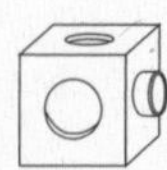 to solve.

9. Craig has 4 blocks.
Lisa has 8 blocks.
How many blocks do they have in all?

(A) 8
(B) 10
(C) 12
(D) 14

10. Melinda has 18 apples.
She gives 5 to John.
How many apples does Melinda have now?

(A) 9
(B) 12
(C) 13
(D) 17

Stop

Name ______________________________

Write the correct answer. Add or subtract.

1. $\begin{array}{r} 7 \\ +\ 9 \\ \hline \end{array}$	2. $\begin{array}{r} 16 \\ -\ 8 \\ \hline \end{array}$
3. $\begin{array}{r} 7 \\ +\ 6 \\ \hline \end{array}$	4. $\begin{array}{r} 13 \\ -\ 9 \\ \hline \end{array}$
5. Circle the way that does NOT make 15. 19 − 4 9 + 6 17 − 3	6. Circle a way to make 12. 18 − 2 8 + 4 6 + 5

Go On

Name ______________________________

7. Write the other fact that belongs in this fact family.	8. Circle the pair that shows two facts in the same family.
$3 + 8 = 11$ $8 + 3 = 11$ $11 - 3 = 8$ ___ ◯ ___ ◯ ___	$6 + 8 = 14$ $14 - 8 = 6$ $8 - 6 = 2$ $6 + 8 = 14$ $4 + 7 = 11$ $7 - 4 = 3$ $9 + 1 = 10$ $7 + 3 = 10$

For 9 and 10, use 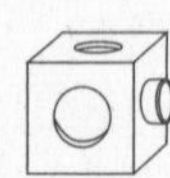 **to solve.**

9. John has 19 tomatoes. He gives 8 to Gail. How many tomatoes does John have left?	10. Rose has 17 pumpkins. Tony has 3 pumpkins. How many pumpkins do they have in all?
___ tomatoes	___ pumpkins

Stop

Choose the correct answer.

1. Which will stack and roll?

Ⓐ 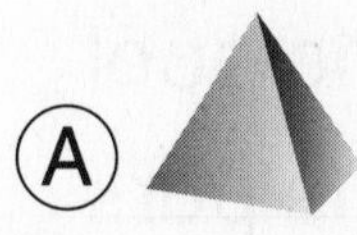

Ⓑ  

Ⓒ 

Ⓓ 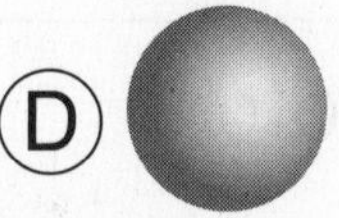

2. Which solid figure has 5 faces?

Ⓐ  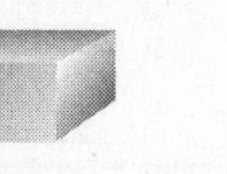

Ⓑ  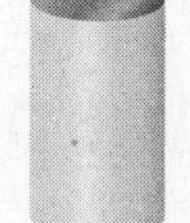

Ⓒ 

Ⓓ 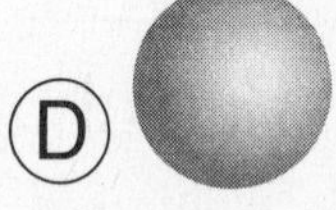

3. Which shape can you make if you trace around a cube?

Ⓐ 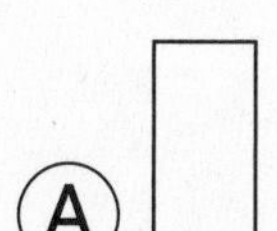

Ⓑ 

Ⓒ 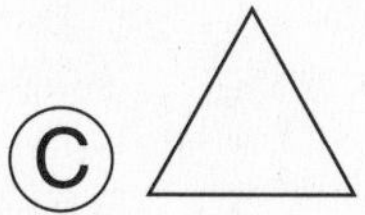

Ⓓ 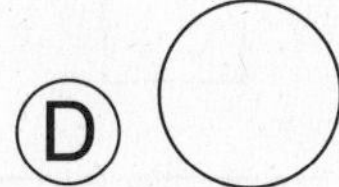

4. Which shape has 4 sides and 4 vertices?

Ⓐ 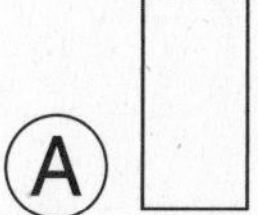

Ⓑ 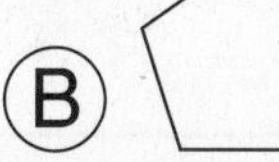

Ⓒ 

Ⓓ 

5. Which picture shows the ladybug below the flower?

Ⓐ 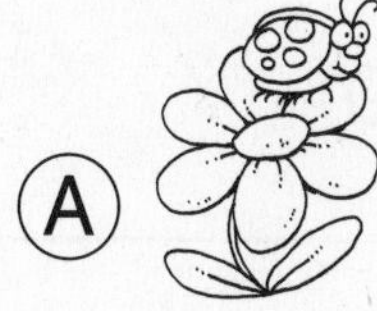

Ⓑ 

Ⓒ 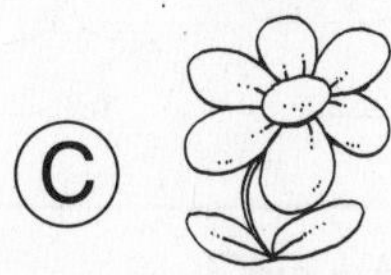

Ⓓ 

6. Which picture shows the bone to the right of the dog?

Ⓐ 

Ⓑ 

Ⓒ 

Ⓓ 

Go On

Name ______________________________

7. Go right 3 and up 2. Where are you?

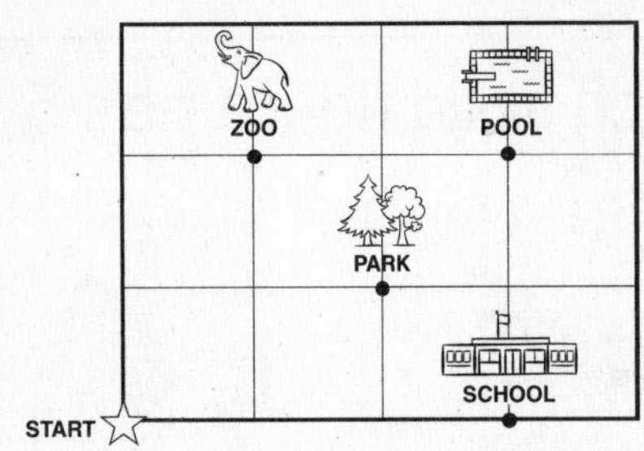

(A) at school
(B) at the zoo
(C) at the pool
(D) at the park

8. Which shows two parts that match?

(A) 
(B) 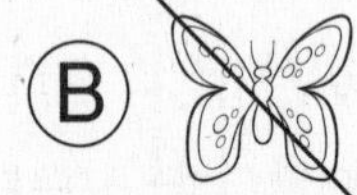
(C) 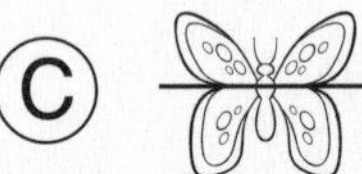
(D) 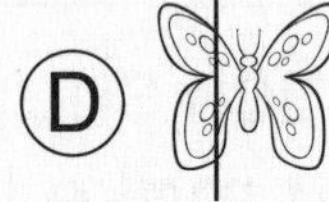

9. Which shape comes next in the pattern?

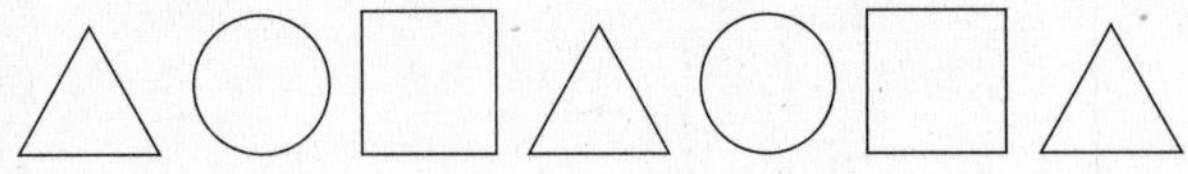

(A) 
(B) 
(C) 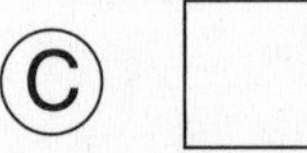
(D) 

10. Which is the pattern unit for this pattern?

(A) 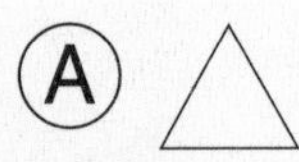
(B) 
(C) 
(D) 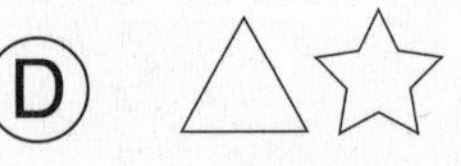

11. Which shape corrects the pattern?

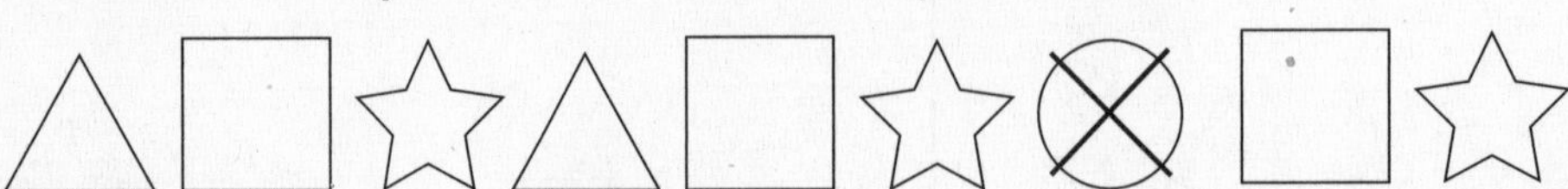

(A) 
(B) 
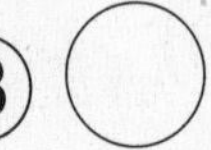
(C) 
(D) 

Go On

12. $\begin{array}{r} 7 \\ +\ 7 \\ \hline \end{array}$

Ⓐ 0
Ⓑ 3
Ⓒ 14
Ⓓ 17

13. $\begin{array}{r} 9 \\ +\ 3 \\ \hline \end{array}$

Ⓐ 13
Ⓑ 12
Ⓒ 11
Ⓓ 6

14. $\begin{array}{r} 4 \\ 7 \\ +\ 3 \\ \hline \end{array}$

Ⓐ 13
Ⓑ 14
Ⓒ 15
Ⓓ 17

15. Use the number line to count back.

15 16 17 18 19 20

$17 - 2 = \_\_$

Ⓐ 19
Ⓑ 16
Ⓒ 15
Ⓓ 14

16. $\begin{array}{r} 4 \\ +\ 4 \\ \hline 8 \end{array}$ $\begin{array}{r} 8 \\ -\ 4 \\ \hline \end{array}$

Ⓐ 4
Ⓑ 6
Ⓒ 7
Ⓓ 8

Go On

17. Which is in the same fact family as $5 + 6 = 11$?

Ⓐ $11 - 6 = 5$
Ⓑ $1 + 5 = 6$
Ⓒ $6 - 1 = 5$
Ⓓ $16 - 5 = 11$

18. $14 - 8 =$ ___

Ⓐ 12
Ⓑ 8
Ⓒ 7
Ⓓ 6

19. Which is a way to make 17?

Ⓐ $9 - 3$
Ⓑ $9 + 8$
Ⓒ $10 + 8$
Ⓓ $20 - 4$

20. Use ▢ to solve.

Dan picks 14 apples.

Julia picks 6 apples.

How many apples do they pick in all?

Ⓐ 8
Ⓑ 15
Ⓒ 17
Ⓓ 20

Stop

Write the correct answer.

1. Circle the solid figure that will stack.

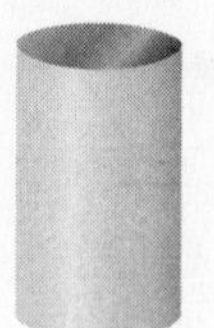

2. Circle the solid figure that has 6 faces.

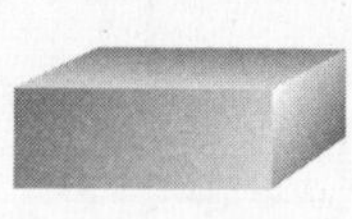
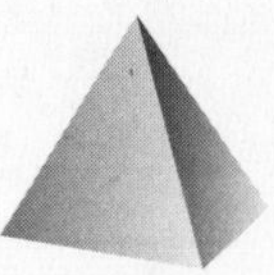

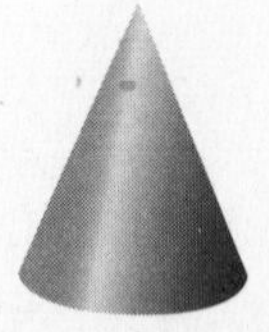

3. Circle the shape that you can make if you trace around a cylinder.

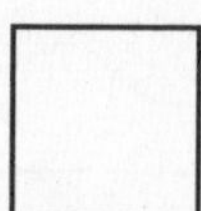
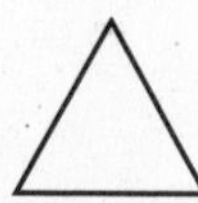
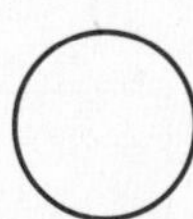

4. Circle the shape that has 5 sides and 5 vertices.

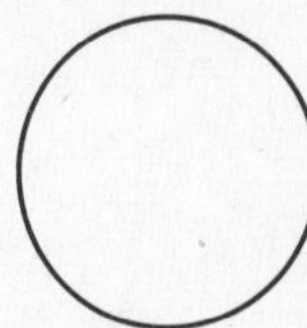
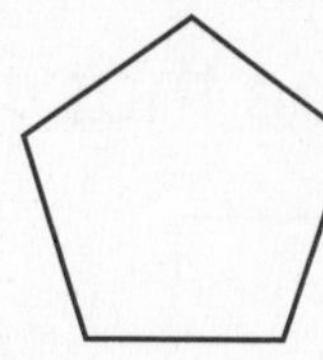
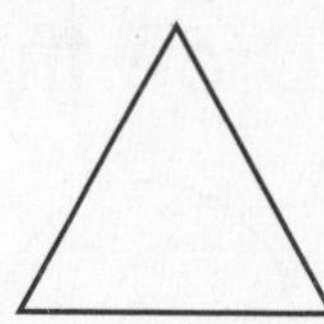

5. Draw an ant below the leaf.

6. Draw a bird to the left of the worm.

Go On

Name ______________________

7. Go right 4 and up 2. Where are you?

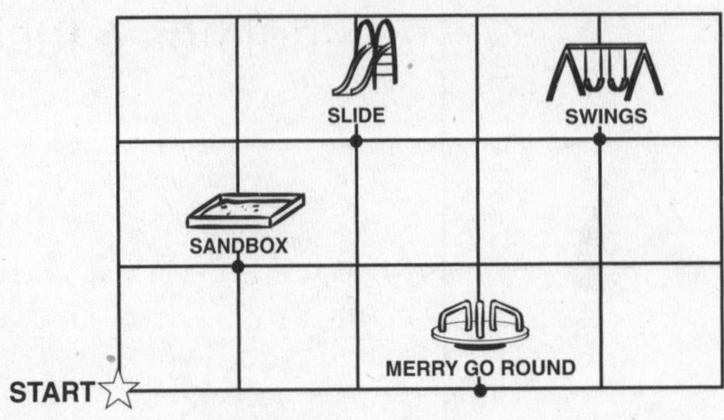

at the __________

8. Draw a line of symmetry to make two matching parts.

9. Draw the shape that comes next in the pattern.

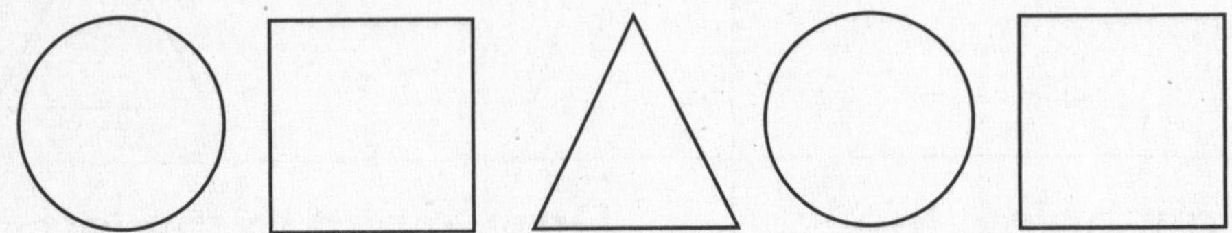

10. Circle the pattern unit.

Go On

Name ______________________

11. Mark an X on the mistake in the pattern.

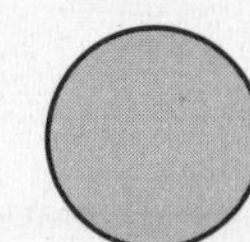 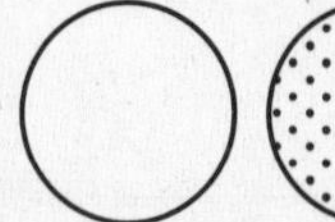 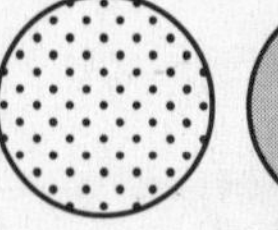 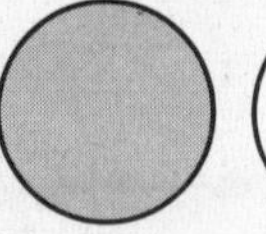  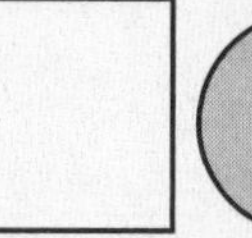 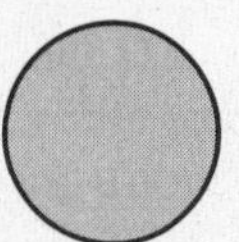 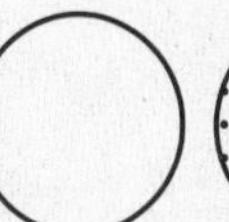 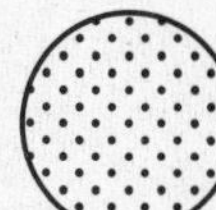

Then circle the shape that corrects the pattern.

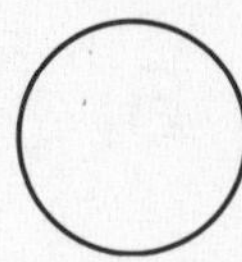 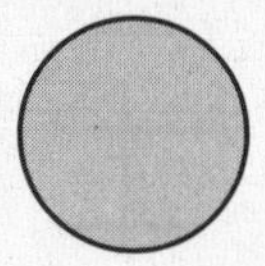 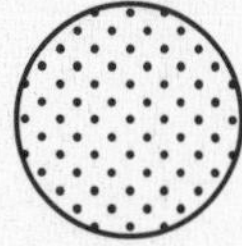 

12.
$$\begin{array}{r} 8 \\ +\ 8 \\ \hline \end{array}$$

13.
$$\begin{array}{r} 9 \\ +\ 4 \\ \hline \end{array}$$

14.
$$\begin{array}{r} 5 \\ 2 \\ +\ 6 \\ \hline \end{array}$$

15. Use the number line to count back.

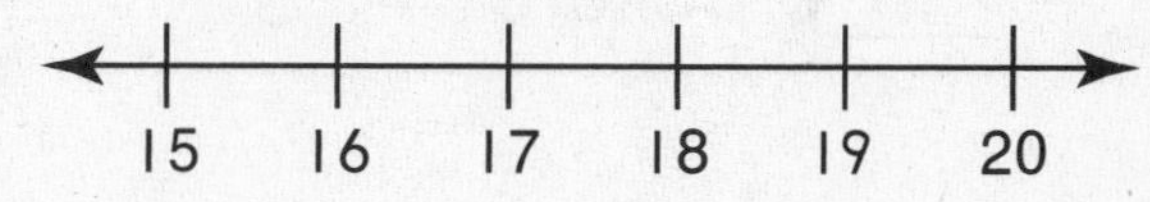

18 − 3 = ___

16. Add. Then subtract.

$$\begin{array}{r} 5 \\ +\ 5 \\ \hline \end{array} \qquad \begin{array}{r} 10 \\ -\ 5 \\ \hline \end{array}$$

17. Write a subtraction fact that is in the same family as 4 + 7 = 11.

___ − ___ = ___

Go On

Name ____________________

18. $15 - 8 =$ ___

19. Circle ways to make 14.

$16 - 2$

$9 + 5$

$19 - 6$

20. Solve. Draw [cube] to help.

Evan has 13 crackers.

He gives 9 away.

How many crackers does he have left?

___ crackers

Stop

Name ______________________

Choose the correct answer.

1. Which picture shows halves?

Ⓐ 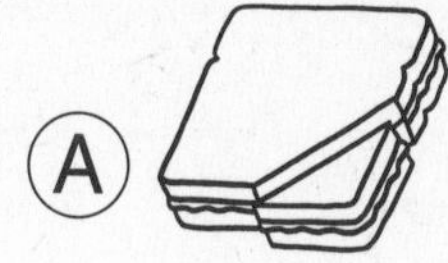
 Ⓒ

Ⓑ 
 Ⓓ

2. Which picture shows 2 equal parts?

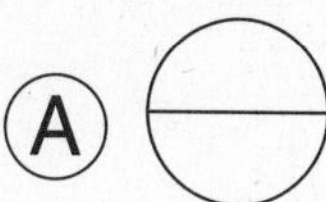 Ⓐ
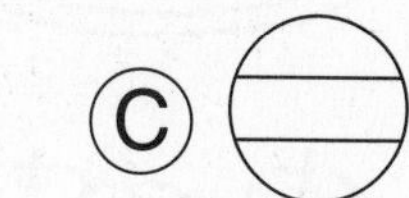 Ⓒ

 Ⓑ
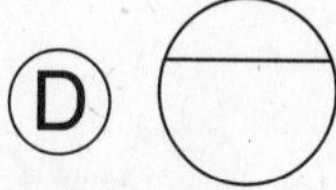 Ⓓ

3. Which is $\frac{1}{4}$ shaded?

 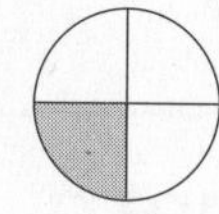
 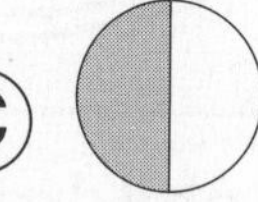

 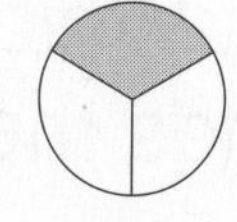
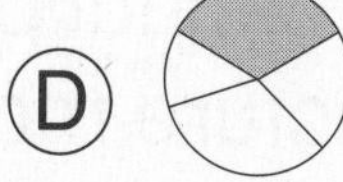

4. Which fraction tells about the shaded part?

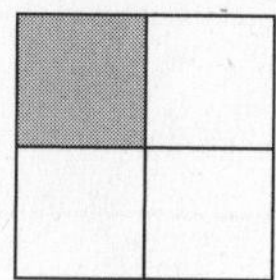

Ⓐ $\frac{1}{2}$ Ⓒ $\frac{1}{4}$

Ⓑ $\frac{1}{3}$ Ⓓ $\frac{4}{4}$

5. Which shows thirds?

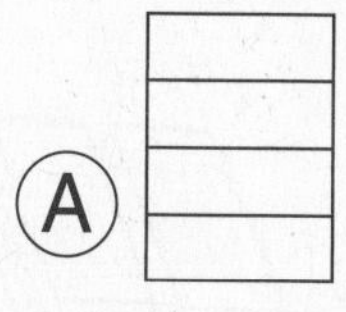
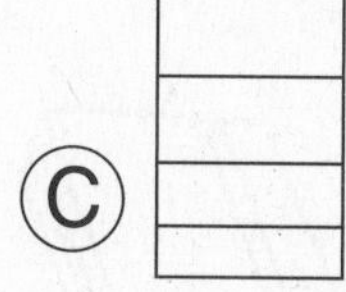

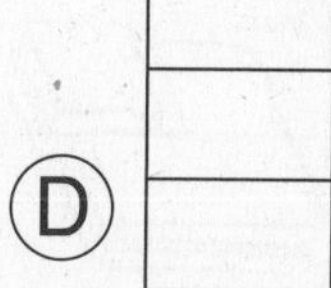

6. Which is $\frac{1}{3}$ shaded?

Ⓑ Ⓓ

Go On

7. Which shows $\frac{1}{2}$ of the apples shaded?

Ⓐ 

Ⓑ

Ⓒ 

Ⓓ

8. Which shows $\frac{1}{3}$ of the apples shaded?

Ⓐ 

Ⓑ 

Ⓒ 

Ⓓ 

9. 3 children share a pizza. Each gets an equal part. Which picture matches the clues?

Ⓐ 

Ⓒ 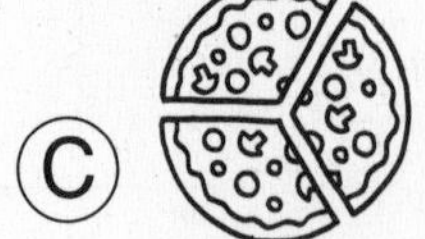

Ⓑ  

Ⓓ 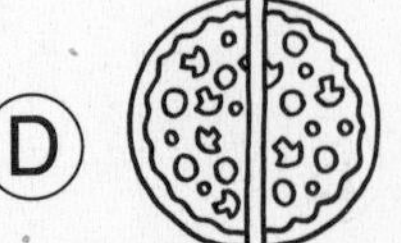

10. 2 children share a sandwich. Each gets an equal part. Which picture matches the clues?

Ⓐ 

Ⓒ 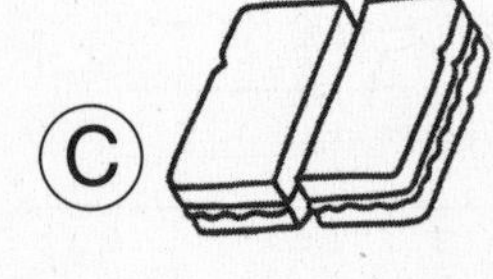

Ⓑ 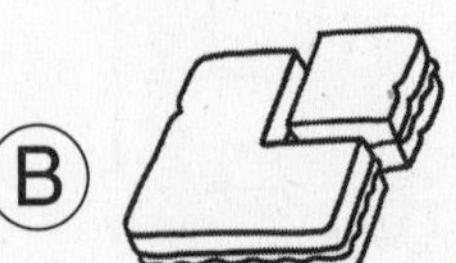

Ⓓ 

Stop

Name ______________________________

Write the correct answer.

1. Find the picture that shows two equal parts. Color one part.

 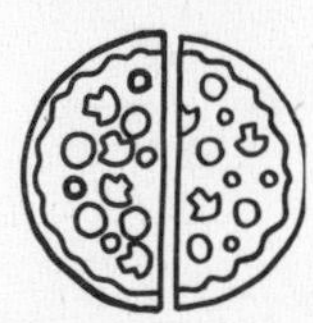

2. Find the picture that shows halves. Color $\frac{1}{2}$.

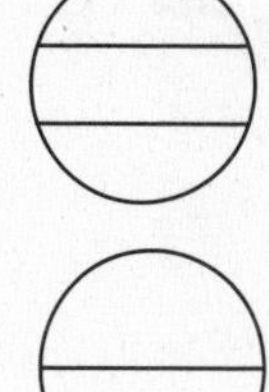

3. Find the picture that shows fourths. Color one fourth.

 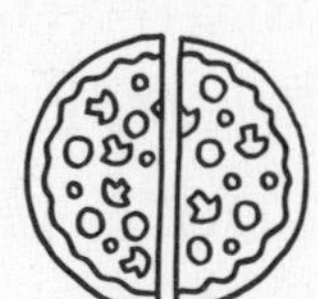

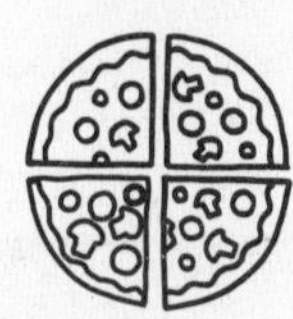 

4. Circle the fraction shown.

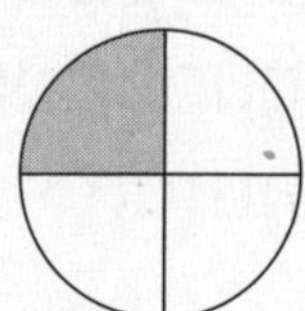

$\frac{1}{3}$ $\frac{1}{2}$ $\frac{1}{4}$

5. Find the picture that shows thirds. Color $\frac{1}{3}$.

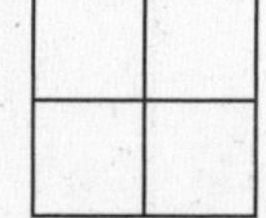  

6. Color one part. Circle the fraction shown.

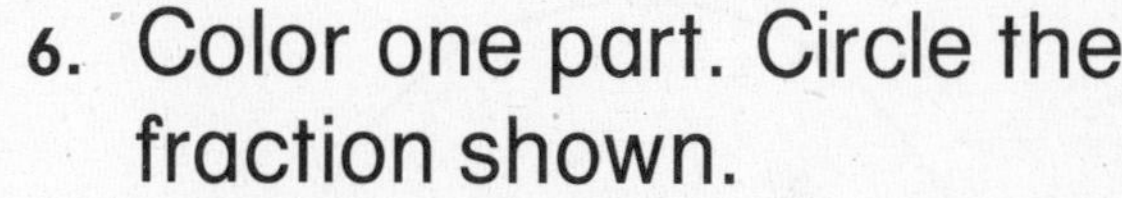

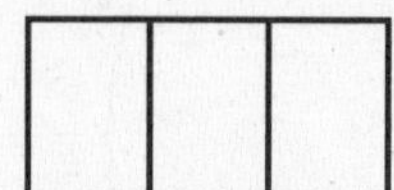

$\frac{1}{3}$ $\frac{1}{2}$ $\frac{1}{4}$

Go On

7. Color $\frac{1}{2}$ of the group of fish.

8. Color $\frac{1}{3}$ of the group of starfish.

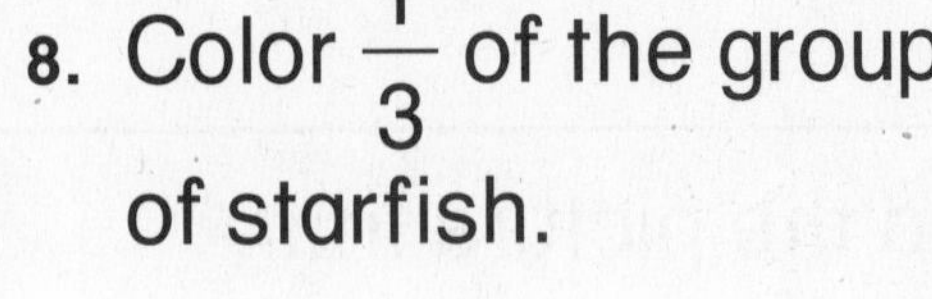

9. 2 children share a pizza. Each gets an equal part. Draw a line to match the clues.

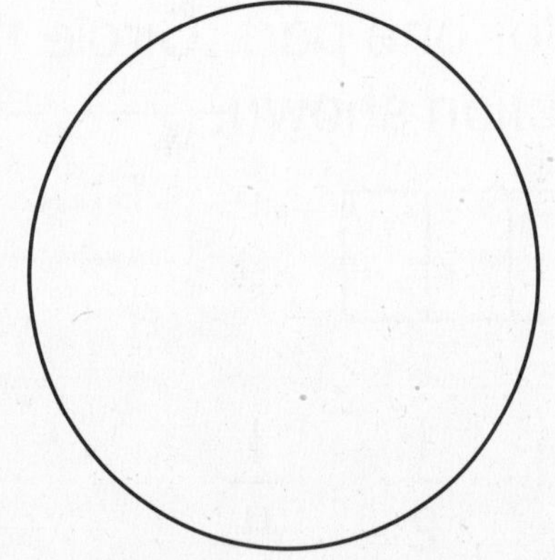

10. 4 children share a sandwich. Each gets an equal part. Draw lines to match the clues.

Stop

Choose the correct answer.

1. Count by ones. Mark the amount.

Ⓐ 60¢ Ⓑ 30¢ Ⓒ 6¢ Ⓓ 5¢

2. Count by fives. Mark the amount.

Ⓐ 60¢ Ⓑ 30¢ Ⓒ 20¢ Ⓓ 6¢

3. Which shows how to count these coins?

Ⓐ 10¢, 20¢, 30¢, 40¢, 50¢, 60¢, 70¢, 80¢
Ⓑ 10¢, 20¢, 30¢, 40¢, 50¢, 60¢, 70¢
Ⓒ 5¢, 10¢, 15¢, 20¢, 25¢, 30¢, 35¢, 40¢
Ⓓ 1¢, 2¢, 3¢, 4¢, 5¢, 6¢, 7¢, 8¢

4. Count by tens. Then count on by ones. Mark the amount.

Ⓐ 8¢ Ⓑ 21¢ Ⓒ 26¢ Ⓓ 80¢

Go On

5. Count. Mark the amount.

Ⓐ 50¢ Ⓑ 30¢ Ⓒ 22¢ Ⓓ 14¢

6. Count. Mark the amount.

Ⓐ 23¢ Ⓑ 13¢ Ⓒ 12¢ Ⓓ 5¢

7. Count. Mark the amount.

Ⓐ 44¢ Ⓑ 40¢ Ⓒ 34¢ Ⓓ 24¢

8. Count. Mark the amount.

Ⓐ 70¢ Ⓑ 35¢ Ⓒ 34¢ Ⓓ 29¢

Go On

Name ______________________

9. April wants to buy a toy for 45¢. List a way to make 45¢. Which coins can she use?

Ⓐ 

Ⓑ 

Ⓒ 

10. Gary wants to buy a toy for 39¢. List different ways to make 39¢. Which coins can he use?

Ⓐ 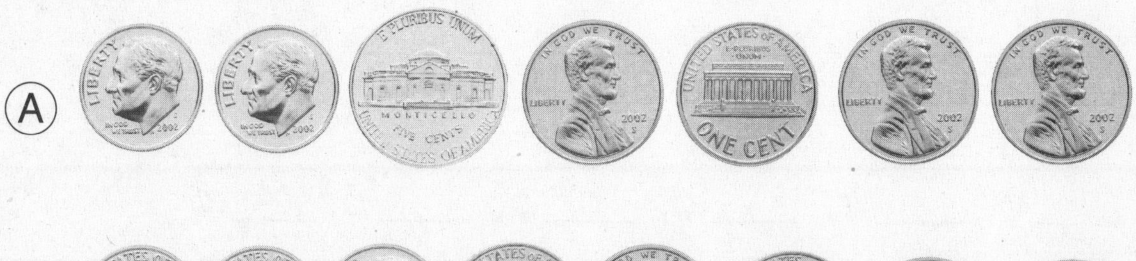

Ⓑ 

Ⓒ 

Stop

Name ______________________________

Write the correct answer.

1. Count by ones. Write the amount.

____ ¢, ____ ¢, ____ ¢, ____ ¢, ____ ¢, ____ ¢, ____ ¢, ____ ¢

2. Count by fives. Write the amount.

____ ¢, ____ ¢, ____ ¢, ____ ¢, ____ ¢, ____ ¢, ____ ¢

3. Count by tens. Write the amount.

____ ¢, ____ ¢, ____ ¢, ____ ¢, ____ ¢, ____ ¢

4. Count by tens. Then count on by ones. Write the amount.

____ ¢, ____ ¢, ____ ¢, ____ ¢, ____ ¢, ____ ¢, ____ ¢, ____ ¢

Go On

Name ______________________________

For 5 to 8, count. Write the amount.

5.      

_____ ¢, _____ ¢, _____ ¢, _____ ¢, _____ ¢, _____ ¢

6.     

_____ ¢, _____ ¢, _____ ¢, _____ ¢, _____ ¢

7.      

_____ ¢

8.    

_____ ¢

Go On

Name ______________________

9. Tyrone wants to buy a toy for 30¢.
Show ways to make 30¢. Draw the pennies, nickels, and dimes that will make 30¢.

Write how many there are of each.

___ dimes ___ nickels ___ pennies

10. Kendall wants to buy a toy for 28¢.
Show ways to make 28¢. Draw the pennies, nickels, and dimes that will make 28¢.

Write how many there are of each.

___ dimes ___ nickels ___ pennies

Stop

Name ______________________

Choose the correct answer.

1. Which group of coins can you trade for 15 pennies?

Ⓑ   

2. Which group of coins can you trade for 20 pennies?

Go On

Name ______________________________

3. Which shows how to count on to find the total amount?

Ⓐ 25¢, 30¢, 35¢, 40¢

Ⓑ 25¢, 35¢, 45¢, 55¢

Ⓒ 25¢, 30¢, 40¢, 45¢

Ⓓ 25¢, 35¢, 45¢, 50¢

4. Count from a quarter. Mark the amount.

Ⓐ 45¢

Ⓑ 40¢

Ⓒ 35¢

Ⓓ 28¢

5. Which group of quarters equals 1 dollar?

Ⓑ   

Ⓒ  

Go On

Name ______________________

6. How many dimes equal  ?

Ⓐ 7 Ⓒ 5
Ⓑ 6 Ⓓ 4

7. Count each group of coins. Which amount is **greatest**?

Ⓑ     

Ⓒ    

Ⓓ    

8. Which shows 20¢ using the **fewest** coins?

Ⓑ  

Go On

9. Which group of coins shows the amount?

30¢

Ⓐ 

Ⓑ 

Ⓒ 

Ⓓ 

10. Which group of coins could you use?

Ⓐ 

Ⓑ 

Ⓒ

Ⓓ 

Stop

Name ________________________

Write the correct answer.

1. Trade 25 pennies for nickels and dimes.

   Use the fewest coins.

   Draw and label the coins.

2. Trade 30 pennies for some nickels and some dimes.

   Use the fewest coins.

   Draw and label the coins.

3. Count on from the quarter to find the total amount.

____ ¢, ____ ¢, ____ ¢, ____ ¢, ____ ¢, ____ ¢, ____ ¢

4. Count on from the quarter to find the total amount.

____ ¢, ____ ¢, ____ ¢, ____ ¢, ____ ¢, ____ ¢

5. For 5 and 6, draw and label the coins. Write how many.
Show how many quarters equal 1 dollar.

____ quarters = 1 dollar

6. Show how many dimes equal 1 half dollar.

____ dimes = 1 half dollar

Go On

Name ______________________________

7. Write the amount for each group of coins.
Circle the amount that is greater.

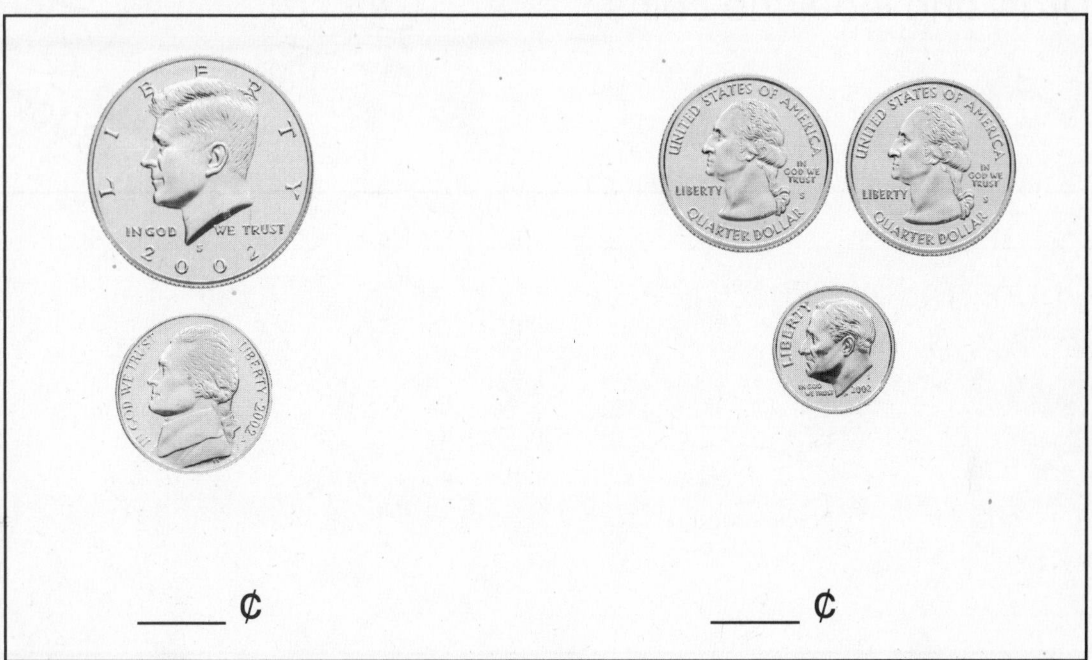

_____ ¢ _____ ¢

8. Show the amount in two ways.
Draw and label the coins.
Circle the way that uses fewer coins.

Go On

Name ____________________

9. What coins could you use?
Use coins to show the amount.
Draw and label the coins.

10. What coins could you use?
Use coins to show the amount.
Draw and label the coins.

Stop

Name ______________________________

Choose the correct answer.

1. What time is it?

Ⓐ 4 o'clock
Ⓑ 3 o'clock
Ⓒ 6 o'clock
Ⓓ 11 o'clock

2. What time is it?

Ⓐ 7 o'clock
Ⓑ 5 o'clock
Ⓒ 4 o'clock
Ⓓ 12 o'clock

3. Which takes more than a minute?

Ⓐ reading a book

Ⓑ writing your name

Ⓒ counting to 5

Ⓓ eating a grape

4. Which takes less than a minute?

Ⓐ taking a walk

Ⓑ riding a bus

Ⓒ going to school

Ⓓ clapping your hands

5. What time is it?

Ⓐ 10:00
Ⓑ 8:00
Ⓒ 6:00
Ⓓ 2:00

6. What time is it?

Ⓐ 12:00
Ⓑ 9:00
Ⓒ 8:00
Ⓓ 4:00

Go On

7. What time is it?

Ⓐ 2:30
Ⓑ 6:30
Ⓒ 10:30
Ⓓ 11:30

8. What time is it?

Ⓐ 3:30
Ⓑ 4:30
Ⓒ 6:30
Ⓓ 9:30

9. At 5:30, where is the hour hand?

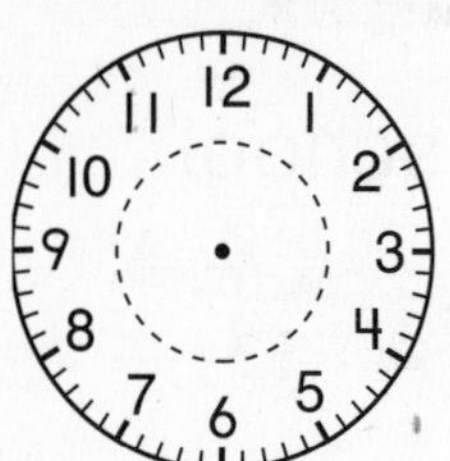

Ⓐ between 5 and 6
Ⓑ between 4 and 5
Ⓒ on the 5
Ⓓ on the 6

10. Which clock shows the same time?

Ⓐ 9:30
Ⓑ 10:00
Ⓒ 10:30
Ⓓ 11:00

Stop

Name ____________________

Write the correct answer.

1. Write the time.  ____ o'clock	2. Write the time.  ____ o'clock
3. About how long would it take to ride home on the bus? Circle your estimate. more than a minute less than a minute	4. About how long would it take to eat a peanut? Circle your estimate. more than a minute less than a minute
5. Write the time.  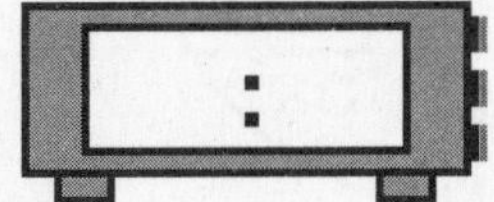	6. Write the time.  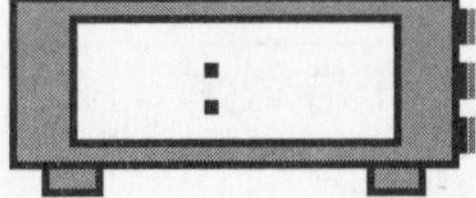

Go On

Name ____________________

7. Look at the hour hand.
Look at the minute hand.
Write the time.

____ : ____

8. Look at both hands.
Write the time.

____ : ____

9. Draw the hour hand and the minute hand on the clock to show 8:30.

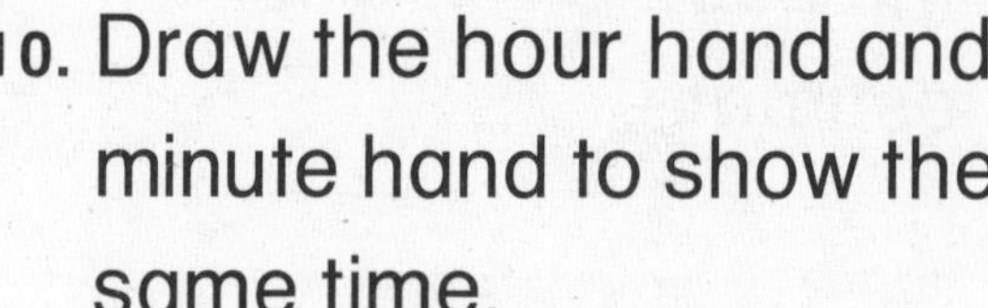

10. Draw the hour hand and minute hand to show the same time.

Stop

Name ______________________________

Choose the correct answer.

1. Which month is just after October?

   (A) July (B) April (C) November (D) January

2. Which day is just after Saturday?

   (A) Sunday (B) Tuesday (C) Wednesday (D) Saturday

3. Which would you do in the morning?

   (A) go home from school
   (B) go to bed
   (C) help make dinner
   (D) eat breakfast

4. Which would you do in the evening?

   (A) get dressed
   (B) go to school
   (C) get ready for bed
   (D) eat lunch

For 5 and 6, use the picture graph.

5. How many children in all chose pears and watermelons?

   (A) 2 (B) 5 (C) 6 (D) 7

6. Which fruit did the most children choose?

   (A) watermelon (B) banana (C) pear (D) apple

Our Favorite Fruits

	Banana	Watermelon	Pear	Apple
8				
7				
6				
5		watermelon		
4		watermelon		
3	banana	watermelon		
2	banana	watermelon		apple
1	banana	watermelon	pear	apple

Go On

Name ______________________________

Use the chart to answer questions 7 and 8.

Simon's Saturday Activities		
Activity	**Start**	**End**
TV		
Practice Piano		
Play		

7. When does Simon practice the piano?

Ⓐ before TV
Ⓑ after TV
Ⓒ after play

8. Which takes the longest amount of time?

Ⓐ TV
Ⓑ practice piano
Ⓒ play

9. Which activity takes about one minute?

Ⓐ tying your shoes
Ⓑ cleaning your room
Ⓒ playing a baseball game
Ⓓ going on a trip

10. Choose the best estimate for the activity.

play a board game

Ⓐ about one minute
Ⓑ about one hour
Ⓒ about one week
Ⓓ about one month

Stop

Name ______________________________

Write the correct answer.

1. Circle the month that is just after June.

   February April
   May July

2. Circle the day of the week that is just before Tuesday.

   Monday Wednesday
   Thursday Saturday

3. Which would you do in the afternoon?

   eat breakfast
   go home from school
   go to bed

4. Which would you do in the morning?

   eat dinner
   eat lunch
   eat breakfast

5. Use the tally table to make a picture graph.

Our Favorite Meal	
Breakfast	𝍸
Lunch	𝍷𝍷
Dinner	𝍷𝍷𝍷

Our Favorite Meal			
5			
4			
3			
2			
1			
	Breakfast	**Lunch**	**Dinner**

6. How many children in all chose dinner or lunch?

   ____ children

Go On

Use the chart to answer questions 7 and 8.

Mindy's After School Schedule		
Activity	**Start**	**End**
Homework		
Play		
Dance Class		
Dinner		

7. Which activity is after dance class? ______________________	8. What does Mindy do just after her homework? ______________________
9. Circle the best estimate for the activity. How much time does it take to go roller skating? about one minute about one hour about one week	10. Circle the best estimate for the activity. How much time does it take to tie your shoes? about one week about one hour about one minute

Stop

Name ______________________________

Choose the correct answer.

1. Which shows $\frac{1}{2}$ shaded?

Ⓐ 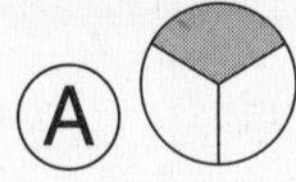 Ⓑ 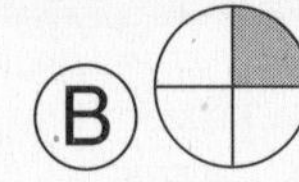 Ⓒ 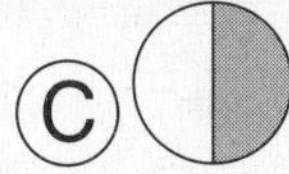 Ⓓ 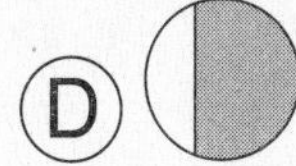

2. Which shows $\frac{1}{4}$ shaded?

Ⓐ 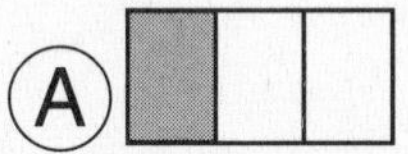 Ⓑ 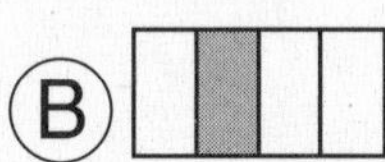 Ⓒ 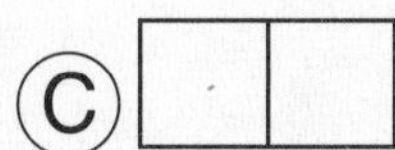 Ⓓ 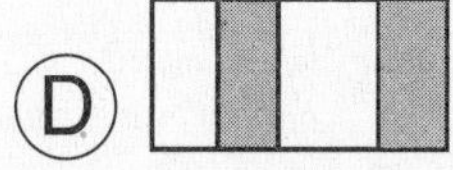

3. 4 children share a pizza. Each gets an equal part. Which picture matches the clues?

Ⓐ  Ⓑ 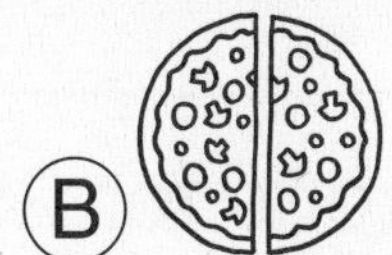 Ⓒ 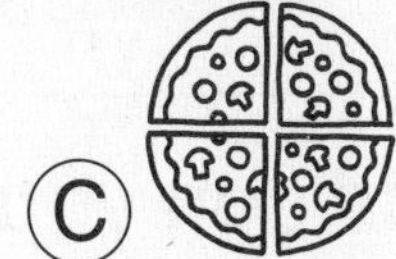 Ⓓ 

4. Which shows $\frac{1}{3}$ shaded?

Ⓐ  Ⓑ  Ⓒ  Ⓓ 

5. Count. Mark the amount.

Ⓐ 60¢ Ⓑ 35¢ Ⓒ 20¢ Ⓓ 6¢

6. Count. Mark the amount.

Ⓐ 60¢ Ⓑ 30¢ Ⓒ 13¢ Ⓓ 6¢

Go On

7. Victor wants to buy a toy that costs 36¢. Which group of coins can he use?

Ⓐ 

Ⓑ 

Ⓒ 

Ⓓ 

8. Which group of coins can you trade for 25 pennies?

Ⓐ 

Ⓒ 

Ⓑ 

Ⓓ 

9. Count on from the quarter. Mark the total amount.

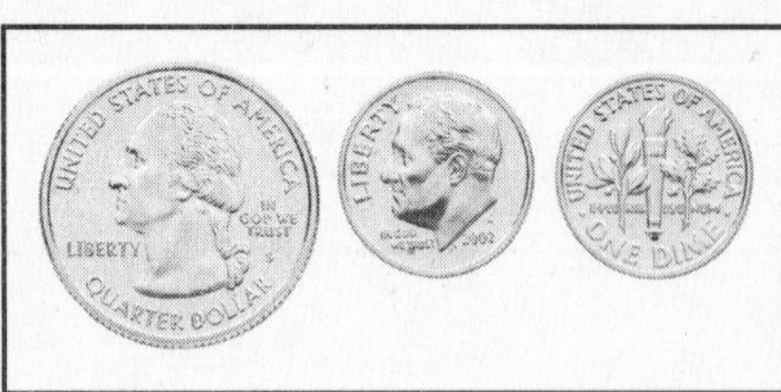

Ⓐ 45¢

Ⓒ 40¢

Ⓑ 35¢

Ⓓ 50¢

Go On

Name ____________________

10. Which group of coins is worth 1 dollar?

Ⓐ 

Ⓒ 

Ⓑ 

Ⓓ 

11. What time is it?

Ⓐ 3 o'clock Ⓒ 12 o'clock
Ⓑ 2 o'clock Ⓓ 4 o'clock

12. Which takes less than one minute?

Ⓐ eating lunch
Ⓑ saying your name
Ⓒ reading a book
Ⓓ getting dressed

13. What time is it?

Ⓐ 11:30 Ⓒ 9:30
Ⓑ 10:30 Ⓓ 8:30

14. Where is the hour hand at 2:30?

Ⓐ on the 2
Ⓑ between 1 and 2
Ⓒ between 2 and 3
Ⓓ on the 6

15. Which month is just after June?

Ⓐ July Ⓒ November
Ⓑ April Ⓓ January

16. Which day is just before Tuesday?

Ⓐ Thursday
Ⓑ Friday
Ⓒ Wednesday
Ⓓ Monday

Go On

Name ______________________

17. Which would you do in the afternoon?

(A) go to bed
(B) eat breakfast
(C) wake up
(D) go home from school

Use the chart to answer questions 18 and 19.

Day Camp Activities

Activities	Start	End
Arts and Crafts	9:00	9:30
Baseball	9:30	11:00
Hiking	11:00	12:00
Lunch	12:00	1:00

18. Which activity is just after baseball?

(A) Arts and Crafts
(B) Swimming
(C) Hiking
(D) Lunch

19. Which activity takes the shortest amount of time?

(A) Arts and Crafts
(B) Hiking
(C) Baseball
(D) Lunch

20. Choose the best estimate. How long does a TV show last?

(A) about one minute
(B) about one hour
(C) about one week
(D) about one month

Stop

Name ___________________________

Write the correct answer.

1. Find the picture that shows halves. Color $\frac{1}{2}$.

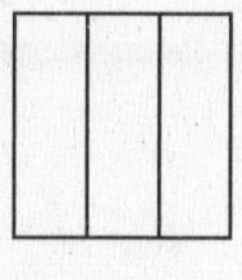
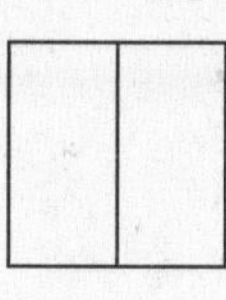
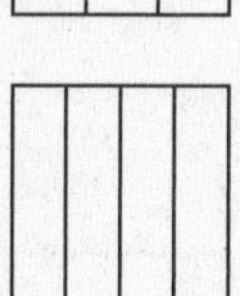
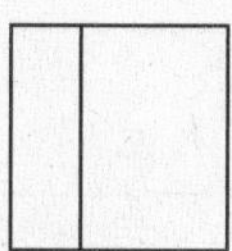

2. Find the picture that shows fourths. Color $\frac{1}{4}$.

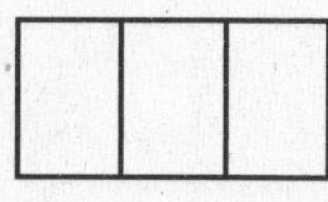
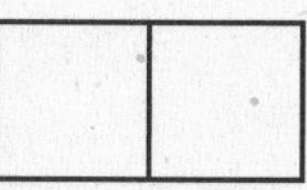
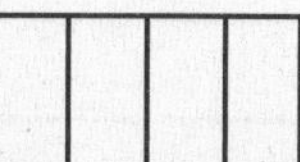
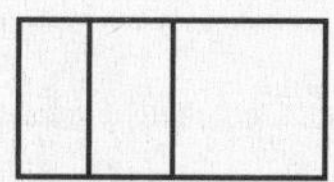

3. 3 children share pizza. Each gets an equal part. Circle the picture that matches the clues.

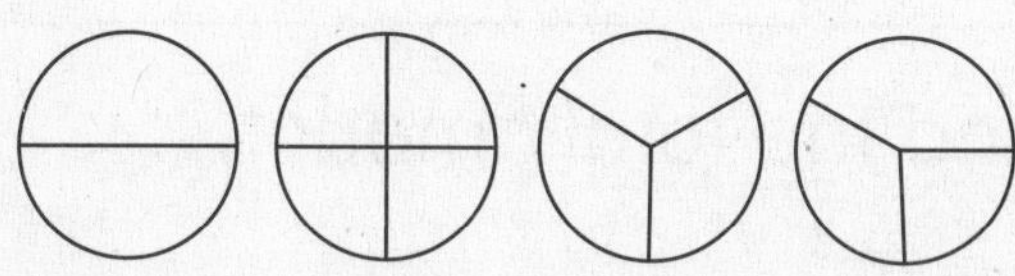

4. Circle the plate that shows $\frac{1}{3}$ of the cherries shaded.

5. Count. Write the amount.

_____ ¢, _____ ¢, _____ ¢, _____ ¢, _____ ¢, _____ ¢, _____ ¢, _____ ¢

6. Count. Write the amount.

_____ ¢

Go On

Name ____________________

7. Emily wants to buy a ball for 24¢. Draw a group of coins she can use.

8. Circle the coins that you can trade for 35 pennies.

9. Count on from the quarter to find the total amount.

_____ ¢, _____ ¢, _____ ¢, _____ ¢, _____ ¢

10. Circle the coins that equal 1 dollar.

Go On

Name ______________________________

11. What time is it?

____:____

12. Choose the best estimate. How long does it take your teacher to bake a cake?

about one minute

about one hour

about one day

13. What time is it?

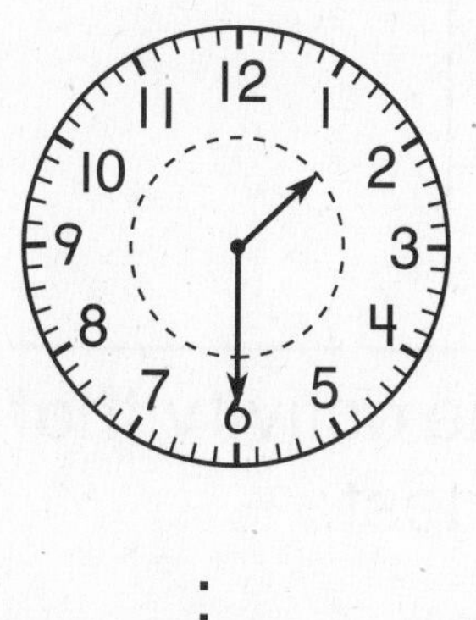

____:____

14. Draw hands on the clock to show 7:30.

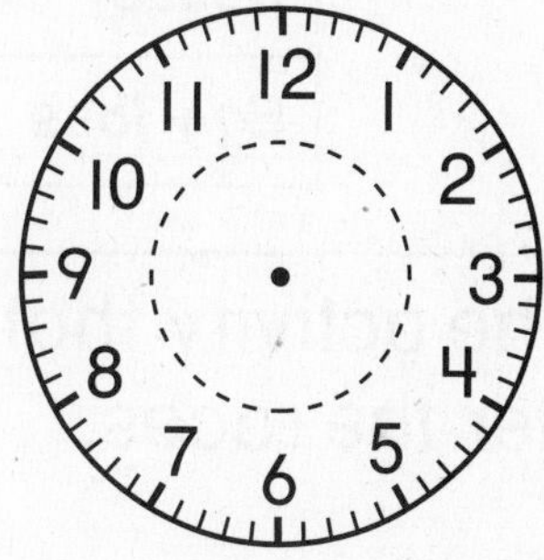

15. Circle the month that is just before March.

January

February

April

May

16. Circle the day that is just after Wednesday.

Tuesday

Monday

Thursday

Sunday

Go On

17. Which would you do in the morning?

wake up
eat lunch
go to bed
walk home from school

Use the chart to answer questions 18 and 19.

Field Day Schedule

Activities	Start	End
Balloon Pop	9:30	10:00
Races	10:00	11:00
Egg Toss	11:00	12:00

18. Circle the activity that is just after the races.

Team Tag
Egg Toss
Balloon Pop
Races

19. Circle the activity that is the shortest.

Team Tag
Egg Toss
Balloon Pop
Races

20. Circle the best estimate. How long does it take to brush your teeth?

about one minute
about one day
about one hour
about one week

Stop

Name ___________________________________

Choose the correct answer.

1. About how many would you use to balance a pencil? Ⓐ 20 Ⓑ 200	2. About how many 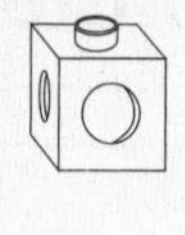 would you use to balance a shoe? Ⓐ 100 Ⓑ 10

For questions 3–6, choose the better estimate.

3.  Ⓐ about 5 pounds Ⓑ about 500 pounds	4.  Ⓐ about 25 pounds Ⓑ about 2 pounds
5.  Ⓐ about 1 pound Ⓑ about 100 pounds	6.  Ⓐ about 10 grams Ⓑ about 10 kilograms

Go On

For questions 7–8, choose the unit you would use to measure the real object.

7. 

half dollar

Ⓐ kilograms

Ⓑ grams

8. 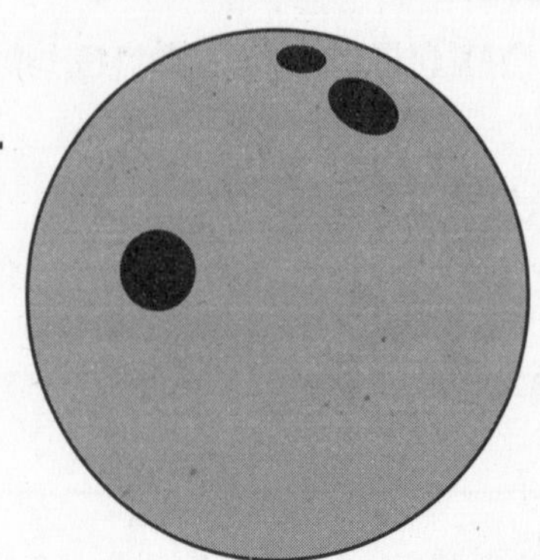
bowling ball

Ⓐ grams

Ⓑ kilograms

9. About how many grams does an  weigh?

Ⓐ 25 grams

Ⓑ 5 grams

10. About how many grams does a dime weigh?

Ⓐ 2 grams

Ⓑ 20 grams

Stop

Name ______________________________

Write the correct answer.

1. Circle how many you would use to balance a quarter. about 5 about 500 	2. Circle how many you would use to balance a box of crayons. about 1 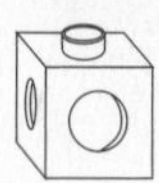 about 10 

For questions 3–6, circle the better estimate.

3.

about 1 pound
about 10 pounds

4.

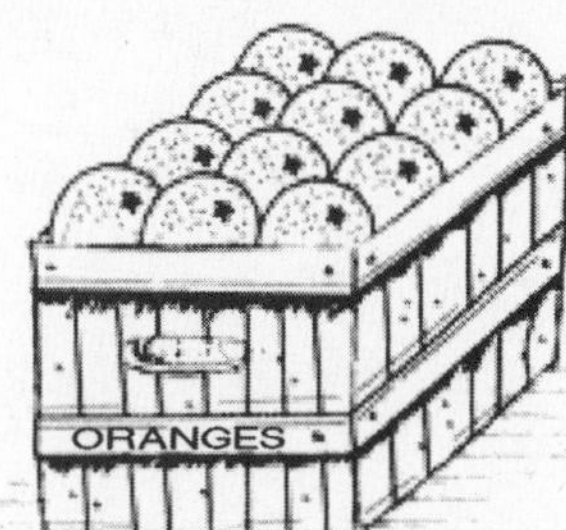

about 1 pound
about 10 pounds

5.

about 1 pound
about 10 pounds

6.

about 5 grams
about 5 kilograms

Go On

For 7–8, circle the unit you would use to measure the real object.

7. eraser grams kilograms	8. computer monitor grams kilograms
9. About how many grams does a cube weigh? I gram I 0 grams	10. About how many grams does a glue stick weigh? 20 grams 200 grams

Stop

Choose the correct answer.

1. About how many   will fill a  ?

Ⓐ 10 scoops
Ⓑ 100 scoops

2. About how many  will fill a?

Ⓐ 200 cups
Ⓑ 20 cups

3. About how many will fill a 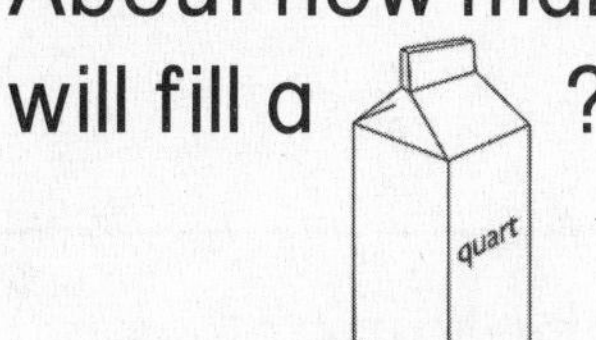 ?

Ⓐ 1 cup Ⓒ 4 cups
Ⓑ 2 cups Ⓓ 8 cups

4. About how many  will fill a 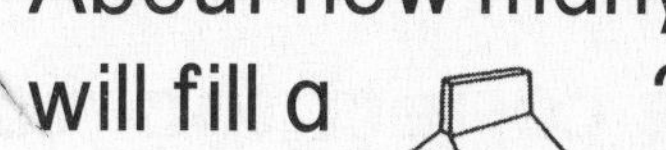 ?

Ⓐ 1 cup Ⓒ 5 cups
Ⓑ 2 cups Ⓓ 10 cups

5. Does this container hold **more than** or **less than** a  liter?

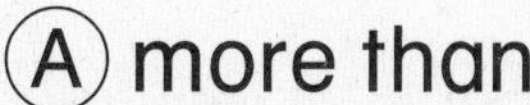

Ⓐ more than
Ⓑ less than

6. Does this container  hold **more than** or **less than** a 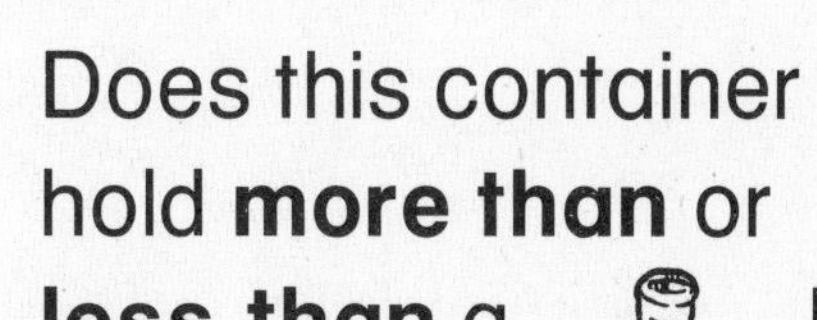 liter?

Ⓐ more than
Ⓑ less than

Go On

Name ______________________________

7. Read the thermometer. What is the temperature?

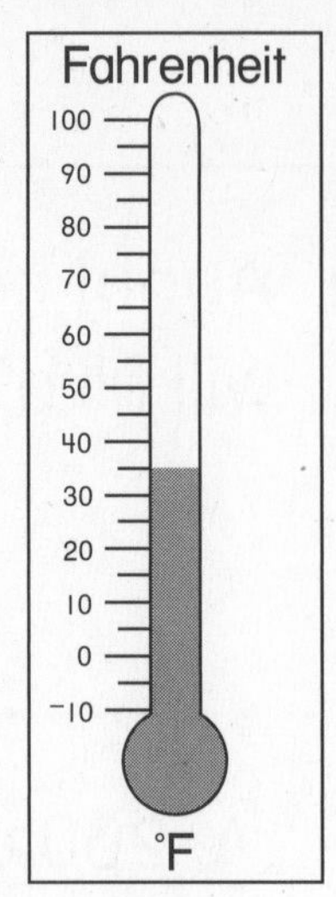

Ⓐ 35°F Ⓒ 53°F
Ⓑ 50°F Ⓓ 65°F

8. Read the thermometer. What is the temperature?

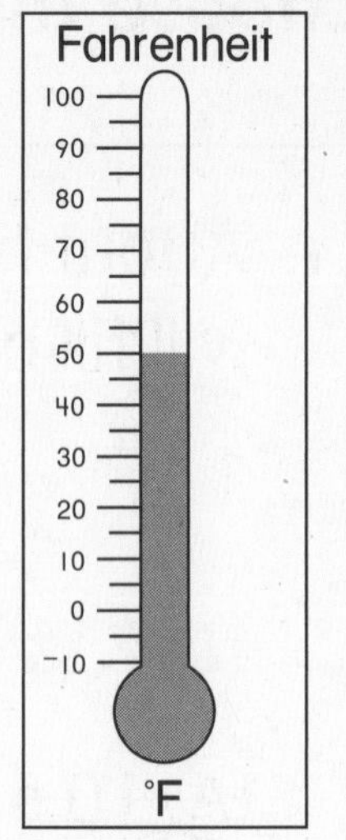

Ⓐ 5°F Ⓒ 45°F
Ⓑ 15°F Ⓓ 50°F

Choose the correct tool to measure.

9. How cold is it outdoors?

Ⓐ 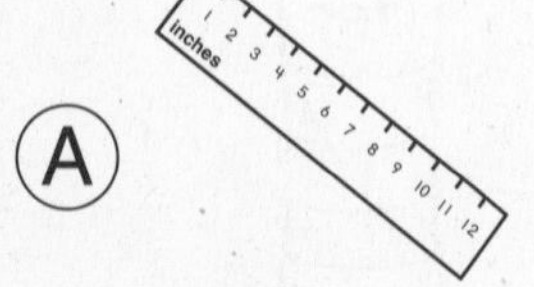
Ⓒ  
Ⓑ 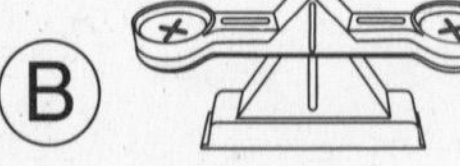
Ⓓ 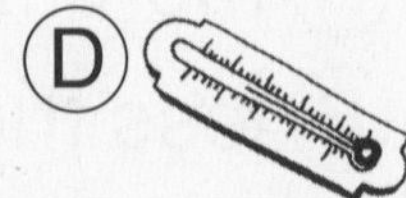

10. Which container holds more?

Ⓐ 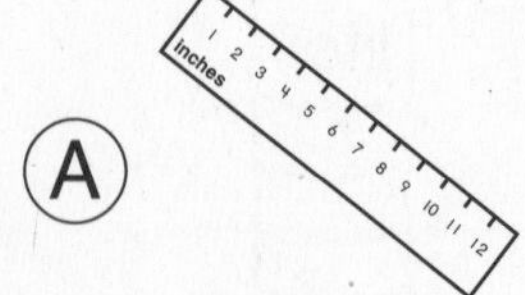
Ⓒ 
Ⓑ 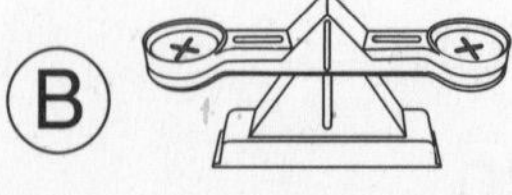
Ⓓ 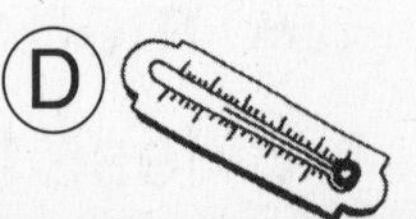

Stop

Name ____________________

Write the correct answer.
For questions 1–6, circle the better estimate.

<table>
<tr>
<td>1. About how many [mug] will fill a [pitcher] ?

about 4
about 40</td>
<td>2. How many [scoop] will fill a [glass] ?

about 50
about 5</td>
</tr>
<tr>
<td>3. About how many cups will fill 2 pints?

4 cups 12 cups</td>
<td>4. About how many cups will fill 2 quarts?

4 cups 8 cups</td>
</tr>
<tr>
<td>5. Does 1 quart hold more than or less than a liter?

more than less than</td>
<td>6. Does 1 gallon hold more than or less than a liter?
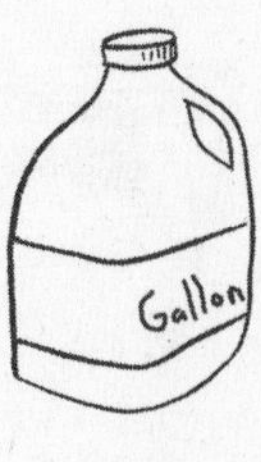

more than less than</td>
</tr>
</table>

Go On

Name ______________________________

Read the thermometer. Then write the temperature.

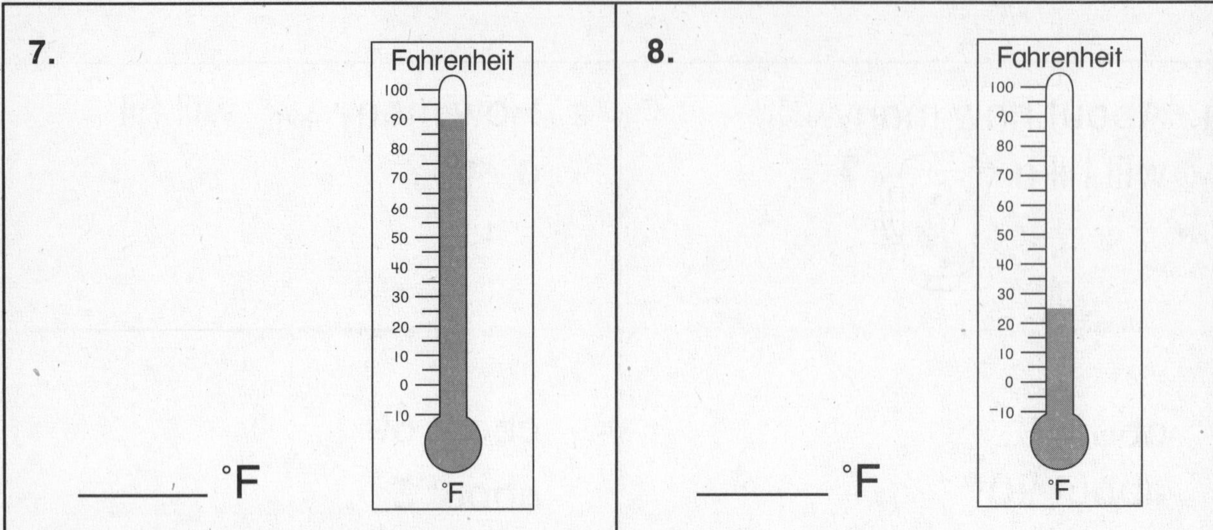

Circle the correct tool to measure.

9. How cold is the water?

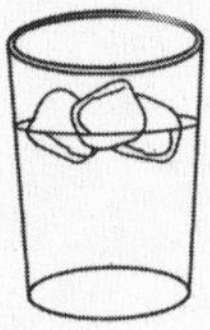

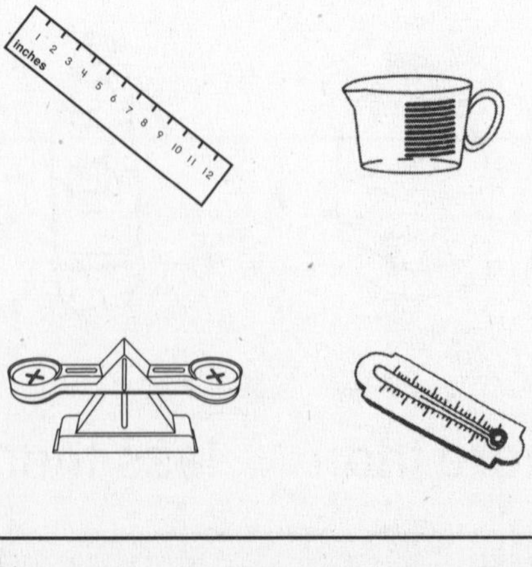

10. Which container holds more?

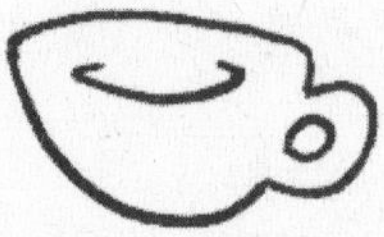

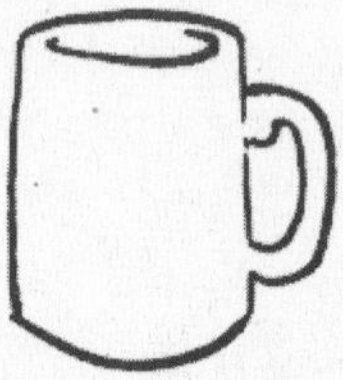

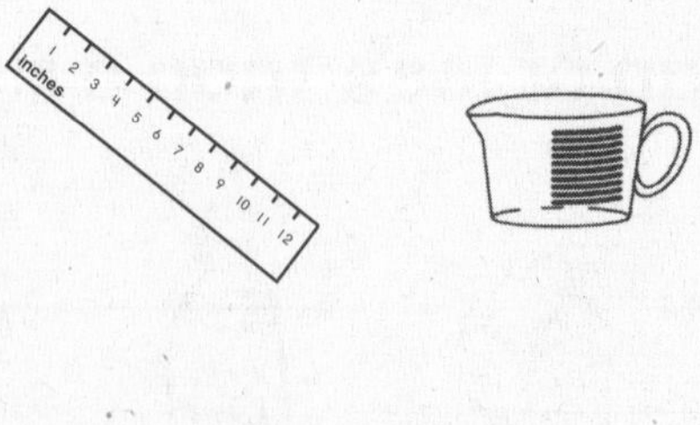

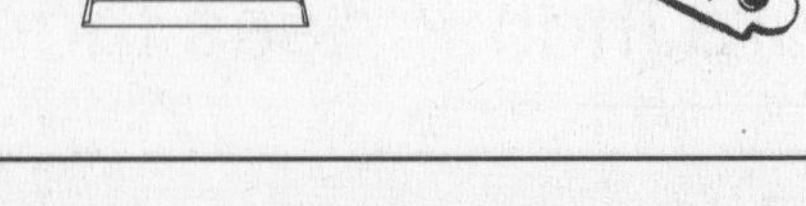

Stop

Choose the correct answer.

1. Add.

$$\begin{array}{r} 50 \\ +30 \\ \hline \end{array}$$

(A) 20 (C) 70
(B) 30 (D) 80

2. Subtract.

$$\begin{array}{r} 50 \\ -20 \\ \hline \end{array}$$

(A) 70 (C) 30
(B) 40 (D) 3

3. Use Workmat 3 and ▢ to add. Find the sum.

	tens	ones
	4	2
+		7

(A) 9 (C) 49
(B) 45 (D) 94

4. Use Workmat 3 and ▢ to add. Write the sum.

	tens	ones
	3	6
−		5

(A) 21 (C) 41
(B) 31 (D) 42

5. Add.

$$\begin{array}{r} 44¢ \\ +35¢ \\ \hline \end{array}$$

(A) 89¢ (C) 51¢
(B) 79¢ (D) 44¢

6. Add.

$$\begin{array}{r} 23¢ \\ +\ 6¢ \\ \hline \end{array}$$

(A) 16¢ (C) 29¢
(B) 25¢ (D) 45¢

Go On

Name ___________________________

7. Subtract.

$$\begin{array}{r} 78¢ \\ -33¢ \\ \hline \end{array}$$

Ⓐ 14¢ Ⓑ 26¢ Ⓒ 38¢ Ⓓ 45¢

8. Subtract.

$$\begin{array}{r} 29¢ \\ -18¢ \\ \hline \end{array}$$

Ⓐ 11¢ Ⓑ 21¢ Ⓒ 37¢ Ⓓ 50¢

Without adding or subtracting, choose the best estimate.

9. Allie had 40 crayons.

She gave 19 to Karen.

About how many did she have left?

Ⓐ 20 crayons
Ⓑ 60 crayons
Ⓒ 80 crayons

10. Lee made 20 cupcakes for the bake sale.

Tia made 12 cupcakes.

About how many did they make in all?

Ⓐ 10 cupcakes
Ⓑ 30 cupcakes
Ⓒ 40 cupcakes

Stop

Name ______________________________

Write the correct answer.

1. Add.

$$\begin{array}{r} 40 \\ +30 \\ \hline \end{array}$$

2. Subtract.

$$\begin{array}{r} 70 \\ -30 \\ \hline \end{array}$$

3. Use Workmat 3 and ▢ to add. Write the sum.

	tens	ones
	5	2
+		6

4. Use Workmat 3 and ▢ to subtract. Write the difference.

	tens	ones
	5	7
−		6

5. Add.

$$\begin{array}{r} 23¢ \\ +24¢ \\ \hline ¢ \end{array}$$

6. Add.

$$\begin{array}{r} 45¢ \\ +13¢ \\ \hline ¢ \end{array}$$

Go On

Name ________________________________

7. Subtract. $\begin{array}{r} 68¢ \\ -65¢ \\ \hline ¢ \end{array}$	8. Subtract. $\begin{array}{r} 93¢ \\ -22¢ \\ \hline ¢ \end{array}$

Without adding or subtracting, circle the best estimate.

9. Mike had 30 toy cars. He gave 9 to Eddie. About how many did he have left? 10 toy cars 20 toy cars 40 toy cars	10. Julia brought 40 cookies to the party. Kenneth brought 22 cookies. About how many cookies were there in all? 15 cookies 50 cookies 60 cookies

Stop

Name ____________________

Choose the correct answer.

1. Is pulling an apple from the bowl **certain** or **impossible**?

Ⓐ certain
Ⓑ impossible

2. Is pulling a tomato from the bowl **certain** or **impossible**?

Ⓐ certain
Ⓑ impossible

3. Is pulling a cherry from the bowl **certain** or **impossible**?

Ⓐ certain
Ⓑ impossible

4. Choose **more likely** or **less likely** to tell how likely a banana is to be pulled from the bowl.

Ⓐ more likely
Ⓑ less likely

5. Choose **more likely** or **less likely** to tell how likely a marble is to be pulled from the bowl.

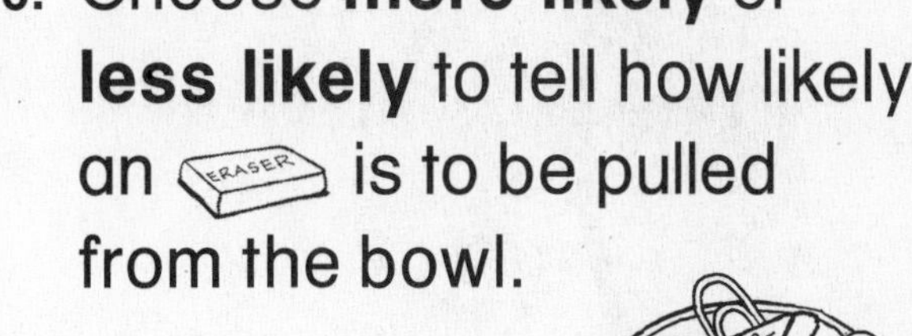

Ⓐ more likely
Ⓑ less likely

6. Choose **more likely** or **less likely** to tell how likely an ERASER is to be pulled from the bowl.

Ⓐ more likely
Ⓑ less likely

Go On

Name ______________________________

7. Which two objects are equally likely to be pulled from the bowl?

  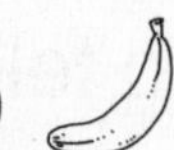

8. Which two socks are equally likely to be pulled from the line?

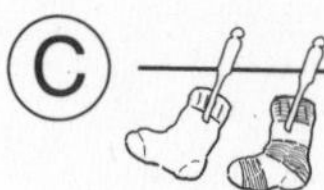

9. Predict. If you spin the pointer 10 times, on which color is it likely to stop more often?

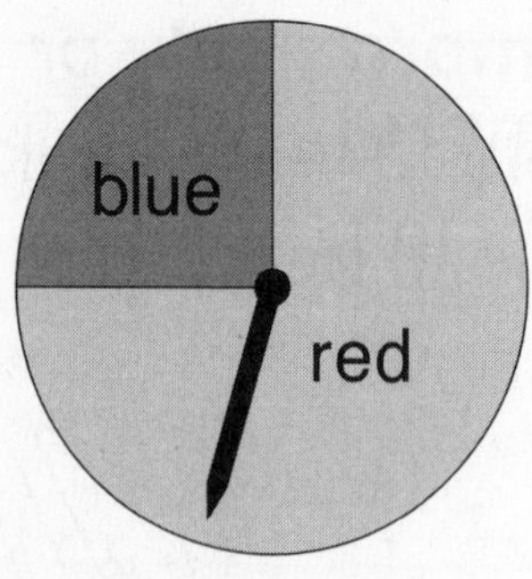

Ⓐ blue

Ⓑ red

10. Predict. If you spin the pointer 10 times, on which number is it likely to stop more often?

Ⓐ 4

Ⓑ 6

Stop

Name ______________________________

Write the correct answer.

1. Is pulling a from the bowl **certain** or **impossible**?

certain
impossible

2. Is pulling a from the bowl **certain** or **impossible**?

certain
impossible

3. Is pulling a from the bowl **certain** or **impossible**?

certain
impossible

4. Choose **more likely** or **less likely** to tell how likely a is to be pulled from the bowl.

more likely
less likely

5. Choose **more likely** or **less likely** to tell how likely a is to be pulled from the bowl

more likely
less likely

6. Choose **more likely** or **less likely** to tell how likely a is to be pulled from the bowl.

more likely
less likely

Go On

Name ___________________________

For 7 and 8, circle the two objects that are equally likely to be pulled from the bowl.

7.

8.

9. Predict. If you spin the pointer 10 times, on which color is it likely to stop more often?

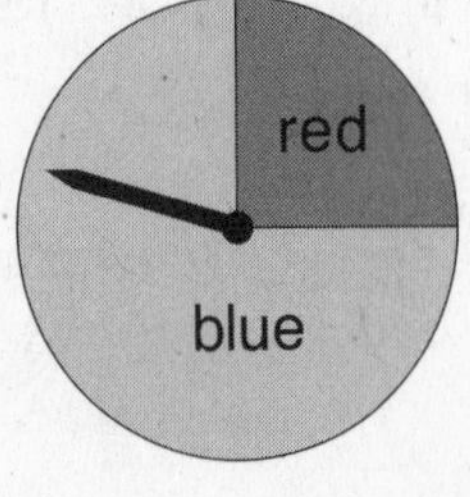

____

10. Predict. If you spin the pointer 10 times, on which number is it likely to stop more often?

____

Stop

Name ______________________________

Choose the correct answer.

1. Which is longest?

Ⓐ 

Ⓑ 

Ⓒ 

Ⓓ 

2. Which unit would you use to measure the real object?

Ⓐ inches Ⓑ feet

3. Use an inch ruler to measure. How many inches long is it?

Ⓐ 2 inches Ⓒ 4 inches

Ⓑ 3 inches Ⓓ 5 inches

4. How many paper clips long is the pencil?

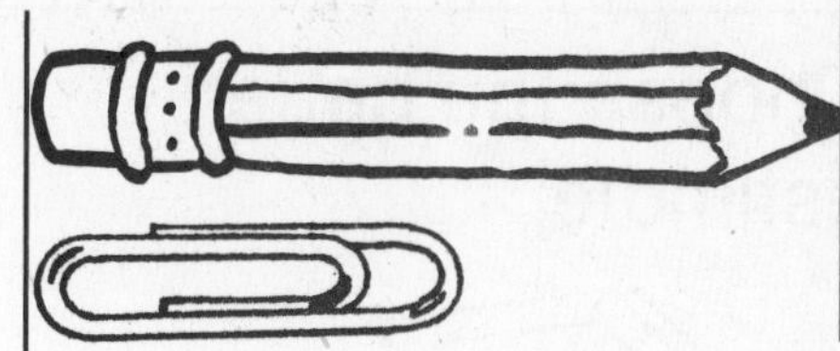

Ⓐ 4 clips Ⓒ 2 clips

Ⓑ 3 clips Ⓓ 1 clip

5. Use a centimeter ruler to measure. How many centimeters long is it?

Ⓐ 6 cm Ⓒ 4 cm

Ⓑ 5 cm Ⓓ 3 cm

6. About how many beads long is the string?

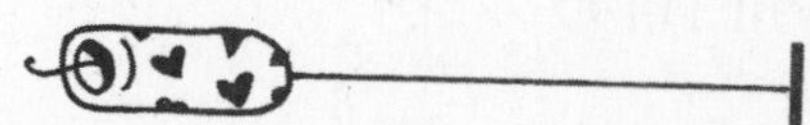

Ⓐ 3 beads

Ⓑ 6 beads

Ⓒ 12 beads

Ⓓ 18 beads

Go On

Name ______________________________

7. Which real object would weigh less?

Ⓐ 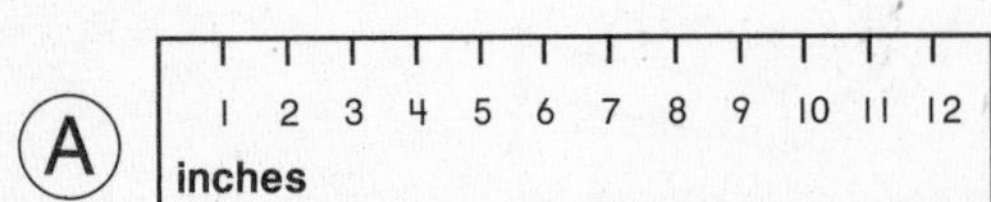

Ⓑ

8. Choose the better estimate.

Ⓐ about 1 pound
Ⓑ about 100 pounds

9. Choose the better estimate.

Ⓐ about 10 kilograms
Ⓑ about 1 kilogram

10. About how many cups will fill a  ?

Ⓐ 4 cups
Ⓑ 8 cups
Ⓒ 10 cups
Ⓓ 16 cups

11. About how many cups will fill a  ?

Ⓐ 1 cup
Ⓑ 4 cups
Ⓒ 10 cups
Ⓓ 16 cups

12. Read the thermometer. What is the temperature?

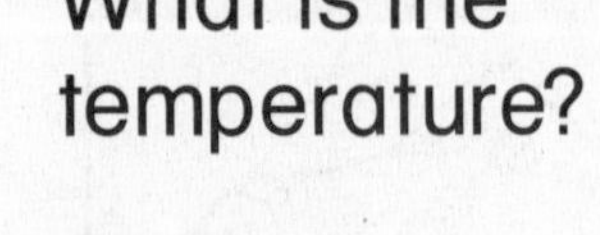

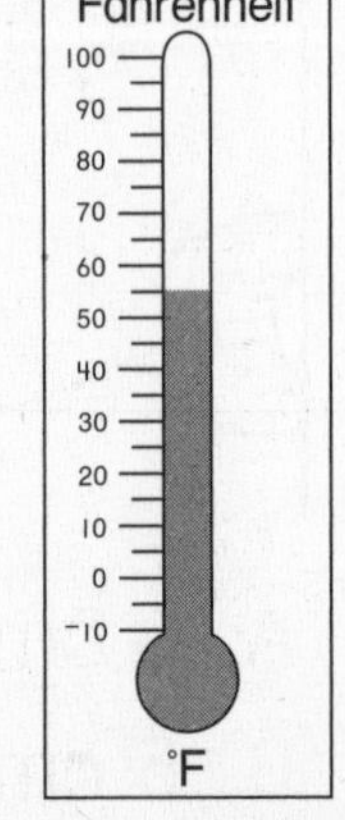

Ⓐ 90°F
Ⓑ 68°F
Ⓒ 55°F
Ⓓ 32°F

Go On

Name ______________________________

13. Which tool would you use to measure which apple is heavier?

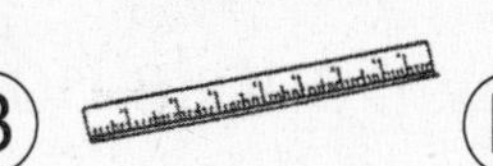

Ⓐ Ⓑ Ⓒ Ⓓ

14.
$$\begin{array}{r} 30 \\ +50 \\ \hline \end{array}$$

Ⓐ 80 Ⓒ 20
Ⓑ 70 Ⓓ 8

15.
$$\begin{array}{r} 60 \\ -40 \\ \hline \end{array}$$

Ⓐ 40 Ⓒ 20
Ⓑ 30 Ⓓ 10

16.

	Tens	Ones
	4	2
+		7

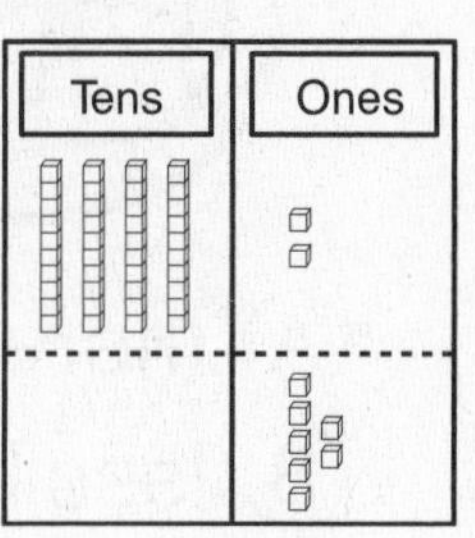

Ⓐ 45 Ⓒ 50
Ⓑ 49 Ⓓ 54

17.

	Tens	Ones
	6	8
−		7

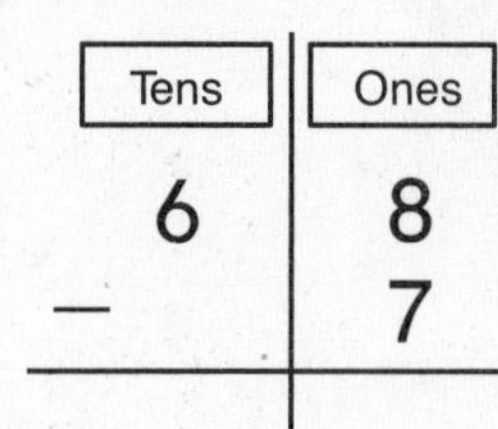
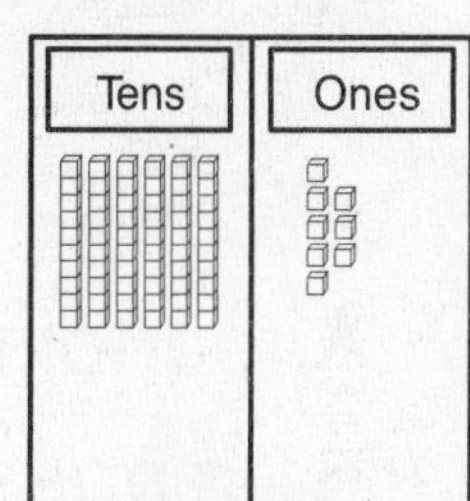

Ⓐ 75 Ⓒ 62
Ⓑ 65 Ⓓ 61

18.
$$\begin{array}{r} 50¢ \\ +25¢ \\ \hline \end{array}$$

Ⓐ 55¢ Ⓒ 70¢
Ⓑ 65¢ Ⓓ 75¢

19.
$$\begin{array}{r} 97¢ \\ -12¢ \\ \hline \end{array}$$

Ⓐ 45¢ Ⓒ 71¢
Ⓑ 56¢ Ⓓ 85¢

Go On

20. Without adding or subtracting, choose the reasonable answer.

Ellen has 4 pencils. Henry has 7 pencils.
How many pencils do they have in all?

Ⓐ about 1 pencil

Ⓑ about 10 pencils

Ⓒ about 50 pencils

21. Is pulling a

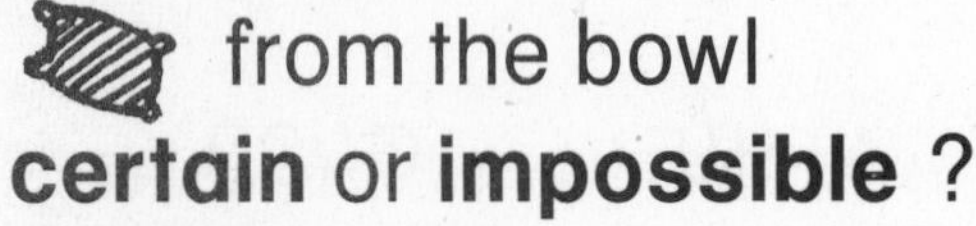

from the bowl **certain** or **impossible** ?

Ⓐ certain

Ⓑ impossible

22. How likely is it to pull a ▯ from the bowl?

Ⓐ more likely

Ⓑ less likely

23. Which two objects are equally likely to be pulled from the bowl?

Ⓐ strawberry and banana

Ⓑ strawberry and apple

24. If you spin the pointer 10 times, on which color is it likely to stop more often?

Ⓐ blue

Ⓑ yellow

Stop

Name ______________________________

Write the correct answer.

1. Circle the longest ribbon.

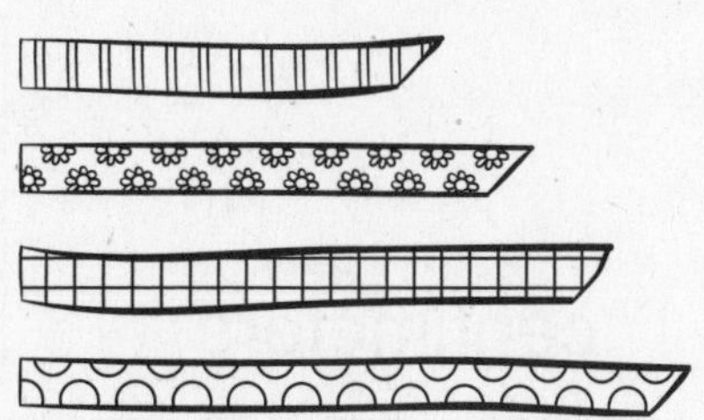

2. Which unit would you use to measure the crayon?

inch foot

3. How many inches long is the corn? Use an inch ruler to measure.

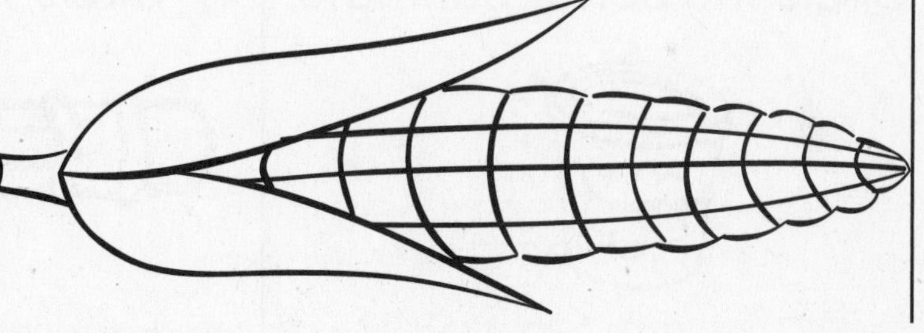

___ inches

4. How many  long is the pickle?

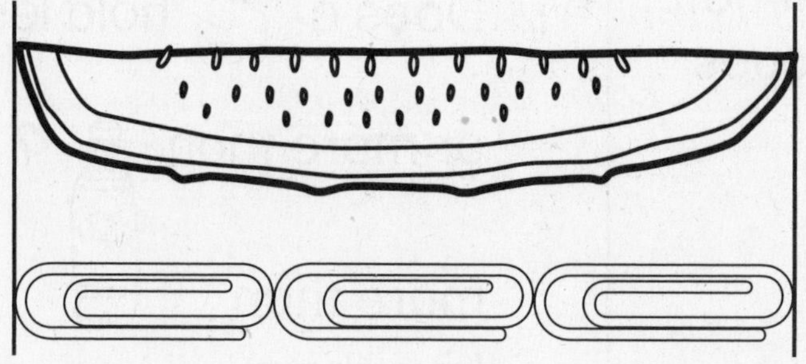

___ paper clips

Go On

5. How many centimeters long is the feather?
Use a centimeter ruler to measure.

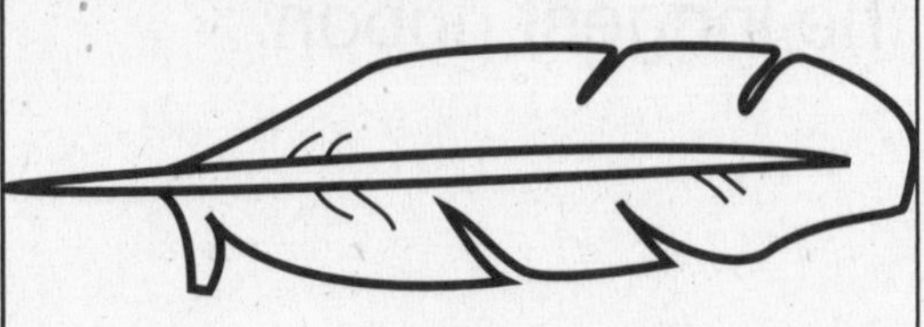

___ centimeters

6. About how many beads long is the string?

about ___ beads

7. Which object is lighter?

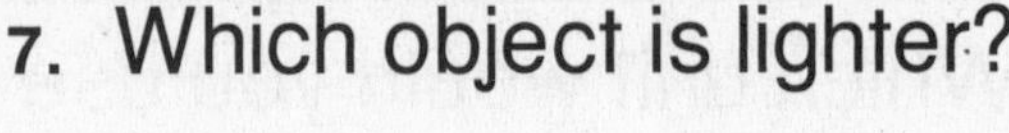

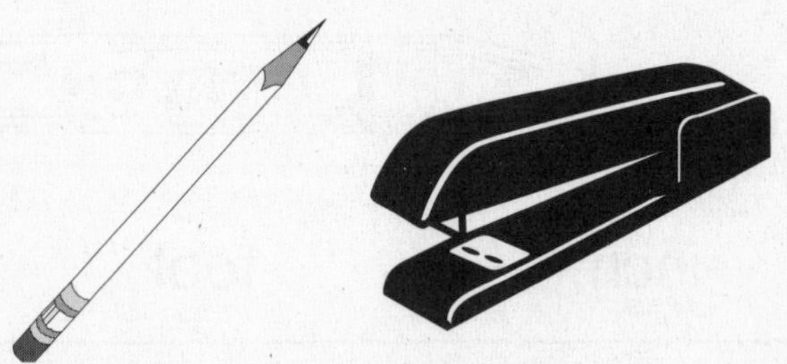

8. Circle the better estimate.

about 1 pound
about 10 pounds

9. Circle the better estimate.

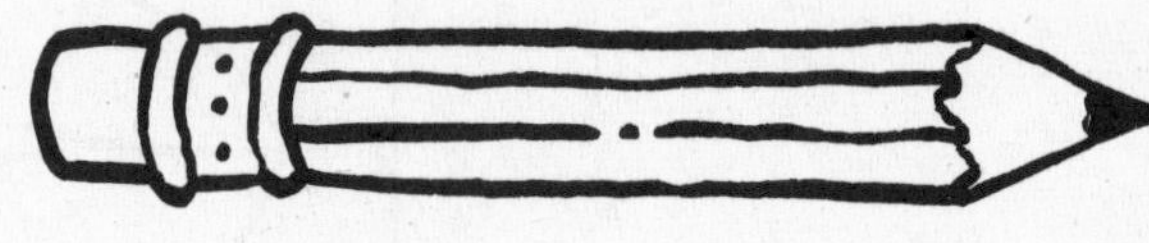

5 kilograms
5 grams

10. Circle the best estimate.
About how many cups will fill a pint?

about 2 cups
about 20 cups
about 200 cups

11. Does a pint hold less or more than  ?

more than
less than

Go On

Name ______________________

12. Read the thermometer. Write the temperature.

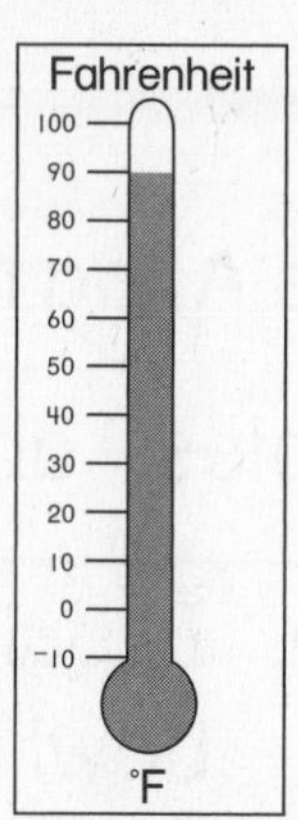

_____ °F

13. Circle the tool you would use to measure how long a book is.

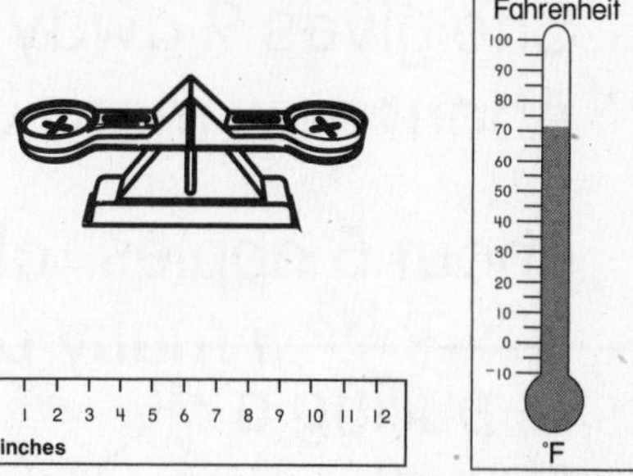

14.

$$\begin{array}{r} 40 \\ +\ 50 \\ \hline \end{array}$$

15.

$$\begin{array}{r} 70 \\ -\ 50 \\ \hline \end{array}$$

16.

Tens	Ones
6	1
−	8

Tens	Ones

17.

Tens	Ones
7	6
−	4

Tens	Ones

18.

$$\begin{array}{r} 54¢ \\ +\ 40¢ \\ \hline ¢ \end{array}$$

19.

$$\begin{array}{r} 51¢ \\ -\ 30¢ \\ \hline ¢ \end{array}$$

Go On

20. Without adding or subtracting, circle the reasonable answer.

Anna has 15 apples.
She gives 9 away.
About how many apples does Anna have left?

about 5 apples about 50 apples about 500 apples

21. Is pulling a [pear] from the bowl **certain** or **impossible**?

certain impossible

22. Is pulling a [black marble] from the bowl **more likely** or **less likely**?

more likely less likely

23. Circle the two marbles that are equally likely to be pulled from the bowl.

24. Predict. If you spin the pointer 10 times, on which color will it stop more often?

yellow green

Stop

Name ______________________

Choose the correct answer.

1. Subtract.

	tens	ones
	5	9
−		4

Ⓐ 23 Ⓒ 55

Ⓑ 43 Ⓓ 65

2. Is pulling a ♡ from the bowl **more likely** or **less likely**?

Ⓐ more likely

Ⓑ less likely

3. Choose the correct number sentence.

6 children are playing. 4 more children join them. How many children are playing now?

Ⓐ $6 - 4 = 2$

Ⓑ $6 + 4 = 10$

Ⓒ $10 - 4 = 6$

Ⓓ $6 + 6 = 12$

4. Choose the correct number sentence.

Adam has 8 berries. He gives away 5 of them. How many berries does he have left?

Ⓐ $3 + 5 = 8$

Ⓑ $8 - 1 = 7$

Ⓒ $8 - 5 = 3$

Ⓓ $5 - 3 = 2$

Go On

Favorite Pets	
Pet	**Total**
cat	II
goldfish	III
dog	~~IIII~~ I

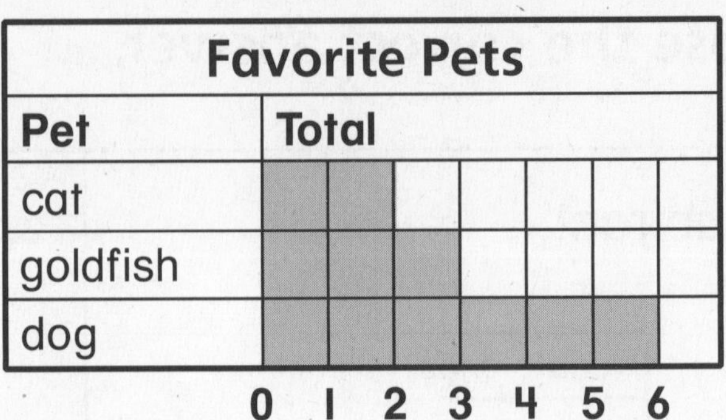

Use the tally table for question 5.

5. How many children have a cat?

Ⓐ 5 Ⓑ 4 Ⓒ 3 Ⓓ 2

Use the bar graph to answer question 6.

6. How many children have a goldfish?

Ⓐ 2 Ⓑ 3 Ⓒ 4 Ⓓ 5

7. Which number is shown?

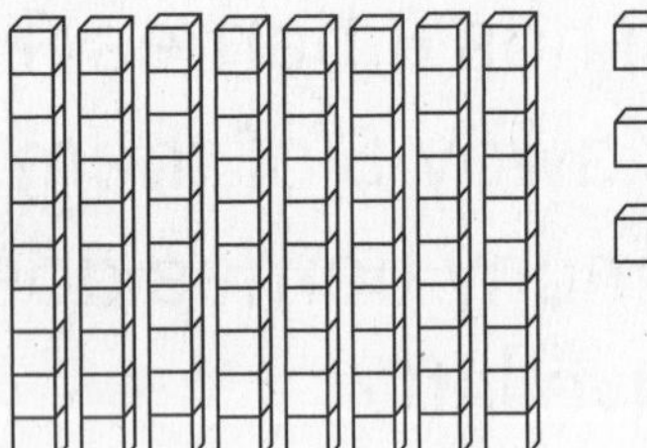

Ⓐ 11 Ⓒ 73

Ⓑ 38 Ⓓ 83

8. Which is a different way to show the number?

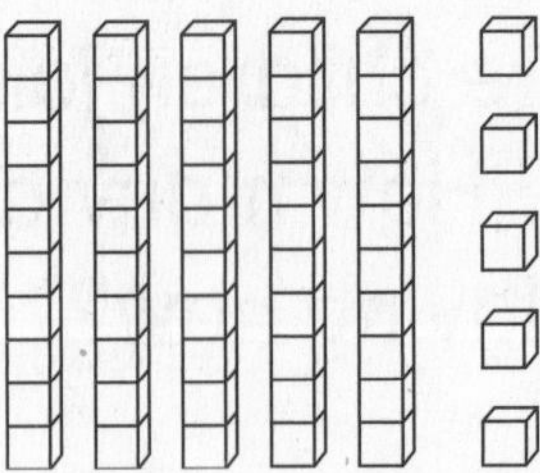

5 tens + 5 ones = 55

Ⓐ 10 + 5 Ⓒ 40 + 4

Ⓑ 20 + 5 Ⓓ 50 + 5

Go On

9. Count by fives.
Which number is missing?

5, 10, ___, 20, 25

(A) 1
(B) 11
(C) 15
(D) 19

10. Find the sum.

$$\begin{array}{r} 6 \\ 4 \\ +\ 7 \\ \hline \end{array}$$

(A) 10
(B) 11
(C) 17
(D) 18

11. How many more cats than dogs are there?

$$\begin{array}{r} 7 \\ -\ 5 \\ \hline \end{array}$$

(A) 12
(B) 10
(C) 5
(D) 2

12. Which is the missing number?

8 + ☐ = 13

(A) 12
(B) 10
(C) 5
(D) 3

13. Which solid figure will stack?

(A) 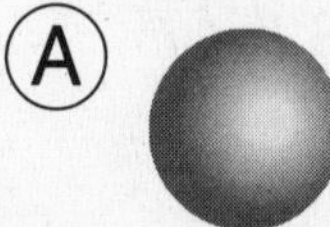

(B) 

14. Which comes next in the pattern?

(A)

(B)

(C) 

(D)

Go On

15. Which fact is in the same fact family as $8 - 2 = 6$?

Ⓐ $6 + 1 = 7$
Ⓑ $6 + 2 = 8$
Ⓒ $6 - 2 = 4$
Ⓓ $8 + 2 = 10$

16. 41¢
+ 34¢

Ⓐ 23¢
Ⓑ 60¢
Ⓒ 67¢
Ⓓ 75¢

17. Which shows thirds?

Ⓐ 
Ⓒ 
Ⓑ
Ⓓ

18. Count. Find the amount.

Ⓐ 15¢
Ⓑ 20¢
Ⓒ 35¢
Ⓓ 45¢

19. What time is it?

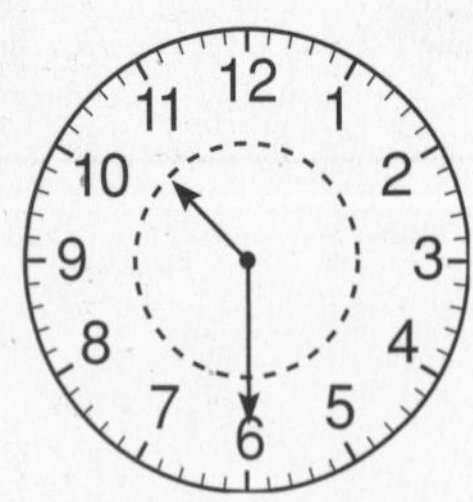

Ⓐ 10:00
Ⓑ 10:30
Ⓒ 11:00
Ⓓ 11:30

20. About how many centimeters long is the picture?

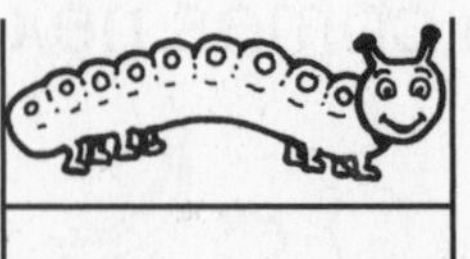

Ⓐ 3 cm
Ⓑ 4 cm
Ⓒ 7 cm
Ⓓ 1 cm

Stop

Name ______________________

Write the correct answer.

1. Subtract.

	tens	ones
	3	8
−		4

2. How likely is pulling a ● from the bowl? Circle **more likely** or **less likely**.

more likely   less likely

3. Write a number sentence to solve.

There are 3 children singing.

5 more children join them.

How many children are singing now?

___ ◯ ___ = ___

4. Write a number sentence to solve.

There are 10 boys playing drums.

8 boys stop playing.

How many boys are still playing drums?

___ ◯ ___ = ___

Go On

Name ______________________________

Favorite Sport	
Sport	**Total**
football	IIII
soccer	III
basketball	~~IIII~~ I

Favorite Sport						
Sport	**Total**					
football	■	■	■	■		
soccer	■	■	■			
basketball	■	■	■	■	■	
	0 1	2	3	4	5	6

Use the tally table for question 5.

5. How many children chose football?

____ children

Use the bar graph to answer question 6.

6. How many more children chose basketball than soccer?

____ children

7. What number is shown?

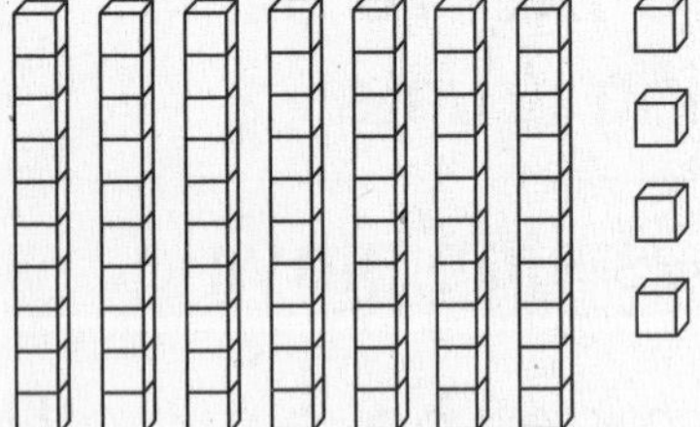

____

8. Write the number in a different way.

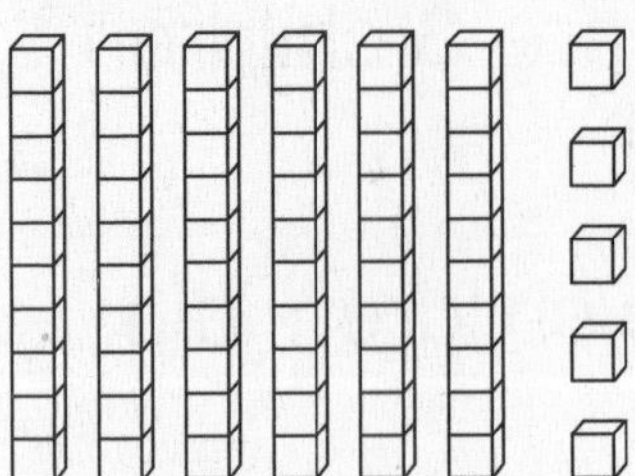

6 tens + 5 ones = 65

____ + ____ = ____

Go On

9. Count by tens. Write the missing number.

30, 40, 50, ___, 70

10. Find the sum.

$$\begin{array}{r} 7 \\ 3 \\ +\ 2 \\ \hline \end{array}$$

11. How many more apples than bananas are there?

$$\begin{array}{r} 9 \\ -\ 6 \\ \hline \end{array}$$

12. Write the missing number.

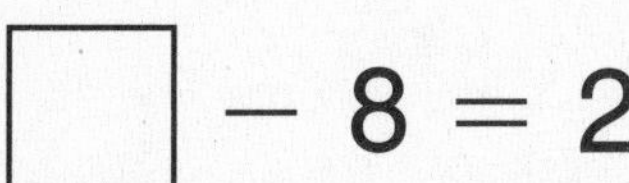

$\square - 8 = 2$

13. Circle the solid that will roll.

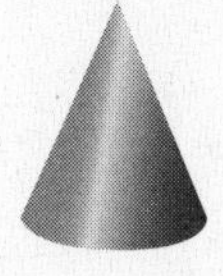

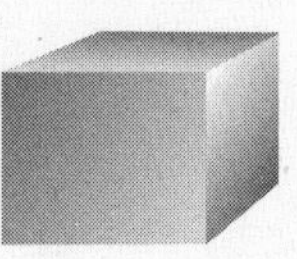

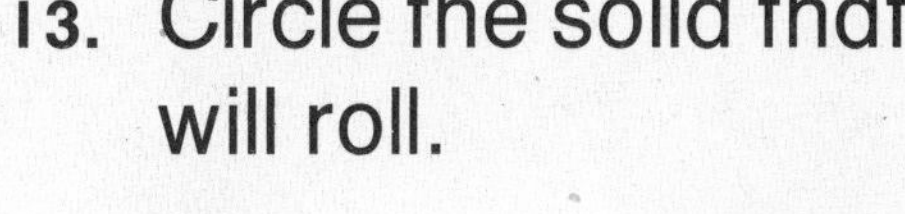

14. Draw what comes next in the pattern.

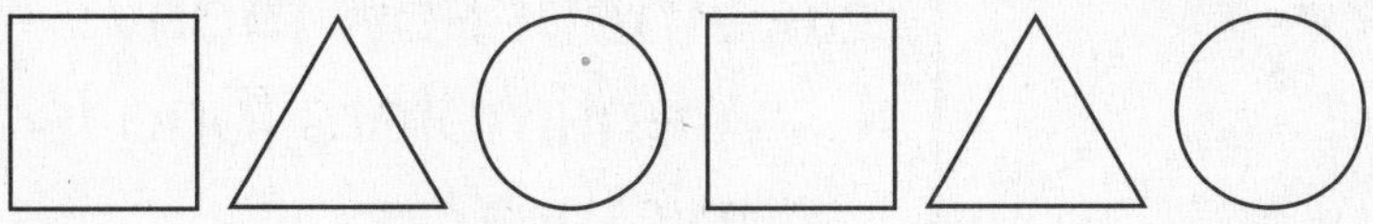

15. Circle the two facts that are in the same family.

$8 + 3 = 11$

$8 - 3 = 5$

$11 - 3 = 8$

16.

$$\begin{array}{r} 70¢ \\ +\ 16¢ \\ \hline \end{array}$$

___¢

Go On

Name ______________________________

17. Which picture shows thirds?

Color $\frac{1}{3}$.

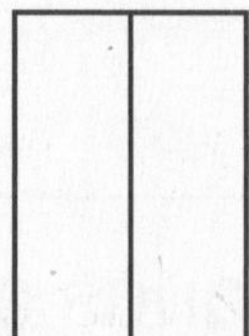
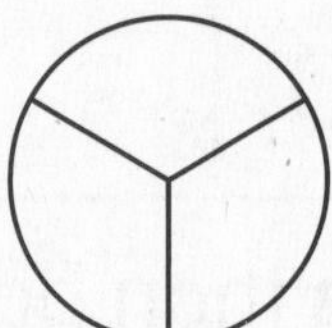
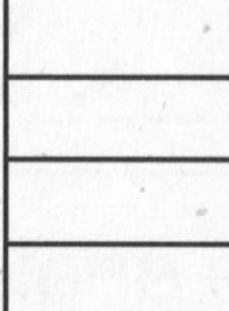

18. Count. Write the amount.

_____¢

19. Read the clock.

Write the time.

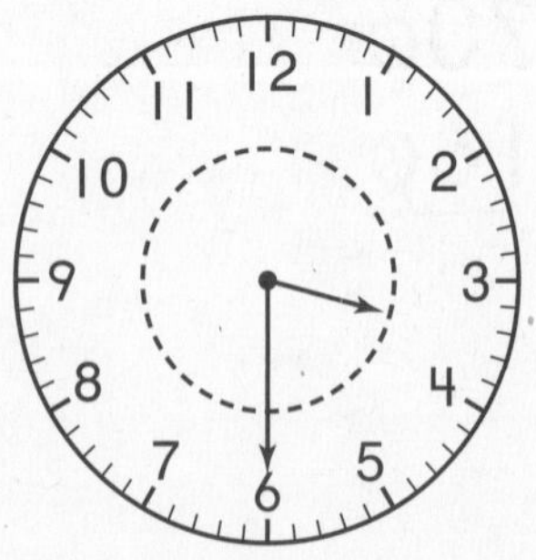

_____ : _____

20. About how many centimeters long is the picture?

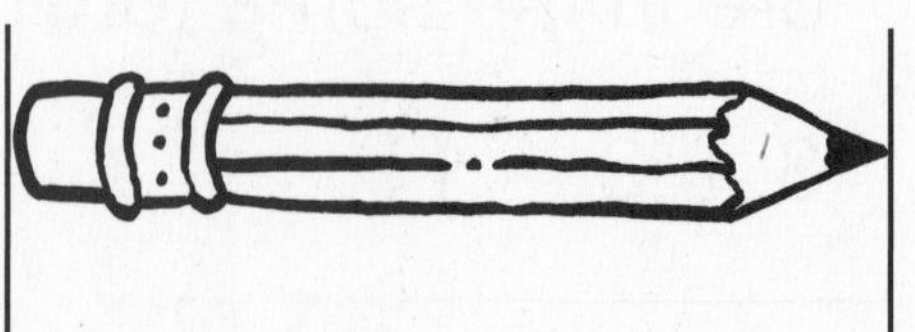

_____ centimeters

Stop

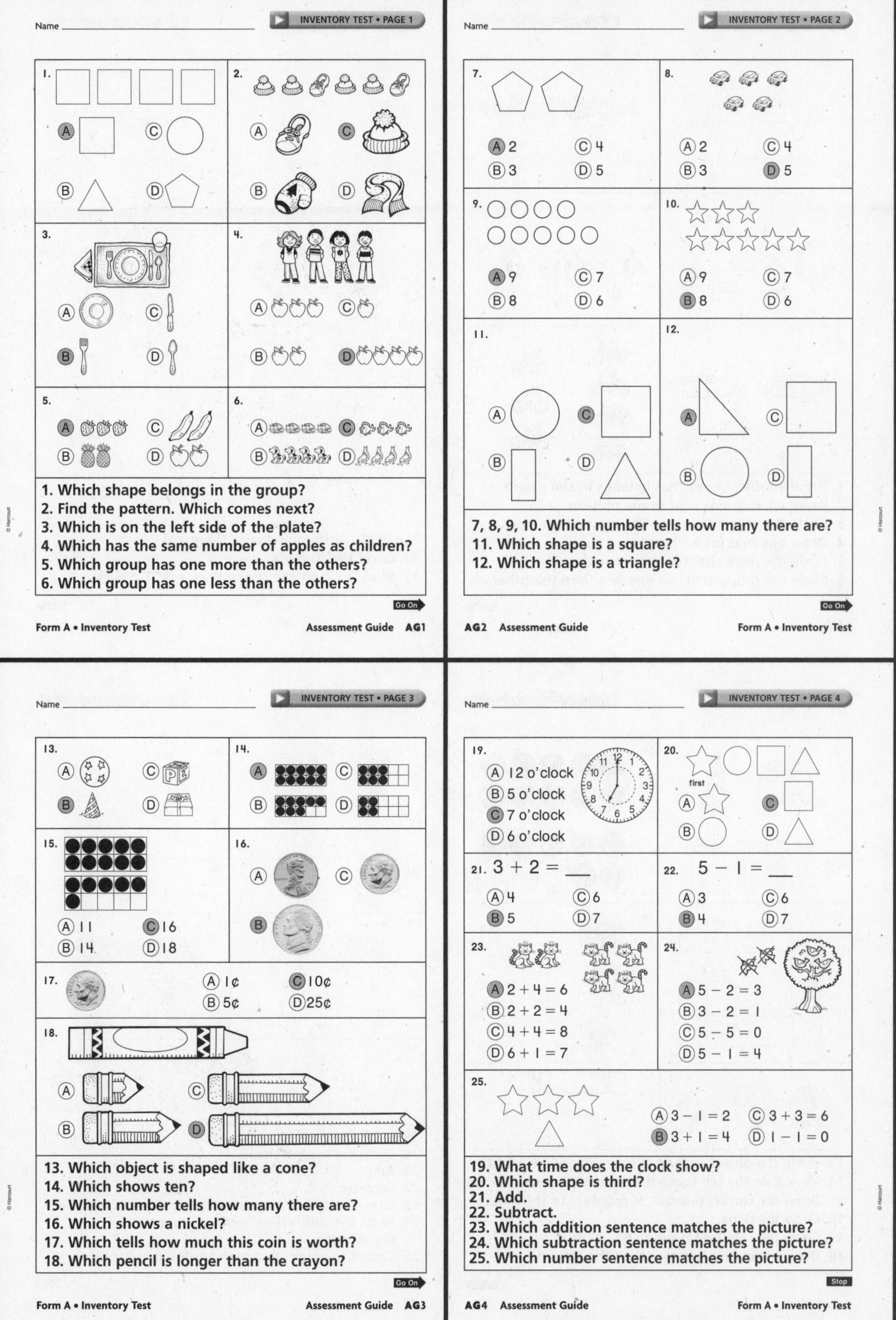

Name ________________ INVENTORY TEST • PAGE 1

1. A B C D
2. A B C D
3. A B C D
4. A B C D
5. A B C D
6. A B C D

1. Which shape belongs in the group?
2. Find the pattern. Which comes next?
3. Which is on the left side of the plate?
4. Which has the same number of apples as children?
5. Which group has one more than the others?
6. Which group has one less than the others?

Go On

Form A • Inventory Test — Assessment Guide AG1

Name ________________ INVENTORY TEST • PAGE 2

7. A 2 B 3 C 4 D 5
8. A 2 B 3 C 4 D 5
9. A 9 B 8 C 7 D 6
10. A 9 B 8 C 7 D 6
11. A B C D
12. A B C D

7, 8, 9, 10. Which number tells how many there are?
11. Which shape is a square?
12. Which shape is a triangle?

Go On

AG2 Assessment Guide — Form A • Inventory Test

Name ________________ INVENTORY TEST • PAGE 3

13. A B C D
14. A B C D
15. A 11 B 14 C 16 D 18
16. A B C
17. A 1¢ B 5¢ C 10¢ D 25¢
18. A B C D

13. Which object is shaped like a cone?
14. Which shows ten?
15. Which number tells how many there are?
16. Which shows a nickel?
17. Which tells how much this coin is worth?
18. Which pencil is longer than the crayon?

Go On

Form A • Inventory Test — Assessment Guide AG3

Name ________________ INVENTORY TEST • PAGE 4

19. A 12 o'clock B 5 o'clock C 7 o'clock D 6 o'clock
20. first A B C D
21. $3 + 2 =$ ___ A 4 B 5 C 6 D 7
22. $5 - 1 =$ ___ A 3 B 4 C 6 D 7
23. A $2 + 4 = 6$ B $2 + 2 = 4$ C $4 + 4 = 8$ D $6 + 1 = 7$
24. A $5 - 2 = 3$ B $3 - 2 = 1$ C $5 - 5 = 0$ D $5 - 1 = 4$
25. A $3 - 1 = 2$ B $3 + 1 = 4$ C $3 + 3 = 6$ D $1 - 1 = 0$

19. What time does the clock show?
20. Which shape is third?
21. Add.
22. Subtract.
23. Which addition sentence matches the picture?
24. Which subtraction sentence matches the picture?
25. Which number sentence matches the picture?

Stop

AG4 Assessment Guide — Form A • Inventory Test

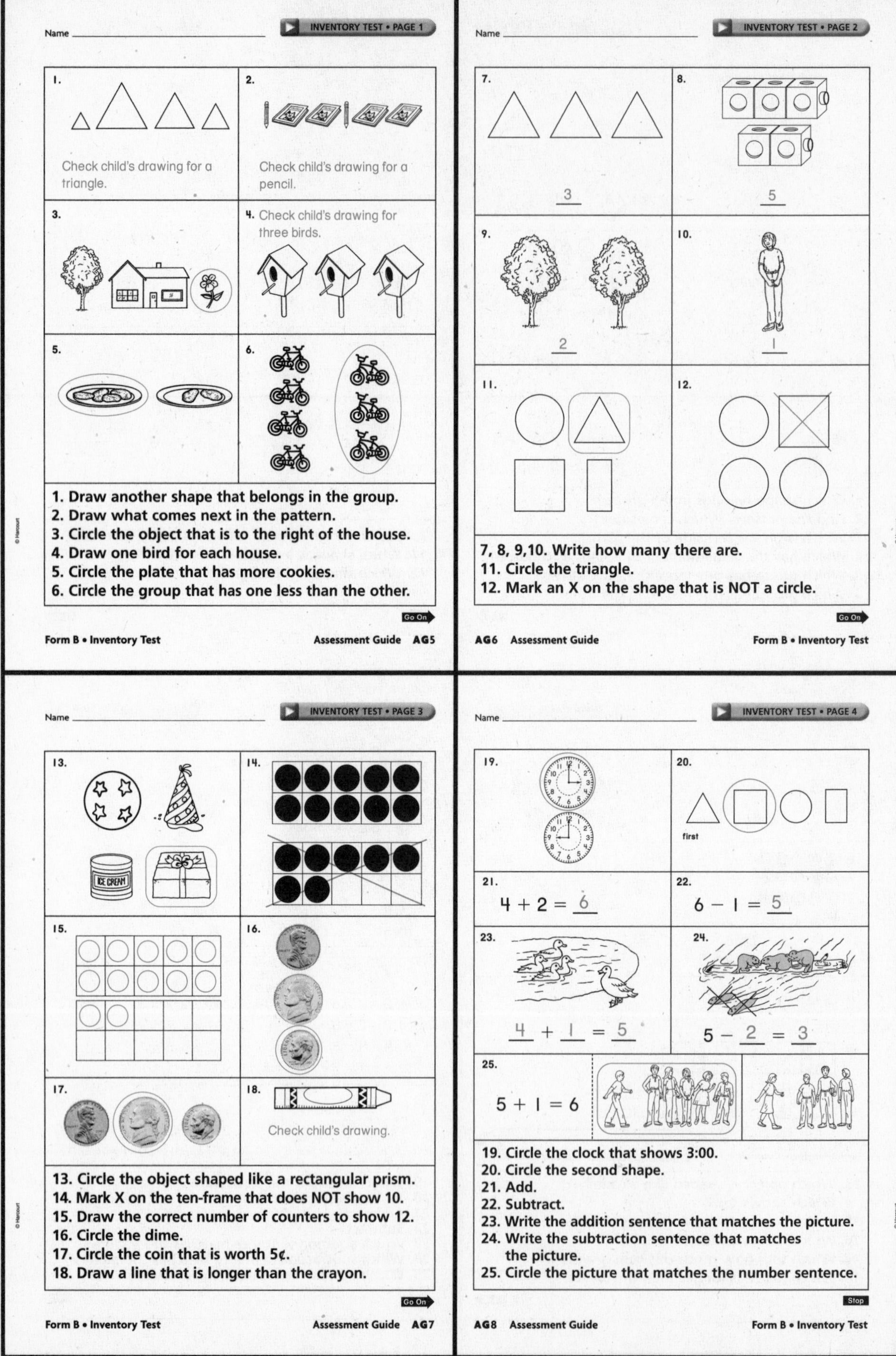

Name ____________________

INVENTORY TEST • PAGE 1

1\. Check child's drawing for a triangle.

2\. Check child's drawing for a pencil.

3\.

4\. Check child's drawing for three birds.

5\.

6\.

1. Draw another shape that belongs in the group.
2. Draw what comes next in the pattern.
3. Circle the object that is to the right of the house.
4. Draw one bird for each house.
5. Circle the plate that has more cookies.
6. Circle the group that has one less than the other.

Go On

Form B • Inventory Test — Assessment Guide AG5

© Harcourt

Name ____________________

INVENTORY TEST • PAGE 2

7\. 3

8\. 5

9\. 2

10\. 1

11\.

12\.

7, 8, 9,10. Write how many there are.
11. Circle the triangle.
12. Mark an X on the shape that is NOT a circle.

Go On

AG6 Assessment Guide — Form B • Inventory Test

© Harcourt

Name ____________________

INVENTORY TEST • PAGE 3

13\. ICE CREAM

14\.

15\.

16\.

17\.

18\. Check child's drawing.

13. Circle the object shaped like a rectangular prism.
14. Mark X on the ten-frame that does NOT show 10.
15. Draw the correct number of counters to show 12.
16. Circle the dime.
17. Circle the coin that is worth 5¢.
18. Draw a line that is longer than the crayon.

Go On

Form B • Inventory Test — Assessment Guide AG7

© Harcourt

Name ____________________

INVENTORY TEST • PAGE 4

19\.

20\. first

21\. 4 + 2 = 6

22\. 6 − 1 = 5

23\. 4 + 1 = 5

24\. 5 − 2 = 3

25\. 5 + 1 = 6

19. Circle the clock that shows 3:00.
20. Circle the second shape.
21. Add.
22. Subtract.
23. Write the addition sentence that matches the picture.
24. Write the subtraction sentence that matches the picture.
25. Circle the picture that matches the number sentence.

Stop

AG8 Assessment Guide — Form B • Inventory Test

© Harcourt

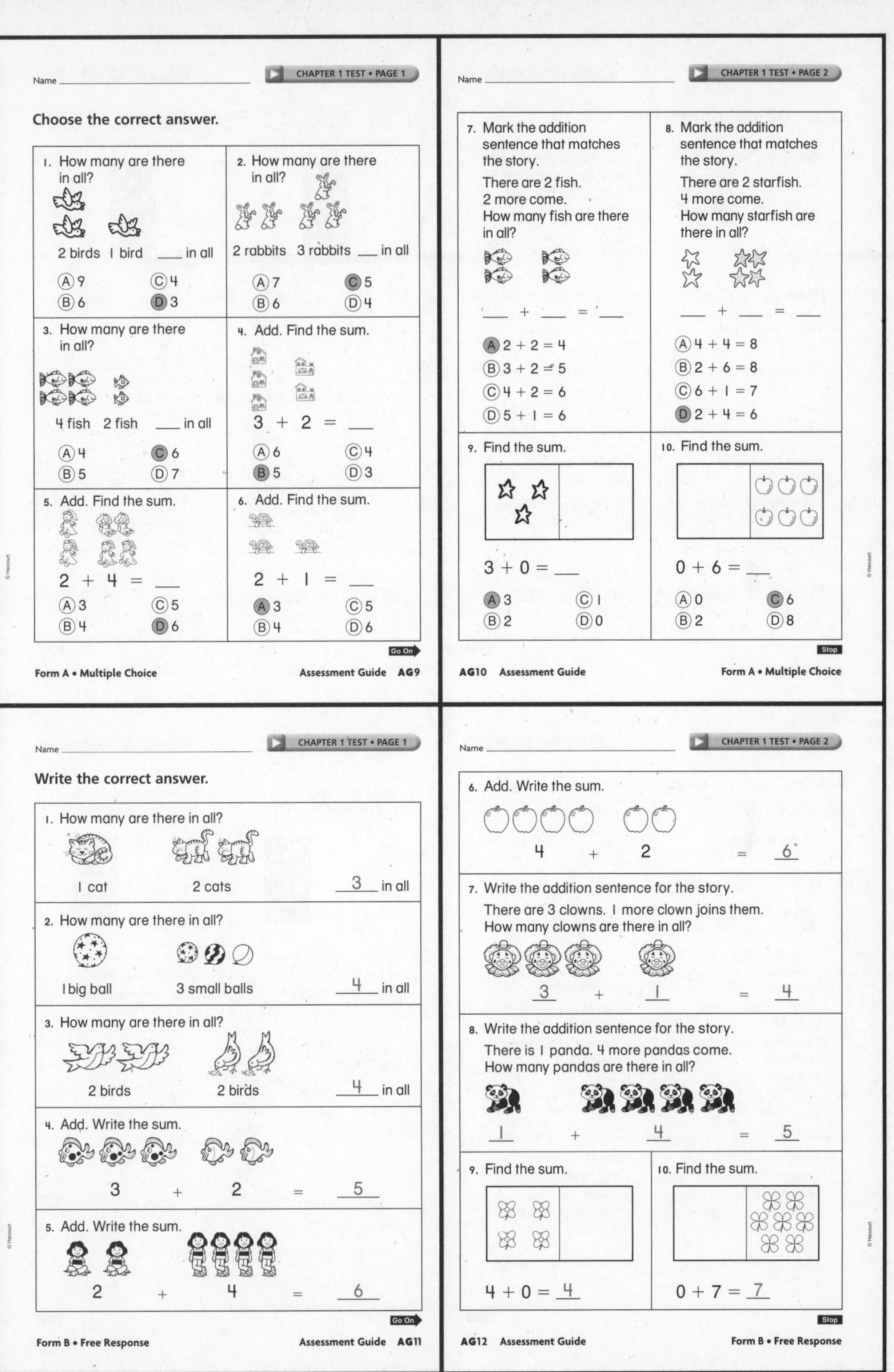

Name ____________ CHAPTER 1 TEST • PAGE 1

Choose the correct answer.

1. How many are there in all?
2 birds 1 bird ___ in all
(A) 9 (B) 6 (C) 4 **(D) 3**

2. How many are there in all?
2 rabbits 3 rabbits ___ in all
(A) 7 (B) 6 **(C) 5** (D) 4

3. How many are there in all?
4 fish 2 fish ___ in all
(A) 4 (B) 5 **(C) 6** (D) 7

4. Add. Find the sum.
3 + 2 = ___
(A) 6 **(B) 5** (C) 4 (D) 3

5. Add. Find the sum.
2 + 4 = ___
(A) 3 (B) 4 (C) 5 **(D) 6**

6. Add. Find the sum.
2 + 1 = ___
(A) 3 (B) 4 (C) 5 (D) 6

Go On

Form A • Multiple Choice Assessment Guide AG9

Name ____________ CHAPTER 1 TEST • PAGE 2

7. Mark the addition sentence that matches the story.
There are 2 fish.
2 more come.
How many fish are there in all?
___ + ___ = ___
(A) 2 + 2 = 4
(B) 3 + 2 = 5
(C) 4 + 2 = 6
(D) 5 + 1 = 6

8. Mark the addition sentence that matches the story.
There are 2 starfish.
4 more come.
How many starfish are there in all?
___ + ___ = ___
(A) 4 + 4 = 8
(B) 2 + 6 = 8
(C) 6 + 1 = 7
(D) 2 + 4 = 6

9. Find the sum.
3 + 0 = ___
(A) 3 (B) 2 (C) 1 (D) 0

10. Find the sum.
0 + 6 = ___
(A) 0 (B) 2 **(C) 6** (D) 8

Stop

AG10 Assessment Guide Form A • Multiple Choice

Name ____________ CHAPTER 1 TEST • PAGE 1

Write the correct answer.

1. How many are there in all?
1 cat 2 cats 3 in all

2. How many are there in all?
1 big ball 3 small balls 4 in all

3. How many are there in all?
2 birds 2 birds 4 in all

4. Add. Write the sum.
3 + 2 = 5

5. Add. Write the sum.
2 + 4 = 6

Go On

Form B • Free Response Assessment Guide AG11

Name ____________ CHAPTER 1 TEST • PAGE 2

6. Add. Write the sum.
4 + 2 = 6

7. Write the addition sentence for the story.
There are 3 clowns. 1 more clown joins them.
How many clowns are there in all?
3 + 1 = 4

8. Write the addition sentence for the story.
There is 1 panda. 4 more pandas come.
How many pandas are there in all?
1 + 4 = 5

9. Find the sum.
4 + 0 = 4

10. Find the sum.
0 + 7 = 7

Stop

AG12 Assessment Guide Form B • Free Response

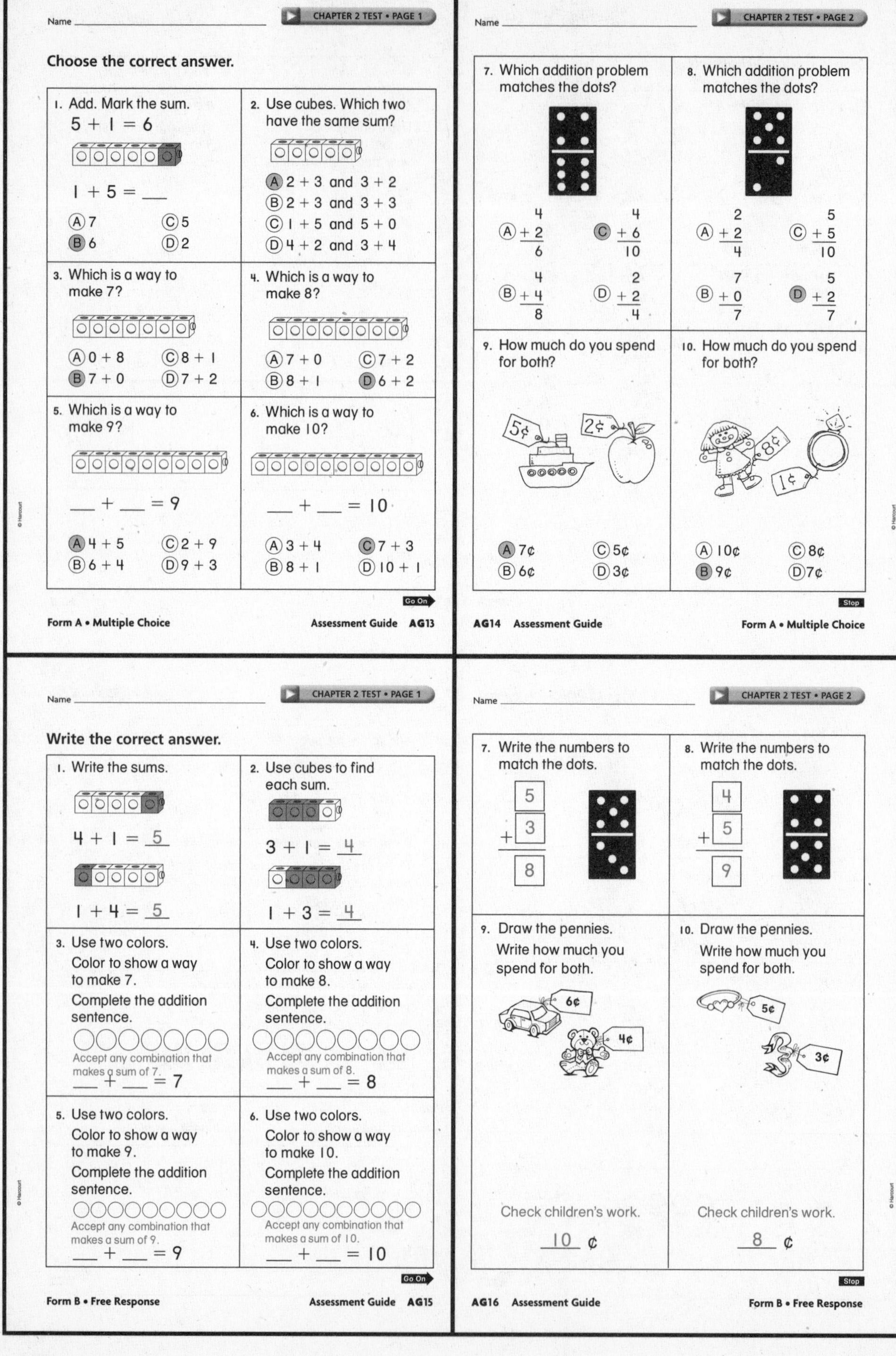

Name
CHAPTER 2 TEST • PAGE 1
Choose the correct answer.
1. Add. Mark the sum.
5 + 1 = 6
1 + 5 = ___
A 7 C 5
B 6 D 2
2. Use cubes. Which two have the same sum?
A 2 + 3 and 3 + 2
B 2 + 3 and 3 + 3
C 1 + 5 and 5 + 0
D 4 + 2 and 3 + 4
3. Which is a way to make 7?
A 0 + 8 C 8 + 1
B 7 + 0 D 7 + 2
4. Which is a way to make 8?
A 7 + 0 C 7 + 2
B 8 + 1 D 6 + 2
5. Which is a way to make 9?
___ + ___ = 9
A 4 + 5 C 2 + 9
B 6 + 4 D 9 + 3
6. Which is a way to make 10?
___ + ___ = 10
A 3 + 4 C 7 + 3
B 8 + 1 D 10 + 1
Go On
Form A • Multiple Choice
Assessment Guide AG13
Name
CHAPTER 2 TEST • PAGE 2
7. Which addition problem matches the dots?
A 4 + 2 = 6
C 4 + 6 = 10
B 4 + 4 = 8
D 2 + 2 = 4
8. Which addition problem matches the dots?
A 2 + 2 = 4
C 5 + 5 = 10
B 7 + 0 = 7
D 5 + 2 = 7
9. How much do you spend for both?
5¢
2¢
A 7¢ C 5¢
B 6¢ D 3¢
10. How much do you spend for both?
8¢
1¢
A 10¢ C 8¢
B 9¢ D 7¢
Stop
AG14 Assessment Guide
Form A • Multiple Choice
Name
CHAPTER 2 TEST • PAGE 1
Write the correct answer.
1. Write the sums.
4 + 1 = 5
1 + 4 = 5
2. Use cubes to find each sum.
3 + 1 = 4
1 + 3 = 4
3. Use two colors. Color to show a way to make 7. Complete the addition sentence.
Accept any combination that makes a sum of 7.
___ + ___ = 7
4. Use two colors. Color to show a way to make 8. Complete the addition sentence.
Accept any combination that makes a sum of 8.
___ + ___ = 8
5. Use two colors. Color to show a way to make 9. Complete the addition sentence.
Accept any combination that makes a sum of 9.
___ + ___ = 9
6. Use two colors. Color to show a way to make 10. Complete the addition sentence.
Accept any combination that makes a sum of 10.
___ + ___ = 10
Go On
Form B • Free Response
Assessment Guide AG15
Name
CHAPTER 2 TEST • PAGE 2
7. Write the numbers to match the dots.
5 + 3 = 8
8. Write the numbers to match the dots.
4 + 5 = 9
9. Draw the pennies. Write how much you spend for both.
6¢
4¢
Check children's work.
10 ¢
10. Draw the pennies. Write how much you spend for both.
5¢
3¢
Check children's work.
8 ¢
Stop
AG16 Assessment Guide
Form B • Free Response
© Harcourt

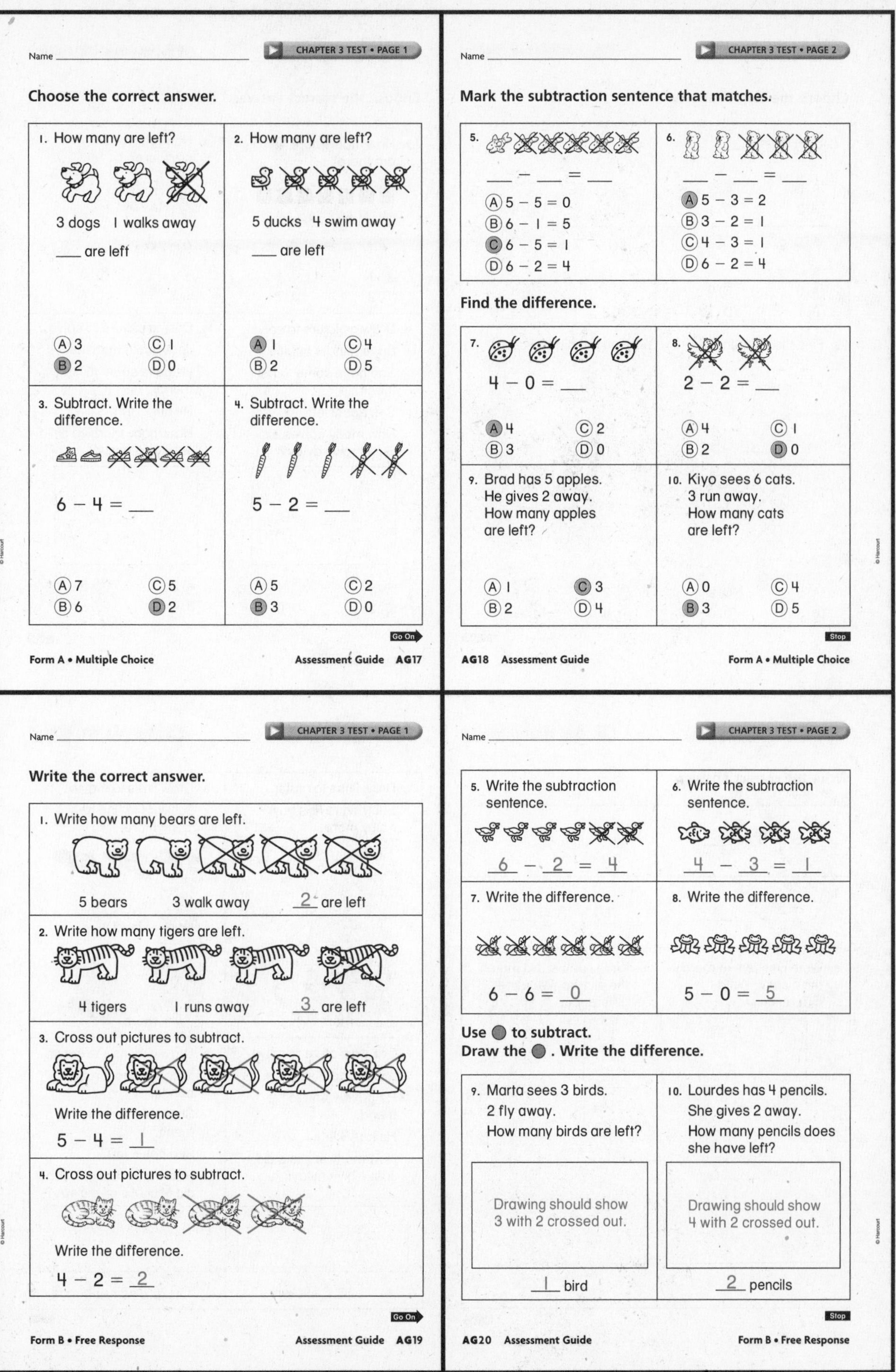

Name

CHAPTER 3 TEST • PAGE 1

Choose the correct answer.

1. How many are left?

3 dogs 1 walks away

___ are left

Ⓐ 3 Ⓒ 1
Ⓑ 2 Ⓓ 0

2. How many are left?

5 ducks 4 swim away

___ are left

Ⓐ 1 Ⓒ 4
Ⓑ 2 Ⓓ 5

3. Subtract. Write the difference.

6 − 4 = ___

Ⓐ 7 Ⓒ 5
Ⓑ 6 Ⓓ 2

4. Subtract. Write the difference.

5 − 2 = ___

Ⓐ 5 Ⓒ 2
Ⓑ 3 Ⓓ 0

Go On

Form A • Multiple Choice — Assessment Guide AG17

Name

CHAPTER 3 TEST • PAGE 2

Mark the subtraction sentence that matches.

5. ___ − ___ = ___

Ⓐ 5 − 5 = 0
Ⓑ 6 − 1 = 5
Ⓒ 6 − 5 = 1
Ⓓ 6 − 2 = 4

6. ___ − ___ = ___

Ⓐ 5 − 3 = 2
Ⓑ 3 − 2 = 1
Ⓒ 4 − 3 = 1
Ⓓ 6 − 2 = 4

Find the difference.

7. 4 − 0 = ___

Ⓐ 4 Ⓒ 2
Ⓑ 3 Ⓓ 0

8. 2 − 2 = ___

Ⓐ 4 Ⓒ 1
Ⓑ 2 Ⓓ 0

9. Brad has 5 apples. He gives 2 away. How many apples are left?

Ⓐ 1 Ⓒ 3
Ⓑ 2 Ⓓ 4

10. Kiyo sees 6 cats. 3 run away. How many cats are left?

Ⓐ 0 Ⓒ 4
Ⓑ 3 Ⓓ 5

Stop

AG18 Assessment Guide — Form A • Multiple Choice

Name

CHAPTER 3 TEST • PAGE 1

Write the correct answer.

1. Write how many bears are left.

5 bears 3 walk away 2 are left

2. Write how many tigers are left.

4 tigers 1 runs away 3 are left

3. Cross out pictures to subtract.

Write the difference.

5 − 4 = 1

4. Cross out pictures to subtract.

Write the difference.

4 − 2 = 2

Go On

Form B • Free Response — Assessment Guide AG19

Name

CHAPTER 3 TEST • PAGE 2

5. Write the subtraction sentence.

6 − 2 = 4

6. Write the subtraction sentence.

4 − 3 = 1

7. Write the difference.

6 − 6 = 0

8. Write the difference.

5 − 0 = 5

Use ● to subtract.
Draw the ●. Write the difference.

9. Marta sees 3 birds. 2 fly away. How many birds are left?

Drawing should show 3 with 2 crossed out.

1 bird

10. Lourdes has 4 pencils. She gives 2 away. How many pencils does she have left?

Drawing should show 4 with 2 crossed out.

2 pencils

Stop

AG20 Assessment Guide — Form B • Free Response

Name ______________________ CHAPTER 4 TEST • PAGE 1

Choose the correct answer.

1. 8 − 6 = ___ Ⓐ 6 Ⓑ 3 Ⓒ 2 Ⓓ 1	2. 7 − 3 = ___ Ⓐ 1 Ⓑ 2 Ⓒ 3 Ⓓ 4
3. 9 − 9 = ___ Ⓐ 0 Ⓑ 1 Ⓒ 9 Ⓓ 10	4. 10 − 7 = ___ Ⓐ 1 Ⓑ 2 Ⓒ 3 Ⓓ 4
5. Find the difference. 5 −3 □ Ⓐ 5 Ⓑ 3 Ⓒ 2 Ⓓ 0	6. Find the difference. 6 −4 □ Ⓐ 2 Ⓑ 4 Ⓒ 6 Ⓓ 10

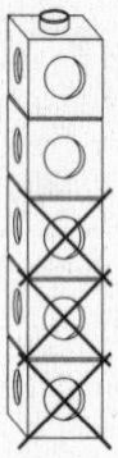

Go On

Name ______________________ CHAPTER 4 TEST • PAGE 2

Choose the correct answer.

7. How many more ■ are there? 7 − 6 = ___ Ⓐ 1 Ⓑ 2 Ⓒ 6 Ⓓ 7	8. How many more are there? 6 − 3 = ___ Ⓐ 1 Ⓑ 2 Ⓒ 3 Ⓓ 6
9. Draw a picture to solve. Susan had 4 apples. She gave some to her friend. She has 2 left. How many apples did Susan give away? Ⓐ 4 Ⓑ 2 Ⓒ 1 Ⓓ 0	10. Draw a picture to solve. Jack had 8 marbles. He gave some to his friend. He has 3 left. How many marbles did Jack give away? Ⓐ 2 Ⓑ 4 Ⓒ 5 Ⓓ 6

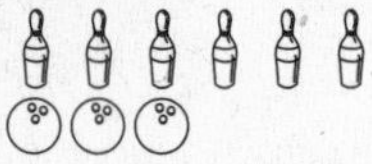

Stop

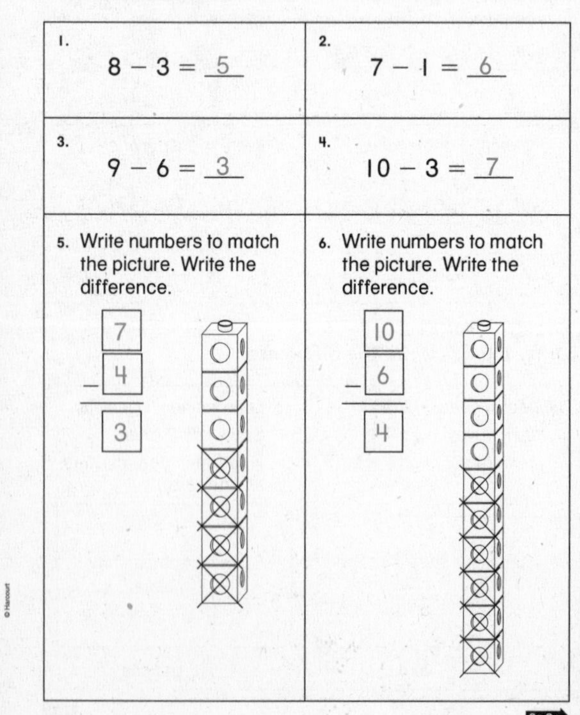
Name ______________________ CHAPTER 4 TEST • PAGE 1

Write the correct answer.

1. 8 − 3 = 5	2. 7 − 1 = 6
3. 9 − 6 = 3	4. 10 − 3 = 7
5. Write numbers to match the picture. Write the difference. 7 − 4 3	6. Write numbers to match the picture. Write the difference. 10 − 6 4

Go On

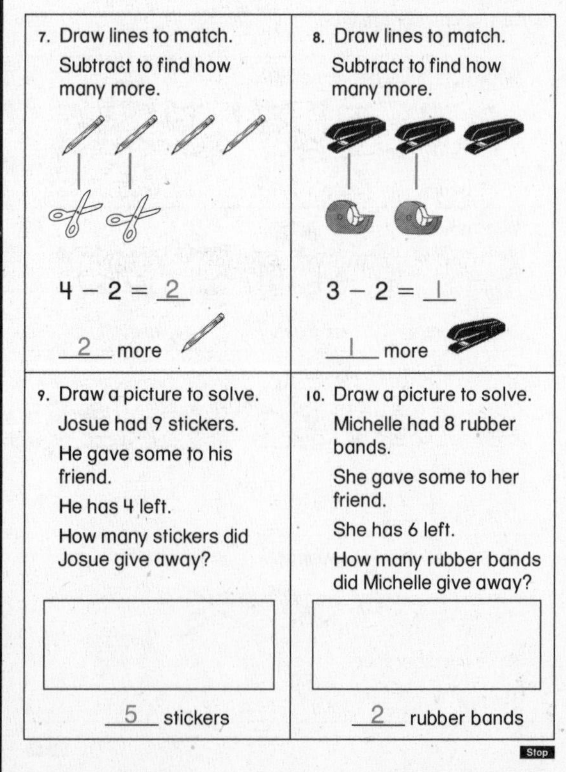
Name ______________________ CHAPTER 4 TEST • PAGE 2

7. Draw lines to match. Subtract to find how many more. 4 − 2 = 2 2 more	8. Draw lines to match. Subtract to find how many more. 3 − 2 = 1 1 more
9. Draw a picture to solve. Josue had 9 stickers. He gave some to his friend. He has 4 left. How many stickers did Josue give away? 5 stickers	10. Draw a picture to solve. Michelle had 8 rubber bands. She gave some to her friend. She has 6 left. How many rubber bands did Michelle give away? 2 rubber bands

Stop

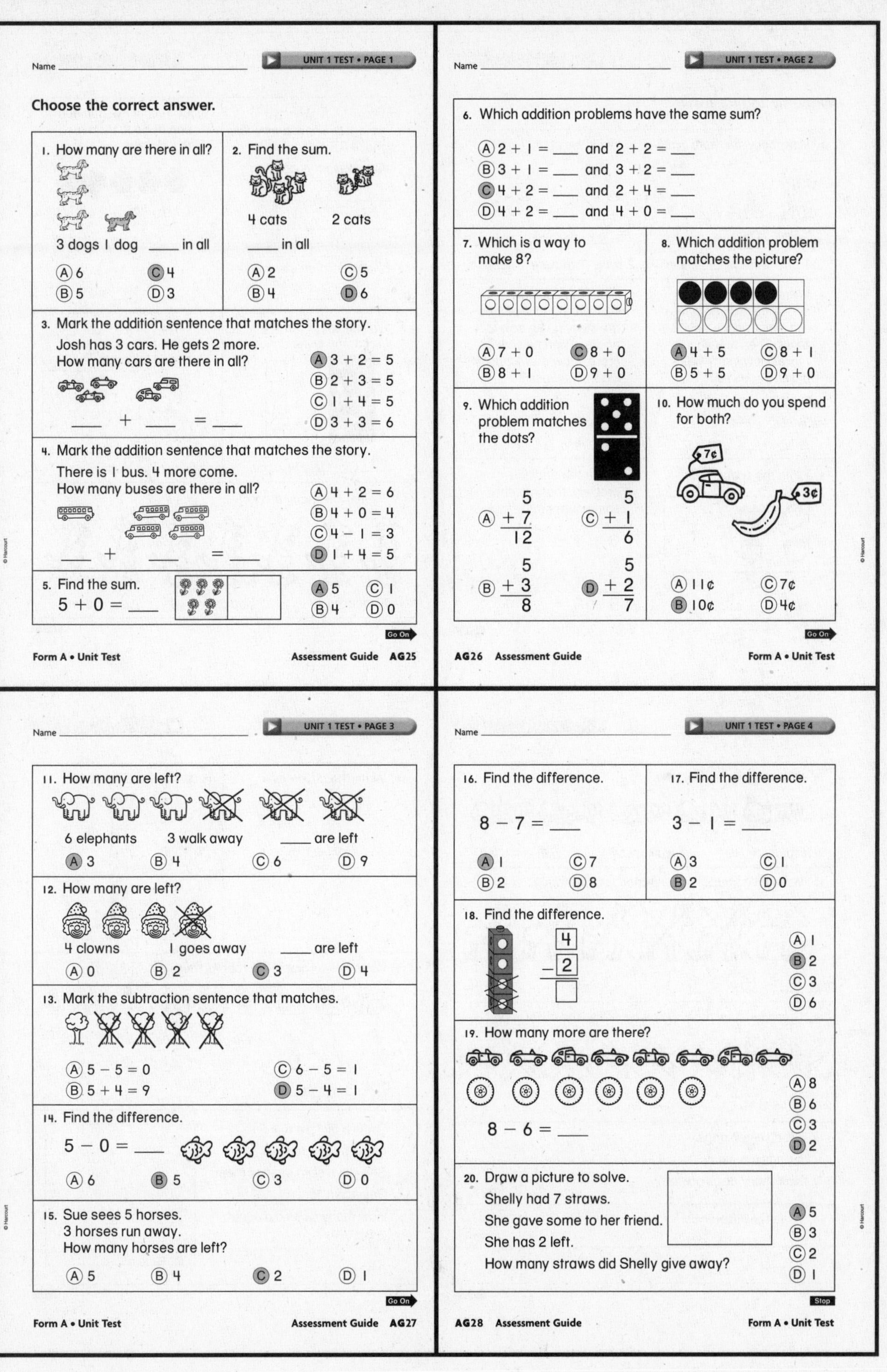

Name ____________ UNIT 1 TEST • PAGE 1

Choose the correct answer.

1. How many are there in all?

3 dogs 1 dog ____ in all

Ⓐ 6 Ⓑ 5 Ⓒ 4 Ⓓ 3

2. Find the sum.

4 cats 2 cats

____ in all

Ⓐ 2 Ⓑ 4 Ⓒ 5 Ⓓ 6

3. Mark the addition sentence that matches the story.

Josh has 3 cars. He gets 2 more.
How many cars are there in all?

____ + ____ = ____

Ⓐ $3 + 2 = 5$
Ⓑ $2 + 3 = 5$
Ⓒ $1 + 4 = 5$
Ⓓ $3 + 3 = 6$

4. Mark the addition sentence that matches the story.

There is 1 bus. 4 more come.
How many buses are there in all?

____ + ____ = ____

Ⓐ $4 + 2 = 6$
Ⓑ $4 + 0 = 4$
Ⓒ $4 - 1 = 3$
Ⓓ $1 + 4 = 5$

5. Find the sum.

$5 + 0 =$ ____

Ⓐ 5 Ⓑ 4 Ⓒ 1 Ⓓ 0

Go On

Form A • Unit Test Assessment Guide AG25

Name ____________ UNIT 1 TEST • PAGE 2

6. Which addition problems have the same sum?

Ⓐ $2 + 1 =$ ____ and $2 + 2 =$ ____
Ⓑ $3 + 1 =$ ____ and $3 + 2 =$ ____
Ⓒ $4 + 2 =$ ____ and $2 + 4 =$ ____
Ⓓ $4 + 2 =$ ____ and $4 + 0 =$ ____

7. Which is a way to make 8?

Ⓐ $7 + 0$ Ⓑ $8 + 1$ Ⓒ $8 + 0$ Ⓓ $9 + 0$

8. Which addition problem matches the picture?

Ⓐ $4 + 5$ Ⓑ $5 + 5$ Ⓒ $8 + 1$ Ⓓ $9 + 0$

9. Which addition problem matches the dots?

Ⓐ $5 + 7 = 12$
Ⓑ $5 + 3 = 8$
Ⓒ $5 + 1 = 6$
Ⓓ $5 + 2 = 7$

10. How much do you spend for both?

7¢ 3¢

Ⓐ 11¢ Ⓑ 10¢ Ⓒ 7¢ Ⓓ 4¢

Go On

AG26 Assessment Guide Form A • Unit Test

Name ____________ UNIT 1 TEST • PAGE 3

11. How many are left?

6 elephants 3 walk away ____ are left

Ⓐ 3 Ⓑ 4 Ⓒ 6 Ⓓ 9

12. How many are left?

4 clowns 1 goes away ____ are left

Ⓐ 0 Ⓑ 2 Ⓒ 3 Ⓓ 4

13. Mark the subtraction sentence that matches.

Ⓐ $5 - 5 = 0$
Ⓑ $5 + 4 = 9$
Ⓒ $6 - 5 = 1$
Ⓓ $5 - 4 = 1$

14. Find the difference.

$5 - 0 =$ ____

Ⓐ 6 Ⓑ 5 Ⓒ 3 Ⓓ 0

15. Sue sees 5 horses.
3 horses run away.
How many horses are left?

Ⓐ 5 Ⓑ 4 Ⓒ 2 Ⓓ 1

Go On

Form A • Unit Test Assessment Guide AG27

Name ____________ UNIT 1 TEST • PAGE 4

16. Find the difference.

$8 - 7 =$ ____

Ⓐ 1 Ⓑ 2 Ⓒ 7 Ⓓ 8

17. Find the difference.

$3 - 1 =$ ____

Ⓐ 3 Ⓑ 2 Ⓒ 1 Ⓓ 0

18. Find the difference.

$4 - 2 =$ ☐

Ⓐ 1 Ⓑ 2 Ⓒ 3 Ⓓ 6

19. How many more are there?

$8 - 6 =$ ____

Ⓐ 8 Ⓑ 6 Ⓒ 3 Ⓓ 2

20. Draw a picture to solve.
Shelly had 7 straws.
She gave some to her friend.
She has 2 left.
How many straws did Shelly give away?

Ⓐ 5 Ⓑ 3 Ⓒ 2 Ⓓ 1

Stop

AG28 Assessment Guide Form A • Unit Test

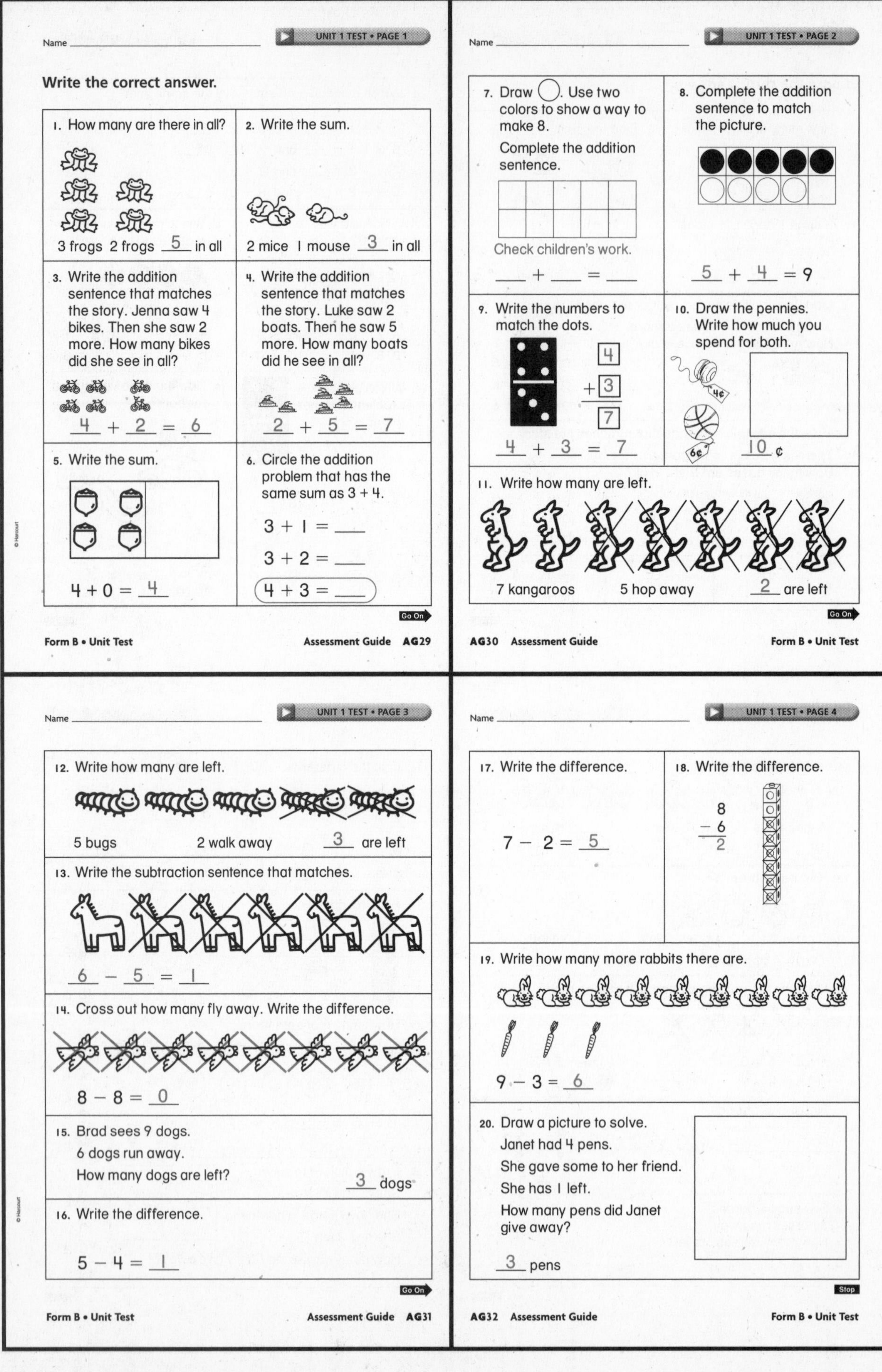

Name ______ UNIT 1 TEST • PAGE 1

Write the correct answer.

1. How many are there in all?
3 frogs 2 frogs 5 in all

2. Write the sum.
2 mice 1 mouse 3 in all

3. Write the addition sentence that matches the story. Jenna saw 4 bikes. Then she saw 2 more. How many bikes did she see in all?
4 + 2 = 6

4. Write the addition sentence that matches the story. Luke saw 2 boats. Then he saw 5 more. How many boats did he see in all?
2 + 5 = 7

5. Write the sum.
4 + 0 = 4

6. Circle the addition problem that has the same sum as 3 + 4.
3 + 1 = ___
3 + 2 = ___
(4 + 3 = ___)

Go On

Form B • Unit Test Assessment Guide AG29

Name ______ UNIT 1 TEST • PAGE 2

7. Draw ◯. Use two colors to show a way to make 8. Complete the addition sentence.
Check children's work.
___ + ___ = ___

8. Complete the addition sentence to match the picture.
5 + 4 = 9

9. Write the numbers to match the dots.
4
+3
7
4 + 3 = 7

10. Draw the pennies. Write how much you spend for both.
4¢
6¢
10 ¢

11. Write how many are left.
7 kangaroos 5 hop away 2 are left

Go On

AG30 Assessment Guide Form B • Unit Test

Name ______ UNIT 1 TEST • PAGE 3

12. Write how many are left.
5 bugs 2 walk away 3 are left

13. Write the subtraction sentence that matches.
6 − 5 = 1

14. Cross out how many fly away. Write the difference.
8 − 8 = 0

15. Brad sees 9 dogs.
6 dogs run away.
How many dogs are left?
3 dogs

16. Write the difference.
5 − 4 = 1

Go On

Form B • Unit Test Assessment Guide AG31

Name ______ UNIT 1 TEST • PAGE 4

17. Write the difference.
7 − 2 = 5

18. Write the difference.
8
− 6
2

19. Write how many more rabbits there are.
9 − 3 = 6

20. Draw a picture to solve.
Janet had 4 pens.
She gave some to her friend.
She has 1 left.
How many pens did Janet give away?
3 pens

Stop

AG32 Assessment Guide Form B • Unit Test

Name ____________________

CHAPTER 5 TEST • PAGE 1

Choose the correct answer.

1. Add.

$$\begin{array}{r} 2 \\ +\,2 \\ \hline \end{array}$$

Ⓐ 2 **Ⓒ 4**
Ⓑ 3 Ⓓ 5

2. Count on. Find the sum.

$$\begin{array}{r} 3 \\ +\,1 \\ \hline \end{array}$$

Ⓐ 13 Ⓒ 3
Ⓑ 4 Ⓓ 2

3. Count on. Find the sum.

$$\begin{array}{r} 7 \\ +\,1 \\ \hline \end{array}$$

Ⓐ 6 **Ⓒ 8**
Ⓑ 7 Ⓓ 17

4. Count on. Find the sum.

$$\begin{array}{r} 5 \\ +\,2 \\ \hline \end{array}$$

Ⓐ 6 Ⓒ 8
Ⓑ 7 Ⓓ 9

5. Add.

$$\begin{array}{r} 3 \\ +\,3 \\ \hline \end{array}$$

Ⓐ 3 Ⓒ 8
Ⓑ 6 Ⓓ 9

6. Add.

$$\begin{array}{r} 5 \\ +\,5 \\ \hline \end{array}$$

Ⓐ 5 **Ⓒ 10**
Ⓑ 9 Ⓓ 11

Go On

Name ____________________

CHAPTER 5 TEST • PAGE 2

7. Use the number line. Count on to find the sum.

$$\begin{array}{r} 6 \\ +\,3 \\ \hline \end{array}$$

Ⓐ 10 Ⓒ 8
Ⓑ 9 Ⓓ 7

8. Use the number line. Count on to find the sum.

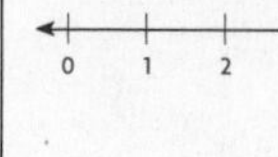

$$\begin{array}{r} 3 \\ +\,2 \\ \hline \end{array}$$

Ⓐ 5 Ⓒ 3
Ⓑ 4 Ⓓ 2

9. Choose the addition sentence that goes with the picture.

Ⓐ 6 − 3 = 3
Ⓑ 6 + 3 = 9
Ⓒ 6 + 4 = 10
Ⓓ 5 + 3 = 8

10. Choose the addition sentence that goes with the story.

There are 2 plates.
There are 5 🍒 on each plate.
How many 🍒 are there?

Ⓐ 5 + 5 = 10
Ⓑ 5 + 1 = 6
Ⓒ 5 + 0 = 5
Ⓓ 5 − 5 = 0

Stop

Name ____________________

CHAPTER 5 TEST • PAGE 1

Write the correct answer.

1. Add.

$$\begin{array}{r} 4 \\ +\,4 \\ \hline 8 \end{array}$$

2. Count on. Write the sum.

$$\begin{array}{r} 3 \\ +\,2 \\ \hline 5 \end{array}$$

3. Count on. Write the sum.

$$\begin{array}{r} 4 \\ +\,2 \\ \hline 6 \end{array}$$

4. Count on. Write the sum.

$$\begin{array}{r} 6 \\ +\,2 \\ \hline 8 \end{array}$$

5. Add.

$$\begin{array}{r} 1 \\ +\,1 \\ \hline 2 \end{array}$$

6. Add.

$$\begin{array}{r} 3 \\ +\,3 \\ \hline 6 \end{array}$$

Go On

Name ____________________

CHAPTER 5 TEST • PAGE 2

7. Use the number line. Count on to find the sum.

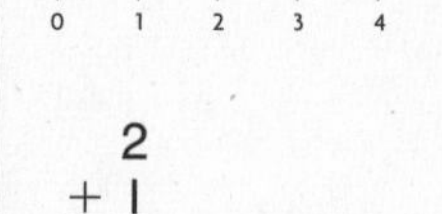

$$\begin{array}{r} 2 \\ +\,1 \\ \hline 3 \end{array}$$

8. Use the number line. Count on to find the sum.

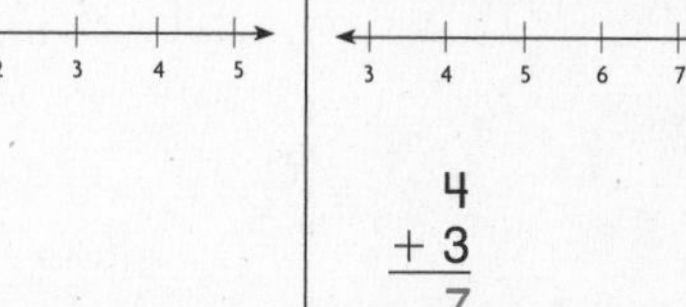

$$\begin{array}{r} 4 \\ +\,3 \\ \hline 7 \end{array}$$

9. Draw a picture to solve. Then write the addition sentence that matches the story.

There are 2 🐒.
4 🐒 come.
How many 🐒 are there?

2 + 4 = 6

10. Draw a picture to solve. Then write the addition sentence that matches the story.

There are 2 🍐 on a plate.
There are 2 🍐 on another plate.
How many 🍐 are there?

2 + 2 = 4

Stop

Name ____________

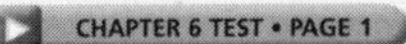

Choose the correct answer.

1. $8 + 2$

Ⓐ 10 Ⓑ 9 Ⓒ 6 Ⓓ 0

2. $5 + 1$

Ⓐ 4 Ⓑ 5 **Ⓒ 6** Ⓓ 7

3. Choose the new fact.

$6 + 3 = 9$ $\quad 3 + 6$

Ⓐ 3 Ⓑ 6 Ⓒ 7 **Ⓓ 9**

4. $4 + 4$

Ⓐ 4 Ⓑ 6 **Ⓒ 8** Ⓓ 10

5. Choose the new fact.

$4 + 3 = 7$ $\quad 3 + 4$

Ⓐ 1 Ⓑ 5 **Ⓒ 7** Ⓓ 9

6. $4 + 1$

Ⓐ 3 **Ⓑ 5** Ⓒ 6 Ⓓ 8

Go On

Name ____________

CHAPTER 6 TEST • PAGE 2

Complete the table.
Follow the rule.

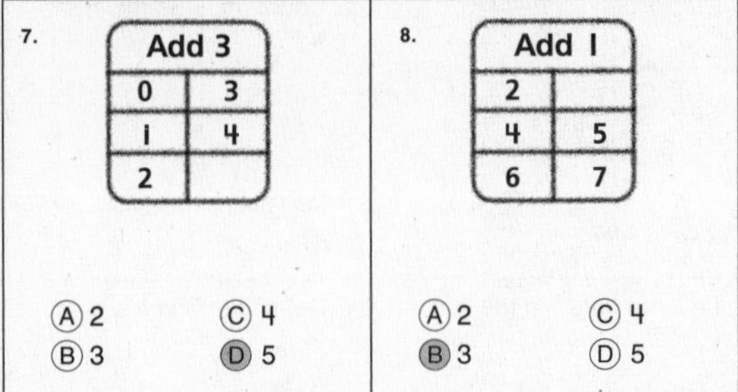

7.

Add 3	
0	3
1	4
2	

Ⓐ 2 Ⓑ 3 Ⓒ 4 **Ⓓ 5**

8.

Add 1	
2	
4	5
6	7

Ⓐ 2 **Ⓑ 3** Ⓒ 4 Ⓓ 5

Choose the correct number sentence to solve the problem.

9. There are 3 red cars. There are 2 blue cars. How many cars are there in all?

Ⓐ $3 + 2 = 5$
Ⓑ $3 - 2 = 1$
Ⓒ $5 + 2 = 7$
Ⓓ $5 + 0 = 5$

10. There are 6 dogs. 4 more come. How many dogs are there in all?

Ⓐ $6 - 4 = 2$
Ⓑ $6 + 0 = 6$
Ⓒ $6 + 3 = 9$
Ⓓ $6 + 4 = 10$

Stop

Name ____________

CHAPTER 6 TEST • PAGE 1

Write the correct answer.

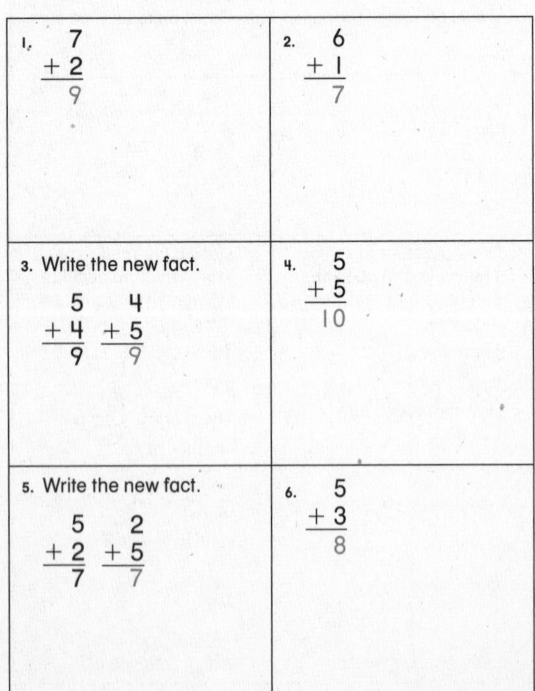

1. $7 + 2 = 9$

2. $6 + 1 = 7$

3. Write the new fact.

$5 + 4 = 9$ $\quad 4 + 5 = 9$

4. $5 + 5 = 10$

5. Write the new fact.

$5 + 2 = 7$ $\quad 2 + 5 = 7$

6. $5 + 3 = 8$

Go On

Name ____________

7. Complete the table. Follow the rule.

Add 0	
1	1
2	2
3	3

8. Complete the table. Follow the rule.

Add 2	
4	6
6	8
8	10

9. Solve. Write the number sentence that matches the story. Draw a picture to check.

Sue has 4 chicks. 2 more chicks come. How many chicks are there in all?

$4 + 2 = 6$

10. Solve. Write the number sentence that matches the story. Draw a picture to check.

There are 5 big birds. 3 little birds come. How many birds are there in all?

$5 + 3 = 8$

Stop

Name ____________ CHAPTER 7 TEST • PAGE 1

Choose the correct answer.

1. Use the number line. Count back to subtract.

0 1 2 3 4 5

2 − 1 = ___

Ⓐ 0 Ⓑ 1 Ⓒ 2 Ⓓ 3

2. Use the related addition fact to find the difference.

7 + 2 = 9

9 − 2 = ___

Ⓐ 9 Ⓑ 7 Ⓒ 2 Ⓓ 1

Count back to subtract.

3. 0 1 2 3 4 5

$5 - 3$

Ⓐ 2 Ⓑ 3 Ⓒ 4 Ⓓ 5

4. 0 1 2 3 4 5

$4 - 2$

Ⓐ 1 Ⓑ 2 Ⓒ 3 Ⓓ 6

5. $9 - 3$

Ⓐ 3 Ⓑ 4 Ⓒ 5 Ⓓ 6

6. $6 - 1$

Ⓐ 5 Ⓑ 6 Ⓒ 7 Ⓓ 10

Go On

Name ____________ CHAPTER 7 TEST • PAGE 2

7. Subtract.

$3 - 2$

Ⓐ 5 Ⓑ 3 Ⓒ 2 Ⓓ 1

8. Use the related addition fact to find the difference.

$5 + 4 = 9$ $9 - 4$

Ⓐ 9 Ⓑ 7 Ⓒ 5 Ⓓ 4

9. Use the picture to solve the problem.
There were 8 mice.
Some of the mice went in a hole.
Now there are 5 mice left.
How many mice went inside the hole?

Ⓐ 8 Ⓑ 5 Ⓒ 4 Ⓓ 3

10. Use the picture to solve the problem.
There were 10 children.
Some of the children got on a bus.
Now there are 4 children left.
How many children got on the bus?

Ⓐ 4 Ⓑ 5 Ⓒ 6 Ⓓ 7

Stop

Name ____________ CHAPTER 7 TEST • PAGE 1

Write the correct answer.

1. Use the number line. Count back to subtract.

0 1 2 3 4 5

$4 - 1 = 3$

2. Use the related addition fact to find the difference.

3 + 5 = 8

8 − 3 = 5

3. Count back to subtract.

$6 - 3 = 3$

4. Count back to subtract.

$5 - 2 = 3$

5. Count back to subtract.

$7 - 3 = 4$

6. Count back to subtract.

$7 - 1 = 6$

Go On

Name ____________ CHAPTER 7 TEST • PAGE 2

7. Subtract.

$8 - 2 = 6$

8. Use the related addition fact to find the difference.

$8 + 1 = 9$ $9 - 1 = 8$

9. Use the picture to solve the problem.
There were 7 worms inching along.
Some worms went inside an apple.
Now there are 4 left.

How many worms went inside the apple?

3 worms

10. Use the picture to solve the problem.
There were 9 children inside the house.
Some children went outside to play.
Now there are 5 left.

How many children went outside to play?

4 children

Stop

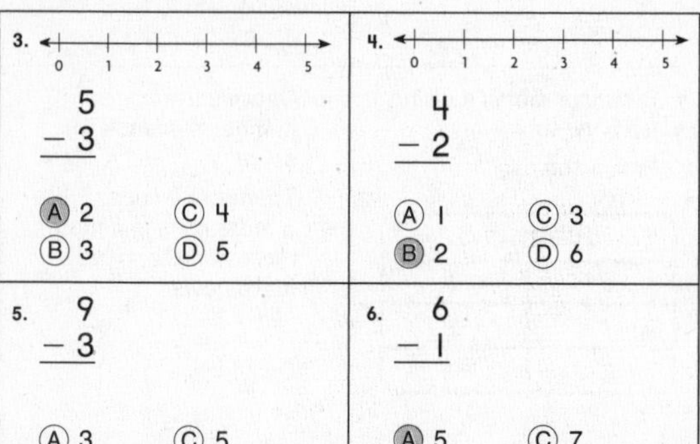

Name ________________ CHAPTER 8 TEST • PAGE 1

Choose the correct answer.

1. $\begin{array}{r} 1 \\ -\ 1 \\ \hline \end{array}$ Ⓐ 0 Ⓒ 2 Ⓑ 1 Ⓓ 3	2. $\begin{array}{r} 2 \\ -\ 0 \\ \hline \end{array}$ Ⓐ 0 Ⓒ 2 Ⓑ 1 Ⓓ 3
3. $\begin{array}{r} 3 \\ -\ 1 \\ \hline \end{array}$ Ⓐ 0 Ⓒ 2 Ⓑ 1 Ⓓ 3	4. $\begin{array}{r} 10 \\ -\ 7 \\ \hline \end{array}$ Ⓐ 0 Ⓒ 2 Ⓑ 1 Ⓓ 3
5. $\begin{array}{r} 5 \\ -\ 3 \\ \hline \end{array}$ Ⓐ 1 Ⓒ 3 Ⓑ 2 Ⓓ 4	6. Find the missing number. 8 − 5 = ◯ 8 − ◯ = 5 Ⓐ 3 Ⓒ 5 Ⓑ 4 Ⓓ 7

Go On

Name ________________ CHAPTER 8 TEST • PAGE 2

7. Subtract. $\begin{array}{r} 9 \\ -\ 7 \\ \hline \end{array}$ Ⓐ 1 Ⓑ 2 Ⓒ 3 Ⓓ 4	8. Which number sentence finishes the fact family? 5 + 4 = 9 4 + 5 = 9 9 − 5 = 4 Ⓐ 9 − 4 = 5 Ⓑ 8 − 3 = 5 Ⓒ 10 − 6 = 4 Ⓓ 8 − 4 = 4
9. What number is missing from the table? Follow the rule. **Subtract 5** 6	1 7	2 8	 Ⓐ 0 Ⓒ 4 Ⓑ 3 Ⓓ 5	10. Choose the correct number sentence to solve. There are 6 lions. 3 more lions join them. How many lions are there now? Ⓐ 6 − 3 = 3 Ⓑ 6 − 4 = 2 Ⓒ 6 + 1 = 7 Ⓓ 6 + 3 = 9

Stop

Name ________________ CHAPTER 8 TEST • PAGE 1

Write the correct answer.
Subtract to find the difference.

1. $\begin{array}{r} 4 \\ -\ 1 \\ \hline 3 \end{array}$	2. $\begin{array}{r} 5 \\ -\ 0 \\ \hline 5 \end{array}$
3. $\begin{array}{r} 4 \\ -\ 2 \\ \hline 2 \end{array}$	4. $\begin{array}{r} 10 \\ -\ 9 \\ \hline 1 \end{array}$
5. $\begin{array}{r} 9 \\ -\ 5 \\ \hline 4 \end{array}$	6. Write the missing number in the circles. 7 − 4 = ③ 7 − ③ = 4

Go On

Name ________________ CHAPTER 8 TEST • PAGE 2

7. Subtract. $\begin{array}{r} 9 \\ -\ 3 \\ \hline 6 \end{array}$	8. Write the number sentence that finishes the fact family. 2 + 5 = 7 5 + 2 = 7 7 − 5 = 2 7 − 2 = 5
9. Complete the table. Follow the rule. 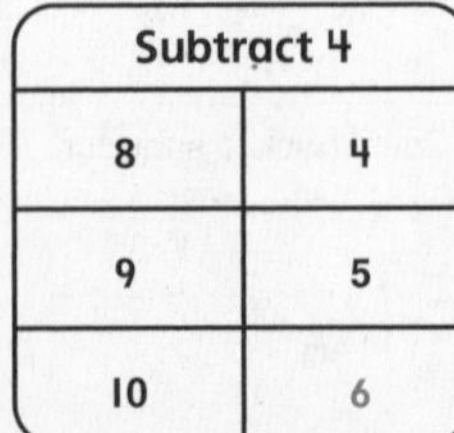 **Subtract 4** 8	4 9	5 10	6	10. Solve. Write the number sentence.  There are 3 bears. 7 more bears join them. How many bears are there now? 3 ⊕ 7 ⊜ 10

Stop

Name ______________________ UNIT 2 TEST • PAGE 1

Choose the correct answer. Add or subtract.

1. $2 + 3 =$ ___

Ⓐ 2 Ⓑ 3 Ⓒ 4 Ⓓ 5

2. $5 + 2 =$ ___

Ⓐ 5 Ⓑ 6 Ⓒ 7 Ⓓ 8

3. $4 - 1 =$ ___

Ⓐ 1 Ⓑ 2 Ⓒ 3 Ⓓ 4

4. $9 - 3 =$ ___

Ⓐ 5 Ⓑ 6 Ⓒ 7 Ⓓ 8

5. $7 + 1 =$ ___

Ⓐ 9 Ⓑ 8 Ⓒ 7 Ⓓ 6

6. $8 - 2 =$ ___

Ⓐ 6 Ⓑ 7 Ⓒ 9 Ⓓ 10

Go On

Name ______________________ UNIT 2 TEST • PAGE 2

7. $5 + 5 =$ ___

Ⓐ 8 Ⓑ 9 Ⓒ 10 Ⓓ 11

8. $3 + 3 =$ ___

Ⓐ 7 Ⓑ 6 Ⓒ 5 Ⓓ 4

9. Which of these is a related subtraction fact for $2 + 7 = 9$?

Ⓐ $9 - 2 = 7$
Ⓑ $7 - 2 = 5$
Ⓒ $10 - 1 = 9$
Ⓓ $7 - 5 = 2$

10. $7 - 1 =$ ___

Ⓐ 5 Ⓑ 6 Ⓒ 7 Ⓓ 8

11. $8 - 6 = 2$
$8 - 2 =$ ___

Ⓐ 8 Ⓑ 6 Ⓒ 3 Ⓓ 0

12. Find the sums.

$$\begin{array}{r} 7 \\ +\,3 \\ \hline \end{array} \qquad \begin{array}{r} 3 \\ +\,7 \\ \hline \end{array}$$

Ⓐ 10 Ⓑ 9 Ⓒ 8 Ⓓ 7

Go On

Name ______________________ UNIT 2 TEST • PAGE 3

13. Complete the table. Follow the rule.

Add 4	
1	5
2	
3	7

Ⓐ 9 Ⓑ 8 Ⓒ 7 Ⓓ 6

14. Which number sentence finishes this fact family?

$5 + 4 = 9$
$9 - 4 = 5$
$4 + 5 = 9$

Ⓐ $9 - 6 = 3$
Ⓑ $5 - 4 = 1$
Ⓒ $3 + 6 = 9$
Ⓓ $9 - 5 = 4$

15. Complete the table. Follow the rule.

Subtract 3	
8	
6	3
5	2

Ⓐ 5 Ⓑ 4 Ⓒ 3 Ⓓ 2

16. Choose the correct number sentence to solve the problem.

Will has 4 mice.
Kate has 2 mice.
How many mice are there in all?

Ⓐ $4 - 2 = 2$
Ⓑ $4 + 0 = 4$
Ⓒ $4 + 2 = 6$
Ⓓ $4 + 4 = 8$

Go On

Name ______________________ UNIT 2 TEST • PAGE 4

17. What are the numbers in this fact family?

$3 + 1 = 4$	$4 - 3 = 1$
$1 + 3 = 4$	$4 - 1 = 3$

Ⓐ 1, 2, 3 Ⓑ 3, 4, 7 Ⓒ 1, 3, 5 Ⓓ 1, 3, 4

18. Use the picture to solve.

There were 9 bees.

Some bees went inside a hive.

Now there are 3 left.

How many bees went inside the hive?

Ⓐ 0 Ⓑ 3 Ⓒ 6 Ⓓ 9

19. Choose the number sentence that goes with the story.

Sam has 8 books.

He gives 4 books to Emma.

How many books does Sam have left?

Ⓐ $8 - 4 = 4$
Ⓑ $12 - 8 = 4$
Ⓒ $12 - 4 = 8$
Ⓓ $8 + 4 = 12$

20. Choose the number sentence that goes with the story.

There are 5 pears in a bowl.

Sue puts in 4 more pears.

How many pears are in the bowl?

Ⓐ $5 + 3 = 8$
Ⓑ $7 + 2 = 9$
Ⓒ $5 + 4 = 9$
Ⓓ $5 + 1 = 6$

Stop

Name

UNIT 2 TEST • PAGE 1

Write the correct answer. Add or subtract.

1. 6 + 2 = 8

2. 4 + 5 = 9

3. 5 − 1 = 4

4. 7 − 6 = 1

5. 8 + 1 = 9

6. 5 − 3 = 2

Go On

Name

UNIT 2 TEST • PAGE 2

7. 4 + 4 = 8

8. 2 + 2 = 4

9. Write a related subtraction fact.
3 + 5 = 8
8 − 5 = 3
or 8 − 3 = 5

10. 10 − 2 = 8

11. 9 − 1 = 8
9 − 8 = 1

12. Count on to find the sums.

$$\begin{array}{r} 2 \\ +\,5 \\ \hline 7 \end{array} \qquad \begin{array}{r} 5 \\ +\,2 \\ \hline 7 \end{array}$$

Go On

Name

UNIT 2 TEST • PAGE 3

13. Complete the table. Follow the rule.

Add 3	
1	4
2	5
3	6

14. Write the number sentence that finishes this fact family.
4 + 6 = 10
10 − 6 = 4
6 + 4 = 10
10 − 4 = 6

15. Complete the table. Follow the rule.

Subtract 2	
9	7
7	5
5	3

16. Write the number sentence that solves the problem.

Maria has 6 fish.
Raoul has 1 fish.
How many fish are there in all?
6 + 1 = 7

Go On

Name

UNIT 2 TEST • PAGE 4

17. Write the numbers in this fact family.
5 + 3 = 8
8 − 3 = 5
3 + 5 = 8
8 − 5 = 3
3, 5, 8

18. Use the picture to solve.
There were 8 bears.
Some bears went inside a cave.
Now 1 bear is left.
How many bears went inside the cave?

7 bears

19. Write a number sentence to solve.
Nick has 9 apples.
He gives 2 apples to Molly.
How many apples does Nick have left?

9 − 2 = 7

20. Write the addition sentence that solves the problem.
There are 6 bananas.
Matt brings 3 more bananas.
How many bananas are there now?
6 + 3 = 9

Stop

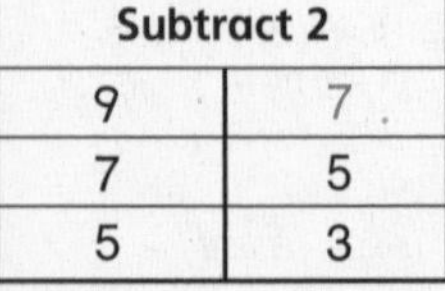

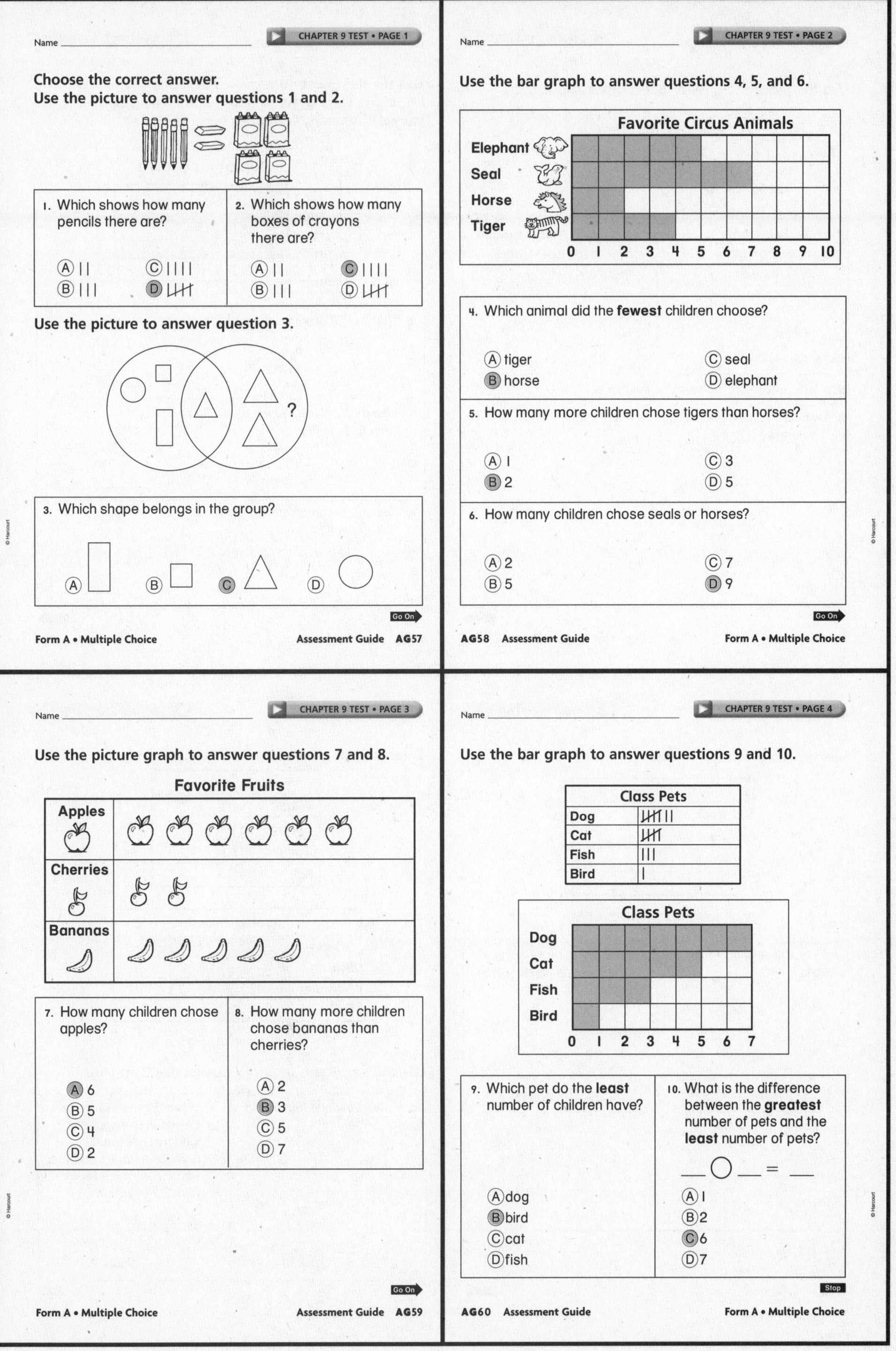

Name ______________________ CHAPTER 9 TEST • PAGE 1

Choose the correct answer.
Use the picture to answer questions 1 and 2.

1. Which shows how many pencils there are?
   Ⓐ || Ⓑ ||| Ⓒ |||| Ⓓ 𝍸

2. Which shows how many boxes of crayons there are?
   Ⓐ || Ⓑ ||| Ⓒ |||| Ⓓ 𝍸

Use the picture to answer question 3.

3. Which shape belongs in the group?
   Ⓐ Ⓑ Ⓒ Ⓓ

Go On

Form A • Multiple Choice   Assessment Guide AG57

Name ______________________ CHAPTER 9 TEST • PAGE 2

Use the bar graph to answer questions 4, 5, and 6.

Favorite Circus Animals

Elephant
Seal
Horse
Tiger
0 1 2 3 4 5 6 7 8 9 10

4. Which animal did the **fewest** children choose?
   Ⓐ tiger Ⓑ horse Ⓒ seal Ⓓ elephant

5. How many more children chose tigers than horses?
   Ⓐ 1 Ⓑ 2 Ⓒ 3 Ⓓ 5

6. How many children chose seals or horses?
   Ⓐ 2 Ⓑ 5 Ⓒ 7 Ⓓ 9

Go On

AG58 Assessment Guide   Form A • Multiple Choice

Name ______________________ CHAPTER 9 TEST • PAGE 3

Use the picture graph to answer questions 7 and 8.

Favorite Fruits

Apples
Cherries
Bananas

7. How many children chose apples?
   Ⓐ 6 Ⓑ 5 Ⓒ 4 Ⓓ 2

8. How many more children chose bananas than cherries?
   Ⓐ 2 Ⓑ 3 Ⓒ 5 Ⓓ 7

Go On

Form A • Multiple Choice   Assessment Guide AG59

Name ______________________ CHAPTER 9 TEST • PAGE 4

Use the bar graph to answer questions 9 and 10.

Class Pets	
Dog	𝍸 ||
Cat	𝍸
Fish	|||
Bird		

Class Pets

Dog
Cat
Fish
Bird
0 1 2 3 4 5 6 7

9. Which pet do the **least** number of children have?
   Ⓐ dog Ⓑ bird Ⓒ cat Ⓓ fish

10. What is the difference between the **greatest** number of pets and the **least** number of pets?
    ___ ◯ ___ = ___
    Ⓐ 1 Ⓑ 2 Ⓒ 6 Ⓓ 7

Stop

AG60 Assessment Guide   Form A • Multiple Choice

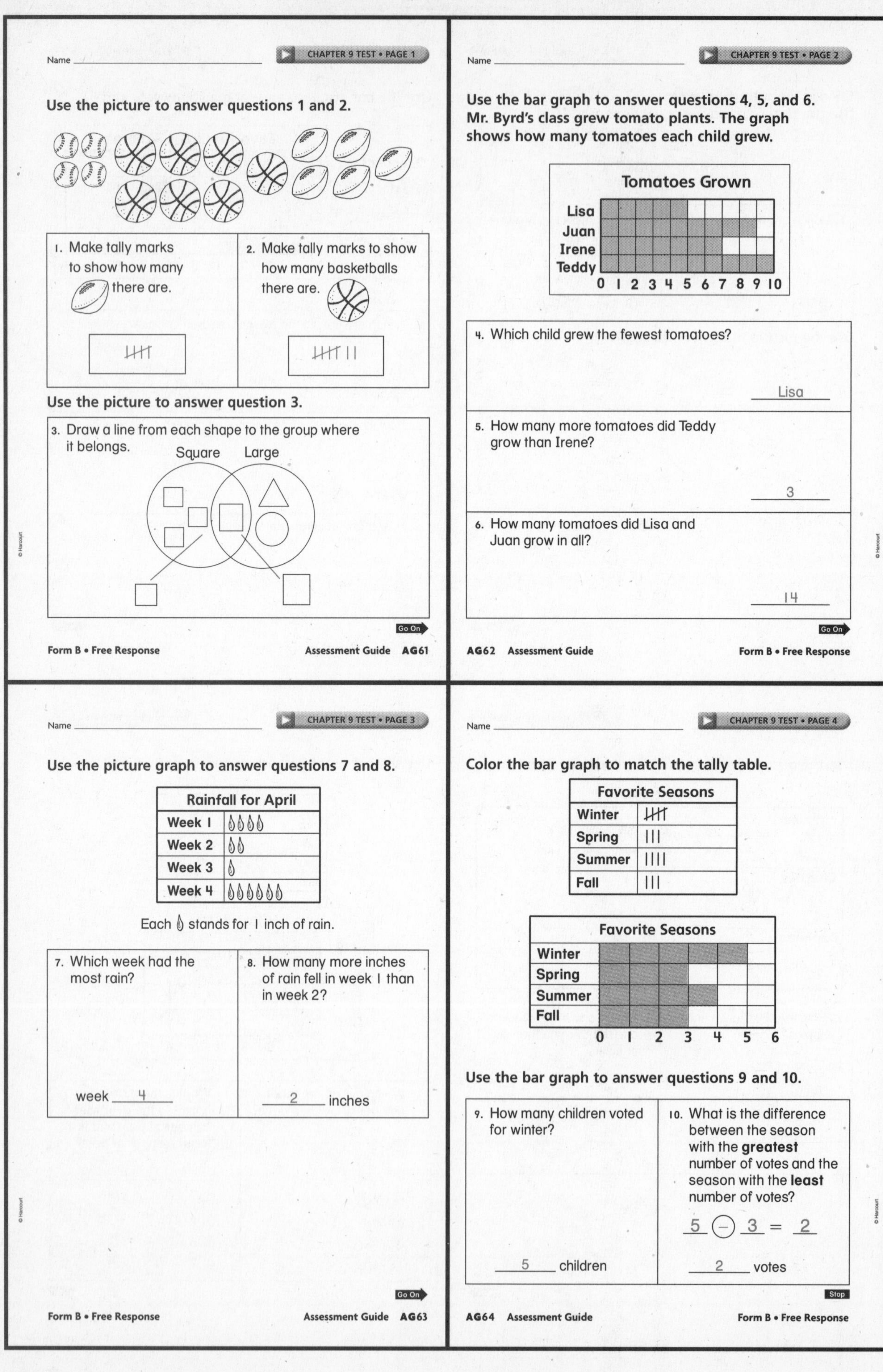

Name ______________________ CHAPTER 9 TEST • PAGE 1

Use the picture to answer questions 1 and 2.

1. Make tally marks to show how many 🏈 there are.	2. Make tally marks to show how many basketballs there are.
卌	卌 ||

Use the picture to answer question 3.

3. Draw a line from each shape to the group where it belongs.

Go On

Form B • Free Response   Assessment Guide AG61

Name ______________________ CHAPTER 9 TEST • PAGE 2

Use the bar graph to answer questions 4, 5, and 6. Mr. Byrd's class grew tomato plants. The graph shows how many tomatoes each child grew.

4. Which child grew the fewest tomatoes?

Lisa

5. How many more tomatoes did Teddy grow than Irene?

3

6. How many tomatoes did Lisa and Juan grow in all?

14

Go On

AG62 Assessment Guide   Form B • Free Response

Name ______________________ CHAPTER 9 TEST • PAGE 3

Use the picture graph to answer questions 7 and 8.

Rainfall for April	
Week 1	💧💧💧💧
Week 2	💧💧
Week 3	💧
Week 4	💧💧💧💧💧💧

Each 💧 stands for 1 inch of rain.

7. Which week had the most rain?	8. How many more inches of rain fell in week 1 than in week 2?
week 4	2 inches

Go On

Form B • Free Response   Assessment Guide AG63

Name ______________________ CHAPTER 9 TEST • PAGE 4

Color the bar graph to match the tally table.

Favorite Seasons	
Winter	卌
Spring	|||
Summer	||||
Fall	|||

Use the bar graph to answer questions 9 and 10.

9. How many children voted for winter?	10. What is the difference between the season with the **greatest** number of votes and the season with the **least** number of votes?
5 children	5 − 3 = 2 2 votes

Stop

AG64 Assessment Guide   Form B • Free Response

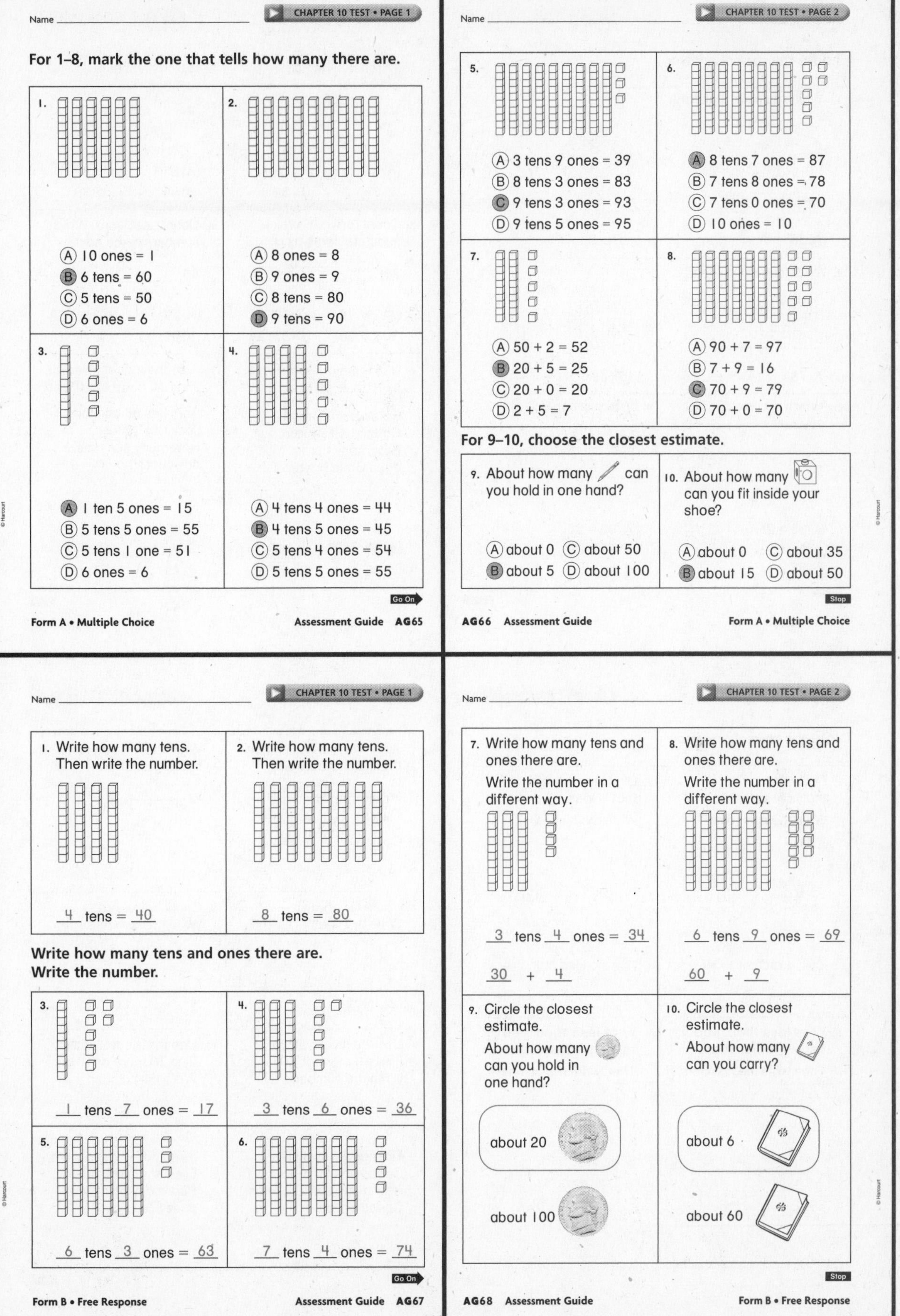

Name ______

CHAPTER 10 TEST • PAGE 1

For 1–8, mark the one that tells how many there are.

1.
(A) 10 ones = 1
(B) 6 tens = 60
(C) 5 tens = 50
(D) 6 ones = 6

2.
(A) 8 ones = 8
(B) 9 ones = 9
(C) 8 tens = 80
(D) 9 tens = 90

3.
(A) 1 ten 5 ones = 15
(B) 5 tens 5 ones = 55
(C) 5 tens 1 one = 51
(D) 6 ones = 6

4.
(A) 4 tens 4 ones = 44
(B) 4 tens 5 ones = 45
(C) 5 tens 4 ones = 54
(D) 5 tens 5 ones = 55

Go On

Form A • Multiple Choice — Assessment Guide AG65

Name ______

CHAPTER 10 TEST • PAGE 2

5.
(A) 3 tens 9 ones = 39
(B) 8 tens 3 ones = 83
(C) 9 tens 3 ones = 93
(D) 9 tens 5 ones = 95

6.
(A) 8 tens 7 ones = 87
(B) 7 tens 8 ones = 78
(C) 7 tens 0 ones = 70
(D) 10 ones = 10

7.
(A) 50 + 2 = 52
(B) 20 + 5 = 25
(C) 20 + 0 = 20
(D) 2 + 5 = 7

8.
(A) 90 + 7 = 97
(B) 7 + 9 = 16
(C) 70 + 9 = 79
(D) 70 + 0 = 70

For 9–10, choose the closest estimate.

9. About how many can you hold in one hand?
(A) about 0 (C) about 50
(B) about 5 (D) about 100

10. About how many can you fit inside your shoe?
(A) about 0 (C) about 35
(B) about 15 (D) about 50

Stop

AG66 Assessment Guide — Form A • Multiple Choice

Name ______

CHAPTER 10 TEST • PAGE 1

1. Write how many tens. Then write the number.
4 tens = 40

2. Write how many tens. Then write the number.
8 tens = 80

Write how many tens and ones there are. Write the number.

3. 1 tens 7 ones = 17

4. 3 tens 6 ones = 36

5. 6 tens 3 ones = 63

6. 7 tens 4 ones = 74

Go On

Form B • Free Response — Assessment Guide AG67

Name ______

CHAPTER 10 TEST • PAGE 2

7. Write how many tens and ones there are. Write the number in a different way.
3 tens 4 ones = 34
30 + 4

8. Write how many tens and ones there are. Write the number in a different way.
6 tens 9 ones = 69
60 + 9

9. Circle the closest estimate. About how many can you hold in one hand?
about 20
about 100

10. Circle the closest estimate. About how many can you carry?
about 6
about 60

Stop

AG68 Assessment Guide — Form B • Free Response

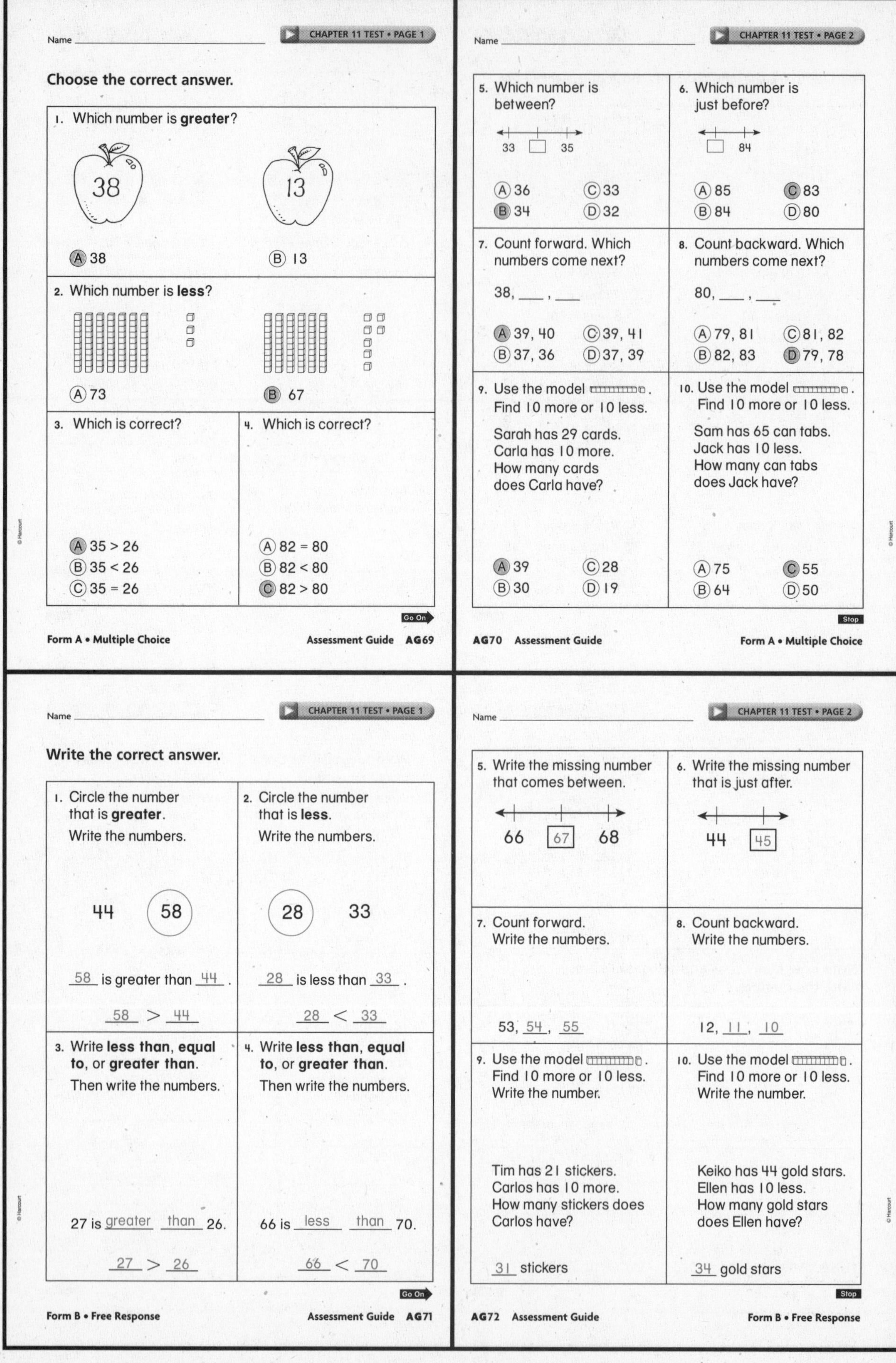

Name ____________ CHAPTER 11 TEST • PAGE 1

Choose the correct answer.

1. Which number is **greater**?

38 13

(A) 38 (B) 13

2. Which number is **less**?

(A) 73 (B) 67

3. Which is correct?

(A) 35 > 26
(B) 35 < 26
(C) 35 = 26

4. Which is correct?

(A) 82 = 80
(B) 82 < 80
(C) 82 > 80

Go On

Form A • Multiple Choice — Assessment Guide AG69

Name ____________ CHAPTER 11 TEST • PAGE 2

5. Which number is between?

33 □ 35

(A) 36 (C) 33
(B) 34 (D) 32

6. Which number is just before?

□ 84

(A) 85 (C) 83
(B) 84 (D) 80

7. Count forward. Which numbers come next?

38, ___, ___

(A) 39, 40 (C) 39, 41
(B) 37, 36 (D) 37, 39

8. Count backward. Which numbers come next?

80, ___, ___

(A) 79, 81 (C) 81, 82
(B) 82, 83 (D) 79, 78

9. Use the model. Find 10 more or 10 less.

Sarah has 29 cards. Carla has 10 more. How many cards does Carla have?

(A) 39 (C) 28
(B) 30 (D) 19

10. Use the model. Find 10 more or 10 less.

Sam has 65 can tabs. Jack has 10 less. How many can tabs does Jack have?

(A) 75 (C) 55
(B) 64 (D) 50

Stop

AG70 Assessment Guide — Form A • Multiple Choice

Name ____________ CHAPTER 11 TEST • PAGE 1

Write the correct answer.

1. Circle the number that is **greater**. Write the numbers.

44 (58)

58 is greater than 44.

58 > 44

2. Circle the number that is **less**. Write the numbers.

(28) 33

28 is less than 33.

28 < 33

3. Write **less than, equal to**, or **greater than**. Then write the numbers.

27 is greater than 26.

27 > 26

4. Write **less than, equal to**, or **greater than**. Then write the numbers.

66 is less than 70.

66 < 70

Go On

Form B • Free Response — Assessment Guide AG71

Name ____________ CHAPTER 11 TEST • PAGE 2

5. Write the missing number that comes between.

66 [67] 68

6. Write the missing number that is just after.

44 [45]

7. Count forward. Write the numbers.

53, 54, 55

8. Count backward. Write the numbers.

12, 11, 10

9. Use the model. Find 10 more or 10 less. Write the number.

Tim has 21 stickers. Carlos has 10 more. How many stickers does Carlos have?

31 stickers

10. Use the model. Find 10 more or 10 less. Write the number.

Keiko has 44 gold stars. Ellen has 10 less. How many gold stars does Ellen have?

34 gold stars

Stop

AG72 Assessment Guide — Form B • Free Response

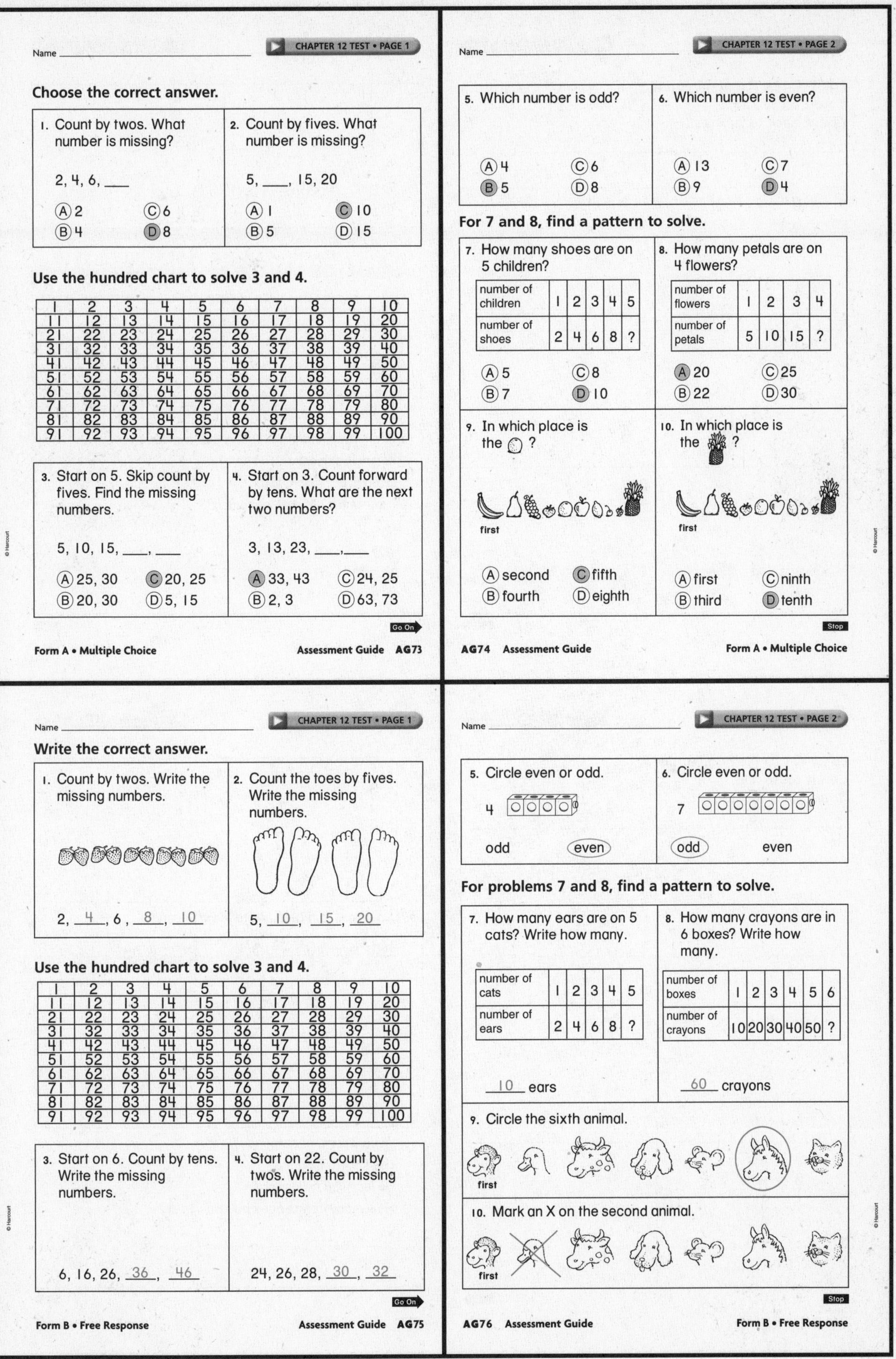

Name ____________________

CHAPTER 12 TEST • PAGE 1

Choose the correct answer.

1. Count by twos. What number is missing?

2, 4, 6, ___

(A) 2 (B) 4 (C) 6 (D) 8

2. Count by fives. What number is missing?

5, ___, 15, 20

(A) 1 (B) 5 (C) 10 (D) 15

Use the hundred chart to solve 3 and 4.

1	2	3	4	5	6	7	8	9	10
11	12	13	14	15	16	17	18	19	20
21	22	23	24	25	26	27	28	29	30
31	32	33	34	35	36	37	38	39	40
41	42	43	44	45	46	47	48	49	50
51	52	53	54	55	56	57	58	59	60
61	62	63	64	65	66	67	68	69	70
71	72	73	74	75	76	77	78	79	80
81	82	83	84	85	86	87	88	89	90
91	92	93	94	95	96	97	98	99	100

3. Start on 5. Skip count by fives. Find the missing numbers.

5, 10, 15, ___, ___

(A) 25, 30 (B) 20, 30 (C) 20, 25 (D) 5, 15

4. Start on 3. Count forward by tens. What are the next two numbers?

3, 13, 23, ___, ___

(A) 33, 43 (B) 2, 3 (C) 24, 25 (D) 63, 73

Go On

Form A • Multiple Choice Assessment Guide AG73

Name ____________________

CHAPTER 12 TEST • PAGE 2

5. Which number is odd?

(A) 4 (B) 5 (C) 6 (D) 8

6. Which number is even?

(A) 13 (B) 9 (C) 7 (D) 4

For 7 and 8, find a pattern to solve.

7. How many shoes are on 5 children?

number of children	1	2	3	4	5
number of shoes	2	4	6	8	?

(A) 5 (B) 7 (C) 8 (D) 10

8. How many petals are on 4 flowers?

number of flowers	1	2	3	4
number of petals	5	10	15	?

(A) 20 (B) 22 (C) 25 (D) 30

9. In which place is the ?

first

(A) second (B) fourth (C) fifth (D) eighth

10. In which place is the ?

first

(A) first (B) third (C) ninth (D) tenth

Stop

AG74 Assessment Guide Form A • Multiple Choice

Name ____________________

CHAPTER 12 TEST • PAGE 1

Write the correct answer.

1. Count by twos. Write the missing numbers.

2, 4, 6, 8, 10

2. Count the toes by fives. Write the missing numbers.

5, 10, 15, 20

Use the hundred chart to solve 3 and 4.

1	2	3	4	5	6	7	8	9	10
11	12	13	14	15	16	17	18	19	20
21	22	23	24	25	26	27	28	29	30
31	32	33	34	35	36	37	38	39	40
41	42	43	44	45	46	47	48	49	50
51	52	53	54	55	56	57	58	59	60
61	62	63	64	65	66	67	68	69	70
71	72	73	74	75	76	77	78	79	80
81	82	83	84	85	86	87	88	89	90
91	92	93	94	95	96	97	98	99	100

3. Start on 6. Count by tens. Write the missing numbers.

6, 16, 26, 36, 46

4. Start on 22. Count by twos. Write the missing numbers.

24, 26, 28, 30, 32

Go On

Form B • Free Response Assessment Guide AG75

Name ____________________

CHAPTER 12 TEST • PAGE 2

5. Circle even or odd.

4

odd even

6. Circle even or odd.

7

odd even

For problems 7 and 8, find a pattern to solve.

7. How many ears are on 5 cats? Write how many.

number of cats	1	2	3	4	5
number of ears	2	4	6	8	?

10 ears

8. How many crayons are in 6 boxes? Write how many.

number of boxes	1	2	3	4	5	6
number of crayons	10	20	30	40	50	?

60 crayons

9. Circle the sixth animal.

first

10. Mark an X on the second animal.

first

Stop

AG76 Assessment Guide Form B • Free Response

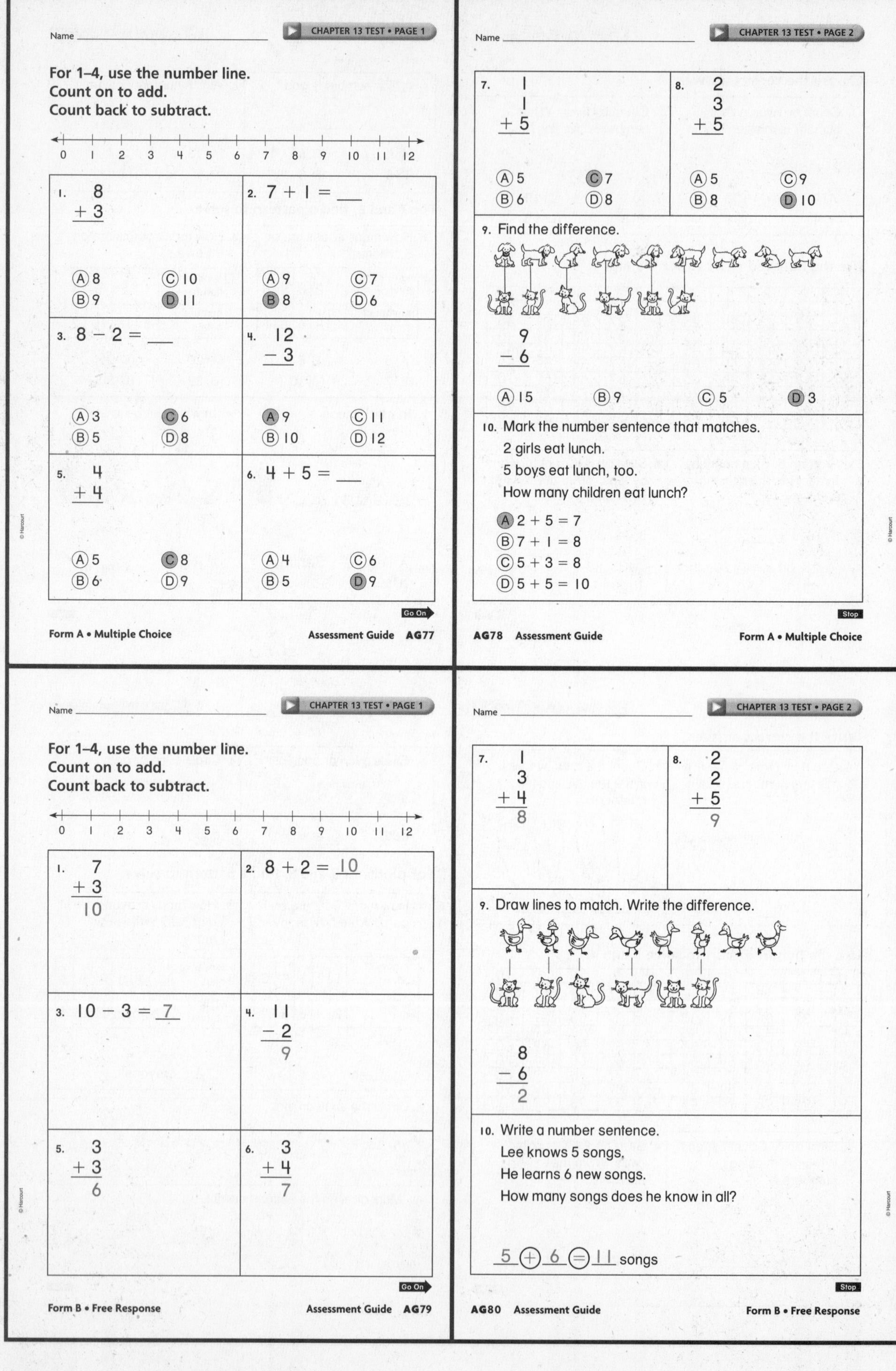

Name ______________________ CHAPTER 13 TEST • PAGE 1

For 1–4, use the number line.
Count on to add.
Count back to subtract.

0 1 2 3 4 5 6 7 8 9 10 11 12

1. $8 + 3$

Ⓐ 8 Ⓑ 9 Ⓒ 10 Ⓓ 11

2. $7 + 1 =$ ___

Ⓐ 9 Ⓑ 8 Ⓒ 7 Ⓓ 6

3. $8 - 2 =$ ___

Ⓐ 3 Ⓑ 5 Ⓒ 6 Ⓓ 8

4. $12 - 3$

Ⓐ 9 Ⓑ 10 Ⓒ 11 Ⓓ 12

5. $4 + 4$

Ⓐ 5 Ⓑ 6 Ⓒ 8 Ⓓ 9

6. $4 + 5 =$ ___

Ⓐ 4 Ⓑ 5 Ⓒ 6 Ⓓ 9

Go On

Form A • Multiple Choice Assessment Guide AG77

Name ______________________ CHAPTER 13 TEST • PAGE 2

7. $1 + 1 + 5$

Ⓐ 5 Ⓑ 6 Ⓒ 7 Ⓓ 8

8. $2 + 3 + 5$

Ⓐ 5 Ⓑ 8 Ⓒ 9 Ⓓ 10

9. Find the difference.

$9 - 6$

Ⓐ 15 Ⓑ 9 Ⓒ 5 Ⓓ 3

10. Mark the number sentence that matches.
2 girls eat lunch.
5 boys eat lunch, too.
How many children eat lunch?

Ⓐ $2 + 5 = 7$
Ⓑ $7 + 1 = 8$
Ⓒ $5 + 3 = 8$
Ⓓ $5 + 5 = 10$

Stop

AG78 Assessment Guide Form A • Multiple Choice

Name ______________________ CHAPTER 13 TEST • PAGE 1

For 1–4, use the number line.
Count on to add.
Count back to subtract.

0 1 2 3 4 5 6 7 8 9 10 11 12

1. $7 + 3 = 10$
2. $8 + 2 = 10$
3. $10 - 3 = 7$
4. $11 - 2 = 9$
5. $3 + 3 = 6$
6. $3 + 4 = 7$

Go On

Form B • Free Response Assessment Guide AG79

Name ______________________ CHAPTER 13 TEST • PAGE 2

7. $1 + 3 + 4 = 8$
8. $2 + 2 + 5 = 9$
9. Draw lines to match. Write the difference.

$8 - 6 = 2$

10. Write a number sentence.
Lee knows 5 songs.
He learns 6 new songs.
How many songs does he know in all?

$5 + 6 = 11$ songs

Stop

AG80 Assessment Guide Form B • Free Response

Name ______________________

Choose the correct answer.

1. Which subtraction sentence is related to $8 + 1 = 9$?

   (A) $9 - 1 = 8$ (shaded)
   (B) $9 - 7 = 2$
   (C) $8 - 8 = 0$
   (D) $9 - 9 = 0$

2. Which fact is related to $12 - 4 = 8$?

   (A) $9 + 3 = 12$
   (B) $8 + 4 = 12$ (shaded)
   (C) $12 - 5 = 7$
   (D) $8 - 4 = 4$

3. Which fact belongs in this fact family?

   4 5 9

   (A) $5 - 4 = 1$
   (B) $9 - 6 = 3$
   (C) $3 + 6 = 9$
   (D) $4 + 5 = 9$ (shaded)

4. Which fact belongs in this fact family?

   6 3 9

   (A) (shaded) $9 - 6 = 3$
   (B) $6 - 3 = 3$
   (C) $9 - 0 = 9$
   (D) $9 + 3 = 12$

Go On

Name ______________________

5. What is the missing number?

   $9 + \_\_ = 10$
   $10 - 9 = \_\_$

   (A) 1 (shaded) (B) 2 (C) 4 (D) 5

6. What is the missing number?

   $\_\_ + 6 = 12$
   $12 - 6 = \_\_$

   (A) 3 (B) 4 (C) 5 (D) 6 (shaded)

7. Find the difference.

   $11 - 7 = \_\_$

   (A) 10 (B) 6 (C) 5 (D) 4 (shaded)

8. Find the difference.

   $12 - 5 = \_\_$

   (A) 6 (B) 7 (shaded) (C) 8 (D) 9

9. Choose a way to solve the problem. Then solve.
   Betty has 10 books.
   She gives 4 to Fred.
   How many are left?

   (A) 4
   (B) 5
   (C) 6 (shaded)
   (D) 9

10. Choose a way to solve the problem. Then solve.
    Jed has 9 crayons.
    Mary has 2 crayons.
    How many are there in all?

    (A) 12
    (B) 11 (shaded)
    (C) 10
    (D) 7

Stop

Name ______________________

Write the correct answer.

1. Write a related subtraction sentence.

   $3 + 7 = 10$

   $10 - 7 = 3$ or

   $10 - 3 = 7$

2. Write the sum. Then write a related subtraction fact.

   $5 + 6 = 11$

   $11 - 5 = 6$ or

   $11 - 6 = 5$

3. Add or subtract. Write the numbers in the fact family.

   $7 + 2 = 9$
   $9 - 7 = 2$
   $9 - 2 = 7$
   $2 + 7 = 9$

   2 7 9

4. Add or subtract. Write the numbers in the fact family.

   $5 + 3 = 8$ $8 - 5 = 3$ $3 + 5 = 8$ $8 - 3 = 5$

   3 5 8

Go On

Name ______________________

5. Write the missing number.

   $3 + 9 = 12$
   $12 - 3 = 9$

6. Write the missing number.

   $3 + 8 = 11$
   $11 - 8 = 3$

7. Write the difference.

   $11 - 4 = 7$

8. Write the difference.

   $12 - 4 = 8$

9. Choose a way to solve the problem. Then solve.
   Jill buys 2 bananas.
   Jamal buys 7 bananas.
   How many bananas do both children buy?

   Check children's work.

   9 bananas

10. Choose a way to solve the problem. Then solve.
    There are 11 carrots.
    Karen eats 3 of them.
    How many are left?

    Check children's work.

    8 carrots

Stop

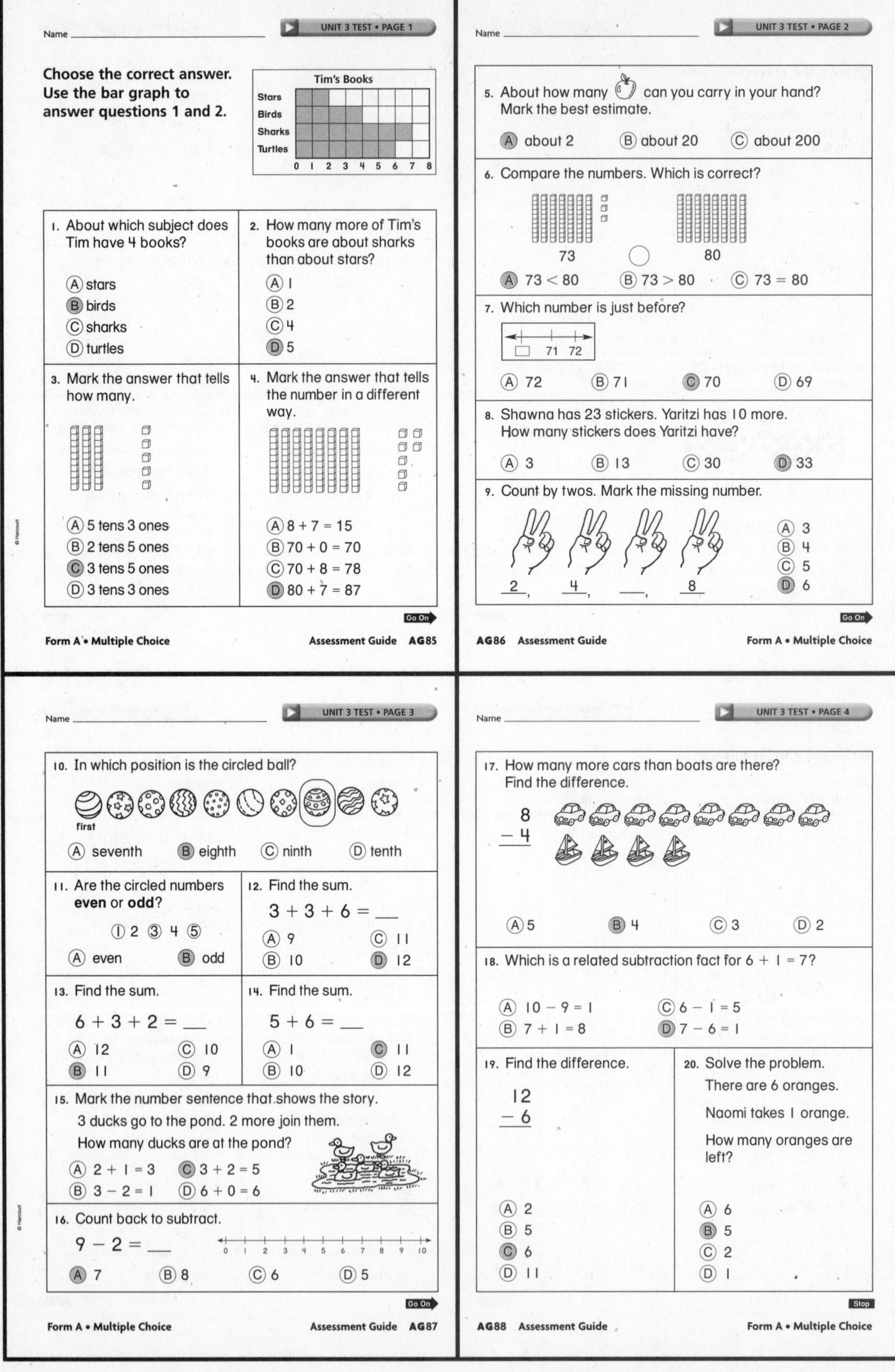

Name ____________________

UNIT 3 TEST • PAGE 1

Choose the correct answer. Use the bar graph to answer questions 1 and 2.

Tim's Books

Stars	2
Birds	2
Sharks	7
Turtles	6

0 1 2 3 4 5 6 7 8

1. About which subject does Tim have 4 books?
   - (A) stars
   - (B) birds
   - (C) sharks
   - (D) turtles

2. How many more of Tim's books are about sharks than about stars?
   - (A) 1
   - (B) 2
   - (C) 4
   - (D) 5

3. Mark the answer that tells how many.
   - (A) 5 tens 3 ones
   - (B) 2 tens 5 ones
   - (C) 3 tens 5 ones
   - (D) 3 tens 3 ones

4. Mark the answer that tells the number in a different way.
   - (A) 8 + 7 = 15
   - (B) 70 + 0 = 70
   - (C) 70 + 8 = 78
   - (D) 80 + 7 = 87

Go On

Form A • Multiple Choice — Assessment Guide AG85

Name ____________________

UNIT 3 TEST • PAGE 2

5. About how many [apple] can you carry in your hand? Mark the best estimate.
   - (A) about 2
   - (B) about 20
   - (C) about 200

6. Compare the numbers. Which is correct?

   73 ○ 80
   - (A) 73 < 80
   - (B) 73 > 80
   - (C) 73 = 80

7. Which number is just before?

   ☐ 71 72
   - (A) 72
   - (B) 71
   - (C) 70
   - (D) 69

8. Shawna has 23 stickers. Yaritzi has 10 more. How many stickers does Yaritzi have?
   - (A) 3
   - (B) 13
   - (C) 30
   - (D) 33

9. Count by twos. Mark the missing number.

   2, 4, ___, 8
   - (A) 3
   - (B) 4
   - (C) 5
   - (D) 6

Go On

AG86 Assessment Guide — Form A • Multiple Choice

Name ____________________

UNIT 3 TEST • PAGE 3

10. In which position is the circled ball?

    first
    - (A) seventh
    - (B) eighth
    - (C) ninth
    - (D) tenth

11. Are the circled numbers **even** or **odd**?

    ① 2 ③ 4 ⑤
    - (A) even
    - (B) odd

12. Find the sum.

    3 + 3 + 6 = ___
    - (A) 9
    - (B) 10
    - (C) 11
    - (D) 12

13. Find the sum.

    6 + 3 + 2 = ___
    - (A) 12
    - (B) 11
    - (C) 10
    - (D) 9

14. Find the sum.

    5 + 6 = ___
    - (A) 1
    - (B) 10
    - (C) 11
    - (D) 12

15. Mark the number sentence that shows the story.

    3 ducks go to the pond. 2 more join them.

    How many ducks are at the pond?
    - (A) 2 + 1 = 3
    - (B) 3 − 2 = 1
    - (C) 3 + 2 = 5
    - (D) 6 + 0 = 6

16. Count back to subtract.

    9 − 2 = ___

    0 1 2 3 4 5 6 7 8 9 10
    - (A) 7
    - (B) 8
    - (C) 6
    - (D) 5

Go On

Form A • Multiple Choice — Assessment Guide AG87

Name ____________________

UNIT 3 TEST • PAGE 4

17. How many more cars than boats are there? Find the difference.

    8
    − 4
    - (A) 5
    - (B) 4
    - (C) 3
    - (D) 2

18. Which is a related subtraction fact for 6 + 1 = 7?
    - (A) 10 − 9 = 1
    - (B) 7 + 1 = 8
    - (C) 6 − 1 = 5
    - (D) 7 − 6 = 1

19. Find the difference.

    12
    − 6
    - (A) 2
    - (B) 5
    - (C) 6
    - (D) 11

20. Solve the problem.

    There are 6 oranges.

    Naomi takes 1 orange.

    How many oranges are left?
    - (A) 6
    - (B) 5
    - (C) 2
    - (D) 1

Stop

AG88 Assessment Guide — Form A • Multiple Choice

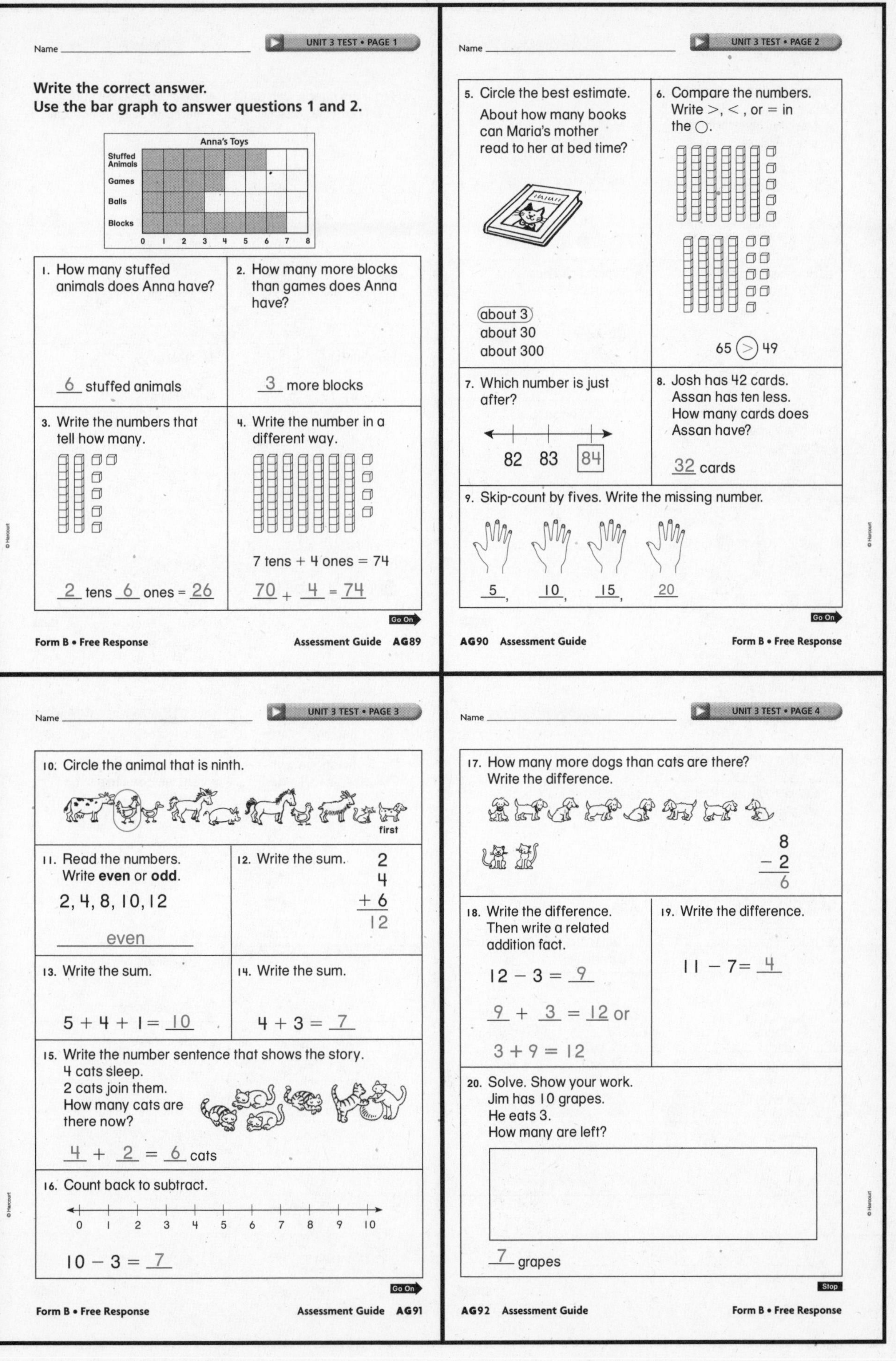

Name ______________________ UNIT 3 TEST • PAGE 1

Write the correct answer.
Use the bar graph to answer questions 1 and 2.

1. How many stuffed animals does Anna have? 6 stuffed animals	2. How many more blocks than games does Anna have? 3 more blocks
3. Write the numbers that tell how many. 2 tens 6 ones = 26	4. Write the number in a different way. 7 tens + 4 ones = 74 70 + 4 = 74

Go On

Form B • Free Response — Assessment Guide AG89

Name ______________________ UNIT 3 TEST • PAGE 2

5. Circle the best estimate. About how many books can Maria's mother read to her at bed time? (about 3) about 30 about 300	6. Compare the numbers. Write >, <, or = in the ○. 65 (>) 49
7. Which number is just after? 82 83 [84]	8. Josh has 42 cards. Assan has ten less. How many cards does Assan have? 32 cards

9. Skip-count by fives. Write the missing number.

5, 10, 15, 20

Go On

AG90 Assessment Guide — Form B • Free Response

Name ______________________ UNIT 3 TEST • PAGE 3

10. Circle the animal that is ninth.

first

11. Read the numbers. Write **even** or **odd**. 2, 4, 8, 10, 12 even	12. Write the sum. 2 4 + 6 12
13. Write the sum. 5 + 4 + 1 = 10	14. Write the sum. 4 + 3 = 7

15. Write the number sentence that shows the story.
4 cats sleep.
2 cats join them.
How many cats are there now?

4 + 2 = 6 cats

16. Count back to subtract.

0 1 2 3 4 5 6 7 8 9 10

10 − 3 = 7

Go On

Form B • Free Response — Assessment Guide AG91

Name ______________________ UNIT 3 TEST • PAGE 4

17. How many more dogs than cats are there? Write the difference.

8
− 2
6

18. Write the difference. Then write a related addition fact. 12 − 3 = 9 9 + 3 = 12 or 3 + 9 = 12	19. Write the difference. 11 − 7 = 4

20. Solve. Show your work.
Jim has 10 grapes.
He eats 3.
How many are left?

7 grapes

Stop

AG92 Assessment Guide — Form B • Free Response

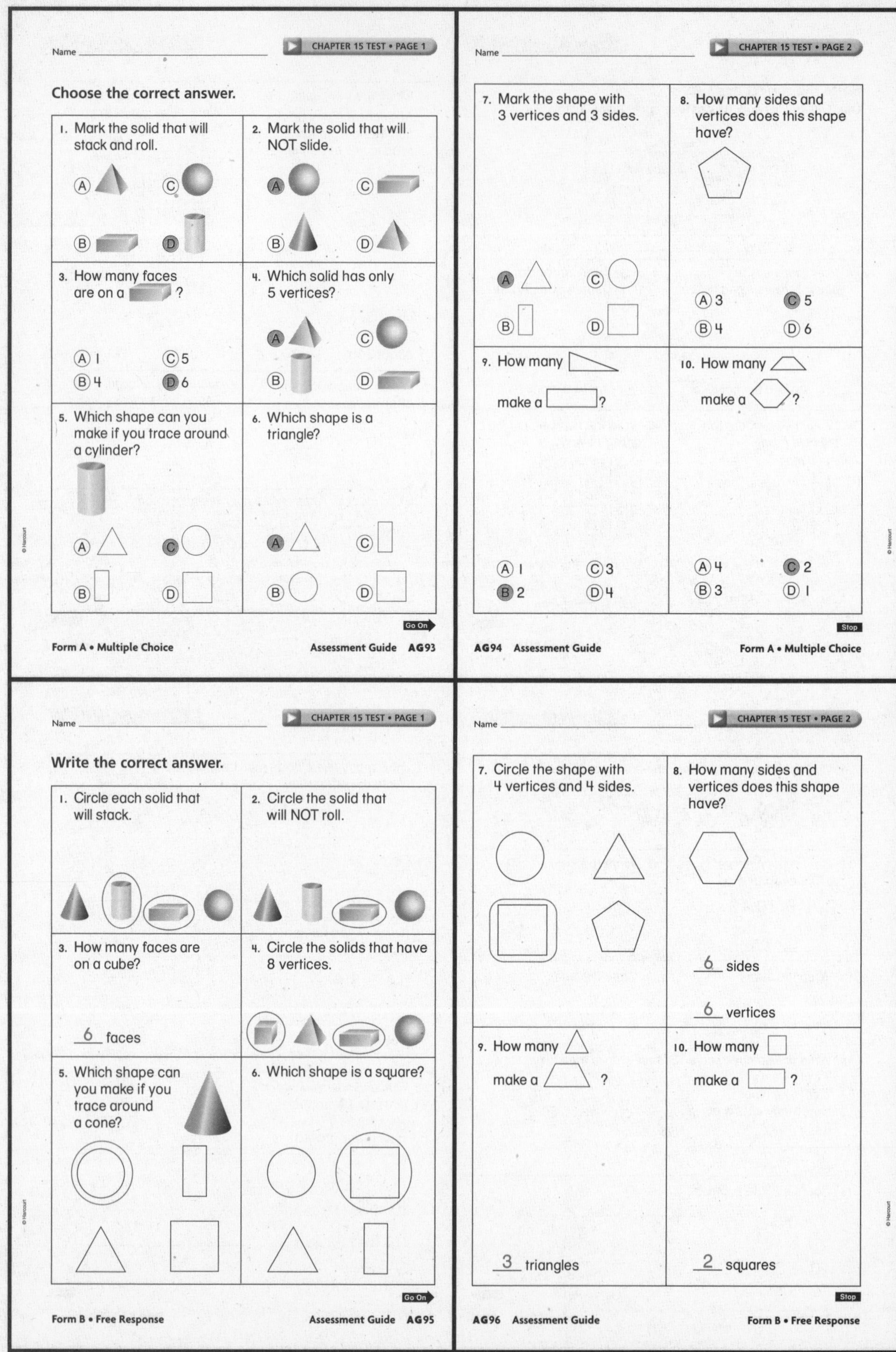

Choose the correct answer.

1. Mark the solid that will stack and roll.
   Ⓐ Ⓑ Ⓒ Ⓓ (D marked)

2. Mark the solid that will NOT slide.
   Ⓐ Ⓑ Ⓒ Ⓓ (A marked)

3. How many faces are on a [box shape] ?
   Ⓐ 1 Ⓑ 4 Ⓒ 5 Ⓓ 6 (D marked)

4. Which solid has only 5 vertices?
   Ⓐ Ⓑ Ⓒ Ⓓ (A marked)

5. Which shape can you make if you trace around a cylinder?
   Ⓐ Ⓑ Ⓒ Ⓓ (C marked)

6. Which shape is a triangle?
   Ⓐ Ⓑ Ⓒ Ⓓ (A marked)

Go On

7. Mark the shape with 3 vertices and 3 sides.
   Ⓐ Ⓑ Ⓒ Ⓓ (A marked)

8. How many sides and vertices does this shape have?
   Ⓐ 3 Ⓑ 4 Ⓒ 5 Ⓓ 6 (C marked)

9. How many [triangle] make a [rectangle]?
   Ⓐ 1 Ⓑ 2 Ⓒ 3 Ⓓ 4 (B marked)

10. How many [trapezoid] make a [hexagon]?
   Ⓐ 4 Ⓑ 3 Ⓒ 2 Ⓓ 1 (C marked)

Stop

Write the correct answer.

1. Circle each solid that will stack.

2. Circle the solid that will NOT roll.

3. How many faces are on a cube?
   6 faces

4. Circle the solids that have 8 vertices.

5. Which shape can you make if you trace around a cone?

6. Which shape is a square?

Go On

7. Circle the shape with 4 vertices and 4 sides.

8. How many sides and vertices does this shape have?
   6 sides
   6 vertices

9. How many [triangle] make a [trapezoid] ?
   3 triangles

10. How many [square] make a [rectangle] ?
   2 squares

Stop

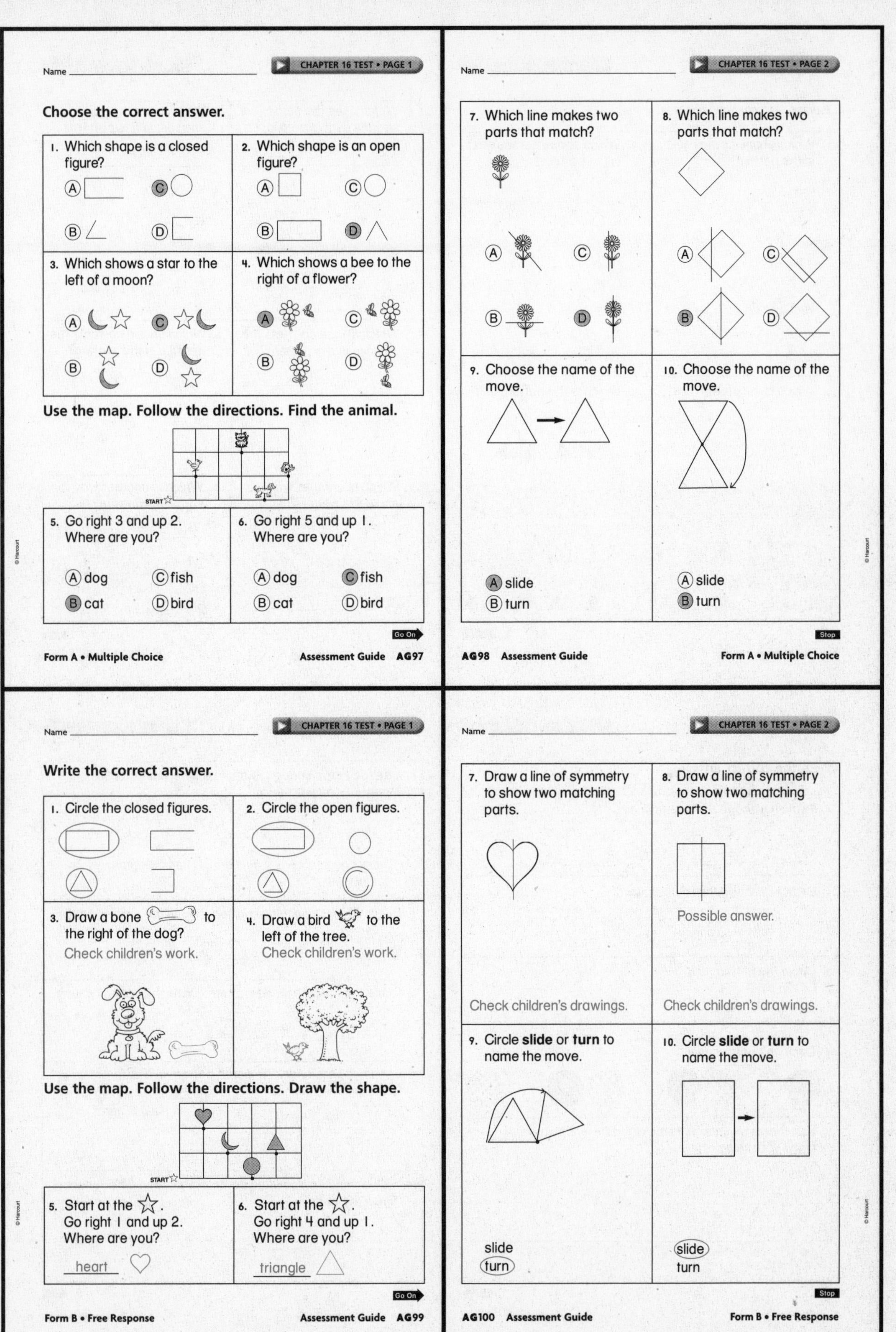
Name

CHAPTER 16 TEST • PAGE 1

Choose the correct answer.

1. Which shape is a closed figure?
   (A) (B) (C) (D)
2. Which shape is an open figure?
   (A) (B) (C) (D)
3. Which shows a star to the left of a moon?
   (A) (B) (C) (D)
4. Which shows a bee to the right of a flower?
   (A) (B) (C) (D)

Use the map. Follow the directions. Find the animal.

START

5. Go right 3 and up 2. Where are you?
   (A) dog (B) cat (C) fish (D) bird
6. Go right 5 and up 1. Where are you?
   (A) dog (B) cat (C) fish (D) bird

Go On

Form A • Multiple Choice — Assessment Guide AG97

Name

CHAPTER 16 TEST • PAGE 2

7. Which line makes two parts that match?
   (A) (B) (C) (D)
8. Which line makes two parts that match?
   (A) (B) (C) (D)
9. Choose the name of the move.
   (A) slide
   (B) turn
10. Choose the name of the move.
   (A) slide
   (B) turn

Stop

AG98 Assessment Guide — Form A • Multiple Choice

Name

CHAPTER 16 TEST • PAGE 1

Write the correct answer.

1. Circle the closed figures.
2. Circle the open figures.
3. Draw a bone to the right of the dog?
   Check children's work.
4. Draw a bird to the left of the tree.
   Check children's work.

Use the map. Follow the directions. Draw the shape.

START

5. Start at the ☆. Go right 1 and up 2. Where are you?
   heart
6. Start at the ☆. Go right 4 and up 1. Where are you?
   triangle

Go On

Form B • Free Response — Assessment Guide AG99

Name

CHAPTER 16 TEST • PAGE 2

7. Draw a line of symmetry to show two matching parts.
   Check children's drawings.
8. Draw a line of symmetry to show two matching parts.
   Possible answer.
   Check children's drawings.
9. Circle **slide** or **turn** to name the move.
   slide
   turn
10. Circle **slide** or **turn** to name the move.
   slide
   turn

Stop

AG100 Assessment Guide — Form B • Free Response

Choose the correct answer.

1. Which shape comes next in the pattern?

Ⓐ Ⓑ Ⓒ Ⓓ

2. Which shape comes next in the pattern?

Ⓐ Ⓑ Ⓒ Ⓓ

3. Which is the pattern unit?

Ⓐ Ⓑ Ⓒ Ⓓ

4. Which is the pattern unit?

Ⓐ Ⓑ Ⓒ Ⓓ

Go On

5. Which uses the same shapes as this pattern?

Ⓐ Ⓑ Ⓒ Ⓓ

6. Which uses the same shapes as this pattern?

Ⓐ Ⓑ Ⓒ Ⓓ

7. Which shape corrects the mistake in the pattern?

Ⓐ Ⓑ Ⓒ Ⓓ

8. Which shape corrects the mistake in the pattern?

Ⓐ Ⓑ Ⓒ Ⓓ

9. Which is another way to show this pattern?

Ⓐ Ⓑ

10. Which is another way to show this pattern?

Ⓐ Ⓑ

Stop

Write the correct answer.

1. Draw the shape that comes next.

2. Draw the shape that comes next.

3. Circle the pattern unit.

4. Circle the pattern unit.

5. Use the same shapes to make a different pattern. Draw your new pattern.

Check children's work. Pattern should use circles and squares.

Go On

6. Use the same shapes to make a different pattern. Draw your new pattern.

Check children's work. Pattern should use triangles and rhombuses.

7. Circle the mistake in the pattern. Draw the correct shape.

8. Circle the mistake in the pattern. Draw the correct shape.

9. Use shapes to show the same pattern in a different way. Draw the shapes.

Children should show an AAB pattern using shapes.

10. Use shapes to show the same pattern in a different way. Draw the shapes.

Children should show an ABB pattern using shapes.

Stop

Name ____________

CHAPTER 18 TEST • PAGE 1

Choose the correct answer.

1. 7 + 7 = 14, so 7 + 8 = ___

Ⓐ 14 Ⓑ 15 Ⓒ 16 Ⓓ 17

2. 6 + 6 = 12, so 6 + 7 = ___

Ⓐ 15 Ⓑ 14 Ⓒ 13 Ⓓ 12

For 3 to 6, use ● and Workmat 7 to add. Find the sum.

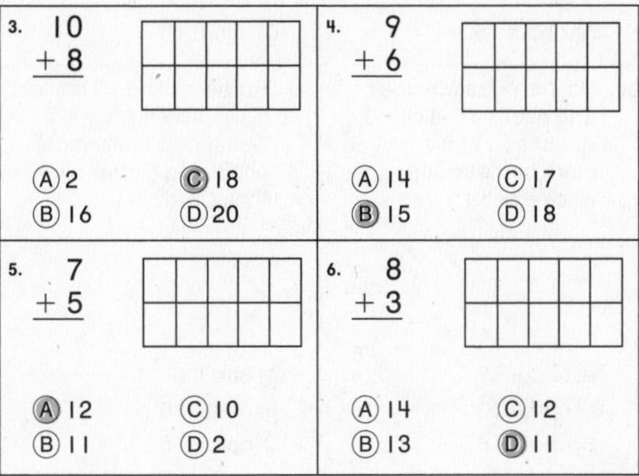

3. 10 + 8

Ⓐ 2 Ⓑ 16 Ⓒ 18 Ⓓ 20

4. 9 + 6

Ⓐ 14 Ⓑ 15 Ⓒ 17 Ⓓ 18

5. 7 + 5

Ⓐ 12 Ⓑ 11 Ⓒ 10 Ⓓ 2

6. 8 + 3

Ⓐ 14 Ⓑ 13 Ⓒ 12 Ⓓ 11

Go On

Form A • Multiple Choice Assessment Guide AG105

Name ____________

CHAPTER 18 TEST • PAGE 2

7. 4 + 7 + 6

Ⓐ 11 Ⓑ 15 Ⓒ 16 Ⓓ 17

8. 3 + 8 + 2

Ⓐ 13 Ⓑ 12 Ⓒ 11 Ⓓ 5

For 9 and 10, use the table.

It tells how many pieces of fruit the children bought.

Fruit	Number
apples	9
peaches	4
bananas	2

9. How many more apples than peaches did they buy?

Ⓐ 8 Ⓑ 6 Ⓒ 5 Ⓓ 4

10. How many apples and bananas did they buy in all?

Ⓐ 12 Ⓑ 11 Ⓒ 8 Ⓓ 6

Stop

AG106 Assessment Guide Form A • Multiple Choice

Name ____________

CHAPTER 18 TEST • PAGE 1

Write the correct answer.

1. 5 + 5 = 10, so 5 + 6 = 11

2. 8 + 8 = 16, so 8 + 9 = 17

For 3 to 6, use ● and Workmat 7 to add. Write the sum.

3. 10 + 5 = 15

4. 9 + 8 = 17

5. 8 + 4 = 12

6. 7 + 6 = 13

Go On

Form B • Free Response Assessment Guide AG107

Name ____________

CHAPTER 18 TEST • PAGE 2

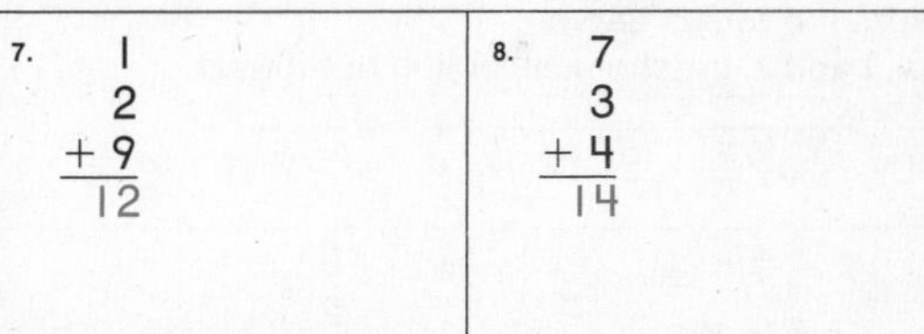

7. 1 + 2 + 9 = 12

8. 7 + 3 + 4 = 14

For 9 to 10, use the table.

It tells how many animals the children saw in the forest.

Animals	Number
birds	5
squirrels	3
rabbits	2

9. How many more birds than rabbits did they see?

5 ⊖ 2 ⊜ 3

3 more birds

10. How many animals did they see in all?

5 ⊕ 3 ⊕ 2 ⊜ 10

10 animals

Stop

AG108 Assessment Guide Form B • Free Response

Name ____________________

Choose the correct answer.
For 1 and 2, use the number line to subtract.

10 11 12 13 14 15 16 17 18 19 20

1. $16 - 3 = \_\_\_$ (A) 13 (C) 19 (B) 14 (D) 20	2. $\begin{array}{r} 19 \\ -\ 3 \\ \hline \end{array}$ (A) 14 (C) 16 (B) 15 (D) 17

Use the related fact to help you find sums and differences.

3. $\begin{array}{r} 8 \\ +8 \\ \hline 16 \end{array}$ $\begin{array}{r} 16 \\ -\ 8 \\ \hline \end{array}$ (A) 6 (C) 12 (B) 8 (D) 16	4. Which is in the same doubles fact family as $9 + 9 = 18$? (A) $9 + 6 = 15$ (B) $1 + 8 = 9$ (C) $19 - 1 = 18$ (D) $18 - 9 = 9$
5. Which addition fact can help you find the difference for $8 - 4$? (A) $4 + 0 = 4$ (B) $5 + 3 = 8$ (C) $4 + 4 = 8$ (D) $8 + 4 = 12$	6. $\begin{array}{r} 12 \\ +\ 7 \\ \hline 19 \end{array}$ $\begin{array}{r} 19 \\ -\ 7 \\ \hline \end{array}$ (A) 2 (C) 9 (B) 8 (D) 12

Go On

Name ____________________

Choose the best estimate.

7. Stefan has 10 tomatoes. He finds 4 more. About how many tomatoes does Stefan have now? (A) about 4 (B) about 10 (C) about 15	8. Laura has 10 carrots. She gives 6 to her friends. About how many carrots does Laura have now? (A) about 5 (B) about 10 (C) about 15
9. Rachel picks 6 berries. She needs 15 in all. About how many more berries does Rachel need? (A) about 5 (B) about 10 (C) about 15	10. Rafael picked 13 apples. Celia picked 7 apples. About how many more apples did Rafael pick than Celia? (A) about 5 (B) about 10 (C) about 15

Stop

Name ____________________

Write the correct answer.
For 1 and 2, use the number line to subtract.

10 11 12 13 14 15 16 17 18 19 20

1. $17 - 3 = \underline{14}$	2. $\begin{array}{r} 18 \\ -\ 2 \\ \hline 16 \end{array}$
3. Write the sum and difference for the pair. $\begin{array}{r} 7 \\ +7 \\ \hline 14 \end{array}$ $\begin{array}{r} 14 \\ -\ 7 \\ \hline 7 \end{array}$	4. Write the fact that is missing from this doubles fact family. $5 + 5 = 10$ $\underline{10} \ominus \underline{5} \circleddash \underline{5}$
5. Write an addition fact that can help you find the difference for $9 - 5$. $4 + 5 = 9$ or $\underline{5} + \underline{4} = \underline{9}$	6. Write the sum and difference for the pair. $\begin{array}{r} 3 \\ +8 \\ \hline 11 \end{array}$ $\begin{array}{r} 11 \\ -\ 3 \\ \hline 8 \end{array}$

Go On

Name ____________________

Circle the best estimate.

7. Sara has 10 cherries. She picks 7 more. About how many cherries does Sara have now? about 5 about 15 about 25	8. Galen has 12 stickers. He gives 8 away. About how many stickers does Galen have now? about 5 about 10 about 20
9. Reese sees 5 bugs. Sam sees 6 bugs. About how many bugs do they see in all? about 5 about 10 about 15	10. Mina has 15 paper clips. Kim has 4. About how many more paper clips does Mina have than Kim? about 5 about 10 about 20

Stop

Name ______________________ CHAPTER 20 TEST • PAGE 1

Choose the correct answer.

1. $8 + 9$ (A) 19 (B) 18 **(C) 17** (D) 16	2. $14 - 7$ (A) 6 **(B) 7** (C) 8 (D) 9
3. $6 + 5$ (A) 12 **(B) 11** (C) 10 (D) 1	4. $12 - 8$ (A) 20 (B) 9 (C) 5 **(D) 4**
5. Which of these is a way to make 20? (A) 4 + 10 (B) 3 + 3 + 1 **(C) 14 + 6** (D) 10 − 9	6. Which of these is a way to make 14? **(A) 16 − 2** (B) 10 + 3 (C) 12 + 1 (D) 20 − 3

Go On

Name ______________________ CHAPTER 20 TEST • PAGE 2

7. Which fact is in the same fact family as 4 + 7 = 11? (A) 11 − 11 = 0 **(B) 11 − 4 = 7** (C) 15 − 4 = 11 (D) 4 + 11 = 15	8. Mark the pair that shows 2 facts that are in the same family. **(A) 9 − 6 = 3, 3 + 6 = 9** (B) 6 − 3 = 3, 3 + 6 = 9 (C) 9 + 9 = 18, 10 + 8 = 18 (D) 8 + 7 = 15, 8 − 7 = 1

For 9 and 10, use [cube] to solve.

9. Craig has 4 blocks. Lisa has 8 blocks. How many blocks do they have in all? (A) 8 (B) 10 **(C) 12** (D) 14	10. Melinda has 18 apples. She gives 5 to John. How many apples does Melinda have now? (A) 9 (B) 12 **(C) 13** (D) 17

Stop

Name ______________________ CHAPTER 20 TEST • PAGE 1

Write the correct answer. Add or subtract.

1. $7 + 9 = 16$	2. $16 - 8 = 8$
3. $7 + 6 = 13$	4. $13 - 9 = 4$
5. Circle the way that does NOT make 15. 19 − 4 9 + 6 (circled) 17 − 3	6. Circle a way to make 12. 18 − 2 (circled) 8 + 4 6 + 5

Go On

Name ______________________ CHAPTER 20 TEST • PAGE 2

7. Write the other fact that belongs in this fact family. 3 + 8 = 11 8 + 3 = 11 11 − 3 = 8 11 − 8 = 3	8. Circle the pair that shows two facts in the same family. (circled) 6 + 8 = 14, 14 − 8 = 6 8 − 6 = 2, 6 + 8 = 14 4 + 7 = 11, 7 − 4 = 3 9 + 1 = 10, 7 + 3 = 10

For 9 and 10, use [cube] to solve.

9. John has 19 tomatoes. He gives 8 to Gail. How many tomatoes does John have left? 11 tomatoes	10. Rose has 17 pumpkins. Tony has 3 pumpkins. How many pumpkins do they have in all? 20 pumpkins

Stop

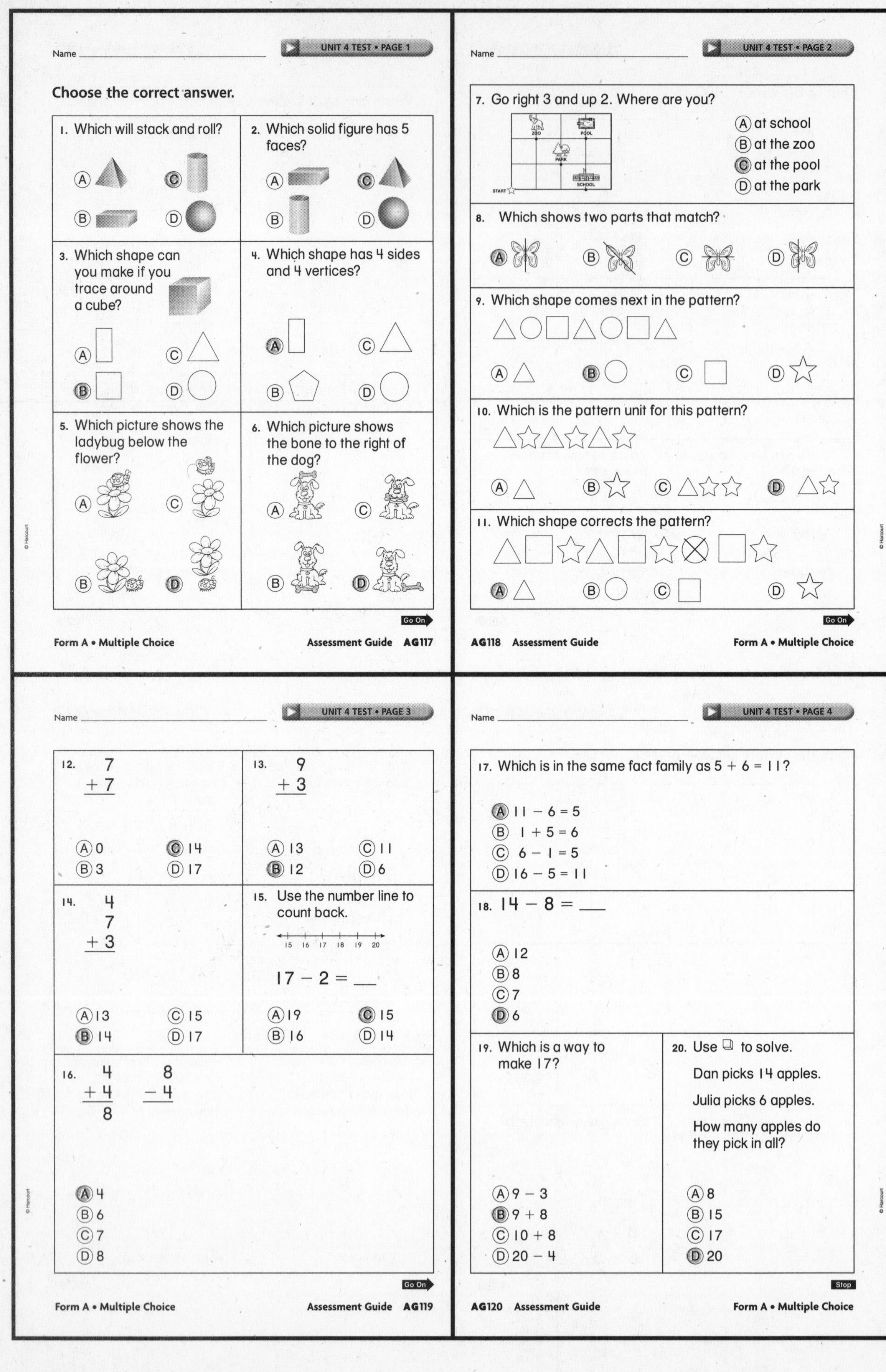

Name ________________ UNIT 4 TEST • PAGE 1

Choose the correct answer.

1. Which will stack and roll?
   (A) (B) (C) (D)

2. Which solid figure has 5 faces?
   (A) (B) (C) (D)

3. Which shape can you make if you trace around a cube?
   (A) (B) (C) (D)

4. Which shape has 4 sides and 4 vertices?
   (A) (B) (C) (D)

5. Which picture shows the ladybug below the flower?
   (A) (B) (C) (D)

6. Which picture shows the bone to the right of the dog?
   (A) (B) (C) (D)

Go On

Form A • Multiple Choice — Assessment Guide AG117

© Harcourt

Name ________________ UNIT 4 TEST • PAGE 2

7. Go right 3 and up 2. Where are you?
   ZOO POOL PARK SCHOOL START
   (A) at school
   (B) at the zoo
   (C) at the pool
   (D) at the park

8. Which shows two parts that match?
   (A) (B) (C) (D)

9. Which shape comes next in the pattern?
   (A) (B) (C) (D)

10. Which is the pattern unit for this pattern?
    (A) (B) (C) (D)

11. Which shape corrects the pattern?
    (A) (B) (C) (D)

Go On

AG118 Assessment Guide — Form A • Multiple Choice

© Harcourt

Name ________________ UNIT 4 TEST • PAGE 3

12. $7 + 7$
    (A) 0 (B) 3 (C) 14 (D) 17

13. $9 + 3$
    (A) 13 (B) 12 (C) 11 (D) 6

14. $4 + 7 + 3$
    (A) 13 (B) 14 (C) 15 (D) 17

15. Use the number line to count back.
    15 16 17 18 19 20
    $17 - 2 =$ ___
    (A) 19 (B) 16 (C) 15 (D) 14

16. $4 + 4 = 8$ $\quad 8 - 4$
    (A) 4 (B) 6 (C) 7 (D) 8

Go On

Form A • Multiple Choice — Assessment Guide AG119

© Harcourt

Name ________________ UNIT 4 TEST • PAGE 4

17. Which is in the same fact family as $5 + 6 = 11$?
    (A) $11 - 6 = 5$
    (B) $1 + 5 = 6$
    (C) $6 - 1 = 5$
    (D) $16 - 5 = 11$

18. $14 - 8 =$ ___
    (A) 12
    (B) 8
    (C) 7
    (D) 6

19. Which is a way to make 17?
    (A) $9 - 3$
    (B) $9 + 8$
    (C) $10 + 8$
    (D) $20 - 4$

20. Use to solve.
    Dan picks 14 apples.
    Julia picks 6 apples.
    How many apples do they pick in all?
    (A) 8
    (B) 15
    (C) 17
    (D) 20

Stop

AG120 Assessment Guide — Form A • Multiple Choice

© Harcourt

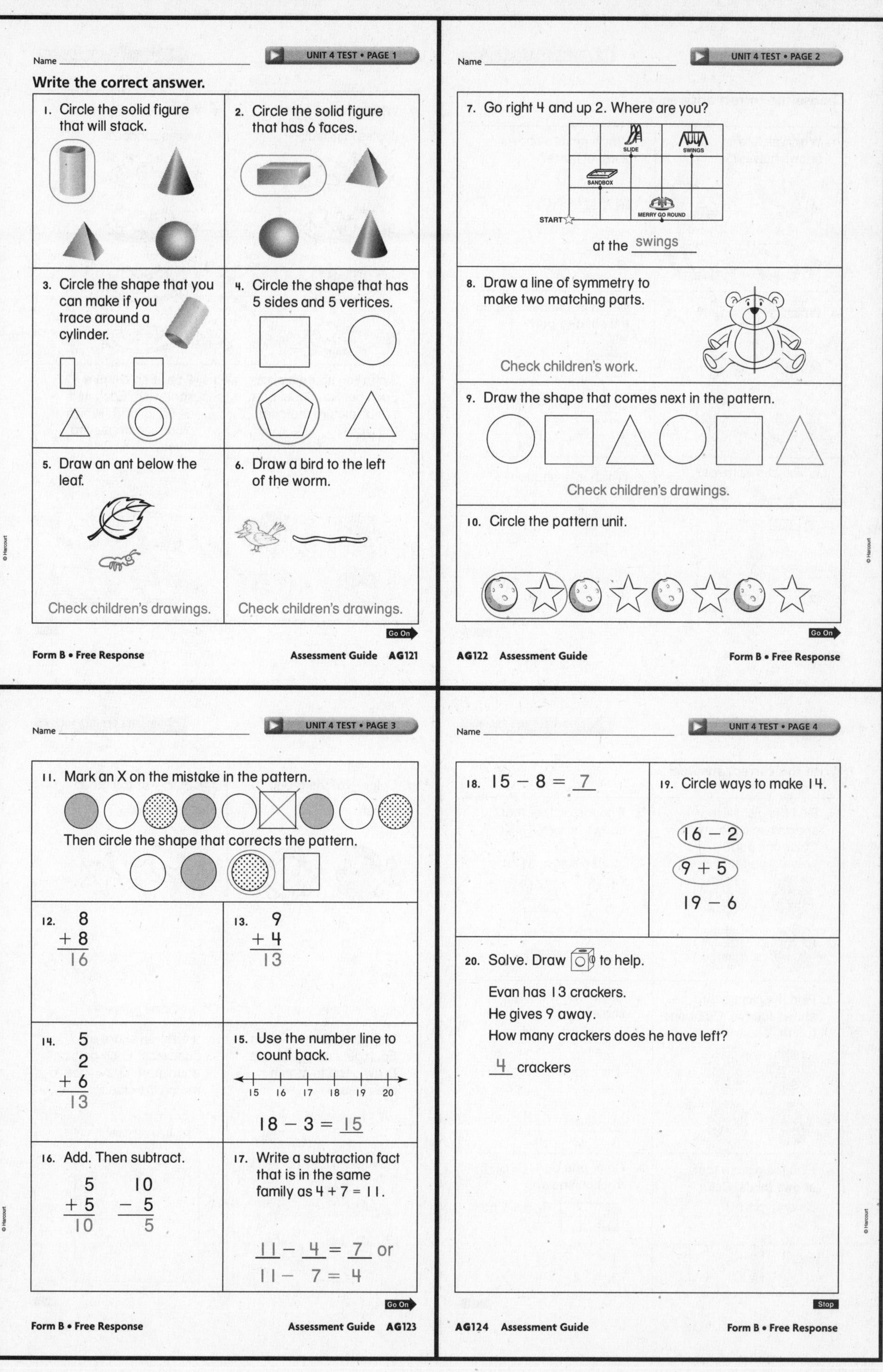

Name
UNIT 4 TEST • PAGE 1
Write the correct answer.
1. Circle the solid figure that will stack.
2. Circle the solid figure that has 6 faces.
3. Circle the shape that you can make if you trace around a cylinder.
4. Circle the shape that has 5 sides and 5 vertices.
5. Draw an ant below the leaf.
6. Draw a bird to the left of the worm.
Check children's drawings.
Check children's drawings.
Go On
Form B • Free Response
Assessment Guide AG121
Name
UNIT 4 TEST • PAGE 2
7. Go right 4 and up 2. Where are you?
SLIDE
SWINGS
SANDBOX
MERRY GO ROUND
START
at the swings
8. Draw a line of symmetry to make two matching parts.
Check children's work.
9. Draw the shape that comes next in the pattern.
Check children's drawings.
10. Circle the pattern unit.
Go On
AG122 Assessment Guide
Form B • Free Response
Name
UNIT 4 TEST • PAGE 3
11. Mark an X on the mistake in the pattern.
Then circle the shape that corrects the pattern.
12. 8 + 8 = 16
13. 9 + 4 = 13
14. 5 2 + 6 = 13
15. Use the number line to count back.
15 16 17 18 19 20
18 − 3 = 15
16. Add. Then subtract.
5 + 5 = 10
10 − 5 = 5
17. Write a subtraction fact that is in the same family as 4 + 7 = 11.
11 − 4 = 7 or
11 − 7 = 4
Go On
Form B • Free Response
Assessment Guide AG123
Name
UNIT 4 TEST • PAGE 4
18. 15 − 8 = 7
19. Circle ways to make 14.
16 − 2
9 + 5
19 − 6
20. Solve. Draw to help.
Evan has 13 crackers.
He gives 9 away.
How many crackers does he have left?
4 crackers
Stop
AG124 Assessment Guide
Form B • Free Response

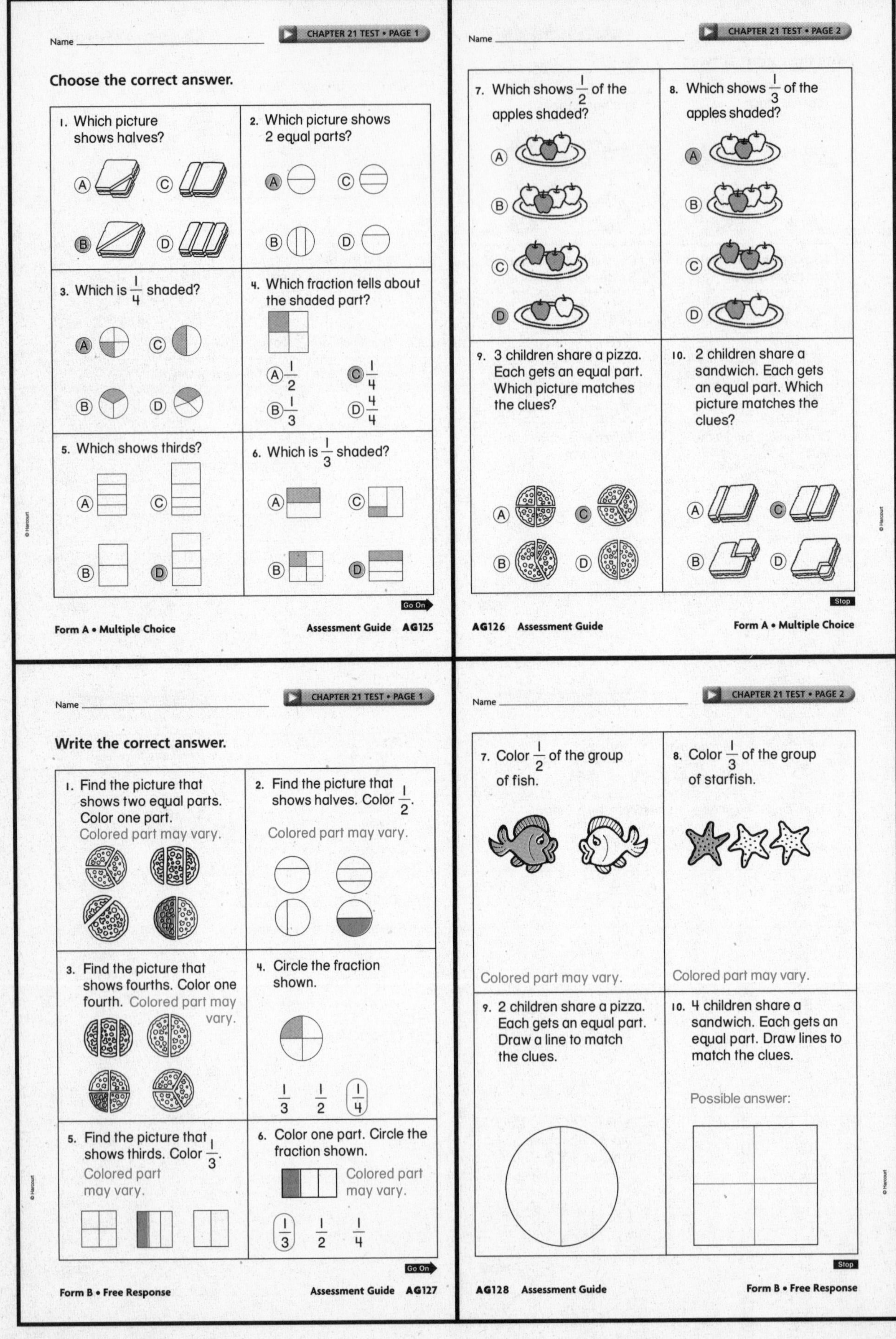

Name
CHAPTER 21 TEST • PAGE 1
Choose the correct answer.
1. Which picture shows halves?
2. Which picture shows 2 equal parts?
3. Which is 1/4 shaded?
4. Which fraction tells about the shaded part?
A 1/2
B 1/3
C 1/4
D 4/4
5. Which shows thirds?
6. Which is 1/3 shaded?
Go On
Form A • Multiple Choice
Assessment Guide AG125
Name
CHAPTER 21 TEST • PAGE 2
7. Which shows 1/2 of the apples shaded?
8. Which shows 1/3 of the apples shaded?
9. 3 children share a pizza. Each gets an equal part. Which picture matches the clues?
10. 2 children share a sandwich. Each gets an equal part. Which picture matches the clues?
Stop
AG126 Assessment Guide
Form A • Multiple Choice
Name
CHAPTER 21 TEST • PAGE 1
Write the correct answer.
1. Find the picture that shows two equal parts. Color one part.
Colored part may vary.
2. Find the picture that shows halves. Color 1/2.
Colored part may vary.
3. Find the picture that shows fourths. Color one fourth. Colored part may vary.
4. Circle the fraction shown.
1/3 1/2 1/4
5. Find the picture that shows thirds. Color 1/3.
Colored part may vary.
6. Color one part. Circle the fraction shown.
Colored part may vary.
1/3 1/2 1/4
Go On
Form B • Free Response
Assessment Guide AG127
Name
CHAPTER 21 TEST • PAGE 2
7. Color 1/2 of the group of fish.
Colored part may vary.
8. Color 1/3 of the group of starfish.
Colored part may vary.
9. 2 children share a pizza. Each gets an equal part. Draw a line to match the clues.
10. 4 children share a sandwich. Each gets an equal part. Draw lines to match the clues.
Possible answer:
Stop
AG128 Assessment Guide
Form B • Free Response

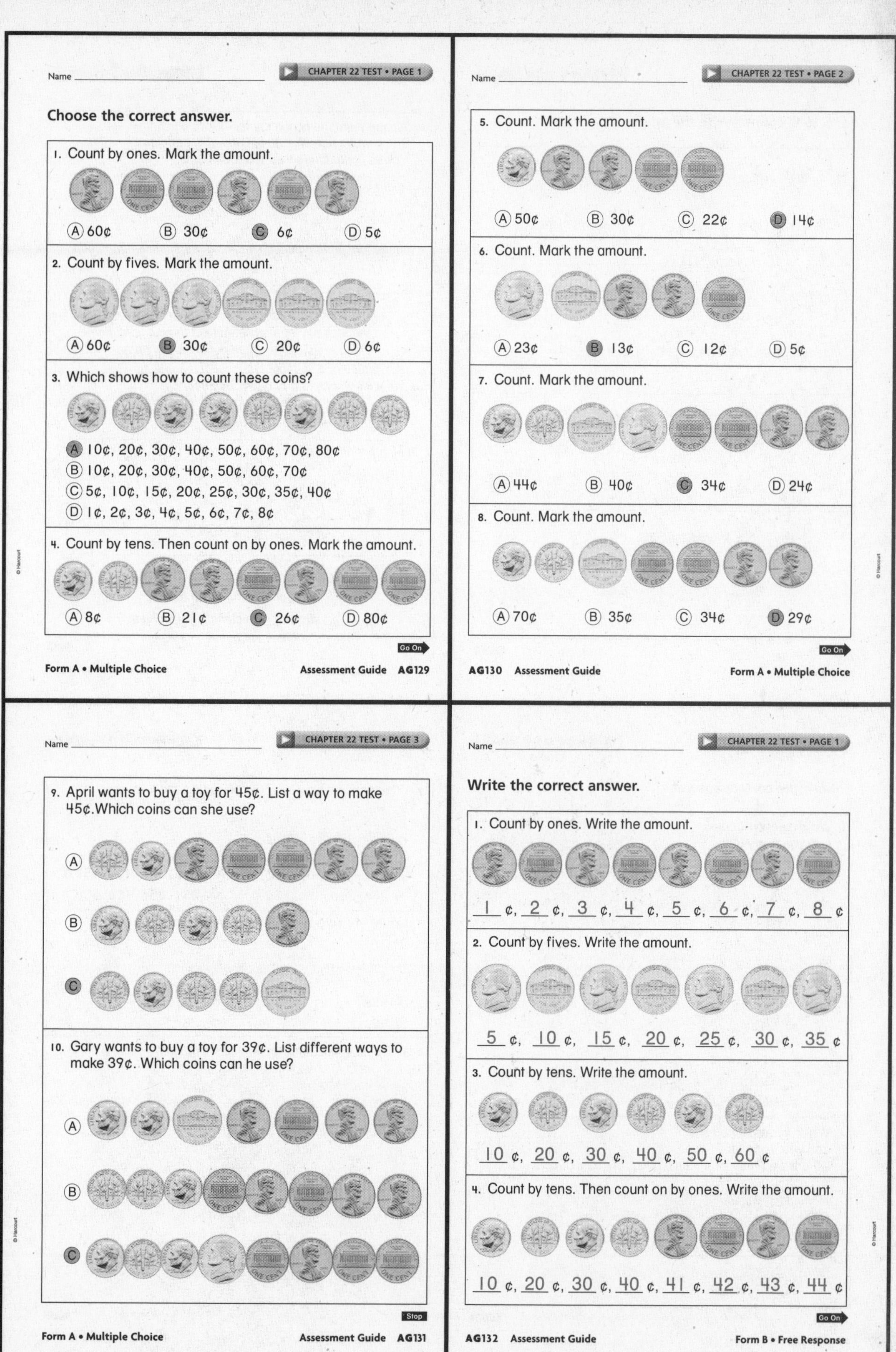

Name ____________________

CHAPTER 22 TEST • PAGE 1

Choose the correct answer.

1. Count by ones. Mark the amount.

Ⓐ 60¢ Ⓑ 30¢ Ⓒ 6¢ Ⓓ 5¢

2. Count by fives. Mark the amount.

Ⓐ 60¢ Ⓑ 30¢ Ⓒ 20¢ Ⓓ 6¢

3. Which shows how to count these coins?

Ⓐ 10¢, 20¢, 30¢, 40¢, 50¢, 60¢, 70¢, 80¢
Ⓑ 10¢, 20¢, 30¢, 40¢, 50¢, 60¢, 70¢
Ⓒ 5¢, 10¢, 15¢, 20¢, 25¢, 30¢, 35¢, 40¢
Ⓓ 1¢, 2¢, 3¢, 4¢, 5¢, 6¢, 7¢, 8¢

4. Count by tens. Then count on by ones. Mark the amount.

Ⓐ 8¢ Ⓑ 21¢ Ⓒ 26¢ Ⓓ 80¢

Go On

Form A • Multiple Choice — Assessment Guide AG129

© Harcourt

Name ____________________

CHAPTER 22 TEST • PAGE 2

5. Count. Mark the amount.

Ⓐ 50¢ Ⓑ 30¢ Ⓒ 22¢ Ⓓ 14¢

6. Count. Mark the amount.

Ⓐ 23¢ Ⓑ 13¢ Ⓒ 12¢ Ⓓ 5¢

7. Count. Mark the amount.

Ⓐ 44¢ Ⓑ 40¢ Ⓒ 34¢ Ⓓ 24¢

8. Count. Mark the amount.

Ⓐ 70¢ Ⓑ 35¢ Ⓒ 34¢ Ⓓ 29¢

Go On

AG130 Assessment Guide — Form A • Multiple Choice

© Harcourt

Name ____________________

CHAPTER 22 TEST • PAGE 3

9. April wants to buy a toy for 45¢. List a way to make 45¢. Which coins can she use?

Ⓐ

Ⓑ

Ⓒ

10. Gary wants to buy a toy for 39¢. List different ways to make 39¢. Which coins can he use?

Ⓐ

Ⓑ

Ⓒ

Stop

Form A • Multiple Choice — Assessment Guide AG131

© Harcourt

Name ____________________

CHAPTER 22 TEST • PAGE 1

Write the correct answer.

1. Count by ones. Write the amount.

1 ¢, 2 ¢, 3 ¢, 4 ¢, 5 ¢, 6 ¢, 7 ¢, 8 ¢

2. Count by fives. Write the amount.

5 ¢, 10 ¢, 15 ¢, 20 ¢, 25 ¢, 30 ¢, 35 ¢

3. Count by tens. Write the amount.

10 ¢, 20 ¢, 30 ¢, 40 ¢, 50 ¢, 60 ¢

4. Count by tens. Then count on by ones. Write the amount.

10 ¢, 20 ¢, 30 ¢, 40 ¢, 41 ¢, 42 ¢, 43 ¢, 44 ¢

Go On

AG132 Assessment Guide — Form B • Free Response

© Harcourt

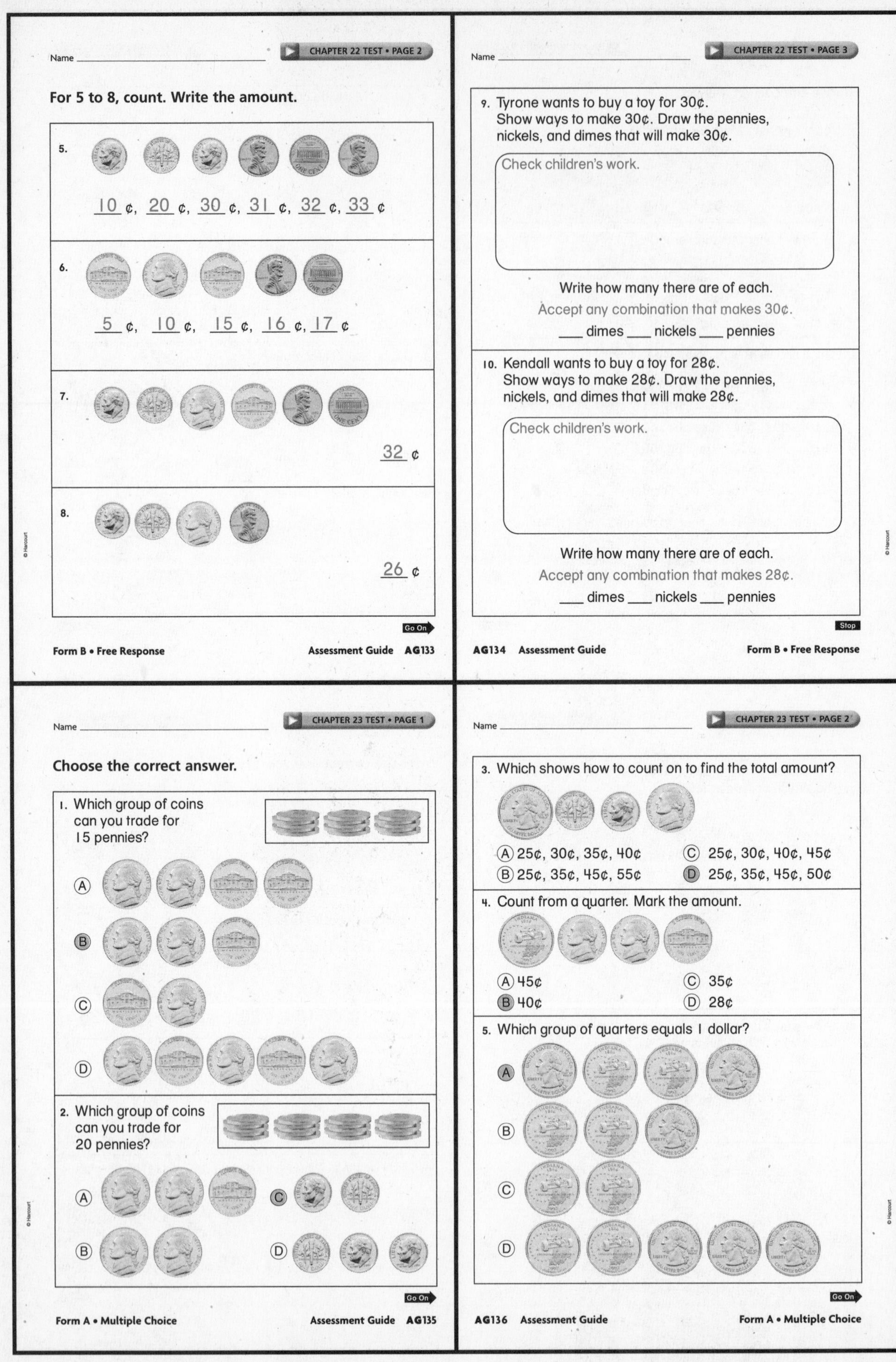

Name ____________________

CHAPTER 22 TEST • PAGE 2

For 5 to 8, count. Write the amount.

5. 10 ¢, 20 ¢, 30 ¢, 31 ¢, 32 ¢, 33 ¢

6. 5 ¢, 10 ¢, 15 ¢, 16 ¢, 17 ¢

7. 32 ¢

8. 26 ¢

Go On

© Harcourt

Form B • Free Response — Assessment Guide AG133

Name ____________________

CHAPTER 22 TEST • PAGE 3

9. Tyrone wants to buy a toy for 30¢. Show ways to make 30¢. Draw the pennies, nickels, and dimes that will make 30¢.

Check children's work.

Write how many there are of each.
Accept any combination that makes 30¢.
___ dimes ___ nickels ___ pennies

10. Kendall wants to buy a toy for 28¢. Show ways to make 28¢. Draw the pennies, nickels, and dimes that will make 28¢.

Check children's work.

Write how many there are of each.
Accept any combination that makes 28¢.
___ dimes ___ nickels ___ pennies

Stop

© Harcourt

AG134 Assessment Guide — Form B • Free Response

Name ____________________

CHAPTER 23 TEST • PAGE 1

Choose the correct answer.

1. Which group of coins can you trade for 15 pennies?

Ⓐ Ⓑ Ⓒ Ⓓ

2. Which group of coins can you trade for 20 pennies?

Ⓐ Ⓑ Ⓒ Ⓓ

Go On

© Harcourt

Form A • Multiple Choice — Assessment Guide AG135

Name ____________________

CHAPTER 23 TEST • PAGE 2

3. Which shows how to count on to find the total amount?

Ⓐ 25¢, 30¢, 35¢, 40¢
Ⓑ 25¢, 35¢, 45¢, 55¢
Ⓒ 25¢, 30¢, 40¢, 45¢
Ⓓ 25¢, 35¢, 45¢, 50¢

4. Count from a quarter. Mark the amount.

Ⓐ 45¢
Ⓑ 40¢
Ⓒ 35¢
Ⓓ 28¢

5. Which group of quarters equals 1 dollar?

Ⓐ Ⓑ Ⓒ Ⓓ

Go On

© Harcourt

AG136 Assessment Guide — Form A • Multiple Choice

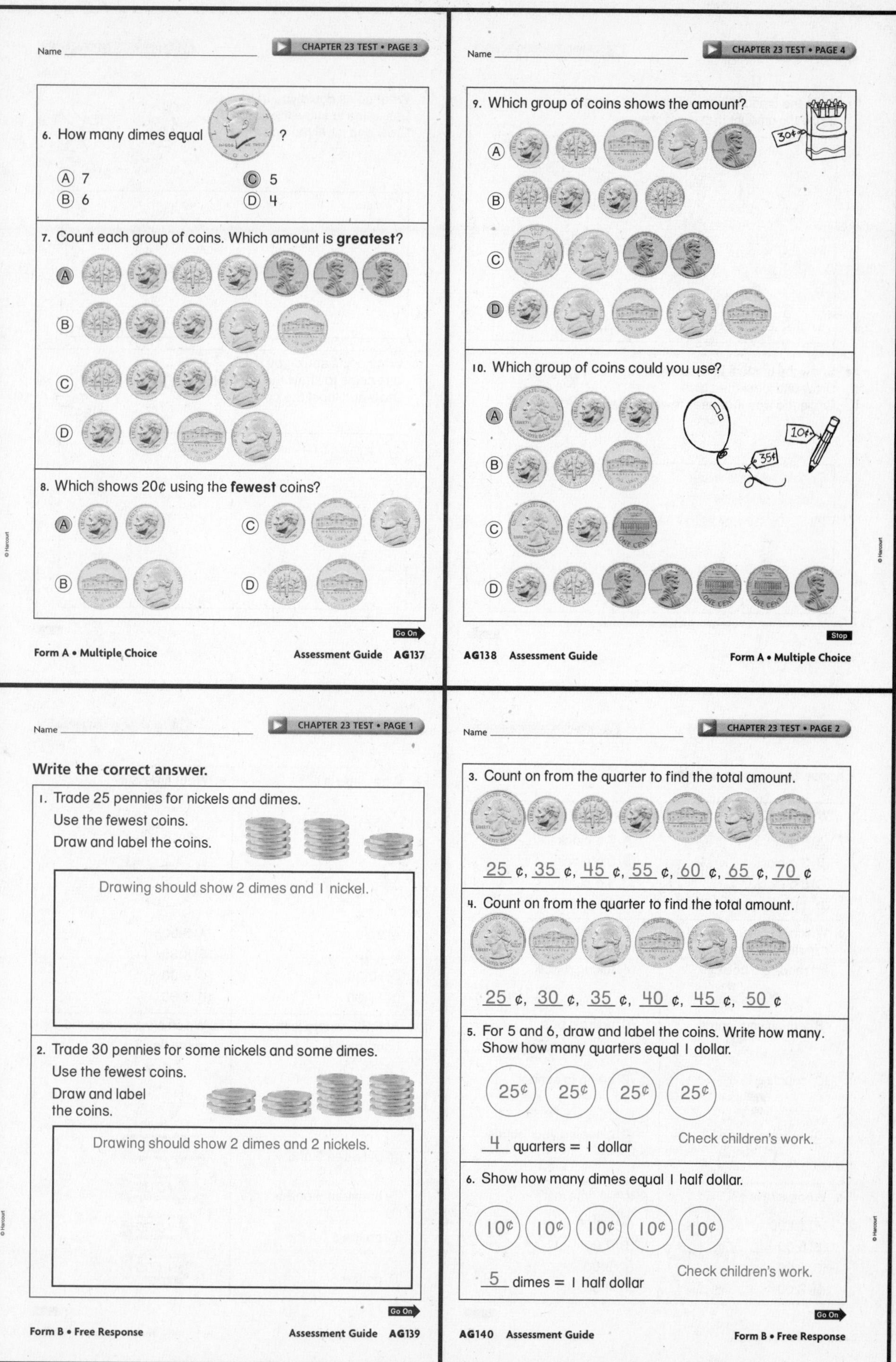

Name ______________________

CHAPTER 23 TEST • PAGE 3

6. How many dimes equal [half dollar] ?

(A) 7
(B) 6
(C) 5
(D) 4

7. Count each group of coins. Which amount is **greatest**?

(A)
(B)
(C)
(D)

8. Which shows 20¢ using the **fewest** coins?

(A)
(B)
(C)
(D)

Go On

© Harcourt

Form A • Multiple Choice — Assessment Guide AG137

Name ______________________

CHAPTER 23 TEST • PAGE 4

9. Which group of coins shows the amount?

30¢

(A)
(B)
(C)
(D)

10. Which group of coins could you use?

35¢

10¢

(A)
(B)
(C)
(D)

Stop

© Harcourt

AG138 Assessment Guide — Form A • Multiple Choice

Name ______________________

CHAPTER 23 TEST • PAGE 1

Write the correct answer.

1. Trade 25 pennies for nickels and dimes.
Use the fewest coins.
Draw and label the coins.

Drawing should show 2 dimes and 1 nickel.

2. Trade 30 pennies for some nickels and some dimes.
Use the fewest coins.
Draw and label the coins.

Drawing should show 2 dimes and 2 nickels.

Go On

© Harcourt

Form B • Free Response — Assessment Guide AG139

Name ______________________

CHAPTER 23 TEST • PAGE 2

3. Count on from the quarter to find the total amount.

25 ¢, 35 ¢, 45 ¢, 55 ¢, 60 ¢, 65 ¢, 70 ¢

4. Count on from the quarter to find the total amount.

25 ¢, 30 ¢, 35 ¢, 40 ¢, 45 ¢, 50 ¢

5. For 5 and 6, draw and label the coins. Write how many.
Show how many quarters equal 1 dollar.

25¢ 25¢ 25¢ 25¢

4 quarters = 1 dollar

Check children's work.

6. Show how many dimes equal 1 half dollar.

10¢ 10¢ 10¢ 10¢ 10¢

5 dimes = 1 half dollar

Check children's work.

Go On

© Harcourt

AG140 Assessment Guide — Form B • Free Response

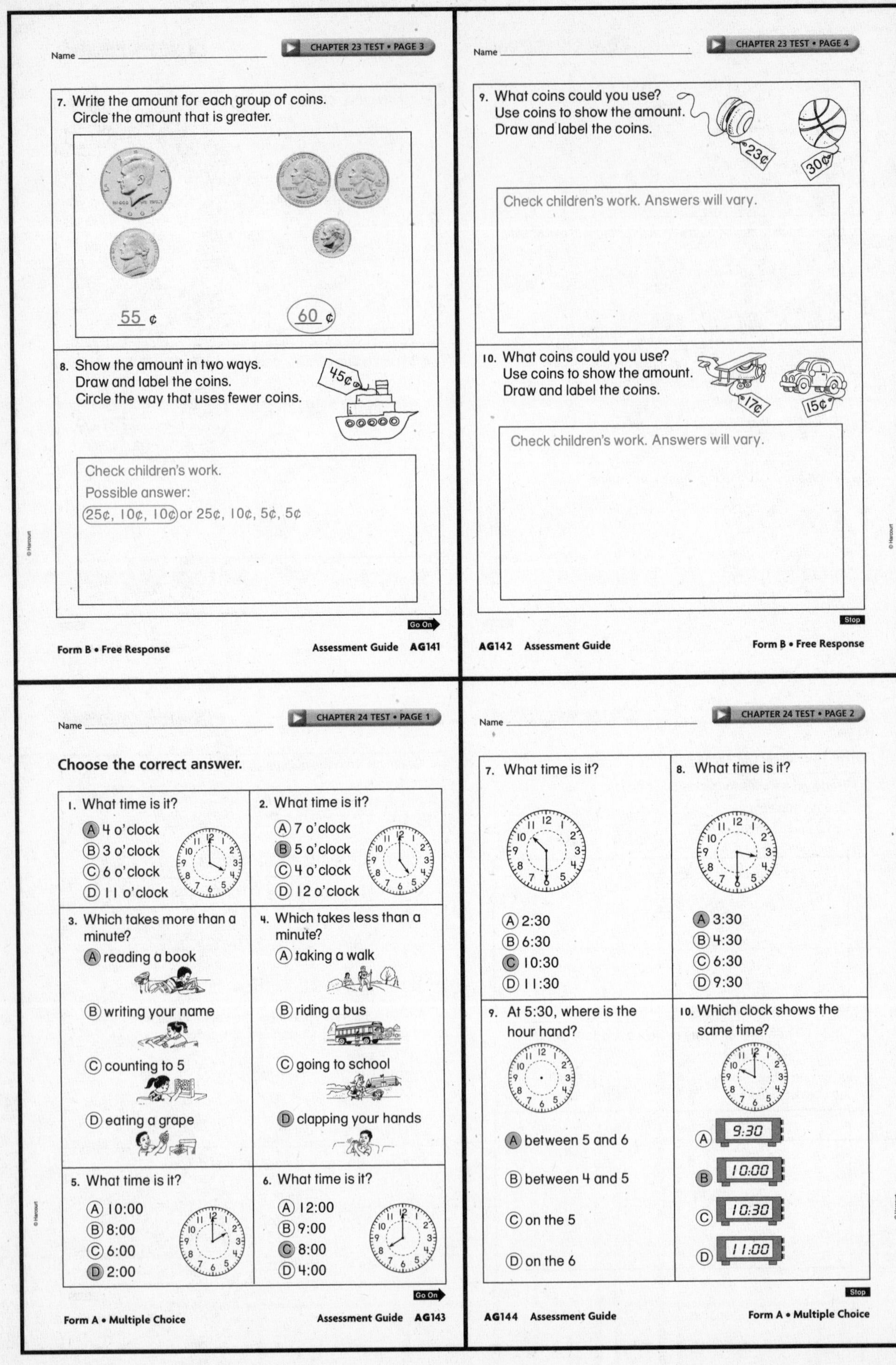

Name

CHAPTER 23 TEST • PAGE 3

7. Write the amount for each group of coins. Circle the amount that is greater.

55 ¢ (60 ¢)

8. Show the amount in two ways. Draw and label the coins. Circle the way that uses fewer coins.

45¢

Check children's work.
Possible answer:
(25¢, 10¢, 10¢) or 25¢, 10¢, 5¢, 5¢

Go On

Name

CHAPTER 23 TEST • PAGE 4

9. What coins could you use? Use coins to show the amount. Draw and label the coins.

23¢ 30¢

Check children's work. Answers will vary.

10. What coins could you use? Use coins to show the amount. Draw and label the coins.

17¢ 15¢

Check children's work. Answers will vary.

Stop

Name

CHAPTER 24 TEST • PAGE 1

Choose the correct answer.

1. What time is it?
(A) 4 o'clock
(B) 3 o'clock
(C) 6 o'clock
(D) 11 o'clock

2. What time is it?
(A) 7 o'clock
(B) 5 o'clock
(C) 4 o'clock
(D) 12 o'clock

3. Which takes more than a minute?
(A) reading a book
(B) writing your name
(C) counting to 5
(D) eating a grape

4. Which takes less than a minute?
(A) taking a walk
(B) riding a bus
(C) going to school
(D) clapping your hands

5. What time is it?
(A) 10:00
(B) 8:00
(C) 6:00
(D) 2:00

6. What time is it?
(A) 12:00
(B) 9:00
(C) 8:00
(D) 4:00

Go On

Name

CHAPTER 24 TEST • PAGE 2

7. What time is it?
(A) 2:30
(B) 6:30
(C) 10:30
(D) 11:30

8. What time is it?
(A) 3:30
(B) 4:30
(C) 6:30
(D) 9:30

9. At 5:30, where is the hour hand?
(A) between 5 and 6
(B) between 4 and 5
(C) on the 5
(D) on the 6

10. Which clock shows the same time?
(A) 9:30
(B) 10:00
(C) 10:30
(D) 11:00

Stop

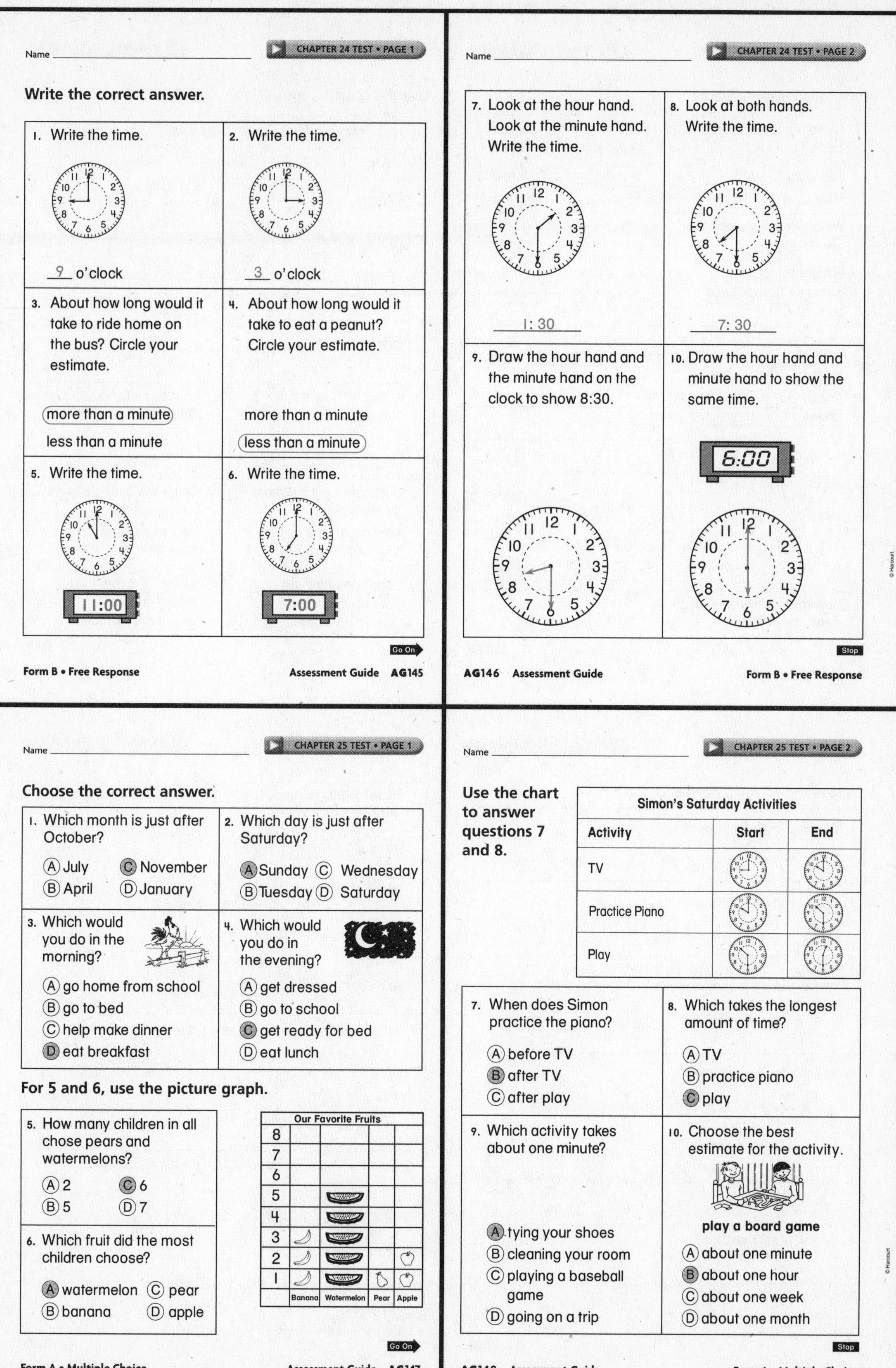

Name

CHAPTER 24 TEST • PAGE 1

Write the correct answer.

1. Write the time.

9 o'clock

2. Write the time.

3 o'clock

3. About how long would it take to ride home on the bus? Circle your estimate.

(more than a minute)

less than a minute

4. About how long would it take to eat a peanut? Circle your estimate.

more than a minute

(less than a minute)

5. Write the time.

11:00

6. Write the time.

7:00

Go On

Form B • Free Response — Assessment Guide AG145

Name

CHAPTER 24 TEST • PAGE 2

7. Look at the hour hand. Look at the minute hand. Write the time.

1:30

8. Look at both hands. Write the time.

7:30

9. Draw the hour hand and the minute hand on the clock to show 8:30.

10. Draw the hour hand and minute hand to show the same time.

6:00

Stop

AG146 Assessment Guide — Form B • Free Response

Name

CHAPTER 25 TEST • PAGE 1

Choose the correct answer.

1. Which month is just after October?

Ⓐ July Ⓒ November
Ⓑ April Ⓓ January

2. Which day is just after Saturday?

Ⓐ Sunday Ⓒ Wednesday
Ⓑ Tuesday Ⓓ Saturday

3. Which would you do in the morning?

Ⓐ go home from school
Ⓑ go to bed
Ⓒ help make dinner
Ⓓ eat breakfast

4. Which would you do in the evening?

Ⓐ get dressed
Ⓑ go to school
Ⓒ get ready for bed
Ⓓ eat lunch

For 5 and 6, use the picture graph.

5. How many children in all chose pears and watermelons?

Ⓐ 2 Ⓒ 6
Ⓑ 5 Ⓓ 7

6. Which fruit did the most children choose?

Ⓐ watermelon Ⓒ pear
Ⓑ banana Ⓓ apple

Our Favorite Fruits (8, 7, 6, 5, 4, 3, 2, 1; Banana, Watermelon, Pear, Apple)

Go On

Form A • Multiple Choice — Assessment Guide AG147

Name

CHAPTER 25 TEST • PAGE 2

Use the chart to answer questions 7 and 8.

Simon's Saturday Activities		
Activity	Start	End
TV		
Practice Piano		
Play		

7. When does Simon practice the piano?

Ⓐ before TV
Ⓑ after TV
Ⓒ after play

8. Which takes the longest amount of time?

Ⓐ TV
Ⓑ practice piano
Ⓒ play

9. Which activity takes about one minute?

Ⓐ tying your shoes
Ⓑ cleaning your room
Ⓒ playing a baseball game
Ⓓ going on a trip

10. Choose the best estimate for the activity.

play a board game

Ⓐ about one minute
Ⓑ about one hour
Ⓒ about one week
Ⓓ about one month

Stop

AG148 Assessment Guide — Form A • Multiple Choice

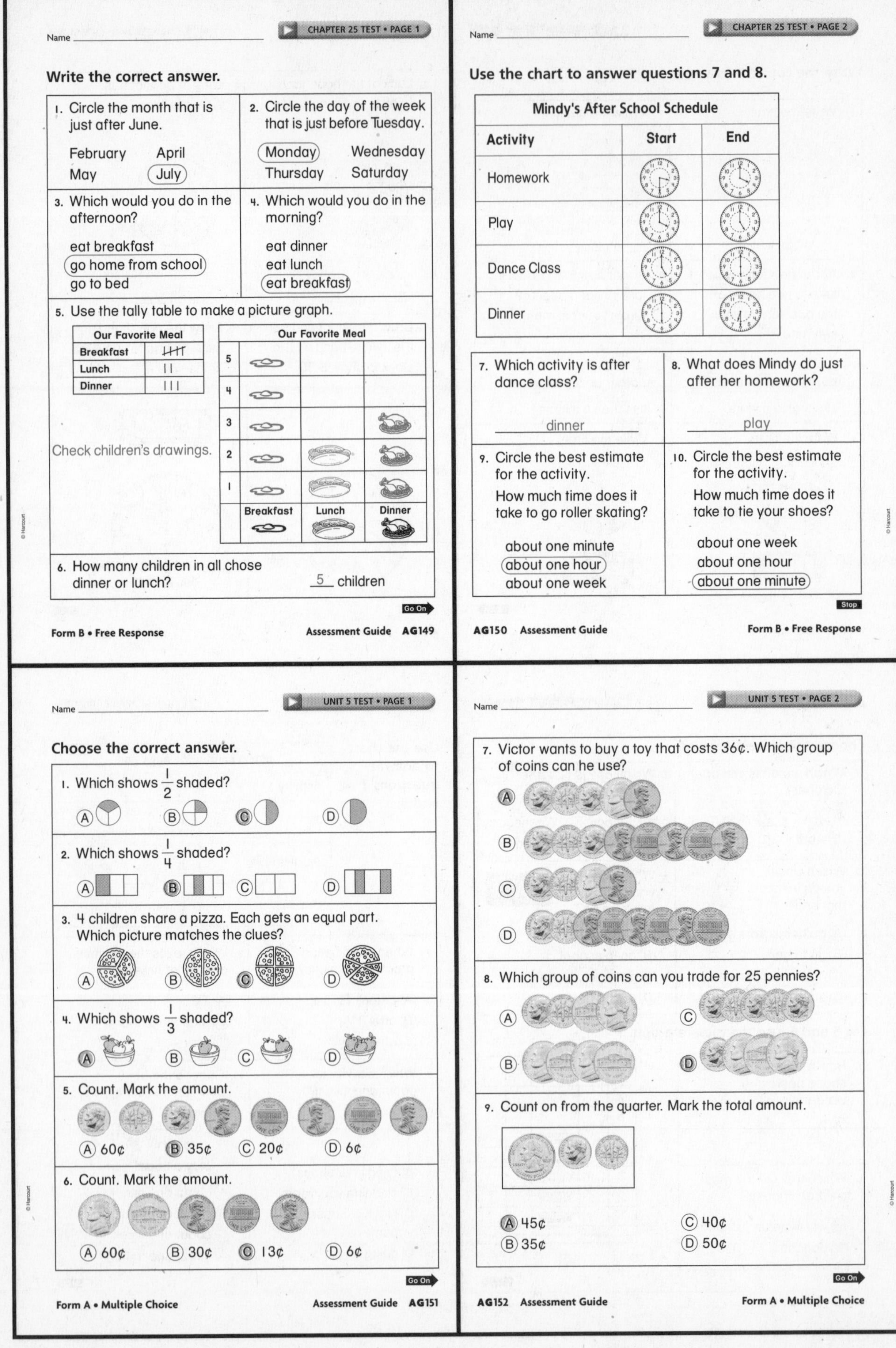
Name
CHAPTER 25 TEST • PAGE 1
Write the correct answer.
1. Circle the month that is just after June.
February April
May July
2. Circle the day of the week that is just after Tuesday.
Monday Wednesday
Thursday Saturday
3. Which would you do in the afternoon?
eat breakfast
go home from school
go to bed
4. Which would you do in the morning?
eat dinner
eat lunch
eat breakfast
5. Use the tally table to make a picture graph.
Our Favorite Meal
Breakfast
Lunch
Dinner
Our Favorite Meal
Breakfast Lunch Dinner
Check children's drawings.
6. How many children in all chose dinner or lunch?
5 children
Go On
Form B • Free Response
Assessment Guide AG149
Name
CHAPTER 25 TEST • PAGE 2
Use the chart to answer questions 7 and 8.
Mindy's After School Schedule
Activity Start End
Homework
Play
Dance Class
Dinner
7. Which activity is after dance class?
dinner
8. What does Mindy do just after her homework?
play
9. Circle the best estimate for the activity.
How much time does it take to go roller skating?
about one minute
about one hour
about one week
10. Circle the best estimate for the activity.
How much time does it take to tie your shoes?
about one week
about one hour
about one minute
Stop
AG150 Assessment Guide
Form B • Free Response
Name
UNIT 5 TEST • PAGE 1
Choose the correct answer.
1. Which shows 1/2 shaded?
2. Which shows 1/4 shaded?
3. 4 children share a pizza. Each gets an equal part. Which picture matches the clues?
4. Which shows 1/3 shaded?
5. Count. Mark the amount.
A 60¢ B 35¢ C 20¢ D 6¢
6. Count. Mark the amount.
A 60¢ B 30¢ C 13¢ D 6¢
Go On
Form A • Multiple Choice
Assessment Guide AG151
Name
UNIT 5 TEST • PAGE 2
7. Victor wants to buy a toy that costs 36¢. Which group of coins can he use?
8. Which group of coins can you trade for 25 pennies?
9. Count on from the quarter. Mark the total amount.
A 45¢ C 40¢
B 35¢ D 50¢
Go On
AG152 Assessment Guide
Form A • Multiple Choice

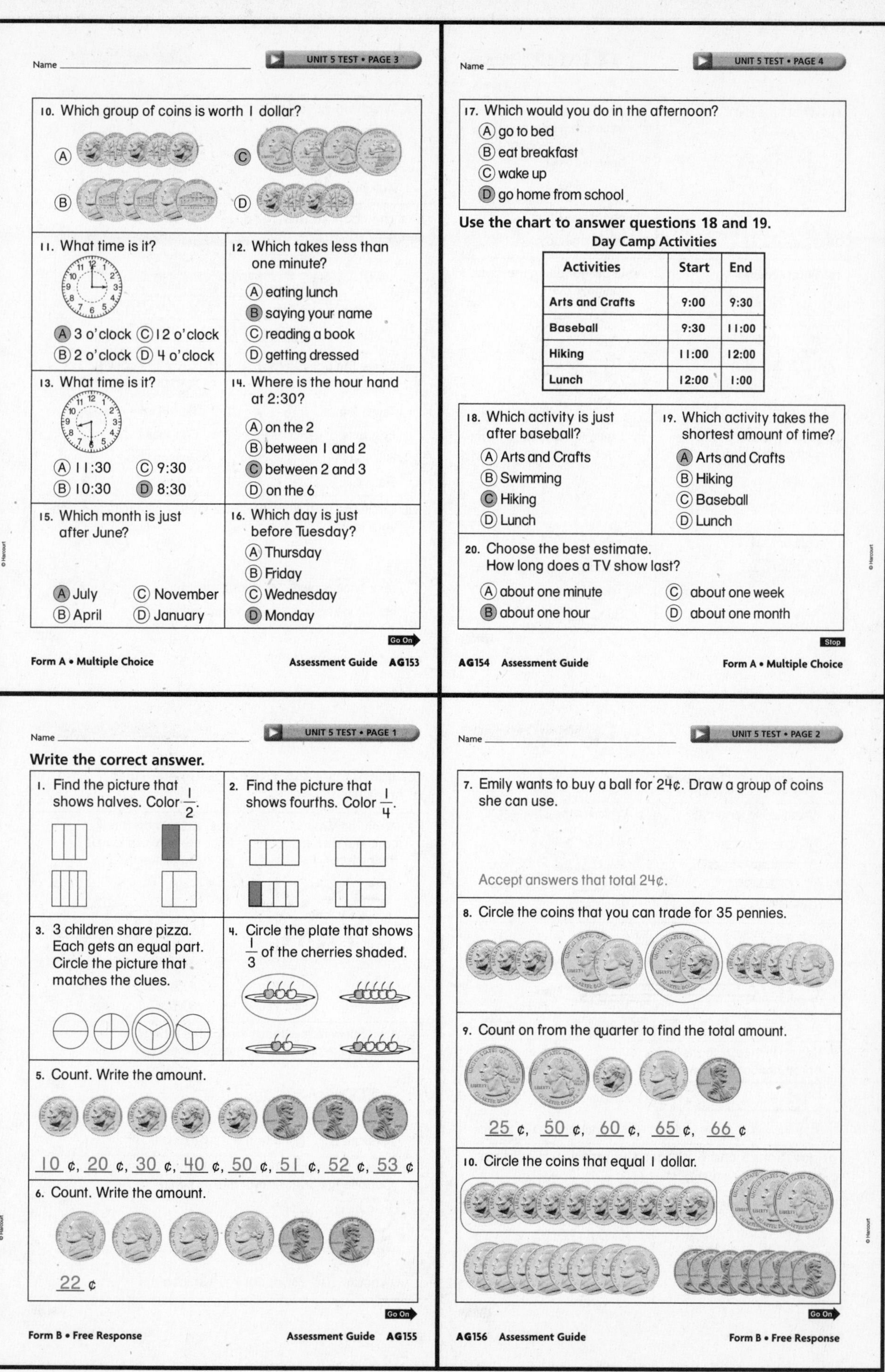

Name ______________ UNIT 5 TEST • PAGE 3

10. Which group of coins is worth 1 dollar?

(A) (B) (C) (D)

11. What time is it?

(A) 3 o'clock (C) 12 o'clock
(B) 2 o'clock (D) 4 o'clock

12. Which takes less than one minute?

(A) eating lunch
(B) saying your name
(C) reading a book
(D) getting dressed

13. What time is it?

(A) 11:30 (C) 9:30
(B) 10:30 (D) 8:30

14. Where is the hour hand at 2:30?

(A) on the 2
(B) between 1 and 2
(C) between 2 and 3
(D) on the 6

15. Which month is just after June?

(A) July (C) November
(B) April (D) January

16. Which day is just before Tuesday?

(A) Thursday
(B) Friday
(C) Wednesday
(D) Monday

Go On

Form A • Multiple Choice — Assessment Guide AG153

© Harcourt

Name ______________ UNIT 5 TEST • PAGE 4

17. Which would you do in the afternoon?

(A) go to bed
(B) eat breakfast
(C) wake up
(D) go home from school

Use the chart to answer questions 18 and 19.

Day Camp Activities

Activities	Start	End
Arts and Crafts	9:00	9:30
Baseball	9:30	11:00
Hiking	11:00	12:00
Lunch	12:00	1:00

18. Which activity is just after baseball?

(A) Arts and Crafts
(B) Swimming
(C) Hiking
(D) Lunch

19. Which activity takes the shortest amount of time?

(A) Arts and Crafts
(B) Hiking
(C) Baseball
(D) Lunch

20. Choose the best estimate. How long does a TV show last?

(A) about one minute (C) about one week
(B) about one hour (D) about one month

Stop

AG154 Assessment Guide — Form A • Multiple Choice

© Harcourt

Name ______________ UNIT 5 TEST • PAGE 1

Write the correct answer.

1. Find the picture that shows halves. Color $\frac{1}{2}$.

2. Find the picture that shows fourths. Color $\frac{1}{4}$.

3. 3 children share pizza. Each gets an equal part. Circle the picture that matches the clues.

4. Circle the plate that shows $\frac{1}{3}$ of the cherries shaded.

5. Count. Write the amount.

10 ¢, 20 ¢, 30 ¢, 40 ¢, 50 ¢, 51 ¢, 52 ¢, 53 ¢

6. Count. Write the amount.

22 ¢

Go On

Form B • Free Response — Assessment Guide AG155

© Harcourt

Name ______________ UNIT 5 TEST • PAGE 2

7. Emily wants to buy a ball for 24¢. Draw a group of coins she can use.

Accept answers that total 24¢.

8. Circle the coins that you can trade for 35 pennies.

9. Count on from the quarter to find the total amount.

25 ¢, 50 ¢, 60 ¢, 65 ¢, 66 ¢

10. Circle the coins that equal 1 dollar.

Go On

AG156 Assessment Guide — Form B • Free Response

© Harcourt

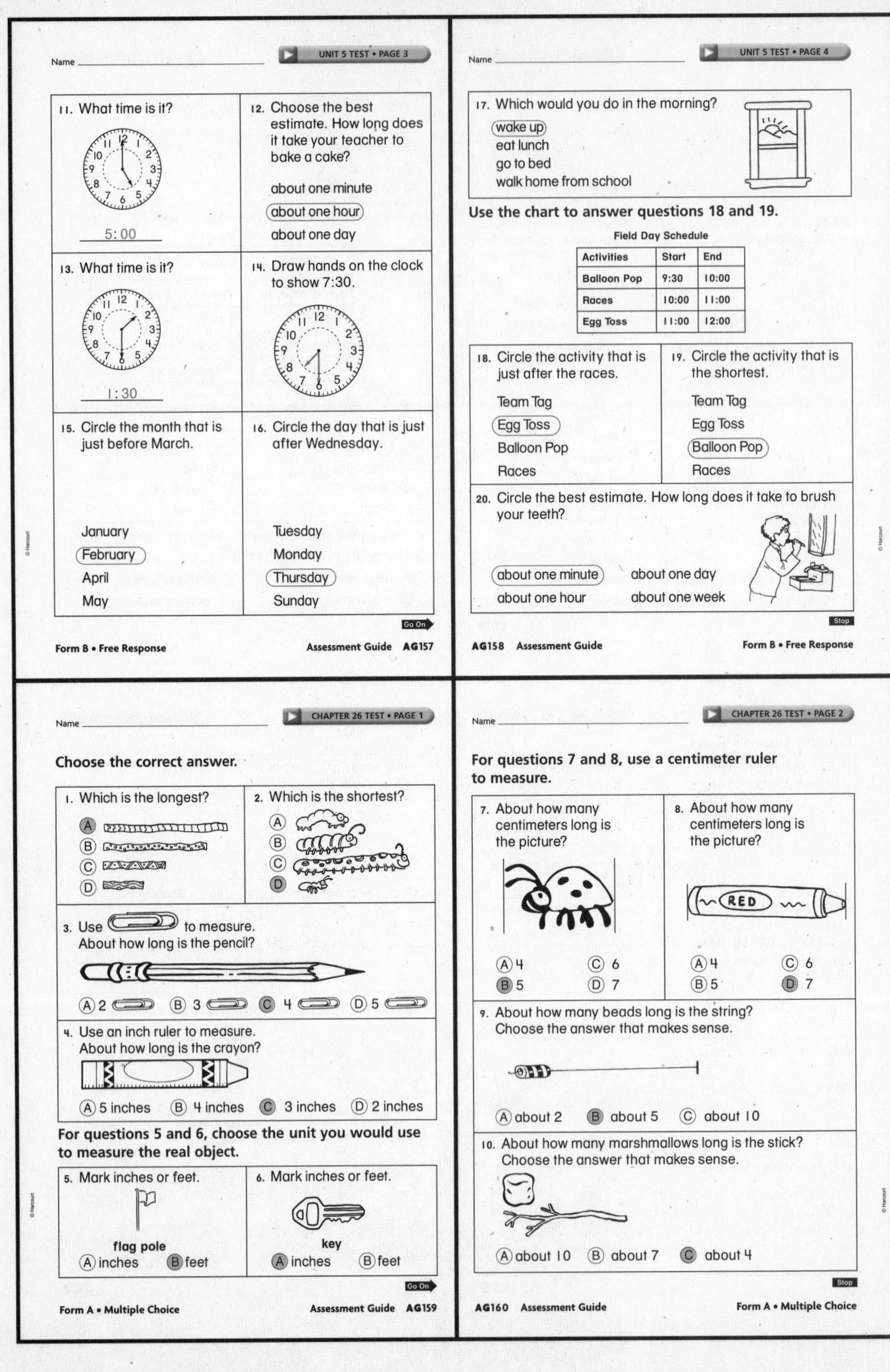

Name

UNIT 5 TEST • PAGE 3

11. What time is it?

5:00

12. Choose the best estimate. How long does it take your teacher to bake a cake?

about one minute
about one hour
about one day

13. What time is it?

1:30

14. Draw hands on the clock to show 7:30.

15. Circle the month that is just before March.

January
February
April
May

16. Circle the day that is just after Wednesday.

Tuesday
Monday
Thursday
Sunday

Go On

Form B • Free Response — Assessment Guide AG157

Name

UNIT 5 TEST • PAGE 4

17. Which would you do in the morning?

wake up
eat lunch
go to bed
walk home from school

Use the chart to answer questions 18 and 19.

Field Day Schedule

Activities	Start	End
Balloon Pop	9:30	10:00
Races	10:00	11:00
Egg Toss	11:00	12:00

18. Circle the activity that is just after the races.

Team Tag
Egg Toss
Balloon Pop
Races

19. Circle the activity that is the shortest.

Team Tag
Egg Toss
Balloon Pop
Races

20. Circle the best estimate. How long does it take to brush your teeth?

about one minute — about one day
about one hour — about one week

Stop

AG158 Assessment Guide — Form B • Free Response

Name

CHAPTER 26 TEST • PAGE 1

Choose the correct answer.

1. Which is the longest?

Ⓐ Ⓑ Ⓒ Ⓓ

2. Which is the shortest?

Ⓐ Ⓑ Ⓒ Ⓓ

3. Use [paper clip] to measure. About how long is the pencil?

Ⓐ 2 Ⓑ 3 Ⓒ 4 Ⓓ 5

4. Use an inch ruler to measure. About how long is the crayon?

Ⓐ 5 inches Ⓑ 4 inches Ⓒ 3 inches Ⓓ 2 inches

For questions 5 and 6, choose the unit you would use to measure the real object.

5. Mark inches or feet.

flag pole

Ⓐ inches Ⓑ feet

6. Mark inches or feet.

key

Ⓐ inches Ⓑ feet

Go On

Form A • Multiple Choice — Assessment Guide AG159

Name

CHAPTER 26 TEST • PAGE 2

For questions 7 and 8, use a centimeter ruler to measure.

7. About how many centimeters long is the picture?

Ⓐ 4 Ⓑ 5 Ⓒ 6 Ⓓ 7

8. About how many centimeters long is the picture?

RED

Ⓐ 4 Ⓑ 5 Ⓒ 6 Ⓓ 7

9. About how many beads long is the string? Choose the answer that makes sense.

Ⓐ about 2 Ⓑ about 5 Ⓒ about 10

10. About how many marshmallows long is the stick? Choose the answer that makes sense.

Ⓐ about 10 Ⓑ about 7 Ⓒ about 4

Stop

AG160 Assessment Guide — Form A • Multiple Choice

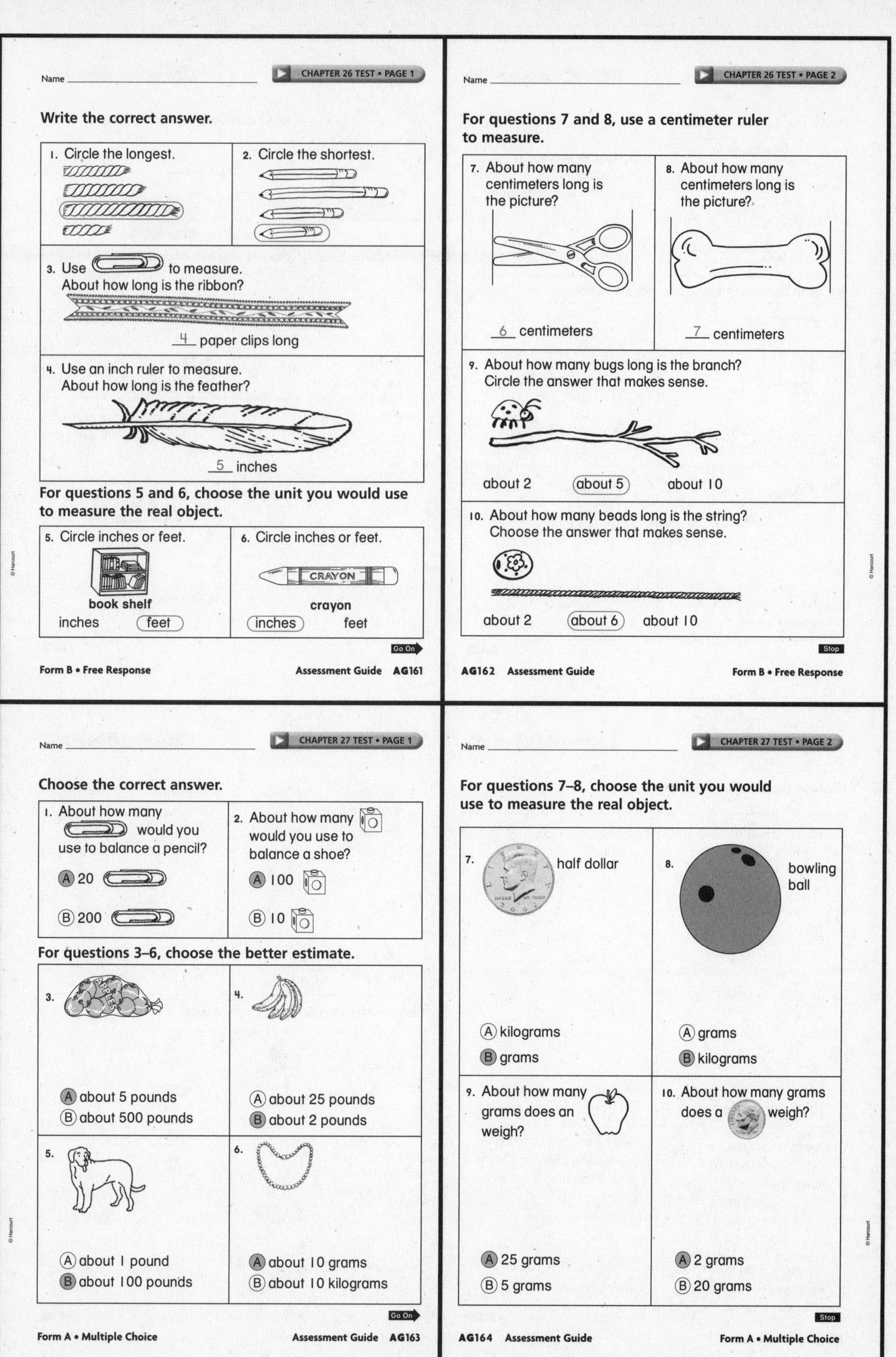

Name
CHAPTER 26 TEST • PAGE 1
Write the correct answer.
1. Circle the longest.
2. Circle the shortest.
3. Use to measure.
About how long is the ribbon?
4 paper clips long
4. Use an inch ruler to measure.
About how long is the feather?
5 inches
For questions 5 and 6, choose the unit you would use to measure the real object.
5. Circle inches or feet.
book shelf
inches feet
6. Circle inches or feet.
CRAYON
crayon
inches feet
Go On
Form B • Free Response
Assessment Guide AG161
Name
CHAPTER 26 TEST • PAGE 2
For questions 7 and 8, use a centimeter ruler to measure.
7. About how many centimeters long is the picture?
6 centimeters
8. About how many centimeters long is the picture?
7 centimeters
9. About how many bugs long is the branch? Circle the answer that makes sense.
about 2 about 5 about 10
10. About how many beads long is the string? Choose the answer that makes sense.
about 2 about 6 about 10
Stop
AG162 Assessment Guide
Form B • Free Response
Name
CHAPTER 27 TEST • PAGE 1
Choose the correct answer.
1. About how many would you use to balance a pencil?
A 20
B 200
2. About how many would you use to balance a shoe?
A 100
B 10
For questions 3–6, choose the better estimate.
3.
APPLES
A about 5 pounds
B about 500 pounds
4.
A about 25 pounds
B about 2 pounds
5.
A about 1 pound
B about 100 pounds
6.
A about 10 grams
B about 10 kilograms
Go On
Form A • Multiple Choice
Assessment Guide AG163
Name
CHAPTER 27 TEST • PAGE 2
For questions 7–8, choose the unit you would use to measure the real object.
7. half dollar
A kilograms
B grams
8. bowling ball
A grams
B kilograms
9. About how many grams does an weigh?
A 25 grams
B 5 grams
10. About how many grams does a weigh?
A 2 grams
B 20 grams
Stop
AG164 Assessment Guide
Form A • Multiple Choice
© Harcourt

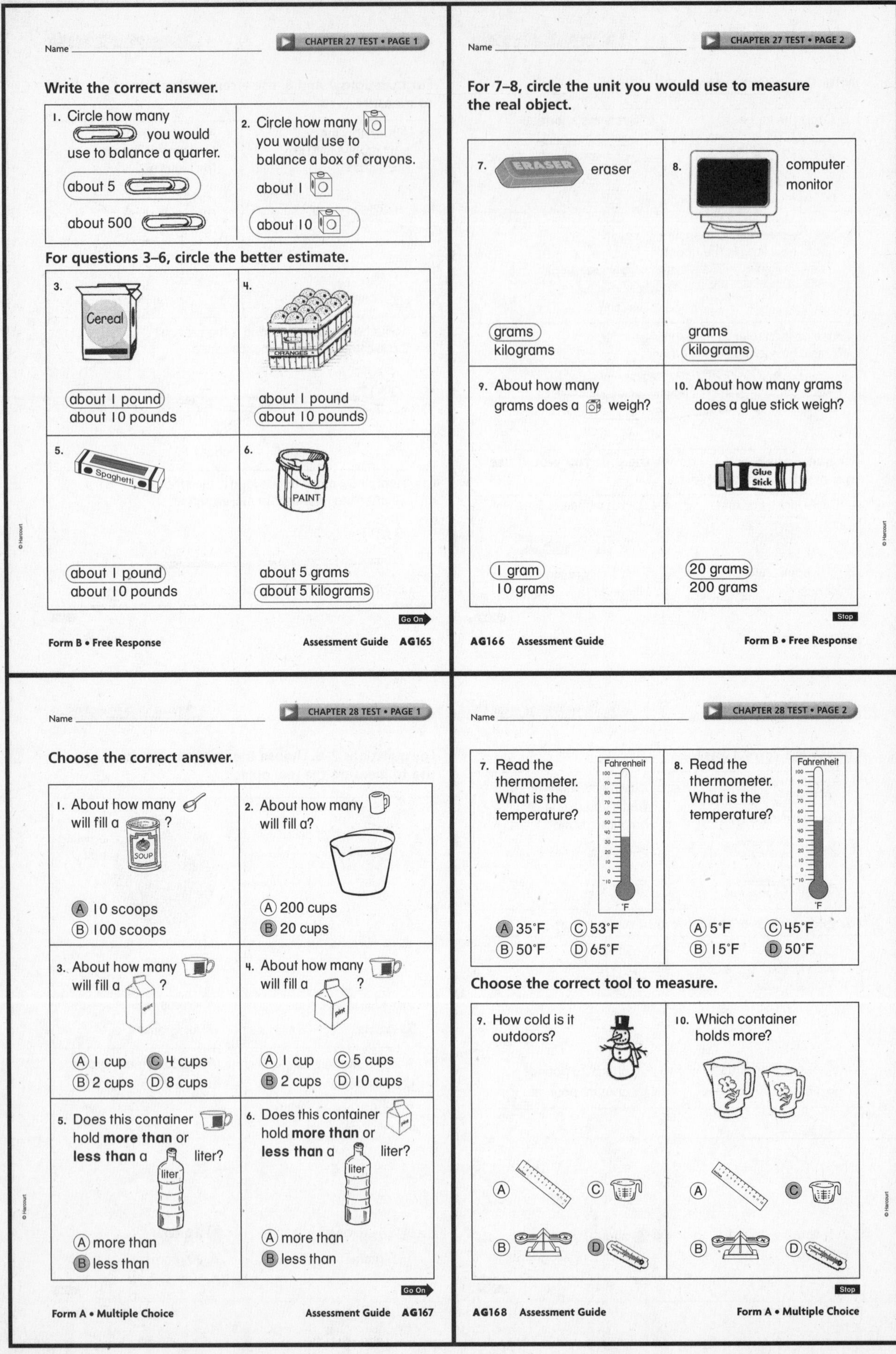

Name

CHAPTER 27 TEST • PAGE 1

Write the correct answer.

1. Circle how many [paper clip] you would use to balance a quarter. about 5 about 500	2. Circle how many [cube] you would use to balance a box of crayons. about 1 about 10

For questions 3–6, circle the better estimate.

3. Cereal about 1 pound about 10 pounds	4. ORANGES about 1 pound about 10 pounds
5. Spaghetti about 1 pound about 10 pounds	6. PAINT about 5 grams about 5 kilograms

Go On

Form B • Free Response — Assessment Guide AG165

Name

CHAPTER 27 TEST • PAGE 2

For 7–8, circle the unit you would use to measure the real object.

7. ERASER eraser grams kilograms	8. computer monitor grams kilograms
9. About how many grams does a [cube] weigh? 1 gram 10 grams	10. About how many grams does a glue stick weigh? Glue Stick 20 grams 200 grams

Stop

AG166 Assessment Guide — Form B • Free Response

Name

CHAPTER 28 TEST • PAGE 1

Choose the correct answer.

1. About how many [scoop] will fill a [SOUP can]? Ⓐ 10 scoops Ⓑ 100 scoops	2. About how many [cup] will fill a [bucket]? Ⓐ 200 cups Ⓑ 20 cups
3. About how many [cup] will fill a [quart carton]? Ⓐ 1 cup Ⓒ 4 cups Ⓑ 2 cups Ⓓ 8 cups	4. About how many [cup] will fill a [pint carton]? Ⓐ 1 cup Ⓒ 5 cups Ⓑ 2 cups Ⓓ 10 cups
5. Does this container [cup] hold **more than** or **less than** a [liter] liter? Ⓐ more than Ⓑ less than	6. Does this container [pint] hold **more than** or **less than** a [liter] liter? Ⓐ more than Ⓑ less than

Go On

Form A • Multiple Choice — Assessment Guide AG167

Name

CHAPTER 28 TEST • PAGE 2

7. Read the thermometer. What is the temperature? (Fahrenheit) Ⓐ 35°F Ⓒ 53°F Ⓑ 50°F Ⓓ 65°F	8. Read the thermometer. What is the temperature? (Fahrenheit) Ⓐ 5°F Ⓒ 45°F Ⓑ 15°F Ⓓ 50°F

Choose the correct tool to measure.

9. How cold is it outdoors? Ⓐ Ⓒ Ⓑ Ⓓ	10. Which container holds more? Ⓐ Ⓒ Ⓑ Ⓓ

Stop

AG168 Assessment Guide — Form A • Multiple Choice

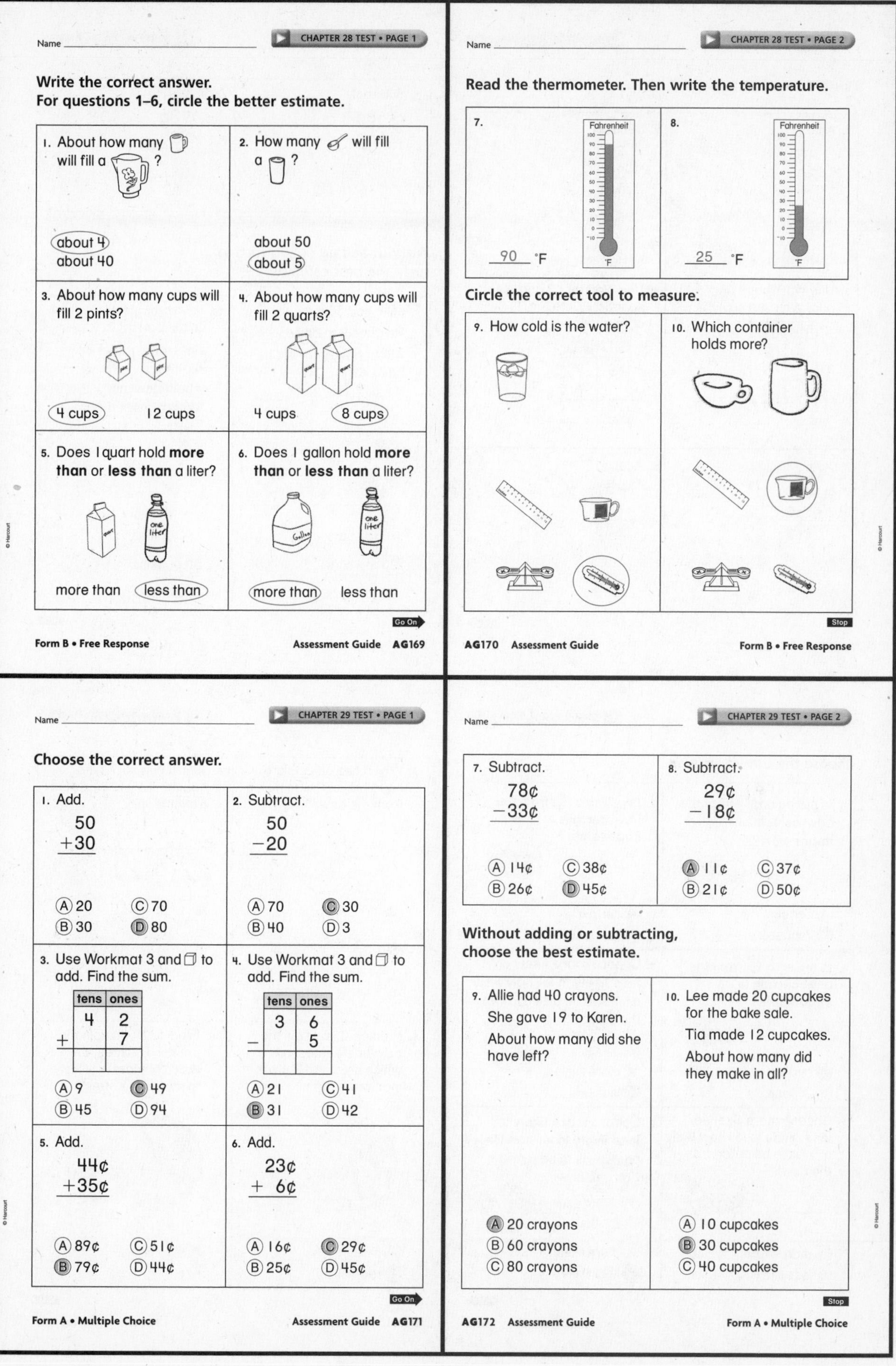

Name

CHAPTER 28 TEST • PAGE 1

Write the correct answer.
For questions 1–6, circle the better estimate.

1. About how many [cup] will fill a [pitcher]? about 4 / about 40	2. How many [spoon] will fill a [cup]? about 50 / about 5
3. About how many cups will fill 2 pints? 4 cups / 12 cups	4. About how many cups will fill 2 quarts? 4 cups / 8 cups
5. Does I quart hold **more than** or **less than** a liter? more than / less than	6. Does I gallon hold **more than** or **less than** a liter? more than / less than

Go On

Form B • Free Response — Assessment Guide AG169

Name

CHAPTER 28 TEST • PAGE 2

Read the thermometer. Then write the temperature.

7. Fahrenheit — 90 °F	8. Fahrenheit — 25 °F

Circle the correct tool to measure.

9. How cold is the water?	10. Which container holds more?

Stop

AG170 Assessment Guide — Form B • Free Response

Name

CHAPTER 29 TEST • PAGE 1

Choose the correct answer.

1. Add. 50 + 30 — (A) 20 (B) 30 (C) 70 (D) 80	2. Subtract. 50 − 20 — (A) 70 (B) 40 (C) 30 (D) 3
3. Use Workmat 3 and [cube] to add. Find the sum. tens ones: 4 2 + 7 — (A) 9 (B) 45 (C) 49 (D) 94	4. Use Workmat 3 and [cube] to add. Find the sum. tens ones: 3 6 − 5 — (A) 21 (B) 31 (C) 41 (D) 42
5. Add. 44¢ + 35¢ — (A) 89¢ (B) 79¢ (C) 51¢ (D) 44¢	6. Add. 23¢ + 6¢ — (A) 16¢ (B) 25¢ (C) 29¢ (D) 45¢

Go On

Form A • Multiple Choice — Assessment Guide AG171

Name

CHAPTER 29 TEST • PAGE 2

7. Subtract. 78¢ − 33¢ — (A) 14¢ (B) 26¢ (C) 38¢ (D) 45¢	8. Subtract. 29¢ − 18¢ — (A) 11¢ (B) 21¢ (C) 37¢ (D) 50¢

Without adding or subtracting, choose the best estimate.

9. Allie had 40 crayons. She gave 19 to Karen. About how many did she have left? (A) 20 crayons (B) 60 crayons (C) 80 crayons	10. Lee made 20 cupcakes for the bake sale. Tia made 12 cupcakes. About how many did they make in all? (A) 10 cupcakes (B) 30 cupcakes (C) 40 cupcakes

Stop

AG172 Assessment Guide — Form A • Multiple Choice

Name ______________________ CHAPTER 29 TEST • PAGE 1

Write the correct answer.

1. Add.
$$\begin{array}{r} 40 \\ +30 \\ \hline 70 \end{array}$$

2. Subtract.
$$\begin{array}{r} 70 \\ -30 \\ \hline 40 \end{array}$$

3. Use Workmat 3 and [cube] to add. Write the sum.

	tens	ones
	5	2
+		6
	5	8

4. Use Workmat 3 and [cube] to subtract. Write the difference.

	tens	ones
	5	7
−		6
	5	1

5. Add.
$$\begin{array}{r} 23¢ \\ +24¢ \\ \hline 47¢ \end{array}$$

6. Add.
$$\begin{array}{r} 45¢ \\ +13¢ \\ \hline 58¢ \end{array}$$

Go On

Name ______________________ CHAPTER 29 TEST • PAGE 2

7. Subtract.
$$\begin{array}{r} 68¢ \\ -65¢ \\ \hline 3¢ \end{array}$$

8. Subtract.
$$\begin{array}{r} 93¢ \\ -22¢ \\ \hline 71¢ \end{array}$$

Without adding or subtracting, circle the best estimate.

9. Mike had 30 toy cars. He gave 9 to Eddie. About how many did he have left?

10 toy cars
(20 toy cars)
40 toy cars

10. Julia brought 40 cookies to the party. Kenneth brought 22 cookies. About how many cookies were there in all?

15 cookies
50 cookies
(60 cookies)

Stop

Name ______________________ CHAPTER 30 TEST • PAGE 1

Choose the correct answer.

1. Is pulling an [apple] from the bowl **certain** or **impossible**?

Ⓐ certain
Ⓑ impossible

2. Is pulling a [orange] from the bowl **certain** or **impossible**?

Ⓐ certain
Ⓑ impossible

3. Is pulling a [cherry] from the bowl **certain** or **impossible**?

Ⓐ certain
Ⓑ impossible

4. Choose **more likely** or **less likely** to tell how likely a [banana] is to be pulled from the bowl.

Ⓐ more likely
Ⓑ less likely

5. Choose **more likely** or **less likely** to tell how likely a [marble] is to be pulled from the bowl.

Ⓐ more likely
Ⓑ less likely

6. Choose **more likely** or **less likely** to tell how likely an [eraser] is to be pulled from the bowl.

Ⓐ more likely
Ⓑ less likely

Go On

Name ______________________ CHAPTER 30 TEST • PAGE 2

7. Which two objects are equally likely to be pulled from the bowl?

Ⓐ [apple] [banana]
Ⓑ [pear] [apple]
Ⓒ [pear] [banana]

8. Which two socks are equally likely to be pulled from the line?

Ⓐ [socks]
Ⓑ [socks]
Ⓒ [socks]

9. Predict. If you spin the pointer 10 times, on which color is it likely to stop more often?

blue
red

Ⓐ blue
Ⓑ red

10. Predict. If you spin the pointer 10 times, on which number is it likely to stop more often?

6
4

Ⓐ 4
Ⓑ 6

Stop

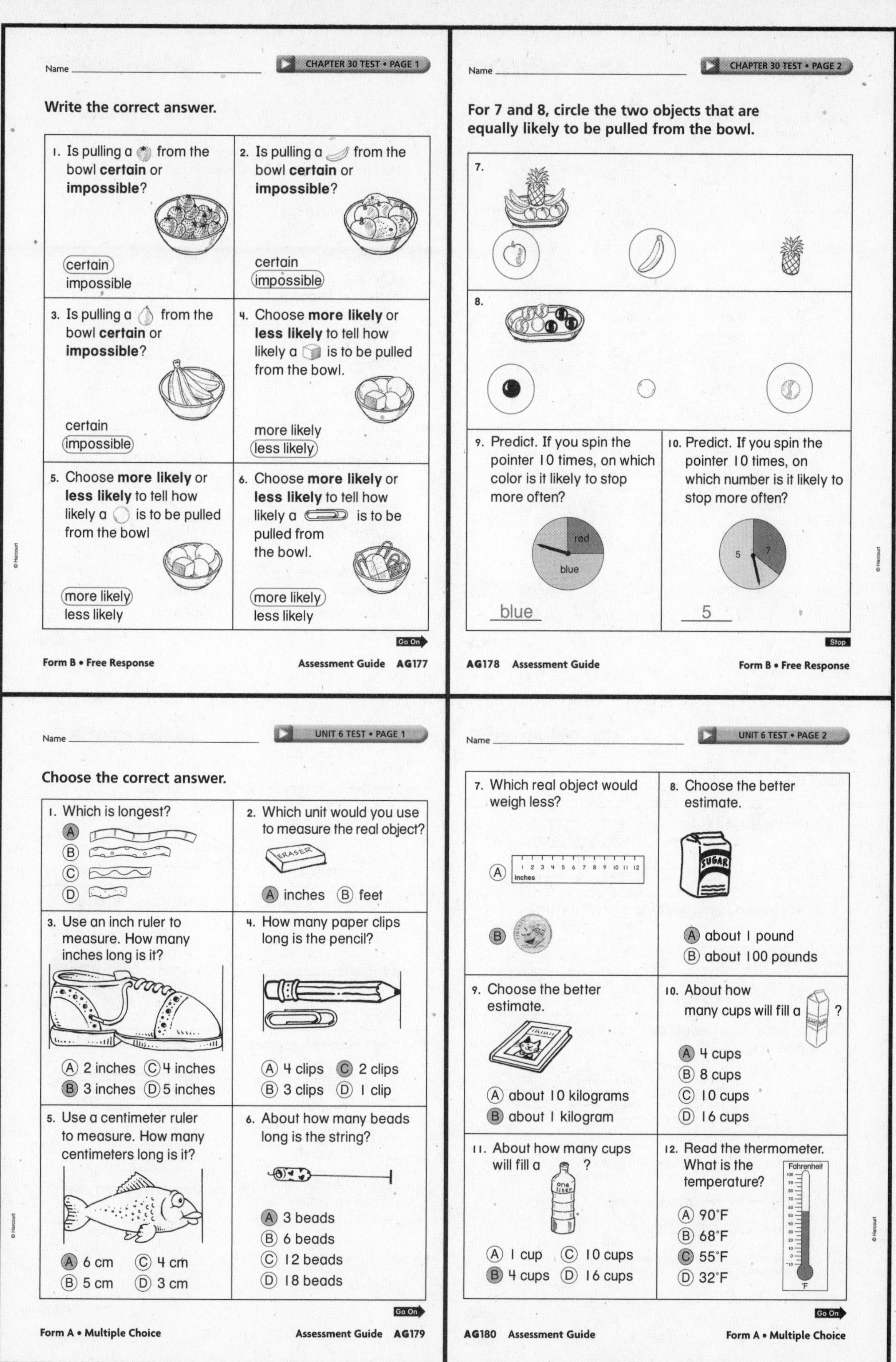

Name ____________________ CHAPTER 30 TEST • PAGE 1

Write the correct answer.

1. Is pulling a [strawberry] from the bowl **certain** or **impossible**?
   (certain) impossible

2. Is pulling a [banana] from the bowl **certain** or **impossible**?
   certain (impossible)

3. Is pulling a [pear] from the bowl **certain** or **impossible**?
   certain (impossible)

4. Choose **more likely** or **less likely** to tell how likely a [cube] is to be pulled from the bowl.
   more likely (less likely)

5. Choose **more likely** or **less likely** to tell how likely a [ball] is to be pulled from the bowl
   (more likely) less likely

6. Choose **more likely** or **less likely** to tell how likely a [paper clip] is to be pulled from the bowl.
   (more likely) less likely

Go On

Form B • Free Response Assessment Guide AG177

© Harcourt

Name ____________________ CHAPTER 30 TEST • PAGE 2

For 7 and 8, circle the two objects that are equally likely to be pulled from the bowl.

7.

8.

9. Predict. If you spin the pointer 10 times, on which color is it likely to stop more often?
   red
   blue
   blue

10. Predict. If you spin the pointer 10 times, on which number is it likely to stop more often?
   5 7
   5

Stop

AG178 Assessment Guide Form B • Free Response

© Harcourt

Name ____________________ UNIT 6 TEST • PAGE 1

Choose the correct answer.

1. Which is longest?
   (A) (B) (C) (D)

2. Which unit would you use to measure the real object?
   ERASER
   (A) inches (B) feet

3. Use an inch ruler to measure. How many inches long is it?
   (A) 2 inches (C) 4 inches
   (B) 3 inches (D) 5 inches

4. How many paper clips long is the pencil?
   (A) 4 clips (C) 2 clips
   (B) 3 clips (D) 1 clip

5. Use a centimeter ruler to measure. How many centimeters long is it?
   (A) 6 cm (C) 4 cm
   (B) 5 cm (D) 3 cm

6. About how many beads long is the string?
   (A) 3 beads
   (B) 6 beads
   (C) 12 beads
   (D) 18 beads

Go On

Form A • Multiple Choice Assessment Guide AG179

© Harcourt

Name ____________________ UNIT 6 TEST • PAGE 2

7. Which real object would weigh less?
   (A) 1 2 3 4 5 6 7 8 9 10 11 12 inches
   (B)

8. Choose the better estimate.
   SUGAR
   (A) about 1 pound
   (B) about 100 pounds

9. Choose the better estimate.
   (A) about 10 kilograms
   (B) about 1 kilogram

10. About how many cups will fill a [carton] ?
   (A) 4 cups
   (B) 8 cups
   (C) 10 cups
   (D) 16 cups

11. About how many cups will fill a [one liter bottle] ?
   (A) 1 cup (C) 10 cups
   (B) 4 cups (D) 16 cups

12. Read the thermometer. What is the temperature?
   Fahrenheit
   (A) 90°F
   (B) 68°F
   (C) 55°F
   (D) 32°F

Go On

AG180 Assessment Guide Form A • Multiple Choice

© Harcourt

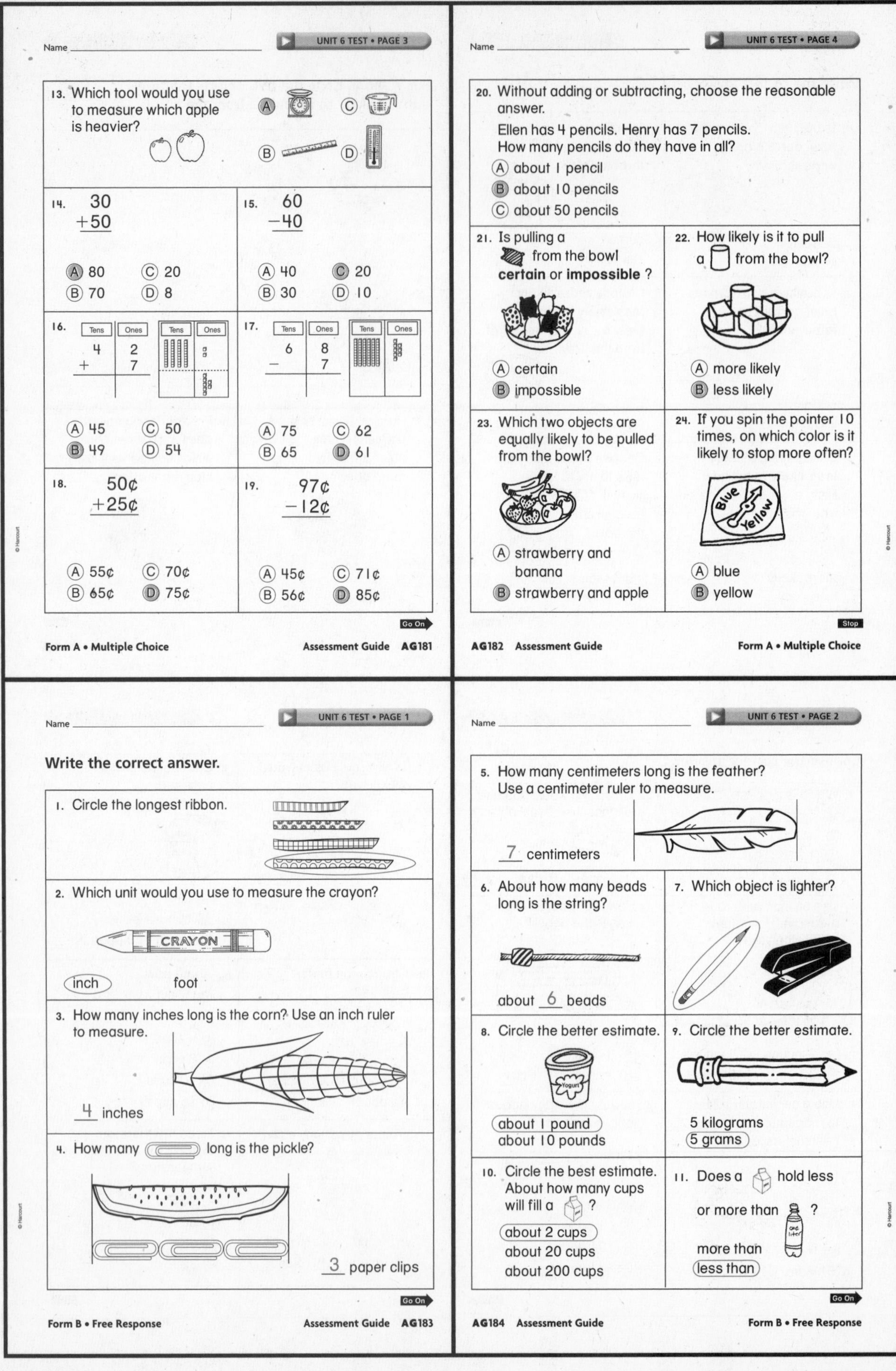

Name ____________________ UNIT 6 TEST • PAGE 3

13. Which tool would you use to measure which apple is heavier?
Ⓐ Ⓑ Ⓒ Ⓓ

14. 30 + 50
Ⓐ 80 Ⓒ 20
Ⓑ 70 Ⓓ 8

15. 60 − 40
Ⓐ 40 Ⓒ 20
Ⓑ 30 Ⓓ 10

16.

Tens	Ones
4	2
+	7

Ⓐ 45 Ⓒ 50
Ⓑ 49 Ⓓ 54

17.

Tens	Ones
6	8
−	7

Ⓐ 75 Ⓒ 62
Ⓑ 65 Ⓓ 61

18. 50¢ + 25¢
Ⓐ 55¢ Ⓒ 70¢
Ⓑ 65¢ Ⓓ 75¢

19. 97¢ − 12¢
Ⓐ 45¢ Ⓒ 71¢
Ⓑ 56¢ Ⓓ 85¢

Go On

Form A • Multiple Choice Assessment Guide AG181

Name ____________________ UNIT 6 TEST • PAGE 4

20. Without adding or subtracting, choose the reasonable answer.
Ellen has 4 pencils. Henry has 7 pencils.
How many pencils do they have in all?
Ⓐ about 1 pencil
Ⓑ about 10 pencils
Ⓒ about 50 pencils

21. Is pulling a from the bowl **certain** or **impossible**?
Ⓐ certain
Ⓑ impossible

22. How likely is it to pull a from the bowl?
Ⓐ more likely
Ⓑ less likely

23. Which two objects are equally likely to be pulled from the bowl?
Ⓐ strawberry and banana
Ⓑ strawberry and apple

24. If you spin the pointer 10 times, on which color is it likely to stop more often?
Blue Yellow
Ⓐ blue
Ⓑ yellow

Stop

AG182 Assessment Guide Form A • Multiple Choice

Name ____________________ UNIT 6 TEST • PAGE 1

Write the correct answer.

1. Circle the longest ribbon.

2. Which unit would you use to measure the crayon?
CRAYON
inch foot

3. How many inches long is the corn? Use an inch ruler to measure.
4 inches

4. How many long is the pickle?
3 paper clips

Go On

Form B • Free Response Assessment Guide AG183

Name ____________________ UNIT 6 TEST • PAGE 2

5. How many centimeters long is the feather? Use a centimeter ruler to measure.
7 centimeters

6. About how many beads long is the string?
about 6 beads

7. Which object is lighter?

8. Circle the better estimate.
Yogurt
about 1 pound
about 10 pounds

9. Circle the better estimate.
5 kilograms
5 grams

10. Circle the best estimate. About how many cups will fill a ?
about 2 cups
about 20 cups
about 200 cups

11. Does a hold less or more than ?
one liter
more than
less than

Go On

AG184 Assessment Guide Form B • Free Response

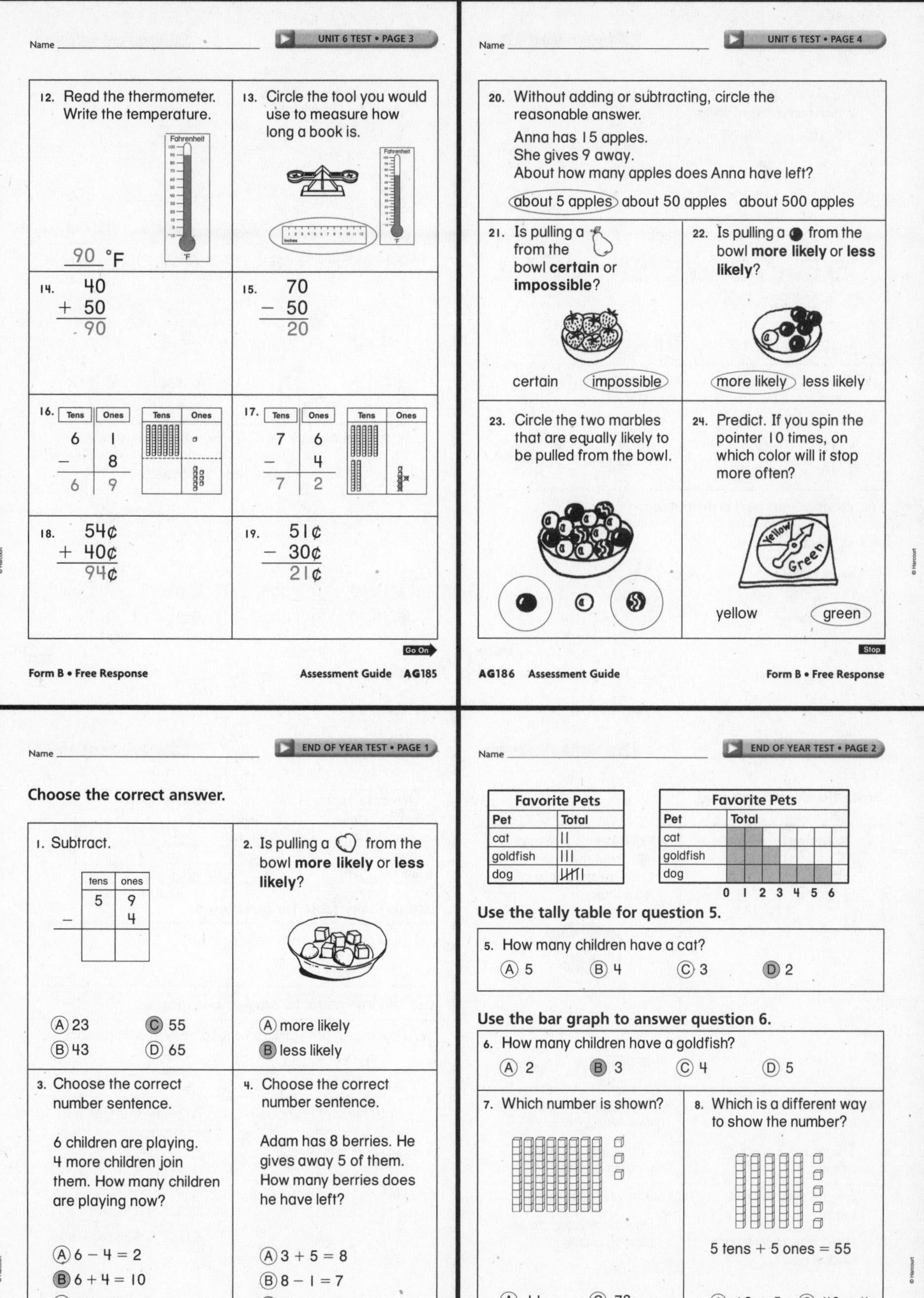

Name

UNIT 6 TEST • PAGE 3

12. Read the thermometer. Write the temperature.

90 °F

13. Circle the tool you would use to measure how long a book is.

14.
$$\begin{array}{r} 40 \\ +\ 50 \\ \hline 90 \end{array}$$

15.
$$\begin{array}{r} 70 \\ -\ 50 \\ \hline 20 \end{array}$$

16.

	Tens	Ones
	6	1
−		8
	6	9

Tens	Ones

17.

	Tens	Ones
	7	6
−		4
	7	2

Tens	Ones

18.
$$\begin{array}{r} 54¢ \\ +\ 40¢ \\ \hline 94¢ \end{array}$$

19.
$$\begin{array}{r} 51¢ \\ -\ 30¢ \\ \hline 21¢ \end{array}$$

Go On

Form B • Free Response Assessment Guide AG185

Name

UNIT 6 TEST • PAGE 4

20. Without adding or subtracting, circle the reasonable answer.

Anna has 15 apples.
She gives 9 away.
About how many apples does Anna have left?

about 5 apples about 50 apples about 500 apples

21. Is pulling a [pear] from the bowl **certain** or **impossible**?

certain impossible

22. Is pulling a [marble] from the bowl **more likely** or **less likely**?

more likely less likely

23. Circle the two marbles that are equally likely to be pulled from the bowl.

24. Predict. If you spin the pointer 10 times, on which color will it stop more often?

yellow green

Stop

AG186 Assessment Guide Form B • Free Response

Name

END OF YEAR TEST • PAGE 1

Choose the correct answer.

1. Subtract.

	tens	ones
	5	9
−		4

Ⓐ 23 Ⓒ 55
Ⓑ 43 Ⓓ 65

2. Is pulling a [cube] from the bowl **more likely** or **less likely**?

Ⓐ more likely
Ⓑ less likely

3. Choose the correct number sentence.

6 children are playing. 4 more children join them. How many children are playing now?

Ⓐ 6 − 4 = 2
Ⓑ 6 + 4 = 10
Ⓒ 10 − 4 = 6
Ⓓ 6 + 6 = 12

4. Choose the correct number sentence.

Adam has 8 berries. He gives away 5 of them. How many berries does he have left?

Ⓐ 3 + 5 = 8
Ⓑ 8 − 1 = 7
Ⓒ 8 − 5 = 3
Ⓓ 5 − 3 = 2

Go On

Form A • End of Year Test Assessment Guide AG187

Name

END OF YEAR TEST • PAGE 2

Favorite Pets

Pet	Total
cat	II
goldfish	III
dog	~~IIII~~ I

Favorite Pets

Use the tally table for question 5.

5. How many children have a cat?

Ⓐ 5 Ⓑ 4 Ⓒ 3 Ⓓ 2

Use the bar graph to answer question 6.

6. How many children have a goldfish?

Ⓐ 2 Ⓑ 3 Ⓒ 4 Ⓓ 5

7. Which number is shown?

Ⓐ 11 Ⓒ 73
Ⓑ 38 Ⓓ 83

8. Which is a different way to show the number?

5 tens + 5 ones = 55

Ⓐ 10 + 5 Ⓒ 40 + 4
Ⓑ 20 + 5 Ⓓ 50 + 5

Go On

AG188 Assessment Guide Form A • End of Year Test

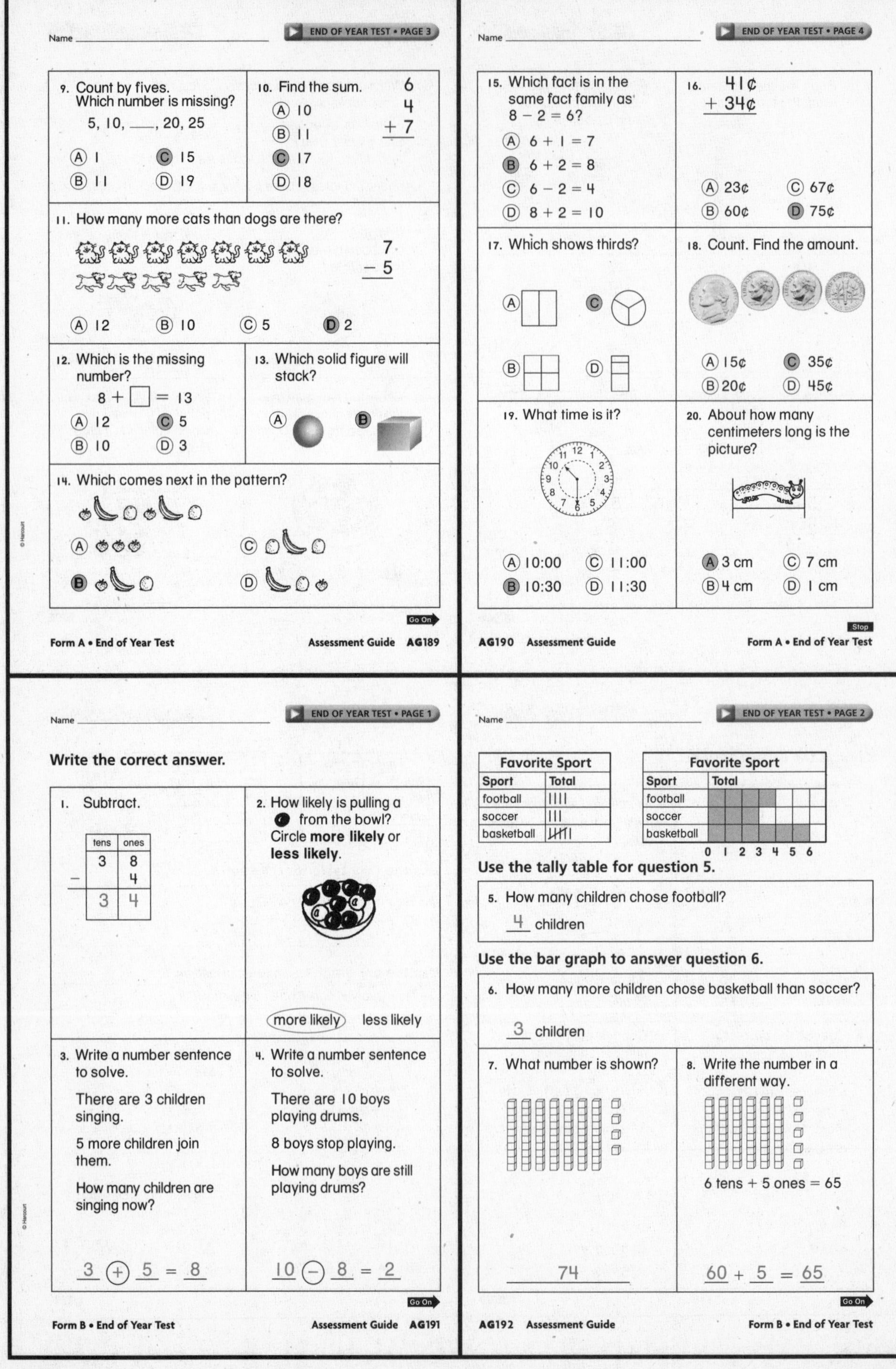

Name
END OF YEAR TEST • PAGE 3
9. Count by fives. Which number is missing?
5, 10, ___, 20, 25
(A) 1 (C) 15
(B) 11 (D) 19
10. Find the sum.
6
4
+ 7
(A) 10
(B) 11
(C) 17
(D) 18
11. How many more cats than dogs are there?
7
− 5
(A) 12 (B) 10 (C) 5 (D) 2
12. Which is the missing number?
8 + □ = 13
(A) 12 (C) 5
(B) 10 (D) 3
13. Which solid figure will stack?
(A) (B)
14. Which comes next in the pattern?
(A) (C)
(B) (D)
Go On
Form A • End of Year Test
Assessment Guide AG189
Name
END OF YEAR TEST • PAGE 4
15. Which fact is in the same fact family as 8 − 2 = 6?
(A) 6 + 1 = 7
(B) 6 + 2 = 8
(C) 6 − 2 = 4
(D) 8 + 2 = 10
16. 41¢
+ 34¢
(A) 23¢ (C) 67¢
(B) 60¢ (D) 75¢
17. Which shows thirds?
(A) (C)
(B) (D)
18. Count. Find the amount.
(A) 15¢ (C) 35¢
(B) 20¢ (D) 45¢
19. What time is it?
(A) 10:00 (C) 11:00
(B) 10:30 (D) 11:30
20. About how many centimeters long is the picture?
(A) 3 cm (C) 7 cm
(B) 4 cm (D) 1 cm
Stop
AG190 Assessment Guide
Form A • End of Year Test
Name
END OF YEAR TEST • PAGE 1
Write the correct answer.
1. Subtract.
tens ones
3 8
− 4
3 4
2. How likely is pulling a ● from the bowl? Circle more likely or less likely.
more likely less likely
3. Write a number sentence to solve.
There are 3 children singing.
5 more children join them.
How many children are singing now?
3 + 5 = 8
4. Write a number sentence to solve.
There are 10 boys playing drums.
8 boys stop playing.
How many boys are still playing drums?
10 − 8 = 2
Go On
Form B • End of Year Test
Assessment Guide AG191
Name
END OF YEAR TEST • PAGE 2
Favorite Sport
Sport Total
football ||||
soccer |||
basketball |||| |
Favorite Sport
Sport Total
football
soccer
basketball
0 1 2 3 4 5 6
Use the tally table for question 5.
5. How many children chose football?
4 children
Use the bar graph to answer question 6.
6. How many more children chose basketball than soccer?
3 children
7. What number is shown?
74
8. Write the number in a different way.
6 tens + 5 ones = 65
60 + 5 = 65
Go On
AG192 Assessment Guide
Form B • End of Year Test

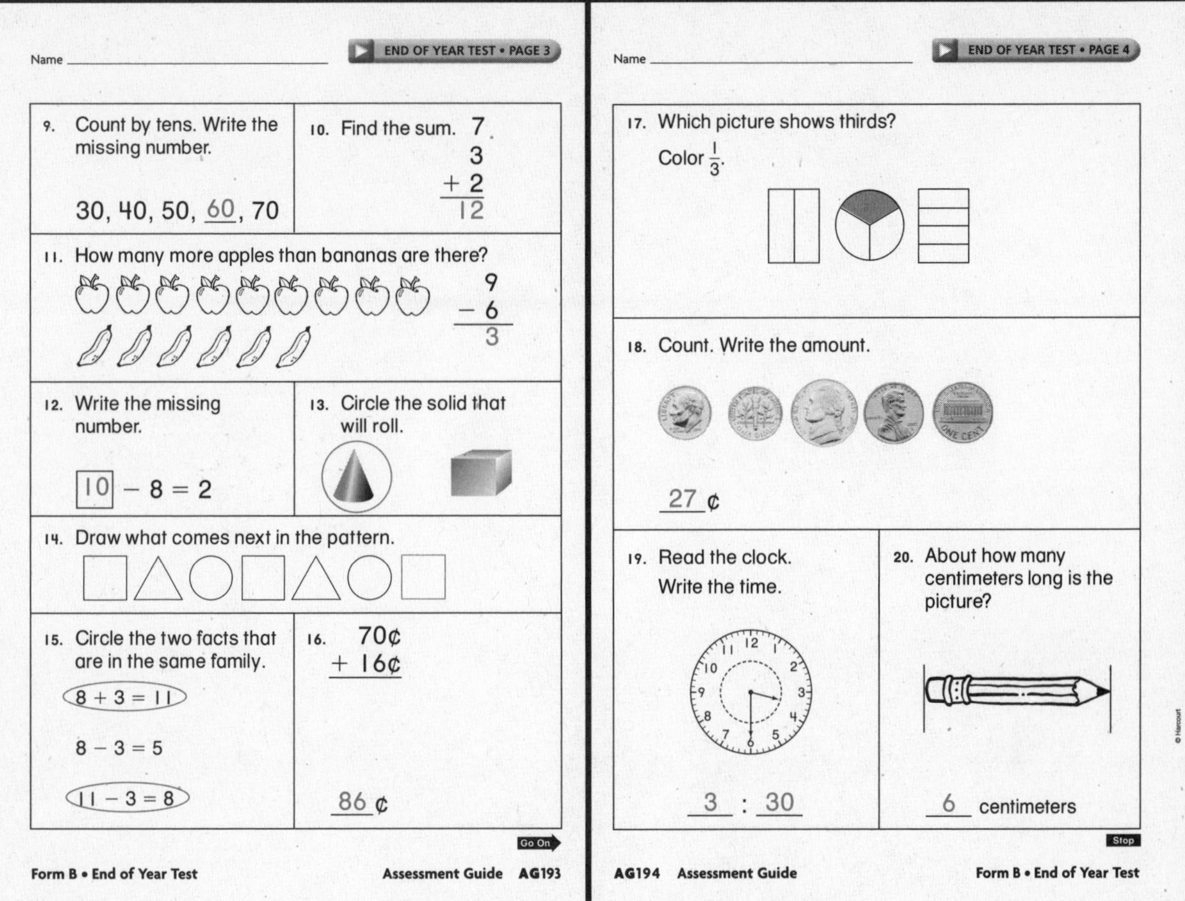

Name
END OF YEAR TEST • PAGE 3
9. Count by tens. Write the missing number.
30, 40, 50, 60, 70
10. Find the sum. 7
3
+ 2
12
11. How many more apples than bananas are there?
9
− 6
3
12. Write the missing number.
10 − 8 = 2
13. Circle the solid that will roll.
14. Draw what comes next in the pattern.
15. Circle the two facts that are in the same family.
8 + 3 = 11
8 − 3 = 5
11 − 3 = 8
16. 70¢
+ 16¢
86 ¢
Go On
Form B • End of Year Test
Assessment Guide AG193
Name
END OF YEAR TEST • PAGE 4
17. Which picture shows thirds?
Color 1/3.
18. Count. Write the amount.
27 ¢
19. Read the clock.
Write the time.
3 : 30
20. About how many centimeters long is the picture?
6 centimeters
Stop
AG194 Assessment Guide
Form B • End of Year Test